The Crew Chief's Son

The Crew Chief's Son

A Trackside Memoir of Early NASCAR

MICHAEL L. CLEMENTS

McFarland & Company, Inc., Publishers
Jefferson, North Carolina, and London

LIBRARY OF CONGRESS CATALOGUING-IN-PUBLICATION DATA

Clements, Michael L.
The crew chief's son : a trackside memoir
of early NASCAR / Michael L. Clements.
p.   cm.
Includes bibliographical references and index.

ISBN 978-0-7864-4954-5
softcover : 50# alkaline paper ∞

1. Clements, Michael L.   2. Clements, Louie.
3. Pit crews—United States.   4. NASCAR (Association)—History.
5. Stock car racing—United States—History.   I. Title.
GV1032.C65A3 2011   796.720973—dc22   2010048297

BRITISH LIBRARY CATALOGUING DATA ARE AVAILABLE

On the cover: (center) The author as a child (second from left) posing with
his father, Louie Clements, and siblings in front of a 1957 Chevy race car;
(bottom) Bob Welborn (49) and Rex White (4) racing in the 1961 Daytona 500

Manufactured in the United States of America

*McFarland & Company, Inc., Publishers
Box 611, Jefferson, North Carolina 28640
www.mcfarlandpub.com*

Table of Contents

It is with a pure heart that I would like to dedicate this book to my parents, Louie and Magdalene Clements. Without their constant attention, nurturing and guidance, I would have never become the man I am today. They were the strength that I counted on while I was "growing up NASCAR."

Special thanks to Rex White, James Hylton, Ned Jarrett, Perry Wood, Bud Moore, Gary Clements, all of my "Darkside" model car friends, and especially to my loving wife Kimberly. Each of you have been a source of information and encouragement when I needed it the most.

Preface

On January 26, 1996, my father, Louis Clements, died in Mesa, Arizona. With him died one of the last remaining links to an era of auto racing that produced the likes of Lee Petty, Cotton Owens, Fireball Roberts, Rex White, the Wood Brothers and a host of other racing legends. These are men who raced for the meager living provided by the newly born sanctioning body, plus the sheer enjoyment and challenge of this demanding sport.

The story that follows is a history of one family and its place in a sport and industry that has grown into a multimillion-dollar enterprise. Today, NASCAR ranks second only to the NFL in audience, though I strongly believe that, like the pioneers of auto racing, the current generation of racers would be out on the tracks racing their hearts out even if the prize money were much less than it is. Drivers like Jimmie Johnson, Jeff Gordon, and Tony Stewart don't race just because of the money. They, like the legends of old, race because it is in their blood.

Racing is in the blood of the Clements clan as well. In fact, my entire life, from childhood to adulthood, has been in and around racing in one form or another. I would like to tell you about these experiences. Some are happy and some are sad. Some are inspiring and some are not. In the end, though, they all add up to a childhood spent growing up with racing, and growing up alongside NASCAR.

This book chronicles the experiences of a close-knit family traveling the highways to all of the NASCAR Grand National races around the country. We laughed together and cried together, had successes and failures, grew as a family and as individuals, all while forming numerous relationships with other drivers and mechanics and their families and friends. Many of these close bonds still exist today, even after 50 years have passed.

Included are more than 180 photographs from our life on the road and at the tracks. Photos of various drivers, crews and the race cars of the day, along with stills from our early home movies, can also be seen. It is my hope that this book will give each reader some insight to the exact nature of the sport during its early days, from the hardships experienced by many racers to the exploits of some who became legends of the sport, and with a particular focus on an overlooked aspect of racing — the people who kept the cars running — as well as those who raced them. While drivers are quick to acknowledge the invaluable contributions of their mechanics and crews, history isn't always so generous. Without the grueling and ingenious work of those crews, the stories of many of the legendary names of NASCAR—family names still involved in racing and heard today in race-day lineups as the flag prepares to drop — might be very different.

I was born into a racing family. Throughout my childhood I was fortunate to meet all the early era pioneers of NASCAR, which was a thrilling experience. As one might expect after a childhood spent around the tracks, I am certifiably race crazy. If it has wheels and an engine, I will race it. As a young boy, I was blessed to have two of the best parents any kid could have hoped for. My parents were strict, but they taught us responsibility, kindness, integrity and a very strong work ethic. My dad would never give up once he started a project, a characteristic that served him well in his career around motor sports. I can't begin to count the number of times I saw him red in the face from hard physical labor, sweat pouring down his face and determination getting more and more pronounced with each swing of the hammer or twist of the wrench. He taught me the basics at a very early age. Our parents made sure that when I was old enough to go out on my own, I was ready to meet the world head-on. (Along the way, I also learned to play guitar well enough to allow me to earn my college spending money playing in a number of bands.)

As noted, my interest in racing extended well beyond my childhood, and shaped much of my life. Over the past 30 years, I have been a contributing editor to three different kart racing magazines. I was lucky enough to win four consecutive national championships in the open classes of kart racing, in which the engines are highly modified and very intricate in detail. My friend Dale Carpenter and I built a laydown kart with four engines on it and took it up to the Bonneville Salt Flats in July of 1992, where we set a world land speed record for four-cycle-powered karts, reaching 144.832 miles per hour. In the course of a career spent working on racing engines, I've earned three patents on internal combustion engine design and still build racing engines for competition karting today.

Today I live in Ocala, Florida, with my wife Kimberly, and in the family tradition I'm still building engines and looking for innovative ways to improve their performance. I hope to bring my latest prototype, an engine powered solely by magnetism, to market soon. But that's the present, and what you're about to read is about an age in racing that's long past, though its echoes are still heard nearly every weekend, at racetracks around the country. I hope it brings back memories and brings you something new, and most of all I hope that you enjoy reading about our experiences growing up in the world of stock car racing.

• *Michael L. Clements* •

CHAPTER 1

1941–1956: The Early Years

In November 1941, my parents were married. About two weeks later they were visiting my mom's dad and her brothers and sisters at their house on Breckenridge Street in Owensboro, Kentucky. They didn't have TV, so that big old wooden-cabinet Philco radio was playing the big band sounds. Out of the blue came the news flash: The Japanese had attacked Pearl Harbor. The United States Pacific fleet was all but destroyed that early Sunday morning.

The next day President Franklin D. Roosevelt spoke to Congress and we declared war on the Empire of Japan. FDR vowed that the United States would prevail in this war, so help us God!

My father, Louie Clements, enlisted in the Army Air Corps but was fortunate enough to remain stateside throughout the war. He was a mechanical wizard and those were in short supply. He traveled all over the U.S. from base to base working on tanks, Jeeps, halftracks, trucks—whatever needed building or repair, he did it. During that time, my mother, Magdalene, was able to go with him on some of these stations, but not all. They missed Christmas a few times, but managed to raise five of us kids.

While stationed in Indianapolis, they could hear the USAC midgets running on Saturday nights from their apartment. The sound was too alluring for Louie. He had to go see what was going on. The racing bug bit him about as hard as the love bug, I think. My dad was just 18 years old then and my mom was a mere 19 years old. Two lovestruck kids, just married, they were involved in

Louie Clements working on the 6-cylinder Chevy Modified driven by G.C. Spencer, Evansville, Indiana, 1946.

Above, left: A Young G.C. Spencer posing with the #34 Chevy known as "The Flying Saucer." *Right:* Right three-quarters view of "The Flying Saucer."

World War II and about to start a family of five kids. I am the fourth of the five born to Louie and Babe. We were Lloyd, David, Cindy, Mike, and Jeff.

February 5, 1951, was a banner day in the Clements home. Well, it was for me, anyway. That's the day that my mom and the Good Lord decided to bring me into this world. Little did I know at the time that I was being born into a NASCAR family.

The big war had ended just over five years earlier. My father, Louis Clements, had been building race cars since returning home from the war. My uncle, Crawford Clements, my dad's younger brother, had served his country during the war, too, and had fought in the Battle of the Bulge in Europe. When he left home, he had a head full of dark, wavy hair. When he returned from Europe after the war, his hair was white. He told my uncle H.A. that during that battle, he thought every breath would be his last.

Together, the two brothers were building modified race cars for a couple of local guys in our hometown of

Rear view of "The Flying Saucer."

Dirt-track Modifieds. The car on the right is the '34 Chevy of G.C. Spencer.

G.C. Spencer drifting through the corner at Owensboro Legion Park.

1936 Chevy Modified.

Modified #A2 driven by Archie Hamilton. Note the overhead valve V8 engine.

Owensboro, Kentucky. Bobby Watkins and G.C. Spencer were their drivers. Bobby drove the Green Hornet, a modified '37 Chevy coupe that was painted green and carried the call letters of the local radio station on its sides. WVJS was kind enough to help out with a tank of gas or a tire here and there. The cool thing about this car was that it also carried our family to church on Sundays before the race.

At this time my dad was working as an auto mechanic and body and fender man for Short Brothers Chevrolet in Owensboro. He was also the painter there. (I believe that Chevy dealership is now named Don Moore Chevy.) After leaving the Chevy dealership, Louie went out on his own and started up his own body shop on Triplet Street in Owensboro. The body shop, located behind a DX gas station, was named "Better Services."

The first race I can remember attending was at Legion Park, right there in Owensboro. I can remember riding with my mom and dad and my two older brothers and my sister in a '36 Chevy. When we got to the track we unloaded the picnic supplies from the trunk, then my dad took the car into the pits to get ready to race. I had to have been around two or three at the time. I asked my mother about it since then and she remembered it the same way.

After the race was over, my dad brought the car back to us, we loaded into it and drove home. This car was my dad's daily driver. It had a modified straight 6 Chevy engine with a straight 3" diameter exhaust pipe right out the back. My dad had drilled some holes in the top and bottom of an oil can and he would slide it up inside the exhaust pipe and then slide a pin behind it to hold the can in place to act as a muffler. My uncle Tommy Payne, my mom's brother, borrowed the car one night and went cruising the town. Legend

Outside our home in Owensboro, Kentucky. Left to right: David, Cindy and "racer" Lloyd. The author was still in his crib just inside the window to the right.

The beginning of the big crash.

The cleanup following wreck. Note the primitive wooden guardrail. To far left is the #75 Ford Modified driven by Buddy Payne.

has it that he removed the oil can and was terrorizing the streets. Well, every policeman in town knew that car was my dad's, so they had a plan. After my Uncle Tom returned it home to my folks, he slipped the oil can back into the exhaust pipe and walked home. Returning the car back to my parents' driveway, Uncle Tommy had had to drive right by the local sheriff's house. Everybody in town knew that car. So, just a few minutes later, the police came knocking at our door. Thinking they had their man, they hauled my dad off to jail, where my Uncle Tommy had to come down and 'fess up. About then was the right time for Louie to tell Tommy where he had left Tommy's Harley lying on the side of the road when my dad had crashed it. I guess the story got to be a little funnier after some time had passed.

The fastest and most successful modified racer they had was a '34 Chevy 3-window coupe known as the "Flying Saucer." G.C. Spencer was the driver of this car and it was built in the Clements Brothers Garage at 206 Locust Street in Owensboro. The real magic in this car, besides having G.C. drive it, was the 302-cubic-inch GMC 6-cylinder engine it had. This engine was quite advanced for its time in a modified dirt tracker. It had about a 16-to-1 compression ratio, fuel injection, Wayne cross-flow head, Spaulding roller cam, dry sump oiling system, and Fenton split exhaust manifolds, and it ran on alcohol instead of gasoline. Famous NASCAR mechanic Harry Hyde once said the Flying Saucer sounded like a "rip saw going through a pine knot." That distinctive sound would later come back to haunt Louie.

Car #75 Buddy Payne starts on the pole at Nashville, Tennessee.

Bob Wente in his rookie year driving the Louie Clements–prepared Kurtis/Offy Midget. Behind the fence, the little girl is my sister Cindy, and to the right of her is my mother Magdalene.

Midget #99 named "The Tilt Action Special," driven by Tom Marshall, tuned by Louie Clements and powered by V8–60 flathead Ford.

Asphalt Midget roadster driven by Shorty Templemen.

Anyway, Spencer won so many races with this car that it started killing the spectator count at five different tracks they ran. In those days they raced at Owensboro, Kentucky; Evansville, Indiana; Bowling Green, Kentucky; Nashville, Tennessee; Cincinnati, Ohio; and Salem, Indiana. There were more, but they escape me at the moment. However, with Spencer beating the flathead Fords everywhere they raced, the promoters began to request he go elsewhere to race. At first, seeing the Chevy beat the Ford drew thousands of paying spectators. But after a few years of this trouncing of the Fords, the spectator count began to fall off.

Remember that distinctive sound of the Flying Saucer? Well, here's the deal. The race track in Owensboro was not far from our home. One afternoon during the week, my mother heard that sound and knew that it was my dad driving it. She loaded us kids in the family's '48 Chevy coupe and headed over toward the track. Upon seeing that it was indeed my father doing the driving, she promptly pulled the car, with all of us still inside it, right onto the track on the straightaway and stopped. Louie had to lock down the race car and slid right up to the side of my mom in the family car. He climbed out of the race car and began to fuss at my mom when she explained to him exactly who ran the show! She told him, "If you're going to kill yourself, you may as well kill us all." He said, "You almost did." And thus ended the race driving career of Louie Clements.

Louie and Crawford also had some other modified Chevys in those days. They named all of their race cars, as was common in the day. One of their '35 Chevy 3-window coupes was called the "Lemon Special." Another was called "Old Jitney." They ran some Chevy 6-cylinder engines before they finally got around to the larger and more powerful GMC 302 engines. One of the cars I remember from those days was a '37 Chevy Master coupe that my dad bought from his younger brother H.A. It was a bit larger in stature than the little 3-window coupes, so we kids called it "The BIG 4." If I remember correctly, Spencer kept racing that car after Louis and Crawford made their way down south to NASCAR country.

For the 1955 and '56 racing seasons we moved to Jasper, Indiana. Louie worked a day job for Eblehar-Structman Chevrolet Dealership. At night and on the weekends he worked for a man named Karl Geilhousen, who was a big USAC and Indy Car fan. They ran two midgets those two years. One was a Ford flathead V8 60 hp driven by Tom Marshall. That car was known as the "Tilt Action Special." Louie also put together a Kurtis midget with an Offy engine for Bob Wente, who later became the USAC National Midget Champion. Karl had bought the car used from Elmer George in Indianapolis.

We traveled to many tracks in the Midwest. The 16th Street Speedway in Indianapolis was the site of the first asphalt-track race I ever saw. I remember telling my dad that this track looked just like the street. I guess that's how a little kid would describe the difference between a dirt track and an asphalt track. It also had the largest crowd of spectators I had ever seen. We got to see an awesome little midget at a gas station the next morning. It was a "Roadster"-style midget and looked just like a baby Indy car. The driver was none other than Shorty Templeman.

The second track that stands out for me, back in the midgets' days anyway, was a quarter-mile high-banked asphalt track in Cincinnati that was called the "Soup Bowl." I still remember seeing the sparks fly from beneath the midgets as they would bottom out through the corners. This race was the first time I actually stayed awake for the entire evening and didn't fall asleep in my mom's lap in the grandstands.

While living in Jasper, Indiana, we got to know the Geilhousen family very well. Karl owned some rental properties and as long as my dad worked on the midgets for Karl, we never had to pay one cent of rent on the home they provided for us. That was pretty cool, but I think my best memory of that period was when we all rode over to the shop to see Spike's birthday present. Karl bought his youngest son, Spike, a brand-new shiny red quarter midget. It had a bright yellow #5 on it and I could barely contain myself. Of course, my family couldn't afford such toys for us kids, but it was really neat just getting to sit in Spike's car. That picture has never left my mind. When I was finally of age to be married and have a five-year-old son of my own, the first thing he got for his fifth birthday was a baby-blue quarter midget. We spent many Saturdays out practicing at the Phoenix South Mountain quarter midget track. I wish we still had that little car.

CHAPTER 2

1957: Auto Factories Get Heavily Involved

As the 1957 racing season was just getting started up, my dad and his brother, Crawford, went down to Daytona for the '57 Speed Weeks. Jack Smith had given them a very high recommendation to the Chevy factory team. He told the Chevy team manager that he would be making a great move to hire those two Clements boys from Kentucky.

About that time, Louie and Crawford were standing off to the side of the mechanics who were working on the 283 fuel-injected Chevys for the big race. They were experiencing problems with detonation, burning pistons and blowing head gaskets. Just as one

Left to right: Cindy, Mike, David and Lloyd Clements at play.

Louie Clements poses with the 1957 Chevy race car and kids, left to right: Lloyd, Mike, Cindy, and David Clements.

of the factory mechanics tossed a blown head gasket into the trash barrel, Louie walked over and pulled it out of the can to get a look at it. He quickly noticed that the fire ring of the gasket was smaller than the bore of the engine. This was actually a head gasket for the '56 Chevy 265 engine and the edges were hanging over into the bore of the larger 283 engine they had for the '57 Chevys. Louie took the gasket and handed it to the Chevy team boss and explained to him what the problem was. Right there, on the spot, Louie and Crawford were hired to come to work for Chevrolet. They installed a set of the proper 283 gaskets and things went pretty smoothly from then on.

The '57 Chevy factory team did pretty well, all things considered. In that particular 1957 beach race, Cotton Owens won it in a Ray Nichels '57 Pontiac. Cotton's teammate, #8 Banjo Matthews, had mechanical problems and ended up finishing in 41st place. But many of the top Chevys remained in the fight and fared well for it. Car #50 was driven that day by Iowan Johnny Beauchamp, and he finished second to Cotton's Pontiac. Finishing fourth was #87 of Buck Baker. Eighth-place finisher was Speedy Thompson in the #46 Chevy. Rex White came in ninth. This gave the Chevy team four of the top 10 finishes that year. Further back in the pack with mechanical problems or an accident were #47 of Jack Smith finishing 34th and Frankie Schneider in the #45 in 40th position. Smokey Yunick had entered a private '57 Chevy Bel Air for Paul Goldsmith to drive. He blew the engine and was credited with a 24th-place finish.

Right after that Daytona Beach and road course race in February of '57, the team

Magdalene Clements with her kids (left, Cindy and Lloyd; right, Mike and David) and the #45 Chevy driven by Frankie Schneider.

We lived in this Chevy wagon during the summer of 1957 and flat-towed the race car across the country. Left to right: Lloyd, Mike, Cindy and David Clements.

Rex White's Chevy factory crew for 1957, outside the wooden shop at Max Welborn Chevrolet. Left to right: Louie Clements, Bill Steele, Rex White, Crawford Clements, Stu McDonald and Hall Moose.

manager took Rex White's black-and-white #44 race car and gave it to another driver for the remainder of the season. Rex, Louie and Crawford were to build a new car for Rex to drive and they had two weeks to get it done. The next race was coming up in Manassas, Virginia, and they needed to be in it. Rex had the idea of installing weight jacks in the front of his car, so they did it. Frankie Schneider was also working on his car in the same shop and he had decided that he did not want the weight jacks in his car. The weight jacks allow a mechanic to simply turn a large ratchet and push up or down on the front suspension springs to set up the chassis with the desired corner weights. This was a huge step in stock car racing because it allowed about an hour's worth of work to be performed in about 30 seconds. And this was the first car in NASCAR history to ever receive such a device. This innovation is still used in the top levels of NASCAR today.

Anyway, the guys worked around the clock, often without the benefit of sleep, to get the car finished up in time for the next race. They pulled into the track at Manassas and unloaded the car and the only adjustment they made for the race was to set the tire pressures. Rex put the car on the pole and ran off with a two-lap victory on the field. Pretty nice payday for the efforts of the team.

For a good portion of the '57 season, we drove around the country following the NASCAR short track series. Mom, dad, and all four kids lived out of a 1957 Chevy 2-door station wagon. We flat-towed the race cars of either Frankie Schneider #45, or Speedy Thompson #46. To me, life just couldn't have gotten any better. I could stand up on top of that old Chevy wagon and watch the races. Every lap those cars made, I made too.

A 1/24th scale model of Rex White's 1957 Chevy "Black Widow."

Phoenix, Arizona, 1995. Left to right: Louis and Crawford Clements standing proudly with the authentic reproduction of the 1957 Grand National Champion car.

Buck Baker's victorious 1957 Chevy after the grueling 200-mile event at Langhorn, Pennsylvania.

In September 1957 my dad moved our family down to Spartanburg, South Carolina, where he and my Uncle Crawford got full time work with Bud Moore and what was left of the Chevy factory team. Louie worked on the '57 Chevy #46 for Speedy Thompson to drive. Crawford worked on the #87 for Buck Baker to drive. They were very much competitive and successful with those cars. Although Speedy won the "Big One" at the Darlington Southern 500 that year, the National Championship went to Buck Baker in the #87 Chevy.

I will always remember our first "home" in South Carolina. It was the interior of the family's 1950 Oldsmobile 88 2-door sedan. We rolled into town, broke, and parked in the front parking lot at Bud Moore's shop. This shop was on Church Street in Spartanburg. It was an old two-pump gas station that was closed down and converted to a race shop. It was small and very crowded inside, but the men who worked there seemed to be as happy as they could possibly be. Hard workers all, they got it done and won the championship that year.

We lived out of that old Oldsmobile for just a few days when Betty Moore found out we were there. She brought us into her home and treated us like family. Bud and Betty Moore are two of the nicest people on the planet. While staying in the car in the parking lot, my two older brothers got to go out behind Bud's shop and sit inside a couple of old worn-out Hudson Hornet race cars. I believe these were cars Bud had put together for Spartanburg's Joe Eubanks to drive. Junkyards have always been a place of fascination for little boys.

Throughout our time living in the southeast, there were always friendly and giving people. After working for a couple of weeks there, my dad finally got a paycheck, so he found us a room in an old house where an elderly lady was renting out rooms. We slept on old blankets and ate whatever we could afford. I don't remember ever hearing even one complaint. If we were poor, we didn't know it. Nobody had bothered to tell us what we didn't have. Sometime later, we got an apartment on Maple Street in Spartanburg. We would live there for five years. Many good memories surround that old apartment building. I started the first grade that September and went to the local Catholic elementary school with my two older brothers and my sister. Along with finding the money to keep the family clothed, fed and sheltered, my folks also paid to keep us in parochial school. That came at a cost, too. We had an old wooden cabinet RCA black-and-white TV. When we came home from school we turned on *American Bandstand*. The big hit in '57 was Buddy Holly's "Peggy Sue." I was just over six years old at the time and was totally unaware that Kimberly, my wife-to-be, was busy being born on June 20, 1957.

The 1957 Darlington Southern 500 was a true story of triumph and tragedy. Speedy Thompson won the race in the #46 Chevy maintained by Bud Moore's garage in Spartanburg. That car was one of the original '57 Chevy Black Widows used by the Chevy Factory Team during the first part of the season. That was right before the edict came down from GM corporate management: "We don't race." Yeah, right...

The tragedy came early in the race when Fonty Flock spun out at the end of the back stretch. Fonty was driving the '57 Pontiac #92 for Herb Thomas. As he sat still, backwards in the middle of the track, Bobby Meyers, driving one of Lee Petty's '57 Oldsmobiles, hit him head-on, full steam. Bobby was killed instantly. We were told that the '57 Olds had aluminum roll bars in it. I don't know if it really did or not, but we were told that. Even with the best roll bars, I don't know that Bobby could have survived that particular accident. Racing lost a great driver that day. Not long after that, Bobby's brother Billy Meyers was racing at Bowman Gray Stadium in Winston-Salem, North Carolina. Billy suffered a fatal heart attack during the race and ran off the track. Certainly 1957 was a tough year for the Meyers family.

I saw my first black man when I entered the first grade. To that point in life, I had never seen a black person. This man, whom we kids called "Jay Van," was the custodian of our school, St. Paul the Apostle. One day after being excused to go to the restroom during class, I exited the men's room and looked up and saw this giant-sized man who happened to be black.

He scared me so bad I almost went potty again, right there. Instead, I ran out the door screaming and ran all the way home. Totally out of breath when I got there, I could hardly tell my mother what I had seen. Once she got me calmed down a bit, she explained to me that not all people are the same color, and this was indeed a natural occurrence.

Left to right: teammates Speedy Thompson and Buck Baker pose with their race cars after the Langhorn, Pennsylvania, race.

After that, things went fine at school. I began to learn about being lifted out of my desk by my ears or having my hands smacked *hard* with a ruler. All in all, looking back on it now, I wouldn't change a thing. I learned life lessons that I still refer to today.

While Rex White and I were talking one day, I mentioned that I had just heard that current NASCAR independent driver Carl Long had been fined by NASCAR for being caught with an engine that was .17 cubic inches too large. While rules are rules and we all understand that, his fine of $200,000 basically put him out of business. He was likely only running that engine because he only had one, and after so much wear, the cylinders needed to be bored a few thousandths to clean them up and get ready for the big race at Charlotte. Certainly, he did not see any horsepower advantage to such a small increase in displacement. So I said to Rex, at least NASCAR just used to disqualify the guys back in our day and didn't hand down monetary fines. Then Rex told me of one time when he was indeed fined by NASCAR. Seems the race was held up in Trenton, New Jersey, and Frankie Schneider had pulled into the gate and was checking in, buying his pit passes and signing the entry form. He noticed that the race only paid $200 to win a 200-lap race. And that particular asphalt track chewed up tires like no other. He mentioned that

This photograph was taken from the grandstand seats at the end of the back straightaway at the 1957 Darlington Southern 500. If you viewed the race from this location you were an eyewitness to a horrific accident that claimed the life of driver Bobby Meyers.

even if he was to win the race, that wouldn't even pay his tire bill. He was told, tough, that's what it pays. So he got back in his truck and turned around and headed out of the track. As Frankie was just about to pull off the track property, Rex was pulling in with his race car and trailer. He asked, "What's up?" When Frankie told him about the deal, Rex said, "Well then, I'll just follow you out of here too." Which he did.

So at the next race, which was Asheville-Weaverville Speedway in North Carolina, Rex and Frankie pulled into the gate and went to sign in to compete. Mary Bruner then informed them that Pat Purcell had levied a $100 fine against both of them for leaving the track at Trenton without racing. Funny thing was, Rex had not yet even bought a pit pass! How do you get fined for a race in which you didn't even register to compete? Rex told Mary Bruner that he didn't have the $100 to pay her, so they agreed that NASCAR would take it out of his winnings for that night's race. Good thing Rex won the race! He made enough to pay the fine *and* still get back home.

One thing about the '57 season that I didn't find out about until a couple of years later was that when Louie and Crawford were working for Speedy Thompson and Buck Baker, it was up to the drivers to go to the NASCAR pay window and collect their winnings for that particular race. Crawford and Baker got along very well. Buck was indeed a gentleman. After Buck collected his winnings, he would always come back to the garage area and pay Crawford his share as was agreed. Well, Speedy Thompson was a different breed. Several times he just didn't feel the need to pay Louie for his work. With Louie having a wife and four kids to feed, this made a great hardship on our family. The way I found out about it was at the Darlington Southern 500 in 1959. Rex had qualified inside second row in the Louie Clements gold-and-white '59 Chevy #4. Starting in the third spot,

Start of the Modified race on the beach at Daytona, 1954. Cotton Owens is on the pole.

Start of the Sportsman race on the beach at Daytona, 1954.

outside front row, was Speedy Thompson in the Paul McDuffie '59 Chevy #22. Fireball was on the pole in Smokey's '59 Poncho #3. While the cars were parked in the garage area (yep, even as a kid I was in the garage area), I walked over and was looking inside that white '59 Chevy Impala #22. My dad saw me and hollered at me, "Get back over here." Never had a problem doing what my dad told me to do, especially when he had that killer tone in his voice. Once back over there I asked him, "What's the deal? I was just looking inside." He said, "If Speedy had walked over to you I would have had to whip his butt right here in the garage. And that would not be a pretty sight." After the race was over he told us kids on the ride home that Speedy owed him quite a bit of money that he was never paid. And given the chance, he intended to get it back in one form or another.

The first NASCAR race I saw was the Daytona Beach and Road Race in February 1954. I have a good many photos from that race. We watched the modifieds run one day and then the Grand Nationals the next day. I was pretty small at the time so I saw most of the race from the top of my dad's shoulders in the palmetto bushes just off the highway portion of the track. We had picnic blankets, coolers, etc., right there on the side of the road. Even in those days the cars were running 120+ mph when they passed us. This was my first time to see palm trees and the ocean, to smell the fresh ocean air and see the sunset at the beach. I loved it and still do to this day. We had driven down to the beach following the Gielhousen family in their new Cadillac. We were riding in our 1950 Olds coupe. I can still remember pulling into the little motel parking lot that Karl's Cadillac was so long he knocked over some flower pots out in front of the motel office. What a way to introduce yourself! That was a trip to remember. Got to watch the races on the *real* beach track and got to go by St. Augustine and drink from the "Fountain of Youth"

Start of the Grand National race on the beach at Daytona, 1954. Hudson on the front row.

on the way home. I gotta tell you, I think that youth fountain is a hoax. I'm 59 years old now and I was four when I drank that water. That makes me think it didn't work!

One thing I will never forget about that day and the same race in '55 was that the Blue Angels did a couple of flyovers while I was up on my dad's shoulders. They absolutely scared me to death! Man, those things were *loud* and fast! Being four or five at the time, it made an indelible mark on me that still gives me cold chills whenever I'm at a NASCAR race and they do the flyover. Except today, I love it.

The first NASCAR race I got to see from the "inside" was the 1957 fall race at Martinsville. We actually got to view the race from the infield in those days. Little did I know it at that time, but I was about to make a friend who would remember me years later. Just recently, while in the Busch garage at Phoenix, I met up with Jim Graham. Jim was working for Morgan Shepherd, trying to help get Morgan in the Busch race at Phoenix in the fall of '07. Jim looked at me several times and then came over and asked, "Is your name Clements?" I said yes and, lo and behold, this was the same kid I played football with in the infield that day at Martinsville. Jim was good friends with the Wendell Scott family and we all hung out together in the infield. We had shared toys, games, food, and whatever we had. What a real treat to see him again after all those years. I mentioned to Jim that this was a long time ago and I was just a real small boy at the time. He said, "I know, man, we ran all over you!"

Bob Welborn won that race that day in Martinsville driving a '57 Chevrolet #49. Jimmy Massey finished second in the Wood Brothers Ford. Lee Petty ran third in a '57 Oldsmobile and Rex White finished fourth with that black-primered #44 Chevrolet. Speedy Thompson was sidelined by an accident after completing 416 laps. My daddy had some work to do that next week!

Modifieds coming down the asphalt at the beach. Note the north grandstand full of people.

At the motel in Martinsville, Virginia. We towed the solid black 1957 Chevy for Speedy Thompson.

Setting up the cars in the pits in Martinsville, Virginia, Louie Clements with his back to the camera.

I know I was at other NASCAR races before that Martinsville race, but I really don't have much memory of them. This Martinsville race was different though. At this race I remember seeing a flat black primered '57 Chevy number 44. Simply because it had that #44 on it made it my favorite. Number 4 was my favorite number and having two number 4's on it made it my double favorite, I guess. As things would have it, that car was driven by Rex White. He would later have a profound effect on my life.

The next race we went to was in North Wilkesboro, North Carolina. Jack Smith won it in a '57 Chevy and Speedy Thompson finished fourth despite blowing a RF tire. Baker finished sixth in the #87 Chevy and Rex came in eighth in the #44 Chevy.

The next race was at Greensboro, North Carolina, and Buck Baker and Speedy Thompson ran first and second in that one. Rex had problems and finished 18th.

Buck Baker won the Grand National Championship that year, just as he had the year before. With Speedy Thompson coming in third in the championship points and Jack Smith finishing up fifth, that gave the Chevys three of the top five positions in the '57 championship season. Rex came in 21st place in the points, having only competed in 9 of the scheduled 42 races for the 1957 season. I believe Rex finished second in the NASCAR short track points that year, though. The NASCAR short track division was Rex's main mission for the season. Rex and Frankie Schneider were assigned by the Chevy factory team to compete in as many of the short track races as they could.

For some of the first half of the '57 racing season, we were still going to some of the USAC midget races with the two cars for Karl Gheilhousen, the Ford V8 60 for Tom Marshall and the Offy for Bob Wente. We hit the road that summer when school let out so we could tow those '57 Chevy factory cars around the country. I can still remember stopping for a couple of days at my Aunt Mary and Uncle Tiny's home in Elgin, Illinois. We were towing the #45 for Frankie Schneider that time. Funny what we remember from various times in our lives. I remember my older brothers talking about finally getting to have some pizza pie. Well, my dad and my Uncle Tiny went out and brought back a couple of pizzas and I have to tell you, that weren't like any pie I ever tasted. This thing had cheese on it and meat and all sorts of things that don't go in pies!

I also remember that little round picture tube on my Aunt Mary's TV. My brother and I watched wrestling on it for a while and then switched channels and actually found a modified race broadcast from Soldier Field in Chicago. What a treat to get to watch race cars on TV!

While still working for Bud Moore, Louie and Crawford were busy building a couple of '58 Chevys for Buck Baker to run at the February beach race. When it came time to put the roll cage in, Bud had acquired some nice heavy-wall 2" tubing. But they had no way to bend it. So, like all good racers, they improvised the best they could. They figured out a way to bend the bars just where they needed to be bent for the main hoop as well as the hoop across the front of the car around the windshield. They watched the local train that came right near the shop and figured out its schedule. Then one day Bud said, "Let's go." He had loaded up the new roll bar tubing, some torches and a couple of race wheels into the truck. Bud and Louie went down to that railroad track and actually welded a race wheel flat down on the tracks. Then they drove the truck to one end of the bar, used the rose bud tip on the torch to make a really hot flame, heated the roll bar tubing up and proceeded to pull that tube to a perfect 90 degree angle. If you look closely at the

Again at Martinsville, prepping the #87 for Buck Baker, his crew chief Crawford Clements.

photos of Buck's '58 Convertible, you will notice the rather large radius on the corners of the main roll bar hoop. And yes, they used the torch to cut the wheel off the train tracks when they were done.

Cotton Owens used to drop over to Bud's shop on occasion and ask questions about his engines. On one visit, Cotton pulled out a pair of his Pontiac heads and let Louie and Crawford look at them to help give him an idea of what might be going on with his engine. They pointed out to him that there were signs of the valves hitting the pistons and he would need to get some valve springs that were a little stronger if he intended to rev the motor that high. Well, Cotton left for a while and then came back to show them the springs he had come up with. I remember my dad telling me that the springs Cotton brought back couldn't be squeezed with a D9 Cat bulldozer. They asked Cotton where he got those springs and he told them he found them at the railroad junkyard. They were looking at these parts and talking out in the parking lot. So they brought Cotton inside the shop and wrote down the phone number for Honest Charlie's Speed Shop up in Chattanooga, Tennessee. They explained to Cotton to just call up Charlie and tell him what you're doing and he will send you what you need. That was his business and most of the racers down south were ordering their parts from Honest Charlie's.

There were some high-performance parts on the market in those days. Most of them came from Vic Edelbrock, Sr., Frank McGurk, Ed Windfield, Ed Iskanderian, Fish Carburetors, and of course there was some help from the factories out the back door, so to speak. For the most part, stock car racers of this era needing a particular part either had to make do with what they had or build their own. This is exactly where innovation in the sport came from. Back in the day, a smart mechanic could "innovate" his car into the winner's circle. Today they call this cheating. But years ago, the men who "innovated" were looked at as heroes. One mechanic would pull a slick trick out of his bag of tricks and even if the other guys got beat by it, they still had that unspoken respect for that innovation. In today's NASCAR garage area, I personally feel that tradition has still carried over to a degree. But most of the old-time gang has long since left the building and many of the newer teams call it cheating when the other teams get caught. If it's on their car, well… they just view it a bit more quietly.

CHAPTER 3

1958: Racing with Cotton Owens

The first official race of the 1958 season was held on a third-mile asphalt track in Fayetteville, North Carolina. It was a 150-lap race with Jack Smith starting on the pole in his '57 Chevy #47. Rex White started fifth on the grid that day and went on to win his first-ever NASCAR Grand National race. Lee Petty was second in his Oldsmobile and Tiny Lund was third driving another '57 Chevy. Buck Baker in #87 and Speedy Thompson in his #46 ended up in eighth and ninth respectively.

Rex brought home $630 for his efforts. Since a week's salary back then was about $65, Rex's payday wasn't too bad.

Louie Clements joined with Cotton Owens pretty soon after coming back home from Daytona in February 1958. The next race was at Concord, North Carolina, and it was won by Lee Petty. Cotton finished seventh that day. He was still driving the old '57 Pontiac built by Nichels Engineering and sponsored by Jim Stephens Pontiac. On April 12, 1958, the Grand Nationals came to run a 200-lapper at the Piedmont Interstate Fairgrounds' half-mile dirt oval in Spartanburg. Since it was close to Cotton's garage and home, Cotton decided to run that race. Cotton finished a dismal 26th place after sitting on the outside pole and then losing a fan belt on the 14th lap. Louie and Cotton ran a bunch of modified races in between the Grand National races they would pick to run. The next day, April 13, they towed down to Atlanta to run at the one-mile dirt speedway. Cotton started fifth and finished 11th. The race was won by Curtis Turner in his 1958 Holman-Moody Ford. On April 18 they ran the Grand Nationals at the Charlotte half-mile dirt track. Curtis Turner started on the pole and once again took home the first-place trophy and money. Cotton started ninth and finished seventh, still running the red-and-white '57 Jim Stephens Pontiac #6.

The first race for Cotton to run the '58 Pontiac he had bought from Smokey was the Martinsville race on April 20. Cotton qualified eighth fastest and ran out of brakes on lap 126. That gave him a 38th-place finishing spot. Bob Welborn won the race in the #4 1957 Chevy of J.H. Petty. Rex White came in second in the other J.H. Petty '57 Chevy. Pretty good days for the Chevys. The pole sitter and fastest qualifier, Buck Baker experienced electrical problems and ended up with a 35th-place finish. The next two races were in Manassas, Virginia, and Old Bridge, New Jersey. Cotton and Louie decided to stay closer to home and run a couple of modified races. I believe that was the Sunday afternoon race where Cotton was running the '38 Plymouth coach with the Hemi in it. He was leading the field, going away with it, until the right front tire blew going into the third corner. That track at Asheville-Weaverville had a high bank and was asphalt. Speeds in the modifieds were up there pretty high. Cotton hit that solid concrete wall and destroyed that old race car that day. I can still remember him walking very slowly and his son, Donnie, holding his dad's hand while they walked up to the smashed spot on the wall after the race.

The race in Manassas was won by good ole Frankie Schneider. He was a whale of a driver and probably the best chassis guy in the business at that time. Second place went to Jack Smith and third was #44, Rex White. The Chevys ran 1-2-3 that day.

Then in Old Bridge, New Jersey, Jim Reed won the race in a Ford with West Coast driver Eddie Pagan running second. Rex White pulled off a third for the bow-tie brigade.

The next race for the Grand Nationals was held at the Greenville-Pickens Speedway on the half-mile dirt oval. This was a 200-lapper, or 100 miles. Jack Smith started on the pole and scored one for the Chevy team. Buck Baker finished second in his Chevy. Cotton Owens ran the #6 Stephens '57 Pontiac again and experienced a broken axle after just 84 laps. The relegated him to an 18th-place finish after qualifying fifth.

The next Grand National race for Cotton was at North Wilkesboro, North Carolina. That was always one of my favorite tracks, especially once I was old enough to start racing and running on the track myself. Junior Johnson won that day, May 18. He was followed closely by Jack Smith in his Chevy #47 and Rex White in his #44. The #6 of Cotton Owens finished sixth that day. This was still the red-and-white '57 Pontiac that had won the Daytona Beach and Road Course race in February 1957.

May 24, 1958, marked the return to the Bowman Gray stadium in Winston-Salem, North Carolina. This is a short, quarter-mile, flat asphalt track around a football field. Handling was everything at this track. Rex White started on the pole in his '57 Chevy #44 but the race was won by Bob Welborn driving his own '57 Chevy #49. Cotton started 11th and finished ninth, two laps down. Glen Wood started fifth and finished seventh in his '57 Ford with that now-famous #21 on the doors. Glen Wood was a top-notch short-track driver. He could flat-out get the job done when the car held up.

One week later, May 30, 1958, NASCAR Grand Nationals traveled to Trenton, New Jersey, for a 500-mile race on a one-mile paved track. Marvin Panch, #98, started from the pole but suffered mechanical woes and finished 23rd in a '57 Ford #98. Cotton started 28th and experienced mechanical problems on lap 196 which sidelined him to a final position of 26th. The race was won by Fireball Roberts driving a '57 Chevy. Second place was Junior Johnson and third was Lee Petty.

The next race on the schedule was slated for way out west in Riverside, California, on the 2.6-mile paved road course. Needless to say, Cotton and Louie didn't tow all the way out there for that one. Jack Smith and Lee Petty did, though. Lee was chasing the points championship that year and was pretty much committed to running every race he could. Jack finished third after starting 40th. Lee Petty started fourth and finished fourth in his 1957 Oldsmobile. West Coast ace driver Parnelli Jones started from the pole but was sidelined in his Vel's Ford on lap 147 for a 26th-place finish. A total of 46 cars started that long 500-mile trek over the infamous road course.

The next race for Louie and Cotton to run was held at Asheville-Weaverville Speedway in North Carolina. Rex White grabbed the pole away from Cotton, who started outside pole this time. Rex drove off with a solid victory in his '57 Chevy #44. Cotton lost a wheel bearing on lap 172 for a 14th-place finish and an $85 payday.

One of the larger races of the year was the 250-mile race at Raleigh, North Carolina, on a one-mile paved track. This was the July 4th race of its day. Fifty-five entries started that race with Cotton Owens on the pole. He was a rocket that day for certain. But, as fate sometimes has it, a mechanical malfunction sidelined him on lap 78 of the scheduled 250 laps for a 45th-place finish. The Chevys finished 1-2-3 that day with Fireball winning, Buck Baker second and Rex White third. Other notables that day were Speedy Thompson fifth and Lee Petty sixth.

July 12, 1958, was another race at Asheville's McCormick Field. This was the site of Rex White's first-ever win back in 1956. I believe that race was actually considered a NASCAR Short Track Series race. Rex would have to wait another year before winning his first "official" Grand National race. If he could add his short track victories to his Grand National victories, his record for number of wins would be much higher on the list, even today. He drove a hastily prepared '56 Chevy that day. It was solid black with an "X" taped on the door. However, on this day, two years later, Jim Paschal started on the pole, Cotton started second and Rex started third. And that too, is the way they

This 1956 Chevy gives Rex White his first NASCAR victory at McCormick Field in Asheville, North Carolina. Note NASCAR's first flagman, Roby Combs (courtesy Phil Combs).

Winner Rex White receiving winning trophy/clock and checkered flag from Roby Combs (courtesy Phil Combs).

finished out at the end of their 150 laps. Those three were the only cars on the lead lap and Cotton brought home a $465 payday.

There was another race four days later in Busti, New York. But Louie and Cotton passed this race up and instead prepared the red '57 Pontiac for the race in Toronto, Canada, on July 18. Rex White grabbed the pole in his '57 Chevy and Lee Petty won the 100-lap race on the third-mile asphalt oval. Second place went to Cotton for a $480 payday and Jim Reed ran third in his '57 Ford. Rex finished seventh, two laps down to the winner.

One notable racer in the field this day was none other than Lee Petty's young son Richard. Richard started his first Grand National race this day and finished 17th after an accident on the 55th lap. What a start for the future "King of Stock Car Racing"!

On July 19, NASCAR held Grand National race #32 for the '58 season. This race was held in Buffalo, New York. Of historical significance, Rex White took the pole with a new qualifying record that day. I doubt this record will ever be broken. You see, this record is for the *slowest* ever pole position speed logged for a NASCAR race. Rex's pole speed was 38.593 mph as they qualified in the rain on a quarter-mile paved oval. Over 50 years later, no one has beat that record yet. Anyway, New Yorker Jim Reed won this race and Cotton Owens finished second with the '57 Pontiac #6. Rex finished fifth and Lee Petty finished sixth.

July 25 would be one of Cotton's better racing days. It had been a while since he had won a race, so it was with great joy and jubilation that he rolled into the winner's circle at Rochester, New York, on the half-mile dirt track. Cotton had two laps on the entire field that day. Buck Baker, Speedy Thompson and Lee Petty finished 2, 3, and 4 for that race. After qualifying on the pole for the race, Rex White experienced overheating problems on the 10th lap and finished 21st.

The next race for Cotton and Louie to run, because they were not running the full Grand National schedule, was the 2.85-mile road course at Bridgehampton, New York. Jack Smith brought his '57 Chevy up from Spartanburg to set on the pole and won the race. Dad and Cotton also came up from South Carolina, started fifth and finished second. Second place for the 35-lap, 100-mile race paid a whopping $525. They ran the '58 Pontiac in this race. Jim Reed was third, Junior Johnson was fourth and Buck Baker came home fifth. One car of note that would have an effect on my future was the eighth-place finisher of Al White, the black #40 1958 Chevy built by Rex White. Although they shared the same last name, they were not related. Five days later there was another Grand National race. This time the venue was back down south in good old Columbia, South Carolina. This would be a 200-lap race on a half-mile dirt track. Speedy Thompson grabbed the pole and the win this time. Bob Welborn ran second and Cotton came away with a fine third-place finish. That payday was worth $350. No wonder these guys had to run so many races each week. They had to run all they could and finish well to make a living. Crashing the race car was a very sad day for any racer back then. They did not have 15 more just like it sitting in the shop back home like today's teams have.

Just three days later, on August 10, the Grand National series came to the Nashville Fairgrounds' half-mile asphalt oval. This was to be a 200-lap race on a blistering hot Tennessee race track. Just as he did every time he ran at Nashville, Rex White grabbed the pole. He won the pole at Nashville for every race there from 1957 through 1963. That was one track where the 5' 4" driver stood taller than all of the other drivers combined. After starting from the pole, Rex had a right front wheel break while leading on lap 162. He ended up with a 23rd-place finish and $85 for his efforts. Hardly seems fair compared to today's money.

The race was won by Joe Weatherly in a 1958 H-M Ford and he collected $1,850 for his winnings. Second went to Bob Welborn. I can specifically remember my dad telling me that Bob Welborn was one of the nicest drivers in the NASCAR garage. They always got along well.

For their efforts in this Nashville race, Cotton and Louie made $60 for a 29th-place finish. Cotton was involved in a crash on lap 61 and that ended their day. It made for a bunch of repair work once they got home too.

Just one week later the next big race came along. This time it was back to Asheville-Weaverville Speedway for the Western North Carolina 500 in the half-mile, high-banked paved track for 250 miles, or 500 laps. Jimmy Massey grabbed the pole with his '57 Pontiac. Lee Petty finished third, stretching out his point lead for that season. About 50 laps into the race, both Cotton and Rex had engine problems with their '57 model race cars. I guess those year-old engines were bound to give up sooner or later. Cotton finished 36th and Rex was credited with 37th place.

The next race we got to attend was the "Big One," the granddaddy of them all, the Southern 500 in Darlington, South Carolina. This race is now a legend. West Coast racer Eddie Pagan sat on the pole in his 1958 Ford #45. During the race, he blew a tire entering turn one, went through the guardrail and landed outside the track, luckily, right side up. Again, Fireball Roberts won the race in his '57 Chevy #22. Again, he was the only car on the lead lap. Fireball was a hero in his own time. Buck Baker started seventh and finished second to Fireball. Third place went to Shorty Rollins driving his '58 Ford #99. Rex finished seventh driving Dave White's '58 Chevy #40. The Chevy 348 engine in that car

Buck Baker posing beside the 1958 Chevy maintained by Crawford Clements and Jess Rhodes.

ran the entire 500-mile race exactly as it was delivered to the Chevy dealer where they bought the car. There was not time to blueprint the engine in any manner. So they went with what they had and fared pretty well with it. As stated earlier, Cotton had crashed his '58 Pontiac earlier during the week's practice sessions. The car was a total mess and couldn't be repaired, so he borrowed a '57 Dodge from Bob Osekie. The engine burned a piston 15 laps into the race, so Cotton was credited with a 43rd-place finish and received a whopping $100 payday. I think Fireball earned $13,220 for his victory and Rex earned $1,045 for his seventh-place finish.

Eddie Pagan was not the only racer to fly outside the track that day. NASCAR officials warned the drivers to steer clear of the gaping hole left in the guardrail by Pagan's Ford. Less than 20 miles later, Eddie Gray's Ford lost traction and sailed right through that same hole in the fence. Then, on lap 210, Jack Smith and his '58 Pontiac #47 sailed right over the wall and tumbled several times out into the grassy area between the parking lot and the track. He was shaken up, but not injured badly. Jack was always one of the nice guys who always took time to play with us kids in the infield or garage area. He was a pretty stout man and he could throw us kids up over his shoulders like a sack of flour. We still miss him today.

The race after Darlington for us was the Charlotte Fairgrounds' half-mile dirt track. This was a scheduled 200-lapper. Cotton started fourth and had some problems during the race. He wound up with a 15th-place finish and a payday worth $70. Buck Baker came away the big winner this day in his '57 Chevy and Speedy Thompson finished second in his '57 Chevy. Lee Petty started on the pole but experienced a few problems and brought home a 10th-place finish. This put Baker decidedly closer to Petty in the points chase for 1958.

On September 7 we were off to Birmingham, Alabama, for a 200-lap race on another half-mile dirt track. Only 18 cars showed up for this race and Cotton set the record and took the pole in his rebuilt '58 Pontiac. Cotton led 189 laps and again experienced some overheating problems with a clogged radiator. In a rare short track appearance, Fireball Roberts won this one in his Strickland-owned '57 Chevy. Baker was second and Petty third. Cotton received $140 and was running at the end in ninth position.

The next race for Cotton and Louie would be the Richmond Fairgrounds track in Richmond, Virginia. Speedy Thompson grabbed the pole with his trusty '57 Chevy, and went on to the win from there. Lee Petty ran second and Baker was fourth. Cotton qualified fifth in his Jim Stephens '58 Pontiac and collected $165 for his seventh-place finish.

At the start of the 1958 season Louie went to Daytona with Bud Moore and my uncle Crawford with the '58 Chevys they had built new for Buck Baker to drive. They had a black one for the Grand National race and a white convertible for the convertible division race. These cars carried the #87 as well as the newly built 348-cubic-inch "W" engines for that year.

Back in those days the cars were inspected by NASCAR inside an old wooden garage building and they might have 8 or 10 race cars in that shop at one time. They had to pull the heads so NASCAR could check the bore and stroke and make sure that nobody was up to anything with the engine's displacement. NASCAR would drill out a couple of bolt heads so they could run a safety wire through them and then stamp them with a lead seal. If that lead seal was still in place after the race, then NASCAR knew that no one had messed with the engines.

When it came time to bolt the heads and intake manifold back onto the new 348 block, Bud Moore told Louie and Crawford to leave certain bolts slightly loose, maybe just a couple of turns. They did as requested and pulled the car out of that garage with the NASCAR lead seal in place. After going a couple miles down the beach to another shop, Bud let Louie and Crawford know what he was up to. Seems that was a clever "cover" to make more horsepower for the racers. Where they had left the center manifold bolts loose, they raised the manifold with a pry bar and slid a hacksaw blade down between the manifold and the heads. They cut those bolts off without harming the seals. Then they installed the special heads and manifold supplied by Mr. Zora Duntov, who was in charge of Chevrolet's Marine division. They put everything back together and glued the bolt heads back into place as NASCAR would expect to see them.

Well, Buck ran very well in that race and pulled off a fourth-place finish with the added horsepower in his 348 Chevy engine. NASCAR opened the hood and looked at the seals and passed the car right through post-race inspection. Isn't racing wonderful?

They also built another '58 Chevy that year. This one was a black Chevy 2-door Del Ray. They ran pretty well at Daytona. Shortly after coming back home after that race, Baker rented a garage in downtown Spartanburg. I remember it was an old wooden building and the race portion of the shop was on the second floor. There was an old concrete ramp that ran up the outside of that building. Once to the top of the building, the cars could turn into a big doorway and enter the garage area. Louie and Crawford spend many long nights in that garage preparing those '58 Chevys for Baker to drive. Now I do not want to tell stories out of school, but this is the way I remember it. While driving at Buck Baker's driving school in the summer of '88, both Buck and Buddy told me this same story again, just the way I heard it back in 1958. Seems that oftentimes, Buck could be found in the company of some pretty "ladies." This night, for some reason, he just happened to bring two of them up to the shop. Louie was inside the race car and Crawford was underneath it. I believe they were changing out the transmission on this particular evening. Well, the Clements boys heard a little commotion going on and stuck their heads out to see what the ruckus was all about. Apparently on a wise hunch, Betty Baker, Buck's wife, had driven down to the shop. She walked in, saw the two women, and pulled a pistol from her purse. No kidding! Her words were, "Duck, Bucky darlin', it's open season on whores!" And so went the ending to that party.

Just a couple of weeks after that, Louie went to work for Cotton Owens. They ran the same '57 Pontiac that Cotton had won Daytona with in '57 and they had also bought the '58 Pontiac right from Smokey Yunick after Paul Goldsmith won the '58 Beach race. They carried that '58 Pontiac home and converted it to a "zipper top" car so they could also compete in the convertible races with it. Cotton qualified on the outside front row for the Darlington Rebel 300 in the spring.

My uncle, Crawford Clements, stayed on to work on Baker's Chevys for that season. After Louie went over to work for Cotton Owens, another Owensboro race mechanic, Jess Rhoads, came down south to work with Crawford on the '58 Chevys for Buck Baker. Jess and Crawford worked together several times throughout the years.

Rex White also built a new '58 Chevy Del Ray that year too. His car was actually built for Dave White (no relation) to drive. But when they got to Darlington for the '58 Southern 500, Dave didn't care for the track. So Rex drove the car for that race and a few

Buck Baker in the 1958 convertible Impala at Martinsville, Virginia.

other races too. That car was black with a white top and the #40 on the side. It had "Transi-Truck Center" painted on the front fenders and it had "Jim Rathmann Chevrolet" on the rear quarter-panels. Remember, all Chevrolet high performance items went through Rathmann's Chevy dealership in those days. Rex told me that due to time constraints, they actually ran the engine exactly as it came from the factory. In fact, the engine was never pulled from the car during its construction. Wouldn't NASCAR racing be different today if they had to do that?

Cotton qualified for the outside of the front row for the '58 Darlington Rebel 300 in that same Pontiac #3 convertible. Fireball Roberts was on the pole with Paul McDuffie's '57 Chevy small block, and Marvin Panch started in the center of the front row with his '58 Ford convertible.

Together Cotton and Louie never had one engine problem for the entire '58 season. Cotton was an excellent driver and he had a good sense of the car too. Together with Louie's abilities with engines and chassis they had many good, successful races that year. In between racing the Grand National races and the convertible races, they also ran as many modified races as they could get to. Cotton was known as the king of the modifieds back then. He had two cars. One was a '38 Plymouth coupe and the other was a sedan. He had the Chrysler Hemi in each of them. One time at Asheville-Weaverville Speedway, a high-banked half-mile asphalt track, Cotton was running the modified. My mother had baked a prune cake and we all had lunch before the race. Cotton had quite the sweet tooth and consumed at least his share of that prune cake. Well, he won the race going away. But as soon as the race was finished, Cotton drove right to the infield outhouse and bypassed the victory lane ceremonies. From then on, we all knew the trick to getting Cotton to win races. Just like Bud and Betty Moore, Cotton and his wife Dot were very nice folks who never passed up a chance to treat us like family. God bless them all.

The 1958 Southern 500 brought about another chapter in racing for me. That was the first time we got to attend a race at Darlington Speedway. We had been told all about it for weeks. It sounded awesome and as a kid, man, I couldn't wait. When we got to the track on Friday evening, we pulled our cars inside and put them in a circle formation. Several of us carloads were part of Cotton Owens's team and all of us kids were going to sleep on the ground on blankets. We were wired. I don't think we actually got any real sleep. But early the next morning, when I woke up, I could smell the bacon and eggs cooking, the coffee brewing, and the stench of clothes that had been slept in. Yep, it was heaven, right there in good old South Carolina.

The 1958 Southern 500 was not the best race for Cotton and Louie, though. During practice for the race, Cotton crashed the Pontiac and actually went out of the track. Jack Smith also crashed out of the track, as did pole sitter Eddie Pagan in his '58 Ford. But those crashes were during the race. As I remember it, Cotton called home and told his wife, Dot, of the accident. He gave her a list of parts that would be needed to put the car back together. Dot called my mom and asked if she wanted to ride down to Darlington to deliver these parts. My mom said yes and I rode down there with them. I don't know how, but Dot knew just the parts that Cotton described to her and we rode out to the shop and loaded the trunk of her car with new control arms, ball joints, brake drums, spindles, all sorts of stuff. By the time we arrived in Darlington, I believe the decision was already made that the car was too badly damaged to repair at the track. So they parked the Pontiac and Cotton borrowed a Dodge from Bob Osekie for the race. Of course I thought that was pretty cool because the Dodge carried the #4 on it. As I remember, the car only ran a few laps in the race before it broke and had to retire.

My two older brothers took me down just inside the first corner where we could barely get a peek of the race cars as they came into the first turn. I was standing there hanging onto the chain link fence watching the cars come by when BOOM! Eddie Pagan's Ford blew a right front tire and creamed the guardrail entering the first turn. His car actually ripped a hole in the fence and went out of the track and down the embankment. I later got to meet Mr. Pagan in person at his shop in Charlotte, North Carolina. This would have been around 1974 when I was racing in the newly formed NASCAR Baby Grand division. I had a good visit with Mr. Pagan and asked him about that crash. He remembered it well, as you might imagine, and went into detail as to how it unfolded. He said he was running pretty well that day and had just opened the trap door that allowed the drivers to inspect their tires as they raced. He saw the dreaded white line on the tire that meant he was out of rubber on that tire. So he decided that he would pit on the next lap. Well, as luck would have it, he never made the next lap. That tire let go just as he entered the first turn at approximately 125 mph. It was carnage enough to strike fear into this 8-year-old kid. Probably shook the driver up a bit too.

Also in 1958 we met Bobby Johns and his father Socrates. We all called him Papa Johns. The grownups called him Shorty Johns.

By this time, my older brothers and I were well into building model cars and painting them up just like our NASCAR heroes. I had a '58 Buick that I had painted like the one that Fireball drove at the beach that year. My dad mentioned that Bobby Johns was coming over for dinner with us that evening and he might feel slighted if we didn't have a car painted up like his. Well, the rush was on. I pulled the frame and interior from that '58 Buick and my brothers began to sand its sides until it looked somewhat like a '57 Chevy. My older brothers were always better than me at building models. They were older, more mature and had more patience than this kid. Anyway, by the time Bobby arrived, we had that Fireball Buick looking pretty close to a blue-and-white #7A Bobby Johns Chevy. The paint was still wet, but Bobby liked it anyway.

In 1958 we three boys used to take our model cars out back and build a banked dirt track and actually get down on our hands and knees and race them. On a few occasions Cotton's son Donnie and his friend Lenny Senn would come over and race with us. We took this race thing real serious, too. There was a line drawn across the infield of the little track. You had to get down on your hands and knees and remain behind that line. You put your left hand on the line and put your right hand on the model car that was yours. Then, without crossing that line, you stretched and gave your car a shove to get it into and around the corner. There was actually a knack to getting these models to slide through the turns, bounce off the other cars, and roll just a few more inches. After each person had taken a turn pushing his car, we would all sit and just look at the placement of the cars for a few minutes. We had to determine which cars were in front of which other cars. Then, we sat them all on the track as close as we could to being just like real race cars would look in those tight quarters. And yes, we had some really hard knock-down and drag-out fistfights over who actually won. But come next week, we were right back at it. The racing blood ran deep in our veins.

The next Grand National race we attended was held at the .4-mile dirt track at Hickory, North Carolina. Lee Petty won it with his '57 Olds #42. Cotton finished eighth in the red '57 Pontiac #6. This was a grueling 250-lap race that took its toll on the racers' equipment. Twenty-seventh-place Bob Welborn broke an axle and Curtis Turner ran his car clean out of tires. Herman "The Turtle" Beam finished 21st, a full 53 laps down to the leaders.

The next day was our next race. The Grand Nationals raced at Asheville Weaverville Speedway that day. Rex White started on the pole and won the race going away with his '57 Chevy #44. Chevys took the top four spots that day. Cotton qualified his '57 Pontiac on the outside pole but a bad wheel bearing dropped him from contention on lap 172 of the scheduled 200 laps. The highest finishing new car in this race was Herb Estes in his 1958 Ford. He came in eighth place after qualifying sixth.

Race #47 for the 1958 season came with good news and bad news. The bad news was that after qualifying the '58 Pontiac on the outside pole for this race at Hillsboro, North Carolina, Cotton had some mechanical issues with the car and dropped out on lap 68 for a 22nd-place finish. The good news? Cotton and Louie had also prepared the older '57 Pontiac for this race too. Cotton asked his longtime friend, Joe Eubanks, also from Spartanburg, to drive the car at Hillsboro. Good thing, too, because Joe qualified seventh and brought that baby home in first place. Yep, we had another winner for the season. Eubanks and second-place Doug Cox were the only two of the 33 cars on the lead lap at the end of the race. That win paid off $800, plus of course the $50 Cotton got for 22nd place.

Race #48 of the season was a bit kinder to Cotton. This time he qualified well in the '58 Pontiac and finished third. That paid $350 for third, plus the $150 Joe Eubanks received for his eighth-place finish. The race was won by #42, Lee Petty, who was on his way to his second Grand National championship. Buck Baker, who was in the hunt for the championship also, finished a fine second place to Petty. Also of note in this race was the 22nd-place finish of Richard Petty in another Petty Enterprises '57 Olds. Richard was still running at the end of the race, although 30 laps down to the leaders.

The next race on the schedule was one of the more popular races of the season at Martinsville, Virginia. This was the home track for Glen and Leonard Wood, who were awesome people and fierce competitors too. Glen Wood sat on the pole and brought his '58 Ford convertible home in ninth place after the 350 of the scheduled 500 laps. The race was shortened because of darkness. NASCAR officials held up the start of the race for over an hour while they figured out who exactly was supposed to start in the 40-car field. Fireball Roberts won his sixth race in nine starts for the '58 season. No wonder we still call him the first-ever NASCAR superstar. Fireball ran the last few laps on a flat tire under the caution flag and later admitted that things might have been different if he had had to complete all 500 laps. Fireball earned $2,875 for his day's work. Second place went to Speedy Thompson, and third was Rex White driving the black-and-white '58 Chevy 348 car #40. I got to spend many days at the old shop sitting in the seat of that car pretending to be Rex White winning another race. I don't think I ever lost a race in that car. I must have been a really good NASCAR driver when I was eight years old! Well, Cotton started 40th and finished 10th in the '58 Jim Stephens Pontiac #3. Buck Baker finished fifth and gained a few points on Lee Petty, who finished seventh. Joe Eubanks started 10th but finished up 34th after being sidelined on lap 96 in the Jim Stephens #6 1957 Pontiac. And our good friend Bobby Johns finished a very respectable fourth place in his '57 Chevy with the 220-hp 283-cubic-inch small-block Chevy.

The last two races of the 1958 season came at a couple of the racers' favorite tracks. Race #50 was held at North Wilkesboro Speedway, a track that would still be racing today if I had my way. It was October 19, 1958. Wilkesboro was, and still is, a five-eighths-mile paved oval with the front stretch running downhill and the back stretch running uphill. It was a very fast track too. Glen Wood snagged the pole again in his #21 Wood Brothers '58 Ford Grand National car. Outside pole was full-time Wilkesboro resident Junior Johnson. Junior was really hard to beat on his home track, or anywhere else for that matter. Junior drove the red #11 1957 Ford this day. Cotton started third and Speedy Thompson started fourth. Junior won the race as the only car on the lead lap at the end of the 160-lap race. He earned $800 for his efforts that day. And that isn't counting what he made with the corn liquor or on the chickens, either! (Just kidding...)

Glen Wood finished second, Speedy was third and Cotton was fourth. Lee Petty was ninth and Baker was 10th, so Lee got the points back that he had lost the week before. Richard Petty also started this race from the 10th position. Not bad for the rookie! But, as fate would have it, an engine overheating problem took him out of the race on lap 35. That spot paid $50.

The last race of the '58 season was held at the very fast and dangerous Atlanta Lakewood Speedway. For the third week in a row, Glen Wood again took the pole position for this race. In a rare performance for the time, our friend Tiny Lund qualified on the outside pole driving Herb Estes's '58 Ford Grand National car #36. By this time, Charlie Griffith had already purchased the '57 Pontiac from Cotton. So Charlie qualified and raced the '57 Pontiac to a 27th-place finish after an accident on lap 88. Cotton's '58 Pontiac was driven that day by Joe Eubanks, who finished 15th, 10 laps down to the winner, Junior Johnson. Junior earned $1,925, which was a very nice payday in 1958 dollars! Fireball was second, Lee Petty was third and sewed up the championship for the season. Joe Weatherly came in fourth. Buck Baker, second place in the season points battle, finished this race in 13th position driving the same black '58 Chevy that Bud Moore, Crawford and Louie Clements had built for him at the start of the season. Who said those 348 Chevys were truck engines? Again, rookie Richard Petty started this race in 35th position and finished in the same spot after a burned piston sidelined him after 29 laps.

I was not in attendance this day in Atlanta. But worthy of note here is one story my dad related to me on the way to school Monday morning. He said that Curtis Turner, the bravest man to ever sit in any race car, was driving down the front chute wide open and just after the flag stand, he "tossed" the car into one of his signature broad slides. Well, the right rear wheel caught a rut and that '58 Ford flipped side-over-side several times, very hard and fast, a roll that looked to be very much unforgiving. It landed right side up, and a minute later, Curtis climbed out of the car, stood upright and took his hands and simply brushed off his Sunday morning three-piece suit and then walked back to the pits asking if anybody had a car that needed a driver. This man was tough as nails, totally without fear. (There was one other driver who would climb in a race car on a dirt track in an expensive three-piece suit. That was none other than Mr. Buck Baker. Buck even wore a good-sized diamond ring when he raced.)

The top 10 in the NASCAR Grand National Points series for the 1958 season were: first, Lee Petty; second, Buck Baker; third, Speedy Thompson; fourth, Shorty Rollins; fifth, Jack Smith; sixth, L.D. Austin; seventh, Rex White; eighth, Junior Johnson; ninth, Eddie Pagan; and 10th, Jim Reed. Cotton Owens finished 17th in the points that year and "King" Richard Petty came away with a 36th-place points finish.

Some other big-time notables for the '58 season were the hit songs we watched and heard on *American Bandstand* when we got home from school each day. Bobby Day had a #1 hit with "Rockin' Robin" and the Big Bopper had a hit with "Chantilly Lace." Anyone really into NASCAR history this far back can still hear these songs in their heads today.

On a sad note, we lost my Grandpa Clements to cancer in 1958. He was a third-generation auto mechanic who owned and operated his shop in the back yard of the family home on 4th Street in Owensboro. His name was Augustine Clements and he was a huge man, extremely tall, and wore a size 13 triple-D shoe. He liked his beer and he liked his boys, too. George, Louie, Crawford, H.A., Kenny, all of them grew up learning mechanics the hard way: from their dad, who as I stated already liked his beer, liquor and big cigars. Granddaddy always had time to pick me up like a sack of flour and throw me over his shoulder. I was never certain that I would live to walk again, but he meant well. I never got to meet my grandmothers, neither of them. They both passed away before I was born. My father, Louie Clements, was given some of his father's hand tools. One day while searching for a particular tool, I came across an old rusty box-end combination wrench. I was in my early thirties by this time and I asked my dad about this old wrench. He said, "Let me see that." He looked at it and pointed out to me the four filed notches in the beam of the wrench. He said, "That was the way your grandfather marked his tools so he could tell which were his when he found them where they shouldn't have been in the first place." My dad then handed the wrench back to me. So, being the loving and caring son I am, I took that rusty old wrench down to the local chrome shop and had it polished and chrome-plated. Then, on Father's Day, I wrapped it up and gave it back to my dad. I can still see the tears in his eyes when he realized what it was. He hugged me like never before. If you haven't guessed by now, my dad was my hero!

Well, my Mom was, too. But we'll get to that in a coming chapter.

The 1959 Chevy Grand National Car #4

The following comes from notes I made when people asked me about the particulars on this '59 Chevy race car. I could tell them from memory as well as some of the old photos I have.

The factory interior door panels were left in it. The dash as well as the door panels were red. I have a color photo of the '59 with the roof cut off for the 1960 Rebel 300. Actually, this car had the roof cut off for the '59 Rebel 300 also. Ken Rush had entered first so he got to run the #4. Rex's entry came in after Ken's, so Rex ran the #40 on the solid white '59 Chevy convertible for this race. In those days, the first guy to enter a race with a desired car number got to run that number. Today, the car numbers belong to the car owners and are sold and traded off when teams are bought and sold. It's about time the #3 came back to cup racing if you ask me. After two-time champion Joe Weatherly was killed, the #8 was not allowed to be retired. And after the "King," Richard Petty, retired he tried to retire the #43 and competed the next season with Rick Wilson driving the number 44 for Petty Enterprises. NASCAR told Petty: Either you use that number, or we will. It's time for RCR to put the #3 back on the track. There will never be another Dale Earnhardt. It's not about that. You just have to realize that if the #8 had been retired after Joe was killed, the Red Nation of #8 Junior fans would have never been.

On the 1959 Chevy Grand National car, the seat was the factory bench seat with the right side back removed. They took the seat to an upholstery shop to have the seat bolsters added. I believe it was either flat, semi-gloss black or dark brown. The car did have the three trap doors for tire inspection and the stock dash gauge cluster was removed and a flat aluminum panel was put in its place to hold the gauges. There were large tach, small water temp, oil temp, oil pressure and even a rear end oil temp gauge. Those cars were bad about losing rear end gears at Martinsville. That particular car was the first-ever NASCAR race car to have hood pins as we know them today. It was also the first to have the rear-end Watts Link setup. They started the season in '59 with weight jacks in the front and Airlift bags in the rear. About halfway through the season, they installed the weight jacks in the rear too.

Rex started third, outside front row, for the '60 Rebel 300. He also finished third. When the race was over I was in the pits and just eight years old. The fans used to come down and peel the decals off the race cars for souvenirs. Sometimes they would reach inside the car and try to unscrew the shifter knob and take it too. My dad stuck me inside the car and told me to smack anybody trying to steal the shifter knob. He sat my sister, Cindy, who was age 10 years at the time, on the fender on a blanket and told her to start yelling at the first person to start to remove a decal. She did, too! She told those folks that her daddy said to leave those stickers alone. And she meant business. Tell you the truth, I believe she could have handled those fans even without dad's help. She is not only my favorite sister, she turned out to be a fantastic mom and a great grandma in more ways than one!

When the fans would peel all the stickers off the cars, that would pull the paint off too, and that meant the car had to be repainted before next week's race. Since my dad was the body man, painter, engine builder, rear gear builder, transmission man, etc., etc., he didn't care much for fans removing the stickers.

Man, my childhood was the best!

CHAPTER 4

1959: The Formation of White and Clements, Inc.

For the '59 NASCAR season, Louie Clements and Cotton Owens built a new 1958 Pontiac Chieftain 2-door sedan. They found a wreck in a local junkyard and it was in good enough shape to build a nice new race car with. The car, chassis, roll cage, engine, and everything else about it was different from the one that Smokey had built. Everything on this car was a fresh start. I can remember seeing the body of the car on a fixture which held it upside down. There was some horrible residue on the inside of the roof from the previous owner. I believe my oldest brother Lloyd went to work with my dad one Saturday and was appointed the task of scraping that stuff out of the roof. (I'll give you a hint: GM didn't put it there, and it was very dark red!) The two men worked hard together, well into the evenings, to get it finished in time for the first annual Daytona 500 on Bill France's new Daytona International Speedway.

Jack Purser, who owned the local Esso gas station, was a Cotton Owens fan and a friend. He offered as much sponsorship as he could to the team. There was a vacant lot on the street corner right next to Purser's Esso station. Many tractor-trailer rigs were parked there in between road trips. These were owned by Spartanburg's W.H. Watson.

The 1958 Pontiac #6 built by Louie Clements and Cotton Owens, driven by Cotton Owens in the inaugural Daytona 500 in February 1959. This car was the fastest qualifier for the first Daytona 500 with an average speed of 143.198 mph (courtesy Dot Owens).

44

He too gave sponsorship dollars to the team. I believe they even loaded Cotton's new race car for the Daytona 500 into one of W.H.'s trucks for the trip down to Daytona. That could have been the first big tractor-trailer rig in NASCAR for all I know. It was certainly the first one that I had ever seen at the track.

Much excitement was in the air looking forward to this big event. France designed the track with a tri-oval in the front stretch so that more fans could get a better view of the cars. He had the banks built up to 31 degrees so the cars could run wide open all the time and the people could see what the cars could really do.

Louie built the Pontiac engine for this race, and once he was at the track and practicing, he just about wore out the screws on the carburetor by changing jets, metering rods, etc., just looking for that last little bit of speed. He apparently did a good job because Cotton logged the fastest official qualifying speed for the inaugural Daytona 500. His speed was 143.198 mph and was the track record set when he qualified.

This car was painted black with a white top and white coves down each side. The hood was adorned with the 285-hp Pontiac factory horsepower rating. The bright "Day-Glo" orange number 6's were on both doors and the roof. To make the numbers as bright as possible, they mixed up some glass beads from highway marker paint into the Day-Glo orange. During the first practice session, the wind and the race motor's vibration pretty much shucked off all of that fancy glow-in-the-dark paint. But they soldiered on.

As we know today, Lee Petty won the race driving a new 1959 Oldsmobile #42 and second place went to Iowa racer #73, Johnny Beauchamp, driving a new 430-cubic-inch Holman-Moody T-Bird which was owned by Roy Burdick. Who would have thought that finishing right in front of Cotton would be Charlie Griffith driving the old '57 Pontiac that Cotton had sold to him just a couple of months earlier? Cotton finished fourth in that first 500-mile Daytona race. Cotton was running in third position, but he was watching the big four-sided scoreboard with the lights showing drivers' positions and the number of laps completed. That scoreboard was updated every 10 laps. So Cotton thought there were 10 laps to go and knew he couldn't make it that far on fuel. He came flying down pit road as the white flag was waving. My dad pointed to the white flag and Cotton jumped back on the throttle but had lost enough momentum that Charlie was able to sneak by for the third spot. All in all, they came away happy with their finish.

Back in January of '59, once Cotton and Louie had completed the new '58 Pontiac race car, Cotton didn't have any more work to do and had no real income. So Louie called up his old friend Rex White and asked if he needed help getting ready for the Daytona 500 race. Rex was behind schedule, so Louie traveled up to Silver Spring, Maryland, to help Rex and Bill Steele complete the '59 Chevy for Rex to run at the new Speed Palace. Rex ran pretty well there, too, but he had some engine problems during the race. The distributor shaft froze up and spun the distributor and pulled off all of the plug wires. He coasted into the pits and parked the car for a 26th-place finish. Rex had finished 10th in his 100-mile qualifier race and Cotton had finished sixth in that same qualifier. Bob Welborn won that race and that put him on the pole for the 500.

Running on the newly constructed high-banked Daytona Super Speedway was a scary but incredible experience for most of the drivers when they first entered the track. Driver Jimmy Thompson was reported to have stated, "There have been tracks that separated the men from the boys. But this is the track that will separate the weak from the

Left to right: Louie Clements, Cotton Owens and an unknown NASCAR official. Louie is rejetting the carburetor before qualifying.

strong long after the boys have gone home!" They were totally in awe of such long straights and high banks.

The Grand National hardtop cars were running a full 10 to 15 mph faster than the convertible cars. It was a scheduled "Sweepstakes" race, which meant that Grand National as well as convertibles would compete against each other. The Grand National cars lined up on the inside of the track and the convertibles took the outside line. By race time, most guys had figured at least some of the nuances of the draft: pull up close behind a faster car and it will break the air for you and your slower car can suddenly run just as quick as the faster car. Richard Petty tried this tactic early on in the race but it seems he was geared to run by himself, because once he tagged onto a faster hardtop car, Petty's '57 Oldsmobile turned more rpms than the old engine could stand. He fell out of the race with a blown engine on lap 8. A total of 59 race cars started that first Great American race. About 35 were still running at the end.

Lee Petty's win was worth an astounding $19,050, a tidy sum in those days. Cotton earned $2,145 for his fourth-place finish. With that much money, he could have paid for his crew chief's motel room for the week. But he didn't. He and his wife had a room of their own. He told Louie to go get a room. Louie did just that, thinking Cotton would

Left to right: Cotton Owens and Louie Clements after setting the fastest qualifying time for the first Daytona 500.

reimburse him later. Not only did Cotton not reimburse Louie for his motel room, he sent about five more guys all down to bunk with Louie for free. These were volunteer help who came on their own ticket. But a driver who is really serious about getting to the top knows he has to pay for good help.

So, once back home after the '59 Daytona, Louie Clements and Rex White struck up a deal. They formed White and Clements Racing. It was a 50/50 corporation and all winnings and all bills were split down the middle. Both men had incentive to treat each other right. They developed great on-track communication skills that helped them run up the highest NASCAR winning percentage until Jeff Gordon came along and broke it some 40 years later. Rex's average finish over the season was 8.8. That is still right there next to Gordon's new record.

The first racer ever black-flagged on the new Daytona Super Speedway was none other than Richard Petty himself. The NASCAR officials told all drivers to run four or five laps around the track on the flat apron before going up on the high banks. Richard either didn't hear that order, or just got excited and drove straight up onto the banking and put the hammer down. Yep, he was black-flagged and brought into the pits to discuss this with Johnny Bruner. Another rather odd reason for being black-flagged at the new track happened to Herman "The Turtle" Beam. Herman, a college graduate and chemist by trade, always built very nice race cars. But he was known for driving just fast enough to stay on the track. He never got in a hurry during a race. But, at Daytona, he forgot to don his safety helmet. After he ran a few laps on the speedway, one of the officials noticed he was not wearing a helmet and he too was black-flagged.

Of note in this first Daytona, too, was the fact that Harold Smith, driving a '59 Studebaker, finished 31st place and still running at the end, although 41 laps down to the leaders. Starting second on the field and first among the convertibles was Shorty Rollins in his '58 Ford convertible #99. Shorty blew an engine on lap 115, giving him a 38th-place finish.

One very important point needs to be made here. There have been many stories about who actually "discovered" the draft or slipstream. That was the effect that was made by having two or more cars run close together, bumper to bumper, inline with each other. Many people said Richard Petty discovered it in 1959, as it was his first race at the new speedway. Many reporters have stated that Junior Johnson discovered the draft during the 1960 Daytona 500 when he ran an underdog '59 Chevy 348 against the much superior 1960 Pontiacs. Junior did indeed fall in behind Cotton's '60 Pontiac during practice and discover that he could run that old Chevy just as fast as the Pontiacs if he would just pull in behind them when they passed him. So, by race day, Junior had a plan and he stuck to it. His '59 Chevy #27, built by Florida's Ray Fox, was 10 to 12 mph slower than those awesome Pontiacs. But running right up against their rear bumpers, he could stay right with them. He pretty much hitchhiked his way to victory lane that day by making the draft work to his advantage.

Being a true motor sports history buff myself, I did a little research of my own. While reading an excellent book by Dick Wallen called *Board Tracks, Guts, Gold, and Glory*, I read a very well-written story about an early board track motorcycle racer by the name of Ira Vail. He was a factory-sponsored racer in his day. This would be during the early 1920s. Ira would run that race bike wide open on the steep banks of the board tracks and sometimes exceed 140 mph! When catching some slower racers on their motorcycles, he noticed that when he got right behind them, they were actually breaking the air for him. It was like racing with no wind. He could pull up behind one bike and then use his momentum to slingshot right by that bike. He kept doing this, bike after bike, until he had pretty much lapped the field. When asked how he did it, he could only explain it as

#73 Johnny Beauchamp, driving Roy Burdick's 1959 T-Bird, was originally flagged as the winner but later reinstated in 2nd place behind Lee Petty.

"climbing the rope." That was his way of describing what is historically known as the first case of any racer in any brand of motor sports experiencing what we call "the draft."

The next race for Rex and Louie would be the 200-lapper at the half-mile dirt oval at Concord, North Carolina. After taking the pole for this race, Buck Baker lost an engine on the 15th lap for a 18th-place finish. Crawford was still crew chief for Baker at this time. As I remember, that car was sponsored by Thor Chevrolet. It had a distinctive rocket painted down the side of the car. Curtis Turner drove the wheels off his #41 T-Bird for the win that day. Rex ran the '59 Chevy #4 and finished 14th after suffering a broken rocker arm on the old 348 engine.

Rex's next race was held at the Bowman Gray Stadium in Winston-Salem, North Carolina. This was certainly one of Rex's favorite tracks. He always ran well there. On this day, he took the pole with a new qualifying record and finished third in the race. Jim Reed won the race, still running his '57 Ford. Lee Petty finished second in his '57 Oldsmobile. Bob Welborn and Buck Baker rounded out the top five.

The next race on the schedule was April 4 at Columbia, South Carolina, on a half-mile dirt track. Rex and Louie didn't have this race on their schedule, but this is still a very noteworthy race because Buddy Baker, the son of two-time NASCAR Grand National champion, started his first race on this day. Buddy drove his father's '58 Chevy #89 but fell out with chassis problems after 53 laps. That earned him a 14th-place finish and $85 cash. The race was won by Jack Smith in his Bud Moore '59 Chevy. Second went to #11, Ned Jarrett, who went on to make quite a name for himself in the sport.

The next race was race #10 for the season and it was held at North Wilkesboro, North Carolina. Dad and Rex did not enter that race on this occasion. The race was won by Lee Petty, followed by Jack Smith, and third was Cotton Owens. Herman Beam brought his '57 Chevy #19 home in sixth place, a full 13 laps down to the leaders.

Reading, Pennsylvania, was the next race for Dad and Rex to run. Rex was blistering fast that day, but halfway through the race the old 348 Chevy broke a push rod. That was the weak link in the Chevrolet "W" motors. Both the 348s and the 409s were called "W" motors because of the shape of the heads and valve covers. The valve train was always their soft spot. The ports were horrible for stock car racing purposes. They did pretty well drag racing, but that's a whole other story. Rex ended up with a 19th-place finish that day. Junior Johnson won the race at Reading, followed by Speedy Thompson and Tiger Tom Pistone driving his yellow '59 T-Bird #59.

Tom was a short driver who had come down south from the very rough-and-tumble world of Soldier Field racing in the greater Chicago area. He had learned to be tough up there. He was a fierce competitor too. I have a vivid memory of my brother helping me up to see inside that car of Pistone's. After climbing up to look inside that '59 T-Bird I could clearly see that he had actually bolted a couple of 2 × 4 pieces of wood to the pedals to help him reach them.

Things didn't get any better for Rex the next week either. This time the race was at Hickory, North Carolina, on the .4-mile dirt oval. Rex qualified fifth and lost the transmission after just 27 laps. Not a good payday at all. But Junior Johnson got his second win in a row that evening. Joe Weatherly drove Curtis Turner's '59 T-Bird to finish second and Lee Petty ran third in a '57 Olds. Junior's was the only car to complete the required 250-lap distance. Our good friend from Kentucky, G.C. Spencer, started a very respectable fourth, but finished 14th after losing a transmission on lap 179. He was paid $85 for his effort.

Martinsville, Virginia, played host to the 13th race of the '59 season, the Virginia 500. That's 500 laps on a half-mile paved oval. Bobby Johns and Joe Lee Johnson grabbed the front-row starting positions. Both were still running their older '57 Chevys. Those Chevys were quite possibly the best race cars NASCAR has ever seen. They were always tough to beat. But on this day, it was once again Lee Petty taking home the bacon. Petty won by a whopping five laps over second-place Johnny Beauchamp. It wasn't a close call this time!

Richard Petty had a very good run that day for a seventh-place finish, and track and hometown favorite Glen Wood finished 11th. Rex started off with a very good run there just as he always did. But mechanical problems brought him into the pits a few times and he wound up with a 15th-place finish, still running at the end.

Race number 15 of the season rolled around to the Fairgrounds track in Nashville. Once again, Rex White grabbed the pole position just as he did for seven straight years at that track. The '59 Chevy #4 was still solid white for this race. Rex and Louie had not yet come up with the "Gold Thunder" paint scheme. Rex handily won the race with Junior Johnson finishing second. They were the only two cars on the lead lap. The race was 200 laps on the half-mile paved oval. Tommy Irwin ran third and Buck Baker and Joe Lee Johnson rounded out the top five. What I remember about that day in Nashville was that Rex pitted on the back stretch of the quarter-mile oval inside the half-mile track. I remem-

Louie and Rex in victory lane after another 1959 win in Nashville, Tennessee.

ber seeing my dad take a hammer and chisel, and hammer grooves into the inside of the wheel beads. He said the car was spinning the wheels inside the tires coming off the corners and he was just trying to add a little grip to the rims. I also remember that Louie had a wet shop rag tied over his head. He wore a flat-top haircut in those days and it was hotter than blazes that day. Not a drop of shade to be found... unless you had grandstand seating!

The 17th race of the season was held at Ascot Stadium in Los Angeles, California. I believe Jim Reed was the only eastern driver to make the trip out there, probably because he was chasing the short-track points championship. Reed easily sat on the pole but cooked the engine after 137 laps. That was good for a 29th-place finish and a $134 payday. Not much for the long trek across country he made. The race was won by Parnelli Jones driving the Vel's '59 Ford. Second was Lloyd Dane, whom I recently got to meet at a "Legends of NASCAR" reunion. He was very personable and a joy to speak with over 40 years after this race. Third place went to our west coast friend, Marvin Porter, who was driving his own '57 Ford. Ron Hornaday, Sr., finished 23rd that day driving a '57 Chevy.

We missed the next two races, which were held at Hub City Speedway in Spartanburg and Greenville-Pickens Speedway, also in South Carolina.

Shortly after the 1959 Nashville race we see (left to right) Rex White, mechanic Paul McDuffie and his driver Joe Lee Johnson.

Lee Petty won the next two races on the schedule. The season race #20 was in Atlanta on the old one-mile Lakewood dirt track. This was a good day for the Petty clan as son Richard finished second. Together, the Pettys earned a rather decent sum of $3,600 for this 1959 race. I truly believe, with everything I have seen growing up in NASCAR over the years, that Lee Petty was the first man to figure out how to make a living racing stock cars. He was ruthless behind the wheel and an all-around extremely tough competitor every place he raced. In my opinion, he made Dale Earnhardt look like a Girl Scout. No offense to the Earnhardt fans. I was one myself. But most of those Earnhardt fans never got to see Lee Petty, Curtis Turner, or Buck Baker race. These men took no prisoners. By the way, Baker finished third this day.

Race #21 was contested at the Columbia Speedway in the capital city of South Carolina. The track was a half-mile dirt oval and the race went for 200 laps. Again, it was won by Lee Petty, followed by Tommy Irwin and Buck Baker in third.

Our next race was back in Winston-Salem, North Carolina, at the flat quarter-mile paved oval of Bowman Gray Stadium. Lee Petty grabbed the pole, but Rex beat him to the first turn and was never threatened during the entire 200 laps. That win was worth

Louie and Rex in victory lane again.

$675. Second place went to Ken Rush, a very good short-track driver himself. Bob Welborn finished third in his '57 Chevy. Richard Petty qualified third but broke after only 14 laps for a 24th-place finish. Still on our team at this time was the black '58 Chevy #40 driven by Dave White. Dave finished 13th and was running at the end of the race. Favorite Glen Wood qualified fifth but a blown engine sidelined him on lap 165 for a 19th-place finish.

I clearly remember my older brother and me standing up against the pit side of the guardrail watching Glen Wood, Lee Petty, and our hero Rex White practice before the race. If you were a kid who came in the gate with a race team, you could sometimes get away with a lot of shenanigans in those days. During the race, though, I went to the scoring tower with my oldest brother Lloyd to score the race. We both would score at least one car each for the modified race that always ran before the Grand Nationals competed. Then, when the Grand National cars took to the track, Lloyd scored Rex and I would score whoever Morris Metcalf would ask me to score. It was fun and I wouldn't trade it for anything.

My wife and I recently took a day trip over to see the track at Bowman Gray. It is still operational today and the track still has that Roman coliseum feel to it. While showing my wife the dirt areas where we pitted many years ago, I happened to kick up a spot of dirt and found a 1960s Chevy small block rod cap. Yes, it was all dirty and rusty.

But one trip through my glass bead blaster and it looks like a trophy on my shop wall today.

Race #25 for the '59 season was back in Asheville-Weaverville, North Carolina. Again, this was a high-banked paved track with a concrete retaining wall. It was a very fast track too. On this day, June 28, 1959, Glen Wood grabbed the pole position and Rex

White qualified fourth. Rex managed to grab the lead on the first lap and led all 200 laps for a fine and well-deserved victory. This win paid $900. Second place and the only other car on the lead lap was Lee Petty, this time in a new 1959 Plymouth. I guess he was letting Richard use up all the '57 Oldsmobiles by this time. Third went to Junior Johnson, still running his '57 Ford that would later be bought by Ned Jarrett. Our friend and shop mate Dave White ran the #40 1958 Chevy to a 10th-place finish, 15 laps down to the leaders.

Now, this is one of those times where I have to 'fess up to being a culprit. My brother David and I were told by my father while still at the shop to load a floor jack and a spare race tire and wheel in the trunk of that '58 Chevy for Dave White. We towed up to Asheville from Spartanburg and when we got to the track, it was just understood that everyone who loaded something would now unload it. Right? Wrong. It wasn't until the race was over and victory lane ceremonies were over that we walked back down to just inside turn #4 where our pit was located. David opened the trunk to the '58 Chevy and looked at me and said, "Oh-oh!" We had never removed that 60- or 70-pound floor jack or the spare tire and wheel. Dave White ran 185 laps with them still inside the trunk. We tried to forget about it. This would not have been a funny thing to mention on the ride home. So, almost 35 years later, when my dad was pretty ill and in the hospital bed, I spoke up and told him about it. I don't know if my brother ever said anything to my dad about this or not. But when I mentioned it, my dad, who was very sore from having had a broken back and muscle and joint pain, laughed until it hurt him.

The next weekend brought with it the

Winner's trophy from 1959 at Bowman Gray Stadium.

annual Firecracker 250 at Daytona on the still-new Super Speedway. It turned out to be the Fireball Roberts Show. Fireball won the race driving the black-and-gold '59 Pontiac put together by Smokey Yunick at the request of Bunkie Knudsen, who was the head of Pontiac Performance Development at the time. This was still the number 3 car. Fireball didn't start driving the #22 Yunick cars until 1960. This particular '59 Pontiac that won this race just happened to be the same car that would carry Floridian Bobby Johns to what was "almost" his first Daytona 500 victory the next February. We'll get to that when we discuss the 1960 season.

On this day in Daytona, Fireball was challenged several times, first by Peruvian driver Eduardo Dibos in a Holman-Moody '59 T-Bird. He was also challenged by Joe Weatherly in a T-Bird and Jack Smith in a '59 Chevy #47. Johnny Allen finished third in a '59 Chevy #22. By this time, Johnny Beauchamp was no longer involved with the #73 Roy Burdick '59 T-Bird. Roy had enlisted the services of his son Bob to drive the car, and with that 430-cubic-inch Lincoln engine on board, Bob Burdick finished in sixth place after starting second. The #6 of Cotton Owens finished eighth after making the switch from the 285-hp Pontiac to the newer 350-hp T-Bird. Rex White had a strong horse this day but mechanical problems sent him to the pits a couple of times too many. He finished the race, still running in 23rd position, 14 laps down to the winner. Lee and Richard Petty both fell out early with blown engines in their '59 Plymouths. Fireball collected a whopping $7,050 for this victory.

The 100-lap, 250-mile race proved to be just too short of a race to satisfy the race fans. Just a few years later the race was extended to become the Firecracker 400. (The 1964 version of this race turned out especially well for the Clements family. Hang in here till we get to '64 and I'll tell you all about it.) Another worthy note on this race was that Tiger Tom Pistone was leading Fireball Roberts by almost a full lap when he ran out of fuel on lap 48. He was trying to make it to lap 50 for his pit stop, which would have probably given him the win. Driving the yellow #59 Rupert Safety Belts T-Bird, Tom finished a fine seventh place. By the way, did you know that Tom Pistone was the only driver in NASCAR to ever wear a life jacket while racing there? He couldn't swim and had an immense fear of crashing into Lake Lloyd. The lake was built there because they needed the dirt to build those high banks. After the big old hole was dug in the infield, someone had the idea to just fill it with water and name it Lake Lloyd. Tommy Irwin did crash during one of the 100-mile qualifying races and he landed his '59 T-Bird right square in the lake. He got out OK and was unharmed. Driver Jim Hurtubise brought his houseboat down one year and kept it in the lake throughout speed weeks. He stayed right there at the track. These were the days before motor homes and those huge multimillion-dollar motor coaches used by the drivers today.

During the summer of '59, Rex and Louie were asked by the promoter of the Nashville Fairgrounds Speedway to bring the '59 Chevy Grand National car up for a USAC race at the Fairgrounds Speedway. The promoter paid them $250 to bring the car up for Tony Bettenhausen to drive. I believe they also got to keep the money won by the car. Adjusting the seat was about all they had to do to the car. When the 200-lap race came to a conclusion, Tony had finished second. I wish I could remember who won the race.

A couple of things I do remember about that race were two stories my dad told me about it. I was not at this race, so anything I know about it came from my dad or Rex or

Tony Jr. when I met him years later. During practice for the race, Rex was standing out by the pit wall watching some of the guys make some test laps. Louie was over in the pits working on the '59 Chevy with some last-minute checklists. Rex ran over to Louie and said, "Come with me. You are about to see the darnedest wreck you've ever seen!" Bill Cheesbourg, from Arizona, was an Indy car driver and this day he was driving a '57 Ford USAC stock car. Coming off the fourth corner, he was smoking the right front tire so much that they knew he was just minutes away from knocking the wall down. Fortunately, he pulled into the pits and got out of the car and just threw his hands up in the air. He was stumped. Rex and Louie both walked over and introduced themselves and asked if he could use some help. He gladly accepted the assistance from them. They measured the wedge in it, checked tire pressures and sent Bill to get a new right front tire. Then Louie adjusted the front sway bar. Bill went back out and the car drove well, and he came back in the pits very much appreciative of the help. About 22 years later, that little bit of help came back to help us when we were down in Casa Grande, Arizona, racing our late model against Cheesbourg. It was my first race ever in a stock car, and Bill went through the pits and told everyone racing to take it easy on the new kid and explained to them why. He told Carl Trimmer, a local hotshot, that Louie had forgotten more about racing than any of them would ever know. That was a great confidence booster to this kid.

In Louie's other story about the Nashville USAC race, Eddie Skinner entered the pits during the race, jumped out of his race car and threw the hood open. Rex and Louie both ran over to him and asked, "What's wrong?" Skinner said, "We've got to slow this thing down before someone gets hurt!" No kidding. He actually said that. Racing had to have been more fun in those days!

July 21, 1959, brought about the 27th race on the NASCAR season. This time the show was at Heidelberg Raceway near Pittsburgh, Pennsylvania. (All of us little Catholic school kids knew all about Pittsburgh. That's where the Franciscan nuns were from. They seemed to brag about Pittsburgh as much as they taught us about math, history and English.) This track was a quarter-mile dirt oval and the scheduled distance was 200 laps or 50 miles. New Yorker Jim Reed won the race in his blue '59 Chevy #7. Rex White ran second, which was fine with us. They were the only two cars on the lead lap at the finish. Lee Petty, Marvin Porter, and Cotton Owens rounded out the top five. Marvin Porter was a west-coast racer who had just moved down south to race in the mainstream of the NASCAR Grand National series.

It was also right at this same time that a young racer from Harlan, Iowa, came to live in our house with us. His name was Tiny Lund. He and his first wife, Ruthy, lived with us for a few weeks until they could get settled into a home for themselves. Tiny needed a place to work on his race car, so Rex and Louie gave him a spot in their shop. It was starting to get crowded in that shop about that time. They not only had the new white '59 Chevy for Rex to race, but they also had the '58 Chevy for Dave White, the '58 Pontiac that Elmo Henderson had bought from Cotton Owens, and the '57 Ford of Marvin Porter's. I think racers shared help from team to team more like family in those days. They towed down the road together, stopped to eat together, and when we got to the track, the teams' wives and children all got to be in the same area. This helped us get to know each other, put faces with names and share supplies for some of those long weekends away from home.

Just about every Saturday during the school year, I could go down to the shop with my dad if I was up and ready to go in time. Not a problem! I loved that place. We got to racing the creepers on the concrete floors and making too much noise one day and my dad came out and told my brothers and me that creeper racing was now off limits in the shop. Well, the very next Saturday, my dad was working in the engine room on one of those pesky old 348 Chevys and he heard the ruckus of creeper racing coming from the main garage. He came through the door with fire in his eyes, and I am reasonably certain we were about to be reprimanded quite sternly by him. Then he noticed that Marvin Porter was pushing me on my creeper and Tiny Lund was pushing my brother on his creeper. Louie just looked dazed, shook his head and walked away.

Another high point about spending Saturdays at the shop was that we all went to lunch together as a group every Saturday at noon. We would pile into the back of the old '57 Chevy pickup truck and my dad would drive us down to the El Circle Restaurant that was on the north side of the Herron traffic circle in Spartanburg. This was still part of the old Asheville highway then. The restaurant was owned and operated by Alex Rammantamman. Yep, long last name, but he was a real friend to the racing community and many times held racing banquets in the back room of his establishment, usually at his own expense. Of course, Jim Foster, the local sports writer for the *Spartanburg Herald* was in attendance and would write up a nice story for the newspaper, complete with photos of all the drivers involved. That had to be worth something.

Once at the restaurant we could order anything we wanted. You had to order by number from the menu, which was a mimeographed piece of paper each day that listed all the specials for that day of the week. I would usually order a country-style steak with mashed potatoes and gravy and whole kernel corn. Add a big ol' cold Pepsi to that order and I was in hog heaven. The trip back to the shop in the back of that old truck got a bit scary one time, though. Rex and Satch (Sonny Steel) got to play-fighting and trying to throw each other out of the truck while going down the road. At first it looked like a friendly scuffle. Then it got to looking really serious and I was scared that one of those guys was actually going overboard. My brother Lloyd grabbed me and slid me up between himself and the cab of the truck. He was always looking out after me. Glad we got back to the shop before one of them happened to actually go overboard! Those guys were always playing tricks on each other.

The half-mile dirt oval at Charlotte, North Carolina, was the scene of the next Grand National race, the 28th of the season. Rex and Louie didn't run this race, but two of the cars from the shop did. The 200-lap race was won by Jack Smith in his Chevy, but Tiny Lund, driving his old worn-out '57 Chevy, was still running at the end and brought home a respectable 11th-place finish. Elmo Henderson finished 22nd after experiencing overheating problems on lap 160. Our good friend G.C. Spencer finished 27th after losing the rear differential gears on lap 114. G.C.'s son Terry had a Go Kart and his mom would bring him and his kart over to our neighborhood from time to time to race with my cousin Gary and me. I'll tell you, the entire world was about racing then!

The 29th race was held at Myrtle Beach, South Carolina, at Rambi Speedway. This was August 1, 1959. I know the relief felt by Mr. Ned Jarrett that day. He had written a bad check just a few days earlier to buy the '57 Ford from Junior Johnson. Ned won this race, which paid him $800. Jim Paschal and Tommy Irwin finished second and third respectively. Richard Petty fell out after only four laps, giving him the 27th position in the 27-car field. The next race, #30 for the season, Ned won again. This time the race was back at the Charlotte Fairgrounds and Ned brought home another $800, making a total of $1,600 in two days. He scraped up the last $400 to make good on the check he had written for the race car. No doubt, Gentleman Ned was on a mission that weekend. Herman Beam ran the entire race with no problems and finished in eighth place, 12 laps down to the winner. After mechanical problems, Richard Petty and Buddy Baker finished 20th and 21st. Cotton blew an engine on the first lap and finished last place, 29th position.

One week later we were back up to Nashville Fairgrounds for the half-mile paved oval 300-lap race. Just as regular as clockwork, Rex White took the pole again. With Louie Clements turning the wrenches and Rex White doing the driving, these guys were amazingly fast on the short tracks in their day. Rex was one of the very best in the business at knowing his car and what it took to set up the chassis. Louie was the best at building racing engines. He was also the best body and fender man in the business. My dad told me more than once that Rex taught him everything he knew about chassis setup. Before leaving the sport, Louie too was known for being a great chassis guy.

Good fortune was not in the cards for Rex on this day, though. He grabbed the lead on the start and led the race past the halfway mark when the rear end gear burned up. Racers were not allowed gear coolers and pumps in those days. I think, from my memory at least, it was Ralph Moody who finally convinced Big Bill France to allow better, stronger suspension components and gear coolers. Ralph showed France the records and said that the way things are going, with the auto manufacturers building more and more horsepower, pretty soon there would be nobody left to finish a race. France eventually gave in and more cars began to complete the long-distance races.

Joe Lee Johnson, a heck of a nice guy, won this race at Nashville in his '57 Chevy small block convertible. It was his first Grand National win and everyone there was happy for him too. Larry Frank finished second in a Chevy and #10 Elmo Langley came home third. Rex was credited with a 24th-place payday. Mechanical problems once again sidelined Richard Petty and Buddy Baker. They finished 29th and 30th. Each one would go on to become a superstar of the sport, but their beginnings were certainly filled with struggles. They both paid their dues. This had been the 31st race of the season. As I remember it, it was a blistering hot day at the fairgrounds. I remember it well because my mother told me it was over 101 degrees Fahrenheit that day. That was the first time I had ever heard of temps being over 100 degrees. That wouldn't be the last time, though. We moved out to Phoenix, Arizona, in June of '66.

On August 16, we traveled back up to Asheville for the Western Carolina 500 on the high-banked asphalt track there. Rex was always fast on this track and he generally ran well and brought home good money. On this day, three-time convertible champion Bob Welborn won the race by three full laps over the field. Rex grabbed the pole with another new track record but finished the 500 laps behind Welborn, Lee Petty, Jack Smith and Joe Lee Johnson. My dad told me several times just what a nice man Bob Welborn was. I do remember when Bob crashed his '59 Chevy in the Southern 500 that year that dad and Rex loaned him their trailer to get his wrecked race car back home. During this point in NASCAR history, most of the race cars were still flat-towed with a tow bar hooked to the back of a pickup truck or maybe a station wagon. Rex was among the first to realize the benefits of towing the race car from track to track on a trailer to save on wheel bearings, tires, rear end gear, brakes, etc. Welborn's win this day was worth $3,200. Rex was paid $800 for his pole position and fifth-place finish. Our friend Marvin Porter finished ninth, with Bobby Johns coming in 10th. Forty-one cars started the 500-lapper and I do believe I personally knew at least half of them. G.C. Spencer finished 12th but had a much better run going before running out of fuel right at the end of the race. This was an official sweepstakes race, meaning that both Grand National as well as convertible points were up for grabs. So in the big picture, Welborn won the convertible points with Johnson garnering second-place convertible points. Petty, Jack Smith and Rex White earned the first three points-paying positions for the Grand National division.

Race #33 for the season came five days later, back at my favorite track. Bowman Gray Stadium was the quarter-mile flat asphalt track where Rex won five times in a row. This race would be no different. Rex took the pole, got the lead on the start and was never even threatened for the win. Man, he flat-out knew how to get around that track. I was there the day that my dad got inside the car with Rex, who took him for a few laps at full speed. Louie wanted to feel what the car was doing. With Rex strapped into the racing seat and helmet on, Louie just sat in the center of the car on the driveshaft hump and held onto the center roll bar. He loved the ride and told Rex that he could feel the car rolling over onto the right rear wheel coming off the corner. That caused the car to have a little of what the racers called "push" in it. "Pushing" meant that even though the driver was turning the steering wheel, the car was not going where it was aimed. They pulled it into the pits and installed a stiffer right rear spring in the car and then went out and set that Chevy on the pole. These guys were as good as there was in their day.

Finishing second this day was Glen Wood in his Ford, third was Lee Petty in his Plymouth, fourth went to Bob Welborn and fifth went to Jim Reed from New York. Jim was there chasing down some more short-track points. Rex entered as a short-track car too, so he took top points honors for the short-track division that day. Joe Weatherly drove the Wood Brothers team car to a sixth-place finish, followed by Roy Tyner and Tom Pistone. Our team car, driven by Dave White, finished 12th, still running at the end. Only 24 cars started this race. But when you look at the track around the football field, you can understand that 24 cars racing full speed would be quite the crowd.

Buck Baker won the next race at Greenville and Lee Petty won the race after that, which was held back down in Columbia, South Carolina. Rex and Louie had decided to pass up those two races and be more prepared for the upcoming Darlington Southern 500 on Labor Day.

I can remember this 1959 Southern 500, over 50 years ago, just like it was yesterday. But this was not just the Darlington Southern 500; this was also my first entrepreneurial experience. My brothers and I had built many model cars, all painted up like the NASCAR stars. We drove into the track in a brand-new '59 Chevy Impala that was lent to my dad for the weekend. We had the models in the trunk, safely packed in boxes with a towel wrapped around each one to protect our work. Once we got to our infield parking spot that race morning, my mom put a big blanket on the hood of the new Chevy and us boys placed all of our handcrafted creations on the hood for display. And if an admiring passerby had the desire and $3 American, he could buy any one of these cars. These were very close to us in some cases. Once you put so many hours into building something like

View from the front stretch grandstands shortly before the start of the 1959 Southern 500. Car #42 is Lee Petty; in front of him in the white #43 is his son Richard Petty; and to his far left is the #4 Chevy of Rex White.

this, it becomes almost a part of you and you don't really know how to feel when someone buys it. We must have displayed at least 50 models that day and I do believe we sold every one of them too. They cost us 69 cents each and then we painted and built them into race cars. In those days decals were scarce so we had to hand-paint and letter each model. There was a bunch of work that went into those cars. But we came away with a combined total of over $150 for our efforts. It really didn't take too long to sell out, either. The strange thing about it was that darn near every person who looked at the models wanted the same car, and we only had one model of this particular car. They wanted a model of the #43 Plymouth that was being driven this day by Lee Petty's rookie son, Richard. I bet we could have sold 200 of those if we'd had them. Even after we sold out, some grown men, fueled by an excess of adult beverages, kept coming over to our car asking when we would have more models to sell. I believe that day was the start of what today's business of "racing collectibles" is all about. There is some pretty good money in that business. I don't believe we can buy the models for 69 cents anymore. And I know darned well we wouldn't sell them for $3.00 each again. But we learned something, we had fun, and we made a few bucks and a wonderful memory. Thank God and General Motors for those huge Chevy hoods!

I guess this would be a great spot to talk about the actual race we saw. To no one's surprise, Fireball Roberts grabbed the coveted pole position for this one. To everyone's surprise, Elmo Langley drove his white '59 Buick nail head to the second-place starting spot. Speedy Thompson drove Paul McDuffie's '59 Chevy #22 to a third-place qualifying spot. Rex White drove my dad's '59 Chevy #4 to start fourth. This was the first time the car ran in its new gold-and-white paint scheme: gold down the sides; white on the hood, roof and trunk; big red #4's on the doors, roof and trunk. On the hood was painted the factory rating of 320 hp. It was a '59 Chevy Impala 2-door hardtop with the 348 engine, single 4-barrel carburetor and a 4-speed transmission. Starting outside second row was rookie Richard Petty in his first Darlington start. His popularity came around kind of like that of Dale Earnhardt, Jr. His father was very popular with the fans and that automatically made him a fan favorite too.

Fifty cars started the Labor Day classic this year and Jim Reed outfoxed the field and brought his blue '59 Chevy #7 home first. That made for Reed's largest NASCAR payday ever at $17,250. That was a major chunk of change in 1959. I think when my mom sent me to the store around the corner to get her cigarettes, they were only 25 cents a pack. And the store keepers sold them to me when I was just eight years old. Yep, times have changed. I also got to walk right up to Jim Reed's winning '59 Chevy and touch it, look inside it and actually *feel* the car that won the Southern 500. This was the granddaddy of all big-time races. I noticed that particular car had one roll bar running beside the driver between the two upright roll bars. It also had the same horizontal bar on the right door. This was the first time I had seen door bars in any race car that I can remember.

Bob Burdick finished second in his father's '59 T-Bird with that 430-cubic-inch Lincoln engine. Bobby Johns finished third in his father's 283-cubic-inch '57 Chevrolet #72. Richard Petty, with relief driver help from Marvin Panch, finished fourth, and #36, Tommy Irwin from Inman, South Carolina, came home in fifth place. Although Rex qualified fourth and ran very well, the drive shaft went out and he lost several laps in the pits while the crew installed a new one. Mechanics reading this will remember that the Chevys from 1958 through 1964 had what they called the "X" frame. That requires the drive shaft to be a two-piece unit with a bearing support in the center. It was miserably hot that day and the job was tedious work to do on a very hot race car in tight quarters. They got the new drive shaft installed and got Rex back on track for a 17th-place overall finish. Not that bad, considering 50 cars started the race. Bob Welborn crashed and used Rex and Louie's trailer to get his wrecked race car home. Possum Jones drove the black #92 T-Bird of Gerald Duke's. Gerald's son and I were buddies at the tracks and we would

1959 Southern 500 lineup.

play with model race cars and even resort to footraces sometimes. The whole weekend was racing. I think we even had competition over who could drink a Coke the fastest.

Twenty-two of the 50 starters finished the race that day. Our friend G.C. Spencer finished 23rd driving the same car that Speedy Thompson had won the race in back in 1957. Tiny Lund finished 26th after losing a clutch, and Spartanburg man Jack Smith came in 28th after breaking an axle in Bud Moore's '59 Chevy. Buck Baker, who was in a hot contest with Lee Petty over the points championship, finished a fine ninth position. The #42 driven by Lee Petty finished 20th, still running at the finish although down some 45 laps to eventual winner Jim Reed.

Hollywood was there in full force producing a racing movie titled *Thunder in Carolina*. The movie starred Rory Calhoun as an older, seasoned veteran race car driver,

Roy Tyner, the "Flying Indian," was hired by a Hollywood film crew to purposely crash his 1957 Chevy over the guardrail for the movie *Thunder in Carolina*.

Mitch Cooper, who was teaching a young upstart the ropes of the game. Alan Hale, Jr.— remember him as the Skipper on *Gilligan's Island?*— was Mitch Cooper's crew chief in the movie. They actually had several of these '57 Chevy race cars painted up the same with the blue paint, white top and black "V" down the sides. The car carried the #8 and actually made some laps in the real race to get some good film footage for the movie. NASCAR had warned them to keep down low and out of the way. The other movie car was a brand-new 1959 Oldsmobile that must have come right from a new car dealership. I got to get up close and personal with that '59 Olds as well as all the '57 Chevys with the #8 on them. The Chevys were real race cars and they had a few of them so they would have spares. They crashed a few for the movie. That '59 Olds was a new car with the headlights removed, and cardboard tubing for roll bars. They were just taped together. I reached into the car and could actually move the roll bars back and forth. The car numbers and lettering on that car were all watercolor paints. I guess that's so the film company could wash the car and take it back to the dealer or rental car company.

The morning after the race, my mother, sister, little brother and I went to the track and sat in the stands for a while. The film company had given notice to everyone who wanted to, to come back the next day and sit in the stands for free to watch some more filming.

If you have seen the movie, you will remember when the hero, Mitch Cooper, comes

Bobby Johns shown with his blue-and-white 1957 Chevy Grand National car. Young boy in car is family friend Allen.

into the pits. While servicing the car, Alan Hale comes to the driver's window and says, "I can't let you go back out there. You have a cracked brake drum." Then the hero, played by Rory Calhoun, says very loudly, "Put the damn hood down!" Well, right then my mom figured we had heard enough and we left. But I have a VHS copy of the movie and during that pit stop scene, I can still see us right there in the background, sitting on the lower level of the front stretch grandstands.

Seventy-eight thousand people were there that day to watch the 1959 Southern 500. That 1959 Oldsmobile that Lee Petty won the first-ever Daytona 500 with? Joe Caspolich bought it from Petty and drove it to a fine 13th-place finish, 22 laps down to the winner.

Besides the movie *Thunder in Carolina*, there were also a few other hits during 1959. The Flamingos had a number-one hit song called "I Only Have Eyes for You." And, superstar Bobby Darin released "Mack the Knife" for his hit tune of the year.

Just a scant four days after the biggest and most prestigious race of the season, we were all back at the little dirt track in Hickory, North Carolina. Fourteen cars started this race and Lee Petty came away with the winning honors. It was a 250-lap race on a .4-mile dirt track. Buck Baker brought his Crawford Clements–tuned Chevy home in second, still racing Mr. Petty for the points championship. Rex White drove his Louie Clements–

prepared Chevy to a fine third-place finish. Junior Johnson and Brownie King rounded out the top five. It's fairly easy to see why my cousin Gary Clements and I enjoyed going to all these races with our dads and families. Between Louie and Crawford, they usually had both cars up front and that taught the kids in our families to be winners. Not only in racing, but in life also. Our fathers always showed the very best displays of love and courtesy to our mothers. They spent extra money to send us kids to Catholic schools. In the big picture, that was in our best interest. But I came home from school more than once wishing I had just punched a nun in the nose. Of course that would not only have gotten me suspended or expelled, but it would have been signing my own death warrant once my dad found out. Same with Gary: Uncle Crawford took no prisoners either.

So, back to that Hickory race. Our friends Marvin Porter and G.C. Spencer finished 12th and 14th respectively. Marvin was still running at the end, but his old Ford was getting tired. G.C.'s car, a '57 Chevy, broke a crankshaft on lap 74. G.C. had qualified sixth for this race. Finishing in the seventh spot driving a '57 Chevy #62 was our friend, Buck Brigance. In the next two or three years we came to know him better. This man took up where Joe Weatherly left off. It seems that NASCAR has always needed a garage area clown. Weatherly was called the "Clown Prince" of stock car racing. Buck Brigance was the same way. He just had a way of making a ho-hum day into a bright, cheerful, full-of-laughter day. He always had a practical joke up his sleeve. He teased us kids mercilessly in the garage area at Atlanta one time. Many of the drivers and crew guys were just like family to all of us.

Races number 38 and 39 were not in the cards for Rex and Louie. They passed up those two races to concentrate on getting their '59 Chevy #4 in tip-top shape for the upcoming race in Martinsville, Virginia. Cotton won race #38 at Richmond and Eddie Gray won race #39 at Sacramento, California, which was held on the same day. No east-coast drivers entered the Sacramento race.

Hillsboro, North Carolina, would be the scene of race #40 on the schedule. Not having the Chevy ready yet, Rex borrowed a car from friend Beau Morgan. This was a "run hard and put up wet" '58 Ford. Rex qualified the car in the eighth position but broke an axle for a 17th-place finish. That paid $50. I don't think you could buy an axle for $50!

Lee Petty won this race followed in second by Cotton Owens driving his "Thunder Chicken" '59 T-Bird. Richard Petty brought home a very fine third-place finish a full 10 laps down to his father. Buck finished 12th in Crawford's '59 Chevy. The class of the field was no doubt Junior Johnson. He showed up late to the track, probably on purpose to avoid pre race inspection and started shotgun on the field. He drove from 22nd place to seventh place by the fourth lap. But after the race a suspicious NASCAR official checked Junior's car and found an illegal "locked" rear differential gear. That was a trick used many times by many teams in those days. The real trick was to use it with some discretion and not blow the field away like Junior did. When you've got 110 laps to get the job done, why do it in four laps? Looked kind of obvious. I once heard Richard Petty say in an interview, "Cheat neat." That means don't let it look obvious.

Now, onto one of the best races of the year. Certainly the most beautiful track on the circuit in those days was the half-mile asphalt oval at Martinsville, Virginia. This was race #41 on the '59 season and was termed the Virginia Sweepstakes 500. Five hundred

Originally flagged as winner at Martinsville, Virginia, Glenn Wood is shown receiving the winner's trophy and kiss from the race queen.

laps on a half-mile track during these days was a true test of a worthy automobile. Remember, these were truly *stock* cars. No disc brakes, no power steering, no engine oil coolers, no rear gear oil coolers, no dry sump oil systems for the engines, and basically no race parts allowed in the engines. They had to make do with what they had. Drivers ran 500 laps without power steering in 4,000+ pound cars with 5" wide tires and old-fashioned drum brakes! This was indeed a testing grounds for Detroit, man and machines. Forty-seven cars started this 500-lapper and hometown favorite Glen Wood once again grabbed the coveted pole position. Glen was an incredible short-track racer. His brother Leonard was his crew chief. So not too many speed secrets left the Wood Brothers garage in those days. They were and still are two of the nicest guys you could ever meet. Rex White drove my dad's Chevy to qualify for the 14th starting position. Rex and Louie had mapped out their strategy and stuck to the plan: Keep the leaders in sight and wait until after halfway to make the move up front. This was a common strategy for them back then. By lap 165, Rex took the lead for six laps, then pitted and went back into battle. When he came around on lap 306, Rex had taken the lead for good, never to look back. He ran pretty much flat-out for the remaining 194 laps for his seventh win. This win paid $3,250 and plenty of championship points. But finishing in the 10th position was none other than

Moments after Glenn Wood's victory lane ceremony, Rex White was awarded the win after a scoring check; note the wad of cash in Rex's left hand. Left to right: flagman Roby Combs, track owner Clay Earls, unknown, Bill France Sr., race announcer, Rex White. Note tall tail fins on 1959 Cadillac pace car.

Lee Petty, who this day clinched his third National Championship for two in a row. Glen Wood received the checkered flag driving the Wood Brothers 1958 Ford #16. He then went to victory lane, where he was presented with the winner's trophy and the traditional kiss from the race queen. While that was going on, a scoring check was also underway.

Jim Reed, Tommy Irwin and Speedy Thompson rounded out the top five. Buck Baker, who was also deep into the points for the championship, finished in 14th place, still running at the end. Fireball Roberts drove the second Baker entry to a 30th-place finish after burning down a rear end gear on lap 303. Finishing 31st this day was a driver who would have a good influence on my race driving career in later years. It was Ervin Carpenter, who was driving Neil Castle's '56 Ford convertible. Twenty-eight cars were running at the end of this race. And this kid stood very tall walking around the pit area after this one! Yes sir, my daddy's race car put a whoopin' on everybody this day! Of course, you learn early on that bragging is just not the thing to do. I guess that's because the sun never shines on the same dog's butt for long! Humility and grace in winning were taught in our family.

There were three races left in the '59 season to complete the entire 44-race series. Race #42 was two weeks after the big 500 at Martinsville, and this one was contested at Asheville-Weaverville Speedway. I believe there is a school located on that property nowadays. Back in its heyday, it was the site of some of the fiercest races, and also one of the dark moments in NASCAR when a crowd of unruly spectators blocked the track exit gate and refused to let the teams leave the premises after the race. We'll get to that in the next chapter. On October 11, 1959, the NASCAR Grand Nationals rolled into town to put on a 200-lap race on the famed half-mile paved track. Number 36, Tommy Irwin, grabbed the pole in his '59 T-Bird with a lap average of over 78.5 mph. That was pretty quick when you consider how heavy that car was and just how narrow those old race tires were. Starting second was the #16 Ford of Glen Wood. At the end of the 200 laps, Lee Petty and Glen Wood had pulled off a one-two finish. Petty earned $900 for his payday. Third place went to Jack Smith in a '59 Chevy and fourth place was our own little Rex White in the Louie Clements '59 Chevy #4. Number 43, Richard Petty, finished fifth. Other notables were Larry Frank in sixth, Ned Jarrett #88 in eighth, Buck Baker in 12th, Bobby Johns in 21st and Tiny Lund was 27th. Pole sitter Irwin lost an engine on lap 96 for a 28th-place finish. I don't know for certain about this case, but many times a driver trying to catch the eye of a potential sponsor might run a little more rear-end gear ratio to turn a quicker lap and grab the pole. It worked well in the short term, but just could not hold together for 200 laps. The race spanned a time period of 1 hour and 18 minutes.

Race #43 took us all back up to North Wilkesboro, North Carolina, for a 160-lap race on the five-eighths-mile paved and high-banked oval. This was normally the home of Junior Johnson, who lived nearby. Rex White was always a threat to win here too. But today, Lady Luck was back in the Petty camp as Lee Petty brought home his 48th victory in the big leagues. Rex White's #4 Louie Clements Chevrolet finished just seconds behind Petty. And, making it an even better day for the Petty clan, son Richard brought home his '59 Plymouth in third position. These three cars were the only cars on the lead lap at the end. Tom Pistone and Junior Johnson completed the top five positions. Pole sitter Glen Wood finished seventh and Buck Baker brought Crawford Clements's '59 Thor Chevrolet home in eighth place. Twenty-six cars started this one and nineteen were still running at the end.

The final race of the '59 season was run at Concord Speedway, just outside of Charlotte, North Carolina. This was to be a 300-lap grind on the half-mile dirt track. There were no time trials for this race. The driver's drew numbers from a hat to determine their starting positions. Fred Harb, driving an older 1957 Ford, drew the pole position. Cotton Owens drew outside pole and Buck Baker was fortunate to snatch the third-place starting spot on the grid. Rex "borrowed" the old '57 Ford from Beau Morgan, started fifth and finished 15th. The race win went to Spartanburg's Jack Smith, driving the Bud Moore '59 Chevy #47. Second place was once again Lee Petty in his '59 Plymouth, and third place went to Buck Baker in the same '59 Chevy he ran one week earlier. Buddy Baker had a great finish this day when he came home fourth. Glen Wood finished fifth. Richard was seventh, Tiny was 11th, and Herman Beam was 13th, still chuggin' right along. Larry Frank came home 15th and Curtis Turner, always a threat to win when his race car stayed under him, finished 24th after losing a transmission on lap 159. Thirty-four cars started this one and 21st-place Billy Scott was still running at the end in his '57 Chevrolet. This year, 1959, would be the final year of eligibility for the venerable '57 Chevy. It was perhaps one of the best race cars ever built. Many of these now Grand National outdated '57 Chevys would show up in Daytona for the modified-sportsman race coming up in February 1960.

The 1959 Top Ten Grand National points' series ranking was: In first place, Lee Petty. Second place: Cotton Owens. Third went to Speedy Thompson. Fourth place was Herman Beam with 12 top-10 finishes. Fifth went to Buck Baker in Crawford's '59 Chevy. Buck ran 35 races, won one time, had 14 top fives and 19 top tens.

Sixth was Tiger Tom Pistone, seventh went to L.D. Austin, eighth was Jack Smith, and ninth went to Jim Reed, who won more money than everyone except the points champion due to his win in the Southern 500. Rex White was the 10th-place points finisher this year with 23 starts, 5 wins, 11 top fives and 13 top tens. Richard Petty competed in 21 races this year and finished a fine 15th place in the points. It was very obvious to anyone watching and paying attention that the sophomore driver had risen to the occasion by the end of his second season. Richard had become a threat to win now, just as his legendary father was. This next season, 1960, we'll see Richard, Lee and Rex go at it head to head in a very spirited competition for the NASCAR Grand National Points Championship.

In addition, 1959 was a special one for our family in another way. In April of that year my little brother Jeff was born. My sister Cindy and I were full time babysitters. We really loved taking care of the new baby. As I write this today, Jeff is now over 50 years old and a grandfather. But in those days, he was our baby brother. Cindy and I were right there when he sat up on his own for the first time. It was really a sight at some tracks when we pulled in the gate for the race. We now had my dad, my mom, and five kids in that car. And to top that off, we also had our little Chihuahua named Ike (named after "Ike" Eisenhower, the President). And on a few occasions, we even took our pet parakeet in his cage with us. What a tribe we were!

CHAPTER 5

1960: Our Championship Season

As the new season was nearing, excitement filled the air in our shop and our home. We read every day the stories that local sportswriter Jim Foster wrote for the Spartanburg newspaper. There was the usual speculation about who was going to switch automotive brands, which mechanics were going with which drivers, and so forth. But much speculation was roaming around about three new super speedways that were being built. Since Big Bill France debuted his 2.5-mile, high-banked super speedway in Daytona, racers were ready, some "concerned," but mostly anxious to get onto some more of those big tracks and let those race cars stretch their legs out and run for the gold and glory.

Indeed, 1960 brought about three new super speedways. The 1.5-mile Charlotte Motor Speedway was a joint venture and project with Curtis Turner and Bruton Smith. Tim Flock was also involved with the promotion and building and raising funds to see the track through its incredibly expensive construction costs that seemed to rise about every day.

Atlanta was building a brand-new 1.5-mile super speedway too. This would also be a high-banked paved track that would let the racers run wide open. Out in California, B.L. Marchbanks was building a one-and-a-half-mile, high-banked paved oval for his end of the country. Our friend Marvin Porter won the very first race at the new Marchbanks super speedway on June 12, 1960.

During the fall and winter months of '59 and '60, White and Clements Garage in Spartanburg was busy building two brand-new 1960 Chevrolet Impalas for the new Grand National racing season. White and Clements Garage received some sponsorship from Chevrolet through Piedmont and Friendly Chevrolet in Concord and Reidsville, North Carolina. When Chevrolet shipped a 1960 Impala 2-door down to Jim Rathmann's Chevrolet dealership in Melbourne, Florida, Rex drove the '57 Chevy pickup down to tow it home as well as bring home an extra 348 marine engine from Duntov. The other white '60 Impala was built for Monroe Shook, who bought it himself somewhere up in Virginia and shipped it down to Spartanburg. Both cars drove into the shop new and were white with red interiors. Both cars were built exactly alike. One car would receive the gold paint down the sides and be set up for 5' 4" Rex White to drive and make a run for the 1960 Grand National championship. The other car was the one ordered by Monroe Shook of Shook Transfer, a trucking company. Shook asked Dad and Rex who he should get to drive the car and they recommended Emanuel Zervakis from Virginia. They left all of the chrome on the car, as that is how Mr. Shook requested it. The whole body

70

remained white, the wheels were painted gold, and big gold #85s were painted on the doors, trunk and roof of the car. The hoods on both cars were emblazoned with the factory rating of 320 hp. Louie built up race engines for both cars and setup recommendations were given to Zervakis when they picked up the car. If I remember correctly, the race-ready, turnkey race car, including the purchase of the new car to begin with, came to somewhere around $6,000. Man, you can't *paint* one of the cars today for that much money.

The team at White and Clements Garage for this season included Rex, Louie, James Hylton, Ken Miller, Slick Owens, Dean "Goat" Hall, and sometimes Wes Roark and a real big fellow they all called "Griller" for Gorilla. He did the heavy work and handled the complaint department too. These guys won the "Best Appearing Pit Crew" award at the Southern 500 that year. That's the first of that particular award that I remember. My mother and Rex's wife, Edith, went out and bought everyone on the team a pair of bright red slacks, a gold golf shirt and a red straw cap. The backs of the shirts had the #4 embroidered on them. My brothers and I got them too. I think this was the time when my sister Cindy bought a small white button-up shirt for our little brother, hand-wrote each of the Grand National drivers' names on the shirt, and then embroidered over each hand-written name. Anytime someone at the track saw that shirt, they thought it was the real autographs of the drivers. I think Cindy could have made a pretty good business out of making racing shirts.

We were still living at Dr. Black's apartment building on Maple Street in Spartanburg at that time. Just across the drive from us was a white duplex.

In the front portion of it lived our personal doctor and his wife and daughter. This was Dr. Bill Bonner, his wife Gloria, and their daughter Sandy. They were big race fans and went to many of the races with us. Dr. Bonner took my tonsils out and even removed a yucky growth from inside my right eardrum. To this day I have never been able to hear properly with that ear. He was also pretty good at sewing us up with stitches. Being a boy around a race shop, racing bicycles downhill and climbing trees… well, you get the picture.

Living in the rear portion of that duplex were Uncle Crawford, Aunt Dottie and their two sons, Gary and Tony. It was really cool living that close to my cousin Gary. We found something to race every day!

Between the racing seasons of 1959 and 1960, there was much work going on down at the White and Clements Garage. But on Christmas Eve of 1959, when we returned home from midnight mass, I was getting out of the car and noticed a couple of tire tracks that looked sort of small, narrow… Could it be? Do you think my prayers were answered? Well, yes they were. Sitting right in front of that Christmas tree was a brand-new racing Go Kart for our family. It was a new 1959 Putt-Nik kart with a 2.5-hp Lauson 4-cycle engine. I am pretty sure that the kart's name, "Putt-Nik," was a takeoff on the name of the first artificial satellite to orbit our planet. Remember? The Russians had taken the lead in the space race when they successfully launched into Earth orbit their satellite, which they named "Sputnik." This kart gave my brothers and me our first taste of driving in real races. There was an insurance company on Main Street in Spartanburg and we were living on the street right behind them. Since there was no one using their nice paved

Louie and Rex working on the engine, prepping the 1960 Chevy for the Daytona 500.

parking lot on the weekends, it made for a very nice place to race that kart. We took it out a few times to some of the real kart tracks in the Spartanburg area, but mostly played on that parking lot.

My brother drove it down the long hill in front of our dad's shop one day and one of the guys on the crew told him to reach over a spray this diesel starting fluid into the carburetor. That was supposed to make it go faster. Well, it did do that... for about three seconds! Then the rod came out the front of that engine and our racing days were over for a while. Once time allowed, my dad went out to an old junkyard, my favorite place to hang out, and we found a cast iron block Briggs and Stratton 4-stroke engine with a kick starter. It had been used on an old military air compressor. It bolted right onto the kart and we were back in business.

During that portion of the off season when the two new 1960 Chevys were being built, the team also had to rebuild their '59 Chevy so they could use it as a backup car and to run some of the early dirt races during the '60 season. Both the '59 and the '60 Chevys were factory equipped with the same 320-hp 348-ci engines. The chassis were the same too. Only the sheet metal was different. Those two cars made for an excellent combination for a championship run.

1/24th scale model of the 1960 championship car.

What I can easily remember about the year 1960 was that John F. Kennedy was elected President of the United States of America. Lyndon Johnson was his vice-president. Also, the World Series! How would I ever manage to forget about the 1960 World Series? No way possible. The Pittsburgh Pirates played the New York Yankees in the best four of seven games and won the series. With all the nuns in the school being from Pittsburgh, it was a sure-fire deal that we got to listen to the World Series that year. When the Pirates won the series, our school building must have shaken the earth. This was a big deal in Catholic school. Just as big as having Kennedy elected. After all, he was a Catholic too!

The catcher for the Pittsburgh Pirates that year was a man named Smokey Burgess. Our pastor was always treating us altar boys to picnics, special ball games, meals out, and so forth. For this occasion, he invited Smokey Burgess to a formal dinner with all of us altar boys from St. Paul's Church. We each got to meet him and get an autograph. My cousin and I were lucky enough to sit at the same table as him during dinner. Although racing was our first love, we were still boys, and a good neighborhood pickup game of baseball or football was a normal Saturday afternoon activity around 1963.

The big one! The 1960 Daytona 500 was finally upon us. My dad and Rex had the new '60 Chevy race car completely race ready and hauled it down to Daytona for the big speed weeks event. They received a new Chevy one-ton stake-bed truck and $1,000 cash from Piedmont and Friendly Chevrolet, which had dealerships in Concord and Reidsville, North Carolina. This was a good sort of sponsorship in those days. I still recall going over one Sunday afternoon to pick up the truck. On the way home, about an hour's drive, my two older brothers, my sister and I all rode in the back of the truck. It had the stake sides up and a big tarp over top of it. It was *cold* back there! My dad, mom, and little brother rode in the front of the truck. That was OK with us kids though. It was an adventure. So, the White and Clements tow rig for the '60, '61, and '62 seasons was this white

Chevy truck and a dual-axle open car trailer for the race car. Pretty much top of the line for those days.

So it was down to Daytona for speed weeks 1960 for the Clements clan, and everybody else involved in NASCAR too. The nuns at St. Paul's would let us out of school for the week in Daytona. Sometimes they gave us some workbooks to do while down there. Sometimes they would tell my mom that the experience we gained from our travels was also an important education. Either way, we were going!

We loaded up the family wagon with everything under the sun that we might need and headed out down the road. When we got to Daytona it was always late at night. We usually had a room waiting for us at either the Castaway or the Monterey. They were within walking distance of each other and both had everything we needed. It was a bit cold in February for a trip to the beach. But swimming wasn't so much on our minds. Racing was.

They had to get the cars through NASCAR prerace inspection, practice, qualify and then run the two 100-mile qualifying races. After those, they usually ran the modified sportsman races the day before the 500. During this year's race the track officials let 73 cars start the 250-mile event. Carl Burris was on the pole with his '54 Ford. Fireball Roberts and Banjo Matthews were right there with him. If I remember correctly, Bobby Johns and his dad put one of the big horsepower Pontiac motors in their old '57 Chevy Grand National car and ran it as a modified. They had streamlined the body a bit too. In the earliest years at the new Super Speedway at Daytona, there was always a modified-sportsman race the day before the 500. The '53 Studebaker body was very popular with this crowd. They could drop in a hemi or a Grand National Pontiac motor and run pretty fast. The Studebaker was about as slippery through the air as any car available. They made good-looking race cars too.

This same race, the day before the 1960 500, had the largest race car accident in NASCAR history. Over 37 cars were involved in a crash in the fourth turn on the first lap. There were no radio spotters in those days, so as the crash started, the cars just kept piling into the mess. It was really ugly. Very luckily, there was no fire and no one was seriously injured.

Not quite a full lap into the race, all heck broke loose coming off the fourth corner. I think it was Dick Foley's Chevy that swerved a bit side to side and some other drivers tried to avoid hitting him. In all, 37 cars crashed right there in the fourth turn on the first lap. Twelve cars flipped over several times and a total of 24 cars were banged up too badly to get back in the race. Larry Frank, Speedy Thompson, Wendell Scott, and Ralph Earnhardt were all eliminated from the race. It was but for the grace of God that no one was seriously injured or even killed in that crash. The Chevy of Dick Foley went on to finish in a respectable 10th position. Bubba Farr went on to win the race and Carl Burris finished second. Carl's son Wayne Burris and I were friends from our Go Karting days. We spoke one day about that race car that his father had put on the pole at Daytona. He told me that the engine was actually a de-stroked 352 Ford V8 with six 2-barrel carburetors on it. The body had been worked over extensively to "cheat the wind." When he passed away, Carl Burris was buried wearing a new Simpson racing suit. A fitting tribute to a fine racer.

On the Grand National side of things, they got the cars qualified. Fireball Roberts drove the black-and-gold #22 Pontiac to break the magic 150 mph barrier in a stock car. Fireball's speed was 151.556 mph, making him the fastest qualifier for the race. The first qualifying race saw Fireball win in his '60 Pontiac with Cotton Owens right on his bumper, also in a '60 Pontiac. Fred Lorenzen, Joe Weatherly, and Junior Johnson completed the top five. Driving the White and Clements–built white #85 Chevy was Emanuel Zervakis, who brought the car home for a fine eighth-place finish. Richard Petty finished 10th, G.C. Spencer was 14th, Buck Baker came in 15th, David Pearson was 17th, and #33 Reb Wickersham drove his 1960 Oldsmobile to a 25th-place finish; #2 Dave Hirshfield finished 28th driving a '59 Buick. In all, this race saw seven different makes of cars compete. Thirty-seven cars started the race.

The second 100-mile qualifier came up on the grid with 40 cars lined up for the start. Car #47 with Jack Smith at the wheel started from the pole and led every lap in his 1960 Boomershine Pontiac. Bobby Johns, driving the second Smokey Yunick entry, started second and finished there too. Jim Reed, Rex White and Bob Welborn drove their Chevys wide open, drafting those big tin Indians all the way home for third, fourth, and fifth positions. A solid fourth place in the qualifier race was a good sign for the #4 Chevy. We were happy with that. Our friend Elmo Henderson drove that '58 Pontiac flat-out for a 12th-place finish, one lap down to the leaders. Indy car driver Parnelli Jones drove his Vel's Ford #97 to a 22nd-place finish, while Curtis Turner, Ned Jarrett, John Rostek, and Johnny Beauchamp all crashed and did not finish.

Finally, the big day was here. It was February 14, 1960, and everybody who was anybody in the world of motor sports was here for this one. Even CBS Television had sent sports commentator Bud Palmer down to Daytona along with more than 50 technicians to cover the qualifying races for the *CBS Sports Spectacular*. We all knew that show. And we were certainly all awaiting the next show. That would be the second running of the Great American Race, the Daytona 500. We were watching history right in front of us and didn't know it. Legends were being formed in our presence and we didn't realize it.

Rex's niece, Kay, had come down to Daytona to watch the race with us. We had parked my mom's car just inside the fourth corner. Standing on top of that car I was able to see almost the entire track. That beautiful gold-and-white paint on the '60 Chevy made it easy to find on the track. Sixty-eight cars started the 1960 Daytona 500 and only 38 finished the long-distance grind for American factory stock cars. From our position inside the fourth turn, we saw Rex come around one lap with another car to his outside. There must have been about four or five feet in between them. Directly in front of us, we saw the air between those two cars turn into a vacuum and pull the two cars together, side to side. It was really strange seeing firsthand what the drivers were experiencing. Pole sitter Cotton Owens lost his transmission on the 149th lap and was credited with 40th position. Third-place starter Fireball Roberts, who was clearly the fastest car there, started third and blew one of Smokey's hand-built Pontiac engines on lap 51. He was listed as finishing in the 57th position. Second-place starter Jack Smith's Pontiac also fell on some tough times. He finished the race, still running, in 23rd position, nine laps down to the leaders.

Up front, things were shaping up to be a great race. Toward the end of the race, it was looking pretty good for Bobby Johns driving a year-old '59 Pontiac #3. Bobby was leading the race with eight laps to go when a freak thing happened. At speeds of 150 mph, the racers just didn't know exactly everything to expect. The vacuum behind the rear window sucked the window out of the race car. Junior Johnson was right behind Bobby, drafting and hoping for a solid second-place finish. Suddenly Bobby's rear window blew out. Junior says the entire rear end of the '59 Pontiac lifted off the ground and spun Bobby around and down into the infield coming off turn two. Junior drove on past and held on to his 23-second lead for the win. An underdog 1959 Chevy with the 348 Chevy truck motor had just won the Great American Race! Amazing! Bobby recovered to finish second and Richard Petty, Lee Petty, and Johnny Allen rounded out the top five. Rex White finished ninth with drafting help from Curtis Turner and Fred Lorenzen. Fred was driving his own yellow #28 1960 Ford sponsored by Rupert Safety Belts. Emanuel Zervakis brought home the second White and Clements 1960 Chevy in 10th place. We felt pretty good having both cars in the top 10. If my memory serves me right, I believe Uncle Crawford Clements was the crew chief for the 1960 Thor Chevrolet #59 which was driven this day by Tiger Tom Pistone. Tom pulled off a fine 12th-place finish. A few other notables in this race were Buck Baker finishing 18th in his own '60 Chevy #87. Banjo Matthews was 19th in his #93 T-Bird, Larry Frank was 22nd, G.C. Spencer was 31st, and Mel Larson drove the J.D. Braswell/Sun City '60 Pontiac to a 36th-place finish. Mel was an Arizona driver who helped in the founding, construction and management of Del Webb's Sun City, a retirement community in Arizona. A few years later, Mel went on to become the general manager of the Circus Circus Hotel and Casino in Las Vegas, Nevada. I can still remember seeing his 1960 Pontiac. It was metallic blue #35, and he used those 8-bolt magnesium wheels that came factory stock on more expensive Pontiac models of the day.

For his 1960 Daytona 500 victory, Junior Johnson collected a whopping $19,600. That was a fantastic payday in 1960. Rex led the race for 10 laps right around the halfway point. He ran well, but just couldn't hang onto those Pontiacs quite yet. His day would come, though.

Next, it was on to race #6 for the season. This time we raced over on the half-mile dirt track in Charlotte, North Carolina. This is one of those races that you would maybe rather forget. Rex was fast this day, very fast, and he deserved to win the race. But he had to contend with the Petty boys. Lee Petty had engine problems 38 laps into the race. Buck Baker's '60 Chevy was very fast, but he lost an engine on lap 118 and wound up with a 13th finishing spot. The race was scheduled for 200 laps and Doug Yates had his '59 Plymouth running pretty good, but he needed relief. Lee Petty jumped in the car and finished the race for Doug. Lee finished one lap down to the leaders. Rex was leading with 18 laps to go and pretty much had the race won. But Lee Petty, as we stated earlier, was tough as nails and he took no prisoners. He slammed into Rex, almost crashing him. That slam was enough to move Rex up into the marbles, where there is no traction. Just so happened that Lee's son, Richard, a 22-year-old racer, was running second and with Rex moved out of the way, Richard got by. Richard Petty got his first Grand National win that day. Doug Yates was credited with third and Junior Johnson and Joe Eubanks finished out the top five. Richard got $800 for his first win and Rex was paid $525 for second place. Lee was questioned about his tactic of slamming Rex to move him, and he then stated, "Well, that didn't hurt Richard's chance of winning any."

On to race #7. North Wilkesboro was still a family favorite for us all. Rex always ran well there. So did hometown favorite Junior Johnson. But on this day, Lee Petty had a different idea. With 14 laps to go, Lee Petty shoved Junior Johnson right into the wall. I guess that was easier than just racing him clean. Rex White finished second, Glen Wood was third and Ned Jarrett was fourth. Lee Petty was pelted with rocks, pop cans and beer cans— sort of like Jeff Gordon at Talladega a couple of years ago. Petty grabbed the microphone from the track announcer and tried to explain himself and that move. North Wilkesboro is Junior Johnson country. His fans were having no part of the Petty celebration. Even in victory lane, he was pelted again amid a roar of jeers from the crowd. Buck Baker finished 14th, driving his 1960 Chevy #87, and Richard Petty and David Pearson finished 18th and 19th. Petty earned $900 for his win and Rex earned $525 for second place. This was in the '59 Chevy that he had run all the season before. The '60 was still home in the shop being prepped for an upcoming race.

The Arizona State Fairgrounds was the site of the next race on this season. No east-coasters attended this one. Nineteen cars started the race and Mel Larson started from the pole in his 1960 Sun City Pontiac. John Rostek, an excellent short-track racer, won the race in a Ford. Larson was second and Scotty Cain finished third. That was the eighth race of the season.

Columbia, South Carolina, was the battleground for race #9 this year. This race would be set for 200 laps on a half-mile dirt track. Louie had the 348 in a good state of tune and Rex was loaded for bear! Doug Yates grabbed the pole and Joe Weatherly grabbed the outside pole driving the #12 Holman-Moody 1960 Ford. Joe crashed on lap 127 and wound up a dismal 18th position. Rex qualified third and grabbed the lead and never looked back. He was the only car on the lead lap at the end of the 200 laps. I made at least 200 laps on top of that old Chevy pickup truck. Just stood right there and kept turning on my feet. It's a wonder I didn't screw myself right down into the roof of that truck. Anytime Rex was leading, I kept my eyes glued right to that race car. I even remember a few dirt tracks where things were still wet and muddy and Rex would switch on the wiper blade on his side of the car. Sometimes one of the crew guys would toss a bucket of water on the windshield when Rex pitted on those muddy dirt tracks. Buck Baker drove his Chevy home for the second-place money and Doug Yates came in third driving his Plymouth. Lee Petty and Joe Lee Johnson rounded out the top five. Our friends G.C. Spencer and Ned Jarrett finished ninth and 11th respectively. Rex and Louie split $800 on this day. That would buy some groceries. It was always fun to go grocery shopping with my mother after we had a good weekend at the race track. Either my sister or I could usually talk her into a few extra snacks for the week.

April 10 came around and found us all back at Martinsville, Virginia. This was the Virginia 500, and that meant a tough, grueling 500 laps on a half-mile asphalt oval. The track was terribly hard on brakes, rear end gears, engines, transmissions, tires and very, very tough on the fenders too! Once again, Glen Wood grabbed the pole with a blazing-fast lap time. Nearing the end of the 500 laps, Bobby Johns, who was driving my dad and Rex's '59 Chevy #41, was leading the race. Even though Rex was already in a tight points battle with Bobby Johns, when Bobby needed a car for the race, Louie and Rex loaned him their '59 Chevy backup car. It was just more of a "family" back then and less of big business. Rex, Fred Lorenzen, Bobby Johns and Richard Petty swapped the lead eight times in the closing laps. During the last pit stop, Louie knew that both the '60 Chevy

Louie Clements poses with the 1960 Chevy prior to the Virginia 500 at Martinsville. In the background is the #41 1959 Chevy that Rex and Louie loaned to Bobby Johns for this race.

Rex was driving as well as the '59 Chevy that Bobby was driving both needed at least one quart of oil added to the engines. He was going to handle going under the hood on the '60 Chevy for Rex, and Bobby's dad, Shorty Johns, was going to do the same for Bobby. When the cars roared off pit road, Bobby got out first. Louie immediately went over to Shorty and asked, "Did you put the oil in the motor?" Shorty waved him off and said, "No time." Well, Louie knew right then that Bobby would never make it to the end. He just shook his head and went back to watching Rex. Bobby was leading with Richard running second. Just a few laps from the end, the old '59 Chevy motor scattered all over creation. Oil was everywhere and the track crew had a cleanup on their hands. The cars on the track had already made their last stop and they knew they didn't need to pit. That left Richard in the lead with Jimmy Massey, Glen Wood and Rex White in hot pursuit. Add in Bob Welborn for fifth place and that is just how they finished. Richard Petty had won his second race on this season and assumed the points lead this day. The points battle was shaping up to be a good one. Richard earned $3,350 for his workday and Rex made $835 for a fourth-place finish. Rex was actually leading the race when Chevy #29 of Bob Potter spun and Rex couldn't avoid hitting him with the left front fender and knocking it in on the tire. We have a photo of the car during a pit stop right after that collision and Louie is using his bare hands to pull the fender off the tire. I do believe my daddy could have broken an anvil with his bare hands had he wanted to. More folks than me

The photograph that made Louie Clements quit smoking.

Rex poses with the 1960 Chevy prior to the start of the Martinsville 500.

have seen it too. My dad later saw the photo and said, "I look just horrible with that damn cigarette hanging from my mouth." On the ride home from a race a few weeks later, he tossed out his cigarettes and lighter and quit cold turkey. Never smoked again. He was a tough man who could make up his mind to do something and nothing would stop him.

Thirty-seven Grand National stock cars started the Virginia 500 and twenty-one were still running at the end. Emanuel Zervakis ran the other White and Clements '60 Chevy to a ninth-place finish. Zervakis was also a Virginia boy. He went on to start his own company and did very well with it. It was called Stock Car Products. They built complete chassis to individual components for all sorts of race cars.

Hickory, North Carolina, was a .4-mile dirt short track. Rex and Louie took the older '59 Chevy up there for this 250-lap event. This would be race #11 of the season. Rex snookered the start and led for 187 laps until the rear end gear burned down. That took him out of the race and he was credited with a 14th-place finish, which paid $85. Fords ran first and second with Joe Weatherly winning and Ned Jarrett running second. Richard finished third with Bob Welborn fourth and Tom Pistone fifth. Junior Johnson broke a rear axle and finished dead last this day. Joe earned $800 for his day's work.

In Wilson, North Carolina, they had a half-mile dirt oval track that played host to the stars of NASCAR several times. April 17, 1960, was one of those days. Emanuel Zervakis and Buck Baker qualified very well and captured the front-row starting spots. Ned Jarrett and Rex White snatched up the second row. It was shaping up to be a very good race. After the dust settled at the completion of the 200-lap contest, Joe Weatherly was victorious, driving the red-and-white #12 Holman-Moody 1960 Ford. Lee Petty was second, Tom Pistone was third and Rex finished a fine fourth place. Joe earned $1,275 for his win and Rex's fourth place was worth $275. Boy, have times changed or what?

Buck Baker finished fifth, but the racer who was flagged as the winner, Emanuel Zervakis, was found to have an oversized fuel tank and was DQ'd and sent to the back with no money and no points. He was allowed to keep his pole position as the oversized tank had little to do with that. Only 19 cars started the race and four fell out.

Race number 13 of the season saw us all back to the flat quarter-mile asphalt track at Bowman Gray Stadium in Winston-Salem, North Carolina. Bowman Gray was and still is a flat asphalt track around a football field. Rex won five straight races at that track. We used to love to go there because Rex ran so well there and often times won. The track is still there and operational today.

Once again, Glen Wood was fast enough to take the pole and Rex started second. Wood got the jump on the start and led all 200 laps. Rex ran second, right on Glen's tail, for the entire 200 laps. Points leader at this stage in the season was Richard Petty, with his father Lee Petty in second. Rex was in third at this, the 13th race of the season. Glen won $600 for first place and Rex brought home $475 for second. Junior Johnson lost an engine early on in the race and was credited with a 15th-place finish. As usual for this quarter-mile track, my older brother Lloyd and I were in the scoring tower for the race. Again, we scored the modifieds first and then the Grand Nationals when it was their turn to shine. The snack bar was right below us. So for Lloyd to send me down a couple times during the race to grab a couple of Pepsis and hot dogs was fairly common. Seems the more I write about it, the more I miss it. My dad and brother are gone now, and there

The championship rig after the Martinsville 500.

has been more than one time while writing this book that I've had to take a break and remember the present. Life was great then, and it is still great today.

Greenville-Pickens Speedway in Greenville, South Carolina, is a fine asphalt half-mile track today. It has a nice paved pit area and nice amenities for the fans too. But in 1960, it was still a little half-mile dirt oval with wooden fences and worn-out rest rooms. But we were there to race, so that's all that mattered. Curtis Turner took the pole position with his patented long slide into the corners. He would run that H-M '60 Ford wide open down the front chute and toss the car sideways at the flagstand! Man, it was awesome watching this man drive a race car. You've heard of No Fear? This man invented No Fear! Lee Petty was just like him, only meaner. Lee drove his '60 Plymouth to qualify for the outside of the front row. Richard started third and Little Davy Pearson started fourth. They all called him Little Davy until he won the World 600 the next season.

So we had 22 cars taking the green flag. Fords, Chevys, Plymouths, Dodges, Mercurys, one Pontiac and two T-Birds all started the 200-lap race. Ned Jarrett won the race, earning another $800 for his evening's work. Lee and Richard ran second and third. Rex ran the '59 Chevy this night and could run right there with the leaders, just biding his time. But on lap 136, time ran out on the old '59 Chevy. Another rear end gear burned up. Rex was credited with a ninth-place finish. Only six cars were running at the end of this race. Remember, these were still stock cars! It makes a difference.

Let me tell you a bit about what it was like for my mother being the wife of a Grand National crew chief with five kids.

Some days, by noon, the guys still didn't know if they were going to have the race car ready to race that night. Remember, back then we raced three, four or five times a week. Just one or two races made for a pretty soft weekend. Well, with a situation like this, my Mother had to *stay* prepared. The Boy Scout motto is "Be Prepared." I think my mom would have made a fine Boy Scout!

We had a Chevy station wagon and my dad might call up and say, "Be here at the shop in 30 minutes if you're going racing with us." Well it was "game on" when that call came. We each had our job to do. Load the wagon, double-check the food, drinks, water, ice chest. Who's got the baby? Who grabbed the dog? Do we need jackets? Somebody grab the first aid kit! You kids bring your homework and finish it going down the road! We did whatever it took to get to the shop in time to pull out to go racing. If it was a race in, say, Columbia, South Carolina, that was a 90-minute drive down to the track. After the race was over, the payoff window and the bench racing took hours too. Columbia ran Thursday nights. So if we left the track maybe at 2 A.M., we slept on the way home, not in school. One complaint and you got to stay home from the next race.

One thing about the way my mom packed the car was that if *anyone* in the infield, any driver's family or crew member's family, anybody needed anything at all, they all knew to come down to our car. My mom brought everything but the kitchen sink. But we had a water bowl that served that purpose. Everyone in the infield knew that my mom had Band-Aids, hairpins, pencils, paper, crayons, fried chicken, biscuits, and even those little cans of Vienna sausages. One or two of those little sausages with a slice of bread and we were heroes to many racers. Man, life just didn't get any better than that.

Greenville was run on April 23, and the very next day, April 24, we were racing the high-banked half-mile paved track in Asheville, North Carolina. This race was scheduled for 167 laps which accounted for a 100-mile event. Junior Johnson grabbed the pole position driving Glen Wood's #21 Ford. Glen Wood himself qualified his #16 Ford for second place. Jack Smith and Rex White were fast enough for the third and fourth starting spots. Jack Smith, Banjo Matthews, Bob Welborn and Lee Petty traded the lead for a while. At the end of the day, it was Lee Patty in victory lane again. This was Lee's 50th NASCAR Grand National win. Our friend G.C. Spencer brought his old '58 Chevy home for a fine fifth-place finish. He was a complete independent and a top five helped him out tremendously with his finances. Rex finished seventh, Baker was eighth and Richard finished ninth. Both Junior Johnson and Glen Wood broke well before the halfway point and finished toward the rear of the field.

On May 14, 1960, the race for the weekend was none other than the Darlington Rebel 300. Darlington was always a favorite for our family. It was the granddaddy of all stock car races. It had a big track and lots of room in the infield for little boys to run wild and play while waiting for the race to start. The track's management always played "Dixie" and usually had a Civil War re-enactment on the front straightaway before the race. Of course, the race brought on battles of its own.

It's funny, some of the things that stick with you over the years. Even though I was only nine years old at the time, I vividly remember that gold-and-white #4 Chevy of my dad's starting outside the front row. Rex always ran well at Darlington. It was just one of those places that he knew how to get around. Standing up on top of our car in the paddock area gave me an excellent view of the fourth corner from the inside. All of the racers parked their trailers just inside the inside guardrail right inside the fourth turn. Of course these were all open trailers of the day. The racers' families were allowed to park back up

Rex White posing with the 1959 Chevy convertible prior to the 1960 Rebel 300. Rex started third, finished third.

against a fence separating us from the regular infield crowd. There was just enough room to drive a car or maybe a tow truck between our car and those race trailers. Coming around the pace lap, ready to get the green, was Fireball in the Smokey Yunick Pontiac. It was an awesome-looking black-and-gold #22 with intimidating black wheels on it. The car always looked serious. In the center of the front row was Little Joe Weatherly driving the red-and-white #12 Holman-Moody 1960 Ford. The hood on that car was lettered with 360 HP! More factory horsepower than the Pontiacs, Chevys and Plymouths. On the outside of the front row was Rex White driving the White and Clements, gold-and-white 1959 Chevy #4. It was all convertibles in this race. The fans could look right in and actually watch the drivers hands work the steering wheels and the gear shifters. The roar of all 32 engines coming around to get the start and boom!— the green flag flies and the drivers get into their throttles and the race is on. It was always a battle between all of the drivers to see who could lead the first few laps. They knew they couldn't win the race in the first lap, but there were bigger stakes at risk. Their pride was on the line!

Fireball led the first eight laps, then Joe led for three laps, then back to Fireball for about 60 laps. Everyone had settled into his comfort zone and prepared to ride the race out and see just which team had planned the best strategy. Rex kept the Chevy up in the top five all day, drafting all he could to save fuel.

The track was 1.375 miles long in those days, so a 300-mile race would require 219 laps. On the 148th lap came one of those things that sort of burns into one's memory. Johnny Allen, driving a light metallic blue '60 Chevy convertible, crashed entering turn 4. As he hit the guardrail, his car went airborne and sailed right over the Armco rails and outside the track. This happened right in front of me. To make his crash worse, the official NASCAR scoring stand was then located right outside the turn 4 guardrail. Johnny's Chevy hit the end of that scoring stand and knocked one end of it to the ground. It was a very scary and tense moment for everyone there. I guess that goes double for those who were scoring the race that day. To everyone's surprise, no scorers were injured and Johnny escaped with only minor cuts and scrapes. His Chevy was totally destroyed, though. I have a photo somewhere of Johnny walking back to the infield care center with his crew chief at the time, Don Bailey. I think Don is retired now and still runs a hunting lodge up in Wyoming. Johnny went on to race several more years and did quite well for himself in the sportsman series in the '70s.

At the end of the race, Joe Weatherly came across the line first for the win. That was worth $9,250 to him and the H-M team. A very proficient young Richard Petty drove to an excellent second-place finish, and our hero, Rex White, brought the old workhorse '59 Chevy home in third place. That paid $2,900, which was still good money back then. Rounding out the top five were Lee Petty in fourth and Buck Baker in fifth. Between Lee's fourth- and Richard's second-place finish, the Petty Engineering team earned $6,815. No doubt, racing was all business for the Pettys. Other notables were Emanuel Zervakis finishing eighth, #15 Tim Flock was ninth in what had become a rare appearance by this time, and Joe Lee Johnson was 14th. Only 17 cars were still running at the end of the 300-mile contest of men and machines. Pole sitter Fireball Roberts' car suffered a broken suspension part and left him for a 20th-place finish. Tom Pistone, Junior Johnson and Banjo Matthews all fell out due to mechanical failures.

Another Darlington race was in the books, and after loading up the truck, trailer and race car, we all headed up the road, back to Spartanburg. I believe this was the night that my dad pulled into a drive-in restaurant in Florence, South Carolina, and a carhop came out to the car to take our order. We kids all knew what we wanted, but my dad asked this young man for a menu. The kid said, "Yes, sir." He came back about a minute later and said, "We all outta that stuff, sir." Louie said, "What stuff?" The kid said, "That menu stuff." With a straight face my dad said, "Son, a menu is the piece of paper you read to see what types of food are offered." The young man said, "We gots a lot of those things, I'll be right back." He brought back the menus and we all ordered and enjoyed a good laugh. The food was good and the young man was a good sport, too. But we had school the next day. Man, that alarm clock was not my friend. Still isn't.

Two weeks later found us racing at home. This time, race #17 for the season was held at the Piedmont Interstate Fairgrounds in Spartanburg. This was May 28, 1960, and the race was scheduled for 200 laps on the half-mile dirt track. Rex ran the '60 Chevy this time and qualified well and ran up front for almost the entire race. Then the motor overheated and he had to pit twice to add coolant to the radiator to cool the engine down. He was still running at the end of the race, but finished 12th. Not what we had hoped for, but better than it could have been.

At the end of the 200 laps, Jimmy Massey had won the race while driving as a relief

In the garage area at Darlington, a Purolator rep confers with crew chief Louie Clements.

driver for Ned Jarrett. Jarrett got credit for the win. That is the way the NASCAR rules have always been, to my knowledge at least. Second place went to Lee Petty in the #42 Plymouth and third went to hometowner Cotton Owens. Tommy Irwin and rookie David Pearson completed the top five. Pole qualifier Jack Smith, driving Bud Moore's 1960 Boomershine Pontiac, suffered suspension problems on lap 79 and was credited with an 18th-place finish. Herman Beam ran a constant and steady pace and finished 13th, a full 25 laps down to the winner. Slow and steady went the race with Herman. I still remember how pretty his race cars were, though. This year, Herman Beam drove a baby-blue 1960 Ford #19. I don't know that his car ever received even one dent or scratch on it.

During these years of the late '50s and early '60s, there was excitement each year around October and November. The auto manufacturers would make a big promotion of the styling on their new cars. In 1960, the Chevys still had those big horizontal rear fins. But they were shaped a bit different from the '59 Chevys and less pronounced too. The Chevys carried the factory horsepower rating of 320-HP on their hood for the season. The Pontiacs for 1960 were beautiful automobiles. They had way less fin than most other cars. And they had a very potent 389-cubic-inch engine which was factory rated at 333 horsepower. They made much more than that in race tune. The 1960 Plymouths still had those big tall straight-up tail fins in the rear, very pronounced, which probably helped to keep them from spinning out on the super speedways. Their factory horsepower rating was 325 hp. Then we had the 1960 Fords. These cars carried the most factory horsepower of any car in competition. They were rated at 360 hp and their Ford bodies were very nice-looking with a rear window sloping similar to the Chevys and Pontiacs. They also had small horizontal rear wings on their quarter panels. The 1959 T-Birds that raced in the '60 season had a distinct disadvantage when it came to aerodynamic down force. Their roofs hung out over the front of the windshield, making for a "trap" for the air to collect in. Then in the rear of the roof, they had that flat back window which was horrible for smooth airflow over the top of the car. However, they were allowed to run the 430-cubic-inch Lincoln V8, which was factory rated at 350 horsepower. I'm sure they put out a bit more than that before they left the Holman-Moody shops in Charlotte.

Hillsboro (now Hillsborough), North Carolina, was next on the list with race #18 of the season. Rex chose to run the newer 1960 Chevy this weekend. He ran well and kept the car up front until one of those pesky 348 rockers broke. They left him on seven cylinders for the rest of the race. Richard and Lee Petty occupied the front row and Lee brought home the big money. Richard finished sixth, three laps down to the "Old Man," as Lee was being called then. Ned Jarrett, Jack Smith, Tommy Irwin and Buck Baker filled out the top five in finishing order. Junior Johnson finished ninth and Rex finished the race, still running, but in the 11th spot. Curtis Turner was 17th in his Wood Brothers Ford and Joe Weatherly finished 19th in his Holman-Moody 1960 Ford. Bunkie Blackburn and Doug Yates rounded out the field of 23 entrants. Petty earned $900 for his win. Rex made $125 for his 11th-place finish.

June 5, 1960, saw us all at the Richmond Fairgrounds for a 200-lap race on a half-mile dirt track. Ned Jarrett grabbed the pole in his 1960 red #11 Courtesy Ford. Cotton Owens qualified outside pole with his #6 1960 Pontiac. Those '60 Pontiacs were really stout and just plain difficult to outrun. At the end of the day, once again, Lee Petty brought home the bacon. His win was worth several very nice points in the season-long points battle, but also another $900 in cash. Not bad at all. Rex ran the '60 Chevy again, this time with a fresh engine in it. He finished second, and he and Lee Petty were the only two cars on the lead lap at the end. Ned Jarrett, Doug Yates and Glen Wood finished out the top five this week. Richard was sixth, Buck was eighth, and Junior Johnson was 14th. Only 19 cars took the green flag. Rex earned us $525 for his second-place finish.

Race number 20 for the season was held out at the new Marchbanks Super Speedway in Hanford, California. Only two east-coast drivers went out to compete. Our friend Frank Secrist took the pole with a speed of 93.04 mph. Frank would later have a greater impact on my life. Joe Weatherly drove the 1960 Ford #97 normally driven by Parnelli Jones. Joe finished a fine second spot with his Vel's Ford. Rex White, hot into a points battle, flew to California and borrowed a car for the race. This was a 1959 Ford and he finished a respectable ninth place with that car. But in the end, it was our good friend Marvin Porter who drove his privately owned and operated '59 Ford to victory, earning a nice well-rounded $2,000 for his day's work. Ron Hornaday, Sr., finished 22nd, driving a 1960 Ford. Seven thousand spectators saw the 33 drivers take the green flag this day.

This next race is a history book in itself. Much has been written about this race and what *could* have been from many different angles. But in the end, it was the Longest Day, the new NASCAR Marathon known forever as the first World 600 at the newly constructed Charlotte Motor Speedway. I only hope I can do this race justice. We were right there watching everything our own eyes could take in. But to be honest, I was totally on sensory overload the whole day. The words awesome and incredible don't begin to describe this day. The word "punishing" seems to do a better job. Every race car, every driver, each and every crew man and race fan, was worn completely out by the time this one was over.

Bruton Smith, Curtis Turner, and Tim Flock got together and came up with the idea of this new super speedway in the Charlotte area. They had some financial backing to get started. But soon after spending all of their money, they hit solid granite right where they had to grade and build a race track. They had to go rattle the bushes for more financing. The construction of the track got behind schedule, and so strapped for cash that one day the work crews actually pulled their road graders across the surfaces to be graded and said, "We're not grading another foot of your dirt until we get paid." This put the track and the new corporation in great jeopardy and it could have gone into receivership.

But Mr. Curtis Turner had another idea. He took his idea up to visit with Jimmy Hoffa and the Teamsters Union. They told him that if he could organize the drivers into a union, they would give him the necessary financial backing he would need. This is certainly how I understand it, anyway. I have heard this stated from many people and read the same thing from other sources too. So, on with construction. Turner started collecting signatures from the drivers, and the teamsters started to funnel money to the speedway for its completion. I clearly remember my father telling me that when they pulled into the track for the opening days of practice that the inside portions of the back stretch were not yet paved. Much of the work was still being completed right up to the waving of the green flag. When we arrived for the race we parked down inside the first and second turns. There was a huge hole, like strip mining going on, down inside the infield of turns three and four. Down inside of turns one and two, there was a huge mountain of solid granite. Most folks parked wherever they could in the infield and then walked up to the top of that big hill for a better view of the race. The infield remained this way for about 10 years. Leveling out the infield into the beautiful place it is today must have required a million dollars and many man-hours. Practice on the track proved that the asphalt surface had not had time to properly cure. NASCAR worked as hard as they could to patch holes everywhere. It was just too much to overcome.

The race was held on June 19, 1960. Six hundred miles for NASCAR stock cars made this the longest and most challenging event in the history of the sport. Knowing the track was going to tear up and cause big problems for the racers, NASCAR tech officials informed each team that they could build some hastily fabricated screens to help protect the radiators and the driver's side windshields, and they also required big truck-style mud flaps under the rear bumpers in an effort to protect trailing drivers from flying debris. Like you might expect, Fireball Roberts took the pole with a speed of almost 134 mph! That was a fast lap on the skinny tires they ran in 1960. The cars weighed in at over 4,000 pounds, too. This was no cakewalk. Roberts was driving the black-and-gold #22 Smokey Yunick 1960 Pontiac. Starting second, in another '60 Pontiac, was Jack Smith driving for Bud Moore. Curtis Turner started third, outside front row, for the three-abreast start. He was driving the light blue #26 Holman-Moody Ford. Sixty cars qualified and lined up for the start of this race. The purse for this race was up there high enough to attract about any race driver who could find a car in time. Rex ran pretty well in the gold-and-white '60 Chevy #4. He started seventh, inside third row. His sixth-place finish gave him the point lead by 1,110 points over Bobby Johns, who was driving the third entry for Petty Enterprises.

The drivers had been warned very sternly before the race about how to make a proper and legal entry to the pit road. The area between the front stretch and the pit road was still just dirt. No grass had time to grow there at this point. At one point in the race, several cars got together in the front stretch and a chain reaction of cars hitting other cars was complicated because of the dust bowl flying around from the lack of grass there. Many of those cars saw clear daylight and drove up the pit road backwards. A couple of days after the race, once NASCAR got to review the film, they notified Lee Petty, Richard Petty, Bob Welborn, Paul Lewis, Junior Johnson and Lennie Page that they had all been disqualified for their improper entrance to the pit road. Had they noticed the pit road, turned around and driven the correct way around the track, and then entered the pits correctly, things would have been different. But I have a copy of that film and Lee and Richard are shown on the tape, clearly driving down pit road in the wrong direction and then making a U-turn to pit. So naturally, when I was reading that Lee Petty stated that he was spinning out in the dust and just happened to come to a stop right in his pit stall, I threw the B.S. flag on that one.

There are so many good stories that go with this first running of the World 600. Where to begin? Well, for one, Fireball was a rocket ship from the beginning. He led the first 65 laps and then came back after pit stops to lead two more times. I believe he broke either a ball joint or an A-frame, and that put him into the wall pretty hard and took him out of the race. Tom Pistone, Curtis Turner and Junior Johnson also took turns leading the race. But the big leader was Jack Smith. Jack was a big man and a strong man with no fear. He drove the wheels off that Pontiac and worked himself up a 5-lap lead over second place. As stated earlier, the track was tearing up and big chucks of asphalt were flying up into the air and coming through the windshields of some of the race cars. A big chunk came through the driver's side of the front windshield on Rex's Chevy, and when he pitted, the crew laid a new windshield on top of the broken one. They taped it down the best they could with duct tape and it held on for the finish. Many cars were hitting the huge potholes left by the deteriorating pavement. That broke ball joints, A-frames, spindles, and wheels, blew tires, etc. The track was really playing havoc with the racers this day. Jack Smith got the brunt of it all, though. While leading by five full laps, a big chunk of asphalt came up and punched a gaping hole, too large to repair, in his fuel tank. Bud Moore and Pop Eargle tried for several laps to stuff rags into the hole and even went on the search for a bar of Octagon laundry soap. If they had found that bar of soap, it's likely they would have won the race. But they didn't, and they finally threw in the towel on lap 352 of the scheduled 400 laps. Still, with lap money and everything, Jack brought home a decent paycheck of $3,680 for a 12th-place finish.

Joe Lee Johnson from Chattanooga, Tennessee, won the race by four laps over Johnny Beauchamp. Both drivers were running 1960 Chevys. Third was Bobby Johns in the Plymouth #46 and fourth was Gerald Duke in his '59 T-Bird #92. Fifth went to Buck Baker, with his Crawford Clements–tuned '60 Chevy. Rex finished in sixth place, which really wasn't too bad when we consider what all he went through. The pit stop for the windshield took a little longer than it should have. Then, just about 65 laps after that windshield ordeal, Rex saw the fuel pressure gauge fluctuate and thought the fuel pump had gone south. It was just time for another fuel stop, that's all. But he came into the pits completely exhausted and demanded a new fuel pump be installed. Louie and James installed the new pump and Rex lost 25 laps while the work was being done. Rex also got to remove his helmet and get a drink of water and cool down a bit. That break in the action had to feel good. Remember, Rex is only 5' 4" and a small-framed man. These were big 4,000+ pound stock cars with no power steering like they have today. Sad thing is, Rex was only 22 laps behind the winner, Joe Lee Johnson, at the end. And to make matters worse, that old fuel pump wasn't bad after all. He could have won the first World 600. Of the 60 cars that started this race, only 18 were still running at the end of it. There is a good story behind each and every entrant. But that would be a book in itself, now wouldn't it?

Some notable finishers were Banjo Matthews seventh and Tiny Lund in eighth. David Pearson finished 10th and Herman Beam finished 14th. Buddy Baker, Larry Frank and G.C. Spencer finished 19th, 20th and 21st respectively. Ned Jarrett crashed on lap 233 and finished 30th with Tom Pistone right behind him. Elmo Henderson, still running at the end, finished 32nd driving the W.H. Watson '58 Pontiac #70. Fred Lorenzen was 41st and Joe Weatherly was 43rd. Cotton Owens and Johnny Allen were involved in an accident on the sixth lap and they finished 51st and 52nd.

Joe Lee Johnson, driving the red-and-white #89 Chevy, brought home an astounding $27,150 for winning this race, certainly the highest paycheck for the season to any NASCAR driver. Joe Lee's chief mechanic, sadly, only had about two more months to live. The sweetness of this victory did not get to ride with Paul McDuffie for long. My father and many more men always spoke very highly of Paul. He was not only a very talented race car builder, tuner, and crew chief, but they all said he was a very good man, something we can all strive to be. NASCAR announced that 78,000 people were in attendance that day.

I just mentioned Larry Frank. Larry was a family friend and once on a visit to our home, Larry stayed for dinner that night. Well, Rex stayed too and we all sat around the kitchen table for the feast my mom had cooked up for us. Now my mom is the best cook there ever was. She certainly understands what "meat and taters" means! I was seated on the back side of the kitchen table and Larry and Rex were across from me. Right before time to eat, Larry excused himself for a trip to the boys' room. While he was washing his hands, Rex reached over and took his spoon and put a big crater in Larry's mashed potatoes and then filled it with black pepper. He then quickly scooped some mashed potatoes over the pepper to hide it. Once back at the table, we said our grace before the meal and we all dug in to chow down. I watched with big eyes, I'm sure, and Larry stirred up his potatoes well, took a bite of them, then requested the pepper shaker. We really never figured out if he really liked pepper or was just getting back at Rex. Man, all of those racers were always messing with each other's heads.

Not long after the 1960 season started, Rex called up his friend James Hylton from Roanoke, Virginia. I believe that James and Evelyn were living and racing down in Tampa, Florida, at that time. Rex offered James a job as a mechanic working on the team and James took it. He actually got the apartment right across the driveway from Rex and Edith's apartment. That was just east of Converse Girls College on Main Street in Spartanburg. It was bicycle-riding distance from our apartment on Maple Street in Spartanburg. Ken Miller also came to work with the team, as did Wes Roark from California. Marvin Porter brought Wes back with him, I think. Jerry Donald was the gas man and Slick Owens sometimes carried the jack and sometimes helped change the right rear tire.

One time while racing at North Wilkesboro, Rex and Louie sat down and discussed some race strategy. Junior Johnson, driving his Pontiac, was faster. So to win this one they were needing to pull a rabbit out of their hat. That is just what they did, too. Pop Eargle was working with them at the time and he was a huge man. He had worked with Bud Moore for a few years and was a great machinist and mechanic. They figured that they really needed to make one less pit stop than Junior or the Pettys or Glen Wood. So on the last practice session, my dad worked on the carburetor to get the float levels just perfect. And he about wore out the jets in the carb changing them around. He set the car up so it would go up the back stretch — remember, the back chute at Wilkesboro went uphill. With the way he set the carburetor, the float bowls would empty while accelerating down the front chute and up the back chute. The engine went through its rich-to-lean fuel curve. In doing that they saved a great deal of fuel. They knew they were spinning the left rear tire coming off the turns and knew that they would need three left rear tires to complete the race. But they also knew that only two left fronts were necessary. So, on the last stop, after changing the right-side tires, big ol' Pop Eargle leaned on a spot they had marked on the race car and made the car pivot on the jack that was still under the right side of the car. Another crew member leaned over the pit wall and changed the left rear tire without actually coming over the wall. It was legal at the time they did it and they won the race because of it. But later that week, the phone rang and it was NASCAR explaining the new rule. That trick would no longer be tolerated. That's pretty much how all the rules came about in NASCAR. Somebody would come up with something innovative and if NASCAR thought it was OK for the sport, it stayed. If they didn't like it, they outlawed it.

June 26, 1960, saw us back at the little quarter-mile flat track in Winston-Salem, North Carolina. This race was called the NASCAR International Sweepstakes race. They allowed some SCCA race cars and drivers to come and race with the Grand National cars. Lee and Richard Petty qualified for the front row and Glen Wood and Bob Welborn took the second row. Rex qualified fifth this time. The race ran for the scheduled 200 laps and was won by Virginia native Glen Wood in his Ford. Lee Petty was second and Rex White finished third. There were only 18 starters in this one and of those, only 13 were American-made cars. Joe Weatherly actually drove a small compact Plymouth Valiant to a sixth-place finish. That car had the little 225-cubic-inch slant 6-cylinder engine in it. Positions 14 through 18 were filled by a '57 Triumph, a '59 MG, a '54 Corvette, a blown-up '57 Ford and a '52 MG. Just a few years earlier, in 1954, Al Keller, an Indy car racer, actually won a NASCAR Grand National race driving a Jaguar on an airport runway with a temporary road course set up. Mr. Wood earned $1,125 for his win and Rex brought back $415 for his third-place finish.

Sixteen thousand spectators came out for the next race, which saw Jack Smith take the win in the 1960 edition of the Daytona July 4th Firecracker 250 at the Daytona Beach 2.5-mile super speedway. Jack's 1960 Pontiac was equipped with a two-way radio. This was one of the first successful attempts at pit-to-driver communications. Cotton Owens, driving his 1960 Pontiac, was second, while Fred Lorenzen and Lee Petty finished third and fourth. Rex drove an excellent race in the underpowered '60 Chevy and finished sixth for a $1,050 payday. Jack Smith earned $11,500 for his win. Thirty-seven cars started the race under the hot Florida sun. Twenty-four were still running at the end. Second-place qualifier Fireball Roberts blew an engine on lap 40 while the team car to Fireball, with Bobby Johns driving, broke an axle on lap 52. Ned Jarrett, Banjo Matthews, Richard Petty, Jim Paschal, Marvin Panch, Junior Johnson, David Pearson, Tom Pistone, and Buck Baker were all in the race and ran hard. All but Pistone and Baker finished the race. The big money winner from a couple of weeks earlier, Joe Lee Johnson, fell out on lap 25 with a blown engine.

The next two races for the season were held up in northern country. Yes, NASCAR even wanted some Yankee fans to like stock car racing. Race #24 was at Heidelberg, Pennsylvania, and it was a 200-lap race that carried the cars for 100 miles on a half-mile dirt track. Problem was, the sky opened up and the rains fell hard on lap 188. NASCAR called it a day at that point. Lee and Richard finished first and second on this day. That was a paycheck of $1,425 for Petty Enterprises with the one-two punch. Rex qualified third and finished third driving the old '59 Chevy this time. Seventeen cars entered the race and 15 were still running at the end. Ned Jarrett lost an engine in his '60 Ford and was credited with a 16th-place finish. By finishing third, Rex increased his point lead to 2,342 points over Bobby Johns.

One week later we ran at Montgomery Air Base in Montgomery, New York. This was the 25th race of the season and it was titled the Empire State 200. The track was a temporarily laid-out triangular-shaped 2-mile circuit on the flat asphalt of the Air Force base. The flat asphalt track took its toll on tires as Ned Jarrett had to pit three times for fresh tires. The race was won by our own hero, Rex White, this week driving the newer 1960 Chevy Grand National car. Rex was the only car on the lead lap at the end of the grueling contest on this hot New York summer day. The win was worth $2,970, which was a pretty good payout for a race of this nature at this time. Richard, Lee, Ned and Buck completed the top five finishers this day. New York's Jim Reed was running very well and lost his engine 14 laps from the end. Herman "The Turtle" Beam was still running, "steady as she goes, captain" and brought his powder-blue Ford in for a ninth-place finish, 10 laps down to White. The estimated crowd was 5,000.

Rambi Speedway in Myrtle Beach, South Carolina, was the site chosen for round #26 of this season. Another half-mile dirt oval, this race was also a 200-lap event. Ned Jarrett always ran well at Myrtle Beach and he snagged the pole for this one. Junior Johnson in his '60 Chevy #27 qualified second. Tommy Irwin and Rex White started third and fourth. Buck Baker in his Crawford Clements tuned '60 Chevy brought home the gold from this race. Baker and second-place Lee Petty were the only two cars on the lead lap this week. Rex ran very well this evening and finished third, which gave him almost a 3,000-point lead in the championship standings. Junior was fourth and Richard was fifth. Seventeen cars started the race and 13 finished it. Future superstar David Pearson finished 11th driving his own '59 Chevy, which he had bought from Jack Smith. Buck earned $800 for his win and Rex made $375 for third place.

Race number 27 of 1960 took us back down the road about four hours' driving time from Spartanburg. This would be the Atlanta Dixie 300 on the new Atlanta 1.5-mile high-banked super speedway. To no one's surprise, Fireball Roberts qualified his '60 Pontiac #22 for the coveted pole position. Just a tick under 134 mph average lap by Roberts made him the man to beat. Jack Smith in another '60 Pontiac started from the second spot, and Fireball's teammate Bobby Johns started from the third spot on the grid. Fireball took the win in this race too. That was actually uncommon for him with the '60 Pontiac. Under normal circumstances he was plagued with mechanical ailments with his always-fast race car. Not on this day, though. He got the job done, and done well. Cotton Owens was second with Jack Smith third. Bobby Johns drove the other black-and-gold Pontiac home in fourth place, with Fred Lorenzen in a Ford finishing fifth. Pontiac swept the top four spots. Those big Ponchos had a bit more horsepower than their competitors. Rex ran pretty well while he was on the track. But some mechanical ills kept him in the pits too long and he finished 23rd, about mid-pack in the 45-car starting field. Of the 45 starters, 32 cars were still running at the end of the race. It was a very hot and humid day in Atlanta, as one might expect in Georgia in July. At one point, Roberts felt a bit dazed and confused and drove down pit road in what he called a hot, tired, exhausted trance. He drove right past his pit and went back into the race and felt OK after that. He took the lead from Cotton with only 12 laps to go. David Pearson, who finished 32nd place, was the last of the cars still running the race at the end. Thirteen had fallen out with mostly blown engines. Lee Petty finished eighth, Ned Jarrett was 15th, Richard was 20th, Banjo was 25th and Tiny Lind, driving an Oldsmobile, was 30th.

With Rex's 23rd-place finish and Lee Petty's eighth-place finish, Lee closed up the point gap a bit on Rex. Approximately 25,000 spectators saw the lead change hands 12 times.

Just three days later NASCAR placed event #28 down in Birmingham, Alabama, on the quarter-mile paved oval track. If it hadn't been for the hotly contested points battle, several drivers would have stayed home. But there was a points war going down, and Rex needed to be in that race. The '59 and '60 Chevys #4 were not ready to go, so Rex drove down to the track and borrowed a car from our friend L.D. Austin. I remember L.D. as being a tall, thin older gentleman with grey hair. He was always polite and had time for us kids. His race car was an older '58 Chevy, black and white with the #74 on the doors. Rex qualified it for the seventh starting position and brought it home in one piece with a ninth-place finish. Ned Jarrett and Richard Petty grabbed up the two front-row starting spots and then proceeded to finish this 200-lapper in that same order. Lee Petty was third, Joe Lee Johnson was fourth and Johnny Beauchamp finished fifth. They were followed closely by our friends G.C. Spencer and Buck Baker. Driving the #44 Petty Plymouth was Richard's brother Maurice, in a rare appearance. He finished eighth, so Petty Enterprises brought home a total of $1,170. All three of their cars were still running at the end and they made more money than the winner, Ned Jarrett, who was paid $770 for his day's work. Once again I'll say it: Lee Petty was the first racer to figure out how to make a living from stock car racing. Only sixteen cars started the race and 12 were still running at the end. Yes, times have certainly changed. Rex came away with a 1,570 point lead. Remember, during these times, the NASCAR points system rewarded "consistency" much more than on-track performance and winning.

The next three tracks were all venues where Rex performed consistently well. Nashville was next, just four days after the Birmingham race. As regular as clockwork, Rex took the pole again at Nashville. He had a stranglehold on speed when it came to the Fairgrounds track at Nashville. The race was scheduled for 400 laps and Rex had the entire field covered and should have won again this day. But Lady Luck played right into #73 Johnny Beauchamp's hands. Johnny had started outside pole and was getting around pretty well himself that day. While leading the race at the 330-lap mark, Rex ducked into the pits for his final stop of the day. Right-side tires and a load of fuel and he was back out on the track. Just as Beauchamp started to head down pit road, his crew chief, Dale Swanson, notice some light rain starting to fall. He quickly signaled Johnny to stand on the gas and get right back on the track, right in front of Rex. He did just that. And within three laps of caution under the rain, NASCAR dropped the checkers for the #73 Chevy for Beauchamp. Second place was still a good points finish and it paid about $2,400. All things considered, it was a good day. Johnny earned almost $3,700 for his victory. Once again, the race doesn't always go to the swiftest. Sometimes we would be lucky rather than good. Rex raised his points lead by another 60 points this day. Buck Baker was third and Lee Petty was fourth. Joe Lee was fifth and Richard came home sixth. Local Tennessee racer and excellent modified standout Bob Reuther borrowed a '60 Ford and finished 14th on his home track against the big boys of NASCAR. I was fortunate to get to speak with Bob a couple of months before he passed away in 2009. He was still flying his plane and life was good. He was thrilled to hear some of the racing stories from back in the day with him racing against my dad's 1934 Chevy modified with G.C. driving it. We talked for quite a while and he invited me down for a visit. I did not make it in time.

We got a whole week off before the next race at Asheville. This was race #30 for the season and it was called the Western North Carolina 500. Asheville-Weaverville Speedway was a fast race track for its time: high-banked, half a mile, paved... and with concrete walls that were not very forgiving.

Jack Smith grabbed the pole with an average speed of 78 mph with his Bud Moore–tuned 1960 Boomershine Pontiac. He was blistering fast this day. Rex and Louie had the '60 Chevy getting through the corners quicker than anyone else. But the Chevy engine was no match for that famous Pontiac horsepower down the chutes. Rex started outside front row with Johnny Beauchamp and Glen Wood taking the second row starting spots. We always parked just inside the fourth corner when we raced at Asheville. That was our comfort zone, I guess. Rex and Louie always chose that first pit stall as you enter the pits, too. Thirty-four cars started the race and most of the hot dogs were there. Bobby Johns, from Florida, was driving the #5 team car to Cotton Owens for this event. After starting seventh, he rushed to the lead by the fifth lap. I think this could have been an audition for full-time employment. Anyway, he led the race for 166 laps before making his first pit stop. Tom Pistone took over the lead for a while, and then on the 389th lap, Rex White took over the point for the remainder of the race. Rex was the only car to complete the entire 500 laps, finishing a full four laps ahead of second-place Possum Jones driving his #2 1960 Chevy. Third was Emanuel Zervakis driving the white #85 Chevy that had been built by the White and Clements team in Spartanburg. Fourth went to Bobby Johns in a Pontiac and fifth was Jack Smith in another Pontiac. Points contenders Lee Petty and Richard Petty finished eighth and 15th respectively. Of the 34 starters, only 10 cars were still running at the end. Everything from blown engines to broken chassis components to crashes pretty much took out the rest of the players. Rex earned a good-sized paycheck of $3,650 for this win. Junior Johnson finished 30th and made $100. The remaining four racers received nothing for their efforts. This was commonplace for this time period in NASCAR history.

The half-mile dirt track back home in Spartanburg was the scene of this next 200-lap event. The shop wasn't far from the track, and often my dad or Rex or one of the team guys would just drive the race car to the track. I think this was a regular practice for Cotton Owens. The track was practically in his back yard. My Uncle Crawford had his shop out on Interstate 85 that goes north to south from Charlotte down to Atlanta. He once drove the Buck Baker car right to the fairgrounds track from out on the freeway. The police were pretty cool about it. Basically, it was just another type of promotion for tonight's race. Once the 21 cars settled into the pit area they ran some warmup laps and some mud-packing laps to start to get a groove worked in. Qualifying started, and who else but hometowner Cotton Owens, with that Pontiac horsepower, would go out and take the pole position honors? With Cotton on the pole, Gerald Duke put his T-Bird on the outside front row. Starting third was Buck Baker and fourth was #43, Richard Petty. Richard was a quick learner and by this time was a threat to win every race he entered. He came along just at the right time. Once the race started, it was pretty much the Cotton Owens and Lee Petty show. Cotton won this time with Lee running second. Coming in third was Junior Johnson and fourth was the #11 Ford of Ned Jarrett. Rex took good care of the race car and brought it home for a fine fifth-place finish. Not bad, considering only two days earlier he drove the same car and engine to victory up in Asheville. A crowd of 6,000 watched as Richard Petty dropped out on lap 147 with mechanical problems. L.D. Austin and Buck Baker were still running at the end for eighth- and ninth-place finishes. Buddy Baker drove hard, but his 1960 Ford lost its rear end gear on lap 81. David Pearson also lost a rear gear on lap 59 for an 18th-place finish. Bobby Johns had come up to drive the '59 T-Bird #93 for Banjo Matthews. That car suffered from engine overheating on the second lap and that lost many points for Bobby. This race was held on August 16, which allowed only two days for the racers to get back home, make repairs and get back down to Columbia, South Carolina, for race number 32 of the season.

Rex almost always ran very well at Columbia, so he and Louie mapped out a pretty clever strategy to try to snag this win. One hundred and fifty miles on a half-mile dirt track meant 300 laps on this evening. Rex was only 31 years old at the time and Louie was only 38 years old. From where I am sitting at this moment in time, those sound like very young racers to me. Anyway, qualifying time rolled around, and would you believe it? Tommy Irwin grabbed the fastest lap time for the pole and our friend G.C. Spencer, driving a worn-out '58 Chevy, qualified second fastest for the outside front row. Spencer's family and ours were always close and it always felt good to share in their good times too. The racers truly were a big family in those days. Doug Yates started third, and rookie sensation David Pearson started fourth in his '59 Chevy. Once the 26 cars took the green flag it quickly became all about Rex White and Richard Petty. This was a Chevy versus Plymouth battle for NASCAR championship supremacy. In the end, Rex won the race with Petty being the only other driver on the lead lap with him. A big part of the race-winning strategy was that this particular track was known for having a good bit of sand in the dirt. Air filters got clogged up pretty easily and about halfway through the race, when the cars pitted, someone would go under the hood and change the clogged-up air

Rex and Louie, posing with the race queen for an early promotional photograph for Perfect Circle piston rings, at victory lane at Asheville/Weaverville Raceway.

filter for a new one. Louie told Rex that this old motor was really tired anyway, so they just decided to race without any air filter element inside the black air filter canister. They saved precious time by not going under the hood on that stop. The old engine was spraying for mosquitoes by the end of the race, but they made enough money for another engine. Buck Baker, Ned Jarrett and Tommy Irwin completed the top five this day. Lee Petty finished seventh. Cotton Owens experienced some problems and finished 15th. David Pearson, Bobby Johns and Joe Weatherly all had problems too. The excitement for Spencer starting on the front row quickly faded. His '58 Chevy burned down a differential gear 42 laps into the show. He was credited with 26th place. Rex earned $1,000 for this victory. By the way, did you know a fully blueprinted race-ready 348 Chevy engine sold for nearly $800 back then? Mere "chump change" to the price of the new 409 that came out in 1961. Those engines, race prepped, sold for $900 a copy. Today it takes about three of those 409s just to pay for one Cup car crankshaft.

No time to waste, no time to fish; the next race was two days away up in South Boston, Virginia. This race would be 150 laps on a quarter-mile dirt track. Race number 33 of the season saw Ned Jarrett qualify for the pole with Junior Johnson starting outside pole. The schedule back then was so tough on drivers, mechanics, cars and families, only

15 cars took the green flag. This time, instead of his '60 Chevy, Junior drove the same Daytona Kennel Ray Fox Chevy that he had won with in the second annual Daytona 500. This day was no different, except maybe he didn't do as much drafting on the quarter-mile dirt. Junior won the race and was the only car on the lead lap at the conclusion of the event. Possum Jones was second and Rex finished third driving our '59 Chevy. Those older backup cars came in handy when chasing the points championship. Buck, Fred Harb, Richard, and Lee filled out the top seven positions. Bobby Johns was the last car running at the end and he was credited with a 13th-place finish. Only two cars failed to finish this one. The win was worth $810 to Junior, and Rex brought back $410 from the pay window.

A mere three days later seventeen cars took the green flag for another 200-lap race at Bowman Gray Stadium in Winston-Salem, North Carolina. When we turned onto the road leading to the track I remember seeing that big billboard with the Winston and the Salem cigarette packages on it. You knew you were in tobacco country when you got to that spot.

At the track, Glen Wood and Lee Petty qualified on the front row again as Richard and Rex were quick enough to take the second-row spots on the grid. Once the race started, Glen Wood took to flying around that little track. He was chased hard by Lee Petty, who eventually realized he could not keep up the pace that Wood was laying down. Glen won this race for his third straight win at Bowman Gray Stadium. Lee Petty finished second followed by Junior Johnson, Rex White and Buck Baker. Richard ended up ninth and Ned was 11th. Only one car fell out of the race and that was the '58 Chevy of G.C. Spencer. This was the third race in a row in which Spencer finished dead last. Not good for the budget. Wood earned $770 for his win and Rex earned $260 for bringing that old '59 Chevy home in fourth spot.

Almost everyone knows where they were when President Kennedy was killed, or where they were when Neil Armstrong first walked on the moon, or where they were when they first got news of the terrorist attacks of 9/11. Well, this next race is and was one of those days for me. The 1960 Darlington Southern 500 could be a book or a movie on its own merits. Everything surrounding this race was big, both for better and for worse. The good stuff started with the White and Clements team having the '60 Chevrolet Grand National car in top shape and rebuilt ready for this, the granddaddy of all super speedway races. At least in the South it still was. There were parades downtown during the week. Beauty contests were held to crown the "Miss Southern 500" race queen, and every racer who was anybody showed up for this one. This was the big one that paid the big bucks and offered the most prestige. The Daytona 500 had not yet overtaken the Southern 500 in notoriety for the winning driver or winning type of automobile as of this point.

For our part, my mother and Rex's wife, Edith, went out and bought new crew uniforms for the entire race team. Even us kids got them too: red pants, gold golf shirts and small red straw hats. The shirts had each member's name on the front pocket, and on the back of each shirt was a big red #4 like you would see on a high school or college basketball jersey. The White and Clements team was voted winners for the "Best Dressed Pit Crew" contest. This was a new deal cooked up by Big Bill France to help bring some legitimacy to the sport. It certainly helped. After this award, more and more teams began to show up with coordinated crew uniforms. This was the 35th race of the season and it fell on September 5, which would be my son's birthday 14 years later.

Forty-eight cars entered this race and it proved to be a very good, close, competitive race with twists and turns in the plot at every point through the day. This day would also turn out to be one of the most tragic days in NASCAR history. For starters, once again Fireball Roberts grabbed the pole. His black-and-gold #22 Pontiac was a rocket ship and he certainly knew how to get around this track as well or better than anyone. Buck Baker, filling in for Jack Smith, drove the 1960 Boomershine Pontiac to a second-place starting spot. Qualifying third, outside on the front row was Jim Paschal driving the number 44 Petty Enterprises '60 Plymouth.

Before the race started they put on the annual Civil War reenactment right on the front stretch of the track. You can bet that every time they did this spectacle, the Stars and Bars were the winning side. Before coming to the track on this morning we went as a family to the earliest Sunday Mass that we could find locally. Usually my sister Cindy would make it her job to take the motel room phone book and look up the Catholic churches near us and find out which one had the earliest service. Fred Lorenzen is also a Catholic and we often saw him at Sunday morning services too. I always looked for him and usually found him in attendance.

Once the race got under way, Baker and Roberts traded the lead back and forth for the first 75 laps. Then Cotton Owens took over for a few laps, then Richard, and then Bobby Johns led about three laps driving Cotton's second entry, the white #5 Pontiac that he had driven in prior weeks leading up to this event. Rex grabbed the lead for a few laps to earn some lap money and extra points. Then Baker and Petty swapped off the lead between each other several times through the second half of the race. Driving the black #92 T-Bird normally driven by Gerald Duke, Elmo Langley had a strong run going until he was involved in an accident on the front stretch. He hit the inside wall so hard that the rear end of the car was completely caved in up to the rear window. The fuel tank became dislodged and flew out into the track. The track safety crews got things cleaned up and we went back to racing. This accident occurred only 25 laps into the race.

On the 95th lap is when the real tragedy hit. This occurred on the back stretch when the cars of Bobby Johns and Roy Tyner bumped into each other. Up until this day the race cars that ran Darlington pitted right out on the track surface with no barrier between the pits and the roaring race cars. Johns's #5 1960 Pontiac crashed right into the car of Joe Lee Johnson, who was stopped in his pit having his car serviced by his crew. Car owner and chief mechanic for Johnson was Paul McDuffie. He was killed immediately, right on the spot. Chunks of inside retaining wall went flying everywhere. Another team member on the Joe Lee Johnson crew, Charles Sweatland, along with a NASCAR official, Joe Taylor, were also cut down and killed on the spot. This accident happened right in the center of the back stretch pits. Bobby Johns landed upside down toward the end of the back stretch. Joe Lee Johnson immediately withdrew his car from the race. Bobby Johns was not physically injured in the crash, but the race car was a total write-off. Three other pit crew men for Johnson's Chevy were also seriously injured and transported by ambulance to local hospitals.

Our family was parked in the racers' paddock area and I was personally up in the newly built scoring stand, which was just inside the fourth corner. From our position

The championship team at Darlington received NASCAR's first award for the best-dressed pit crew. Left to right: Frank, Griller, Satch, Louie, Rex, James, Jerry, Buddy.

there, all we knew is that a serious accident had occurred. We were not made aware of the severity or the outcome of the wreck until after the race was completed. Our neighbors, who also happened to be our family doctor and his wife, had grandstand seating on the back stretch and witnessed the accident firsthand. Dr. Bill Bonner had actually just installed another new roll of 8mm film into his movie camera and just happened to have the camera on when this accident occurred. I have a copy of that film on tape and it really happened so fast that I doubt anyone killed actually felt any pain. The doctor and his wife described the accident to our family about an hour after the race. I suppose that some fifty years after the fact it is now OK to repeat what they saw. It was very gruesome, to say the least. At least two of the men were cut in half at the waist. The ambulance crews and track cleanup crews actually had to use shovels to pick up and load the body pieces onto the ambulance gurneys. I can't imagine what went through the drivers' heads as they drove past that scene of carnage on the back stretch. You know it had to give them second thoughts about what they were doing. Like professionals do, they shook it off and continued the race as soon as the cleanup was completed.

Just inside the last few laps of the race, things began to happen on the track that made scoring a nightmare at best. With about 20 laps to go, Tiny Lund managed to crash his 1960 Oldsmobile #45 into the front stretch just off the fourth corner. That knocked the front end off that car. This particular Oldsmobile race car was owned by Les Richter,

Richard Petty at speed in the 1960 Southern 500.

who some years later went to work for NASCAR as a chief inspector. When the race resumed, Fireball Roberts and Richard Petty were right on Baker's rear bumper. It started to shape up as a really good finish with the guys in a position to really have to race for the win.

Instead, things went sour for a few of them. Smokey's potent Pontiac, driven by Fireball, blew all to pieces with 11 laps to go. That left Richard in the lead. Then, Richard popped a tire and smacked the wall, which took him out of the win zone. That left Baker leading in the #47 Pontiac, and with a lap and a half to go, the right rear tire let go on the Boomershine Pontiac. He spun out and then got the car going back in the right direction and rode around the track apron for the next two laps. Rex saw Baker with problems and Louie motioned him to go for it! Rex then passed Buck and received two white flags. When he came around again, he received the checkered flag and thought he had won the big one. Louie was standing up on the pit wall motioning Rex to stay in the throttle and make a fast and hard "safety" lap. Rex was watching the flagman and missed Louie's message. He backed off the throttle when he got the checkered flag. Baker came limping around on three wheels and just beat Rex back to the real checkered flag for the win. If Rex had stayed in the gas, he would have won it for certain. But it just wasn't in the cards this day. After being flagged the winner, Rex drove by the pits as was customary in those days and all of the crew jumped onto the car and he drove them down to victory lane and right up on the winner's Hill at Darlington. For a few minutes, we were on top of the world. It took a while, but Joe Epton rechecked the score cards and declared Baker the winner. Even after Rex removed the car from victory lane and drove back down to his pit spot, things were still cool. Second place in the Southern 500 all but sewed up the

1960 championship for the team of White and Clements. That #4 Chevy was really pretty that day.

I spoke with Rex recently about that race and he said that he and Louie had both requested to look at the score cards. After looking them over, it was their feeling that no one could really determine for certain who actually won the race. There were places in the score cards were the scorer would take a restroom break or go get a snack or a drink, and he would just let the score card sit on his desk while he took a break. Once back from the break, he would look over at the person next to him and estimate the number of laps he had been away. The race car could have pitted or another car could have pitted and no one would have known. The scoring sheets kept by the crews in their pits for fuel mileage, etc., were more accurate than the official scoring was. Rex and Louie couldn't protest and claim they had won because they couldn't prove it. But no one could prove the Baker Pontiac had actually won the race either. After that day, we never went racing again without at least one paid scorer for the #4 car. The young man who started coming to every race to score Rex was named Robin. Robin was a friend of NASCAR's chief scorer, Morris Metcalf, as was a man named Randolf Barnes. Rex would pay them about $10 per race to score his car and Morris brought them in to the scoring stand.

Buck Baker earned $19,900 for this victory and Rex was paid some $9,780 for second. They were the only two cars scored on the lead lap at the end on the 500 miles. Jim Paschal was third, Emanuel Zervakis was fourth and Ned Jarrett finished fifth. Pole sitter Roberts ended up ninth and our good friend Elmo Henderson finished a fine 12th place. Sixteen cars were still running at the end of the 500-mile heat fest. California racer Clem Procter drove his 1960 Ford to a 13th-place finish. In later years, he became a regular winner at Riverside and several west coast tracks. I think he was best known for building and racing a 1965 Ford T-Bird for the west coast sportsman class. Approximately 80,000 spectators were in attendance that day. I will always remember actually seeing Rex get the checkered flag and thinking we had won the big one. My mom grabbed up my little brother and told me to keep up. She took off running down the front stretch toward victory lane. Man, we actually tasted that win… for a few minutes anyway.

I'll tell you what else was going on about the time this race was run. Chubby Checker had topped the music charts with "The Twist." That's an all-time hit, sort of timeless to me. Also at the top of the charts were Jerry Butler with "He Will Break Your Heart" (also known as "He Don't Love You [Like I Love You]," and Sam Cooke with "Wonderful World." This kind of helps to put this 1960 Chevy race car into some context.

A mere four days after the '60 Southern 500 we were back up in Hickory, North Carolina, for another 250-lap race on the .4-mile dirt track. Buck Baker qualified for the pole and Junior Johnson was fast enough to start outside front row. Fifteen cars started this race and Junior Johnson's '60 Chevy #27 was the clear winner this day. Second place went to Possum Jones in another '60 Chevrolet and third place went to Rex White in the '59 Chevy. David Pearson finished fourth in his '59 Chevy and Ned Jarrett scored a fifth-place finish for the Ford lovers. Lee Petty was eighth and Richard Petty was 12th. Pole sitter Buck Baker fell out on lap 68 with engine problems. This was race number 36 on the 1960 season and was titled the Buddy Shuman Memorial. Buddy Shuman had been a top-class NASCAR modified driver who had perished in a motel room fire.

The AMA puts on one of the best motorcycle flat-track races in the country, if not

Rex in the pits, with Buddy Payne and Crawford Clements changing left front tire.

Buck Baker, driving Jack Smith's Pontiac, ran the last two laps on a flat rear tire.

the best, each year at the Sacramento Mile dirt track. On September 11, 1960, this track hosted a NASCAR Grand National event. No east-coast racers traveled back for this one. But our friend Marvin Porter, who ran on both ends of the country, did run it. He drove the #97 Vel's '59 Ford and blew a head gasket after just 33 of the scheduled 100 laps. The race was won by Jim Cook driving a 1960 Dodge. He was followed by #4 Scotty Cain, and short-track Champion Lloyd Dane finished third. Ron Hornaday, Sr., finished fourth in a 1960 Ford.

Just five days later, the Grand Nationals were back to Sumter, South Carolina, for a 200-lapper on a quarter-mile dirt oval. Only 13 cars started this race and Ned Jarrett reeled in the win. Pole sitter David Pearson finished second in his own '59 Chevy. Points chasers Rex White and Richard finished sixth and seventh respectively.

Rex normally ran pretty well at the Hillsboro, North Carolina, .9-mile dirt track. This race was #39 of the season and ran for a total of 110 laps. Pole sitter Richard Petty pulled out a clean and well-deserved win on this day. Ned and Rex finished one lap down in second and third place. Of the 18 cars that started, only 10 finished. Winning races was pretty tough during these days when everyone had to run pretty much factory stock equipment. But sometimes, just finishing one was a pretty big deal for some of the guys. They raced so often, worked, raced again, drove up and down the road, and so forth, it was a very tough discipline that tested even the strongest of men. Herman Beam's fourth-place finish this day was probably his best finish for the year. Lee Petty lost a rear end gear and Junior Johnson was involved in an accident.

Martinsville, Virginia, was the site for the Old Dominion 500, race number 40 of this season. This was held on September 25, 1960. Martinsville is the same track today as it was then. It's hard on engines, clutches, brakes, rear end gears, and sheet metal. Always has been, always will be. For this particular round, Mr. Martinsville, Glen Wood, again snapped up the top qualifying spot. Rex White put the Louie Clements gold-and-white #4 Chevy on the outside pole. Thirty-one cars started this race and it was a humdinger too. Right from the green flag, Glen Wood, Rex White, Jimmy Massey in the second Wood Brothers Ford, and Joe Weatherly put on a fine display of racing and racing hard. They would usually do that and then back off a little to save their cars for the end of the long 500-lap race. Bobby Johns's T-Bird, Richard Petty's Plymouth and his daddy Lee Petty's '60 Plymouth all crashed together and fell out of the race on about lap 285. They finished way down the line and all but destroyed their title hopes for the 1960 season. When the 500 laps were completed, Rex White was the winner, earning a ton of those really nice championship points as well as $3,110. The only other driver on the lead lap with Rex was Little Joe Weatherly driving his 1960 Holman-Moody Ford #12. Rounding out the top five were Junior Johnson, Jim Paschal and Buck Baker. Finishing 16th was our friend G.C. Spencer in his Weldon Wagner '58 Chevy #48. Spencer was the last car still running. Positions 17 through 31 had fallen from the race due to accidents, overheating, blown engines, worn-out brakes, etc. This race was Rex's 12th Grand National win.

Race number 41 took us all back up the hill to the Wilkes 200 at North Wilkesboro Speedway in North Carolina. This track was Junior Johnson's home track and he had it figured out very well too. The race was scheduled for 320 laps, which makes up 200 miles on the five-eighths-mile banked asphalt oval. This time, though, it was Rex's turn to take the pole with a new track record. The old 348 stove bolt was laying down some lap times on this day. Qualifying for the outside front row was Richard Petty in his '60 Plymouth #43. Starting third was Jim Paschal and fourth was Buck Baker. Starting back in the 11th spot was Spartanburg's Cotton Owens in his 1960 Pontiac. Twenty-four cars started the race and once again, G.C. Spencer was the last car running, giving him a 17th-place finish.

Rex White won the race in the '60 Chevy with Junior Johnson and Possum Jones both on the lead lap with him. Rex mentioned after the race that Cotton's Pontiac was the fastest thing he had ever seen. Cotton lost his bid for the win when a ball joint broke and forced him hard into the wall on lap 241. Jim Paschal was driving the #44 Petty Engineering '60 Plymouth and giving Rex a good hard run when he blew a tire and crashed hard into the wall, just as Cotton had done earlier. Another blown tire also took Lee Petty out of competition on lap 129.

October 16, 1960, was the big National 400 on the new Charlotte Motor Speedway, which had given the drivers and teams all sorts of problems earlier in the season at the first-ever World 600 race. This was an event with so much press and hype that every race car driver in the country wanted a piece of it. Fifty cars started this one under that hot, humid southern sky. Again, it was not a surprise that Fireball Roberts would win the pole for this race. His pole speed in the #22 Pontiac was over 133 mph average, even on the hot slick track. Pretty quick lap! Starting second would be Jack Smith in another super-tuned 1960 Pontiac. After the fiasco at the World 600 with the hole knocked in his fuel tank, he had a score to settle with this track. Starting third was Speedy Thompson driving the #21 Wood Brothers Ford and fourth would be none other than Rex White driving the Piedmont-Friendly '60 Chevy #4. The stage was set for a real barn-burner. Four hundred miles on a mile-and-a-half track would require 267 laps. There were seven different makes of cars in this race. We had Fords, Chevys, Pontiacs, Plymouths, Dodges, T-Birds, and Oldsmobiles. Remember, in these times, a driver had to race the type of engine that came in the car from the dealer. To me, even as the kid I was at the time, this made for very interesting racing, especially when I got back to school on Monday morning and the other boys would ask me how such and such car did. In school, Sister Mary "Beat Me Up" intercepted many NASCAR notes passed between my friend Brad and me during class. That's OK, though. It gave us something to talk about while staying after school to clap erasers and wash the blackboards.

At the end of the 400 miles, Speedy Thompson won the race, driving for the Woods. Twenty-three-year-old Richard Petty finished second in his Plymouth and Ned Jarrett finished third in his #11 Courtesy Ford. Bobby Johns finished fourth driving Cotton Owens's #5 Pontiac second entry. Junior Johnson was fifth and Rex White finished sixth. Thompson was paid $12,710 for his win and Rex made $2,050 for his sixth-place finish. Other notables were #94 Banjo Matthews in 10th, Johnny Beauchamp 12th in a Chevy, Bob Welborn 14th in a '60 Ford, G.C. Spencer 16th in his tired old '58 Chevy (good for him!), Buck Baker 18th, David Pearson 21st, and Friday Hassler 23rd. Special note about Friday Hassler: In the late '60s and early 1970s, Chevy was not involved in NASCAR racing. Despite the disadvantages of trying to compete without any factory help at all, Mr. Hassler held down the Chevy fort in NASCAR. I watched, live on TV, a qualifying race at Daytona around 1970. I don't remember the exact year. But I do remember that Friday Hassler was driving that familiar #39 Chevelle and driving hard to get into the Daytona 500. There was a horrific accident coming off turn two, starting down the back stretch.

Rex and Louie in victory lane again during the 1960 season.

Friday's Chevelle turned sideways with his door facing oncoming traffic. Cars were coming right at him running better than 170 mph. One couldn't get stopped in time and T-boned the driver's door of that Chevelle. That was the moment that we lost one of my heroes. We just never forget when we lose a hero. God bless you, Mr. Hassler.

Pole sitter Fireball Roberts was involved in an accident on lap 232 and was credited with 23rd position. Johnny Allen was 26th, Chargin' Charlie Glotzbach finished 28th, and Curtis Turner, driving the #26 H-M Ford, was 32nd due to a blown engine. The #89 of Joe Lee Johnson, who won the World 600 earlier in the year, finished 35th due to faulty electrical wiring. Lee Petty was 36th, Jim Reed came home 40th, Jimmy Pardue finished 42nd in the Lowe's '59 Dodge. And #47, second-place starter Jack Smith, finished 44th due to an accident on lap 60. And that left last place, 50th, for Fearless Freddy Lorenzen driving his yellow #28 Ford, which suffered from mechanical failures on the fourth lap. Recorded attendance was just over 29,000. By finishing sixth, Rex White sewed up the 1960 NASCAR Grand National Points Championship. It was "Miller Time" in our pits that evening. That translates to "Dr Pepper Time" when you're nine years old! Man, life just couldn't get any better than this.

There are still a few more races before we can close the doors on the 1960 season. Next on the list came at Richmond, Virginia. This would be another 200-lapper on a half-

In victory lane again, left to right: Rex, Louie and James Hylton.

mile dirt track. This week, Ned Jarrett took fast time and sat on the pole in his red 1960 Courtesy Ford. Outside starting position went to Joe Weatherly, who was this week driving for the Wood Brothers in their '58 Ford. Not to be outdone, Speedy Thompson was on hand to drive the #21 Wood Brothers '60 Ford. Speedy started third and Doug Yates put his #23 Plymouth into the fourth-place starting spot on the grid. A crowd of approximately 7500 spectators was on hand to watch this show. Junior Johnson, Richard Petty and Ned Jarrett were all running very well this day. But when the dust settled, Speedy Thompson had put the Wood Brothers' Ford into victory lane. Buck Baker drove his Thor '60 Chevy to a sixth-place finish and Rex drove the old battle-worn '59 Chevy home in eighth place. In a rare move, Lee Petty made the decision to not start this race and he let his son Maurice run his #42 Plymouth. Maurice did a fine job, finishing just one position behind the new 1960 champion, Rex White. Buddy Baker crashed on the first lap and the second Wood Brothers car, with Joe Weatherly at the controls, experienced engine failure on lap 76 for a 16th-place finish. Thompson brought home $900 for his win and Rex brought back $150 for his eighth-place finish.

    Race #44 for the season carried us back down the road to "Hotlanta." That's what the racers called Atlanta. It wasn't too hot this day, though. This was October 30, 1960. The Atlanta 500 was a 500-mile race on a 1.5-mile asphalt super speedway. The run of

Louie Clements in the garage area working on the 1960 Piedmont Friendly Chevy.

Fred Lorenzen in the #28 car, with Rex White in the foreground during practice for the first Atlanta 500.

500 miles required the cars to make 334 circuits of that big asphalt ribbon. Again, it was no surprise that the black-and-gold #22 driven by NASCAR's first superstar, Fireball Roberts, qualified fast enough for the pole position. His average one-lap speed was just a tick under 135 mph. Second fastest time was turned in by Jack Smith in the red #47 Pontiac. Third on the grid went to another Pontiac, this time Junior Johnson, who had just purchased a race-ready '60 Pontiac from Cotton Owens. Fred Lorenzen broke the Pontiac spell by setting his 1960 Ford #28 in the fourth spot. Forty-five race cars started this 500-mile race and the top 10 ran very close together for most of the day. Roberts, Jack Smith, Joe Weatherly, and the #5 Pontiac driven by Bobby Johns all traded the lead back and forth most of the day. Of the 45 starting cars, only 21 were still running at the end. Pole sitter Fireball Roberts had some of his usual luck. His car broke an axle on the

58th lap. The third-place starter, another of those hot rod Ponchos, broke an axle and left Junior Johnson with a 24th-place finish. As the race began to wind down it became evident that if nothing went wrong, Bobby Johns in the #5 Cotton Owens Pontiac had this one in the bag. And he brought it all the way home that way, too. That win paid him $15,975. Second- and third-place finishers were each one lap down to the winner. Second went to Johnny Allen for one of his better finishes of the year. Third went to Jim Paschal driving the #44 Petty Plymouth. Fourth went to Thompson in a Ford, and our "meal ticket," Rex White, drove that '60 Chevy to a very respectable fifth-place finish which paid him $1,850. Already the champion and still making money. That worked for us.

Lee and Richard Petty finished sixth and seventh with Joe Weatherly, Bob Welborn and Fred Lorenzen completing the top 10. Other notables this day were Hank and Herbie Tillman's #39 Chevy coming home in the 11th spot. Very good for them, too. I remember them as being really big and strong. They looked like they could do well on the pro wrestling circuit. L.D. Austin was 13th and Larry Frank was 15th. Buck Baker's '60 Chevy #87, still being maintained by Crawford Clements and Jess Rhodes, was still running at the end and finished in the 20th position. Of the cars that didn't finish this race, mostly blown engines were the causes. Some broke suspension components and some lost brakes and were involved in accidents. An estimated crowd of 30,000 watched the four-and-a-half-hour contest. In my family, we were happy with our Chevy finishing in the fifth position. But I think we were all happier for Bobby Johns to have won the race. After what he had gone through at Darlington, this was a good healing agent for him and his dad. Bobby was just 27 years old at this time.

The 1960 season was officially completed and Rex and Louie had won their first NASCAR Grand National Championship by almost 4,000 points over second-place Richard Petty. Rex started 40 of the 44 races and won six times. That was the most wins by any driver for this season. He finished in the top five a total of 25 times and had an astounding 35 top-10 finishes. The team's winnings were a NASCAR record at the time of $57,524.85. Yep, we Clements kids enjoyed a really good Christmas that year.

By contrast to Rex's season, Richard Petty also started 40 races and won three of them. He earned 16 top fives and 30 top tens. Not a bad season at all. Just not as good as Rex and Louie had. Bobby Johns was third in the points standings with Buck Baker fourth and Ned Jarrett fifth. Old pro Lee Petty ended up sixth in the points chase. For all of his speed during the season, Fireball Roberts only finished 29th in the points. He had two wins and three top tens. The second '60 Chevy race car built at my dad's shop for this season finished a very fine eighth place in the points standings with Emanuel Zervakis doing the driving.

Some of my memories of the '60 season are very clear visions of particular events. But sometimes, the exact time or place might escape me. If you remember what the grille looked like on the '58 Fords, you will remember that little chrome emblem right in the dead center of it. Coming off the fourth corner at Asheville-Weaverville, I can still see Joe Weatherly driving up under Rex when Rex was in the '60 Chevy. From up on top of the truck, it looked to this kid like Joe was fixing to puncture his radiator with the left rear tip of that '60 Chevy tail fin on each lap. Louie had the Chevy really low on the left rear corner, *really low!* The right front was the highest point on the car. Rex would pull him down the chutes and then Joe would try to drive under him coming off the corner with

Fred Lorenzen (#28) followed by Rex White during Atlanta practice.

Rex and Louie pose for a publicity photograph at the Championship Awards Banquet, 1960.

no success. That must have gone on all day. I believe Joe was driving one of the Wood Brothers' Fords that day.

They also took the '60 Chevy out to the Mesa, Arizona, GM Desert Proving Grounds for testing at least once that year that I remember. Rex, Louie, and James Hylton went together. Chevrolet division also invited Junior Johnson to bring his Chevy out to test. Crawford was with him for this test. Zora Duntov was the man in charge of the Chevrolet Marine division, which was actually a guise for building performance parts for racing. So Mr. Duntov was also there.

Rex receives 1960 championship trophy from NASCAR official Pat Purcell.

When Junior first got a look at the 5-mile test track, he didn't like it and considered not testing. The track was high-banked, paved smoothly, and a perfect 5-mile circle. The cars were much quicker here than at Daytona. What Junior didn't like was the fact that there was no guardrail around it. If a driver were to run off the track, he would either hit the moon or land somewhere a few hundred yards out in the desert, which was known to have a few wild critters running around in it. Still, on with the test. At full throttle they were running better than 155 mph. That was four mph faster than Fireball qualified for the pole at Daytona in his Pontiac. But, as they ran wide open, those 348s

Louie receives NASCAR's Car Owner award and Mechanic of the Year award from Pat Purcell.

would occasionally make a "bloop-bloop" sound which wasn't right. Duntov heard it and shook his head and didn't like it. Louie said, "I can fix it." Zora told him, "If you can fix it, do it." All Louie did was add a second ballast resistor inline with the one that was already there. These were still point-style ignitions and Mr. Duntov had some newfangled points that were supposed to stop that problem. The new points did not cure the problem at all. So Zora saw what Louie had done and said, "Oh, snake medicine." True, it wasn't fixing the cause, but it did mask the effect of the problem. They went back on the track and the bloop noise went away and the car picked up another two miles per

DRIVER OF THE YEAR

Anthony Joseph Foyt, by winning four championship events and racking up 1680 points during the 1960 season, became the youngest driver in history to win the coveted national driving title. At 25, he is only on the threshold of a sparkling career that might well equal or better some of auto racing's all-time great drivers. His rise to the top has been fantastic. He began his career in his native state of Texas in 1953, and reached the big time — Indianapolis — in 1958. He won the 1960 USAC title the hard way, coming from an almost hopeless position in point standings at mid-season to capture four wins, two of them in the closing races of the season. A resident of Houston, A. J. is married and has two lovely children.

MECHANIC OF THE YEAR

Louis L. Clements is a 36-year-old resident of Spartanburg, S. C., and is considered one of the top mechanics in stock car racing today. His rise to the top was very rapid. Until 1957, he was a body mechanic in Kentucky, dabbling in modified racing as a hobby. Showing great potential, he was hired by the Chevrolet factory team in '57 and, when the factories retired from racing soon afterward, he teamed with three other veteran wrench twisters. Lou's biggest year was 1960, when he groomed the '60 Chevrolet which Rex White drove to the NASCAR Championship. This car was the season's biggest money winner and the most consistent finisher. Seldom was it forced out because of mechanical ills. An extremely hard worker who enjoys a reputation for his friendliness. Lou puts together virtually indestructible race machines.

CAR OWNERS OF THE YEAR

Bob Bowes and George Bignotti are a unique car-owning combination, not only because they are 50-50 partners, but because Bignotti serves also as chief mechanic. Between them, and with their outstanding young driver, A. J. Foyt, they followed a successful path during the 1960 campaign to racing's highest honor — the National Championship. In 1961, their Bowes Seal Fast Special will be carrying the numeral "1," signifying the honor bestowed upon its driver and the two men behind him. These men are no newcomers to racing. Bowes follows in the footsteps of his dad, who put the Bowes colors into racing back in 1931, and like his father, Bob is enthusiastic, hard working and sincere. Bignotti has been active in the sport since the end of World War II and has established himself as one of the leading mechanics in championship racing today. Both are married and have families. Bowes lives in Indianapolis, while Bignotti makes his home in Burlingame, Calif.

continued

Center of page quip reporting Louie Clements as Racing's Mechanic of the Year.

Bottom row, left to right: Rex White, Louie Clements, Jack Chrisman, Bob Colvin, Carroll Shelby. Top row, left to right: Max Muhleman, unknown, A.J. Foyt, unknown, car owner George Bignotti, and Bob Bowes.

hour. Not bad for "snake medicine"! Soon it was Junior's turn to make some laps in his car and Duntov had set him up a carburetor that was a "Marine Improvement" to the carbs they had been running in NASCAR. Junior made almost a full lap and it burned a piston and blew the engine. Now this is where it gets good. After Crawford and Louie pulled the heads off and looked at the burned pistons and head gaskets, Louie asked, "Junior, couldn't you feel that happening?" Junior said in his typical fashion, "Yeah, but if I'd told them they wouldn't have believed me"! And he was right. Had it been practice for a race, Junior would have backed off, brought the car in and made repairs. But with the GM engineers, if you're not a fellow engineer, they won't listen to you. They want to see proof. Junior gave them what they needed. I still get a chuckle every time I think of that. Having worked for GM Engineering staff for over 12 years, I know exactly how Junior felt.

Rex and Louie were both informed in plenty of time that the new 1961 Chevys were going to be receiving a newer and larger version of the "W" engine. This would be the infamous 409 that the Beach Boys sang about. The '61 body would be a complete restyle too. So they decided to sell off the '59 and '60 Chevys because they would have had to run the 320-hp 348 engines and this new car coming would be factory rated at 360 hp. The body was much slicker, too.

The 1959 Chevy that Rex raced for two years was sold to a man from South America. It was his intention to race it in Peru and other tracks down his way. We were to be paid for the car when we delivered it to the loading dock in Louisiana to be placed on a cargo ship and taken to South America. The man buying the car was going to meet Rex in Louisiana to inspect the car before loading it. Rex enlisted the help of another NASCAR mechanic, Mario Rossi, to go with him on this trip and help drive the truck down there to deliver the race car. Mario, his wife Janie and their two kids lived across the street from us. At some point as they drove through the night, Rex was riding shotgun and sleeping. Mario was driving and he dozed off too. Well, the stuff hit the fan then. They ran off the side of the road and down the side of a mountain. The race car rolled several times, making a mess of it.

The next morning I was at the shop in Spartanburg with my dad. We were the only two there that morning. He was putting together a fresh engine and showing me each step of the way. I even remember that on this morning he asked me to take that broom over there and use a hacksaw and cut him about two inches off the end of the handle. No problem. Hacksaws and hammers were my specialty. He then took the little round piece of wood I got for him, put it into the lathe and trimmed one end of it to fit inside an old valve spring. Then when he bolted on the timing cover, he put that wooden knob and valve spring in there to take the end play out of the camshaft. He explained to me how the camshaft endplay had caused them to break a timing chain and fall out of one race and that it also didn't help the distributor and ignition timing any to have the cam moving back and forth in the block.

So, what does this have to do with the race car going over the mountain? Right as we finished bolting on that timing cover, the phone rang. It was Rex and he was telling Louie all about the accident. My dad asked, "Are you sure you're OK?" And Mario too?" Then some small talk and he said, "I'll see you in a couple of days." My dad was real quiet when he got off the phone. He looked almost lost for a few minutes. Then he said, "Come with me and bring a couple of rags." We walked around behind the shop and started picking out the best of the scrap fenders, door skins, hood, bumpers, etc., and dragged them back into the fabrication side of the shop. He told me about the accident and said, "I've got to get some new sheet metal fixed up to put on that crashed car before Rex gets back here so we can still meet the deadline for delivery." Then after about 15 minutes of hammering and working on a hood, he said, "I've got another idea." He then got on the phone and called up our friend G.C. Spencer and asked, "What shape is your race car in?" G.C. had a '59 Chevy that was a pretty good car. So, White and Clements picked up G.C.'s car, repainted it and towed it back down to Louisiana for the new owner. Could this story get any worse? Well, yes, it could. The man flying up from Peru in his private plane just happened to run out of luck and crashed his plane right into Lake Pontchartrain. He was killed instantly. No sale on the '59 Chevy. Not this day, anyway.

A man by the name of Harry Leake from Winston-Salem, North Carolina, bought the '59 Chevy from Dad and Rex after they put the new sheet metal back on it. G.C. got his car back and raced it the next season. Harry cut off that '59 body and put a '60 Chevy body on it and ran a few Grand National races the next season. After that, he ran quite

Front row for 1960 Indy 500. On the pole is #6 Eddie Sachs, 2nd is #4 Jim Rathmann, and 3rd is #1 Roger Ward. In the foreground is the Rathmann Xterminator racing kart that my dad got for me from Jim Rathmann.

a bit at Bowman Gray Stadium in the sportsman class while he still owned it. Rex and I both have tried to remember who bought the '60 Chevy and neither of us remember. Rex did tell me that they kept the '60 Chevy to use as a backup car for the '61 season. They worked all season on another '61 Chevy so they would have two of them for the season. But Rex tells me the newer '61 was never completed in time to race it. So it received new '62 sheet metal and ran the '62 season as well as a new '62 they also built.

Another thing we spoke about was the NASCAR Points Banquet that year. Each member of the crew was taken to downtown Charlotte to the finest men's store in town and bought a new tux. Rex, Louie, James, Wes, Ken, and Slick all went to that banquet in style. It was their night to shine. Not only did Rex win the points championship that year, but Louie won mechanic of the year and car owner of the year. Rex was also voted NASCAR's most popular driver of the year. They brought home several huge gold trophies from their night on the town. But there was still more to come.

Motor Life Magazine was a popular motor sports magazine of that era. The magazine voted Rex the "Stock Car Driver of the Year." A.J. Foyt was voted the Indy Car driver of the year. But Louie got what was to me the best of the best award. He was voted "Racing's

Championship team photograph. Left to right: James Hylton, Slick Owens, Wes Roarke, Rex White, Louie Clements and Ken Miller.

Mechanic of the Year." This award was given to the mechanic who was voted by the motor sports fraternity as the number one mechanic in all of motor sports. Louie was voted and given this award ahead of peers such as Carroll Shelby, George Bignoti, Jack Chrisman, Smokey Yunick, A.J. Watson, Ray Nichels, Ralph Moody, Paul McDuffie, and anyone else in the running. After receiving this award, Louie was asked to speak a few words. And a few words was right. He was never one to seek out the spotlight or fame. He got up to the podium and stated that it really was enough for him just to be there among everyone that he considered to be the best. But to receive this award was beyond anything he had ever dreamed of. On his way up to the stage and podium Louie heard A.J. Foyt say to George Bignoti, "You let a damned old hayseed beat you out." That just made him smile. And little did Foyt know at the time that Louie would play a very pivotal role in one of Foyt's biggest NASCAR wins in the next few years. Buck Baker was the first to shake Louie's hand and my dad said something to the effect of, "Aw, it's nice. But it's time to get back to work now." And right then Baker told him, "Don't kid yourself. You will reap the rewards from this for the rest of your life." And he did. This ceremony was held at the Glen-Aire Country Club located in Sherman Oaks, California, on the evening of March 7, 1961. Racing notables from all phases of the sport as well as enthusiastic racing fans from around the country were on hand for this event. I can still remember my dad coming home from that deal with the beautiful wall plaque he received. But the only thing he really said was, "Can you believe I paid $200 for a pair of shoes?" Two hundred dollars was a lot more than they earned in some of the races they competed in. We kids were wearing $5.00 Thom McAn shoes.

One more neat memory about the 1960 season was that Rex drove down to Melbourne, Florida, to Jim Rathmann's Chevrolet dealership to pick up the new '60 Chevy that Chevrolet division of GM had given them to build into a race car for the '60 season. Chevy was still in racing but had to play undercover games to keep the AAA off their backs. Rex picked up a spare 348 engine while he was there. Jim Rathmann and my dad and Rex all became pretty good friends and when Rex and Louie went testing they always invited Rathmann to go with them. So, when preparation time for the 1960 Indy 500 rolled around, it was only natural that Rathmann called them to request help with his car at Indy during the month of May. Both of them really wanted to go and be a part of Rathmann's Indy race, but they were involved by this time in their own battle for the NASCAR points championship. So they couldn't be of much help. The track at Charlotte was not ready in time for the Memorial Day race, so we stayed home and listened to the Indy 500 on the radio. What a treat it was to sit there and hear the announcer say, "And here comes #4, Jim Rathmann, to win his first Indianapolis 500." That #4 "Ken Paul Special" roadster is still my all-time favorite Indy race car. I have since been to the museum at Indy several times and I never tire of just looking at that race car. There must be some magic in that #4!

Another noteworthy race of the 1960 season, according to my memory anyway, was the North Carolina 500 held at Asheville-Weaverville Speedway. That was a half-mile, high-banked asphalt oval. As I remember, Rex and Jack Smith had the front row. Rex won the race going away and was by far the fastest car there. Funny thing is, the whole story didn't come out about it until 1971 when Junior Johnson had built that white Chevy Monte Carlo for the Charlotte World 600. Chargin' Charlie Glotzbach drove the car and put it on the pole. He led about half of the race before blowing a tire and crashing the car too bad to be repaired.

My dad was so excited to hear that Chevy was back into the game that he took some vacation days from his job at the General Motors Proving Grounds in Mesa, Arizona, and drove my younger brother and my mom back to Charlotte for the race. He was on pit road during practice for the race and struck up a chat with his old pal Buck Baker. They got to talking about old times and sure enough, if racers talk long enough, the truth will finally come out. Buck mentioned, "What did you have in the Chevy that day in Asheville?" Louie laughed and told Buck that he had used a set of Jahns high-compression pistons, which gave the engine substantially more horsepower. Baker said, "I knew you were up to something, but I wasn't going to say anything about it because Crawford and I had swollen up our fuel tank to hold almost four gallons more fuel. I made one less stop than Rex and you guys still beat me. Nope, what was I gonna do? Cry foul and then they would check me?"

They both enjoyed a good laugh and life went on.

CHAPTER 6

1961: Trying to Defend Our Championship

After sorting through the fiasco of selling the '59 Chevy to the man from Lima, Peru, crashing that car over a mountainside, getting another car down there for him, only for him to crash his plane and be killed, well, it was time to sit down and re-evaluate things for a bit. The '59 Chevy was sold and they kept the '60 Chevy for the '61 season to serve as a backup car. Chevrolet shipped a new '61 Bel Air Bubble Top car down to White and

Victory lane at Asheville. Rex and Louie after 500 grueling laps.

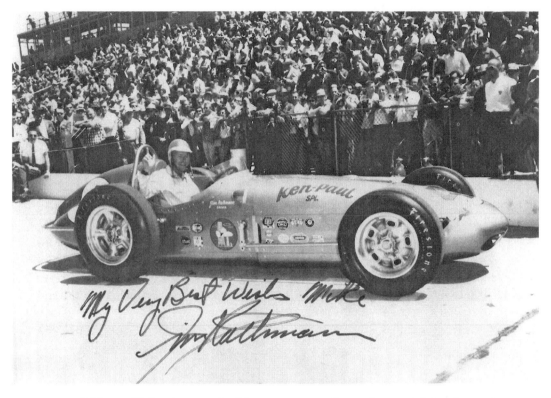

Post-qualifying publicity photograph of front-row starter Jim Rathmann driving the #4 Watson roadster.

Clements to be built into the new car for the '61 season. They also received an extra spare engine. This was a 409 engine with a 4-speed transmission. The car had bucket seats and floor-mounted shifter, a white exterior and a red interior. Once again, it was stripped down of every nut and bolt. We boys used the gas rags and washed all that yucky black tar stuff from the bare frame rails so Rex could weld up every seam in the frame as well as install the weight jacks, shock mounts, etc. All of the Chevys of this period raced with the 6-lug, half-ton pickup suspension, brakes, hubs, etc. Even the rear end housing and gear selections were those available for the half-ton trucks. Available gear selections for each particular make and model of car made a huge difference in which cars were fastest at which tracks during this time. The Pontiacs had the big horsepower advantage. The Chevys and Fords had some good torque. And the Plymouths were in the hands of the Pettys, who could have won racing soap-box cars!

Two of the '61 Chevys were eventually built for the '61 season. The first car that ran the Daytona 500 had to serve double duty and run many smaller races too. It got beat and banged up pretty good. They built another brand-new '61 which was given to them later in the season to have a new car for Darlington and to help wrap up another points championship. Problem was, this new '61 Chevy got very close to being completed but never made it to the track. I do have a perfect memory of its being painted gold and white and sitting over in the engine side of the shop. Just never quite got it completed. I also remember thinking what a shame it was to cut off that brand-new body when they con-

A friend of mine painted this portrait for me depicting my dad with his 1960 championship race car.

verted it to a '62 Bel Air. But those '62 Chevy Bel Air bubble tops are still some of the most sought-after cars for restoration and street rodders today. Beautiful cars!

One good note here is to understand that Chevrolet personnel came to Rex and Louie and said that they wanted to help sponsor another team for the '61 season. They requested that Rex and Louie give them an idea of who they thought would be the best choice for this new team. Both Rex and Louie recommended Ned Jarrett for the job. So Chevrolet contacted Ned and his crew chief, Bud Allman, and set them up as Chevy racers. Ned and Bud both came over to my dad's shop one day that I was there. They spent the entire day there with note pads and a camera, and talking with Rex and Louie about what it takes to make the Chevy into a race car. Nothing was held back. This was all done above board and in the best interest of Chevrolet, who wanted another championship. I would have to say that Ned and Bud were very quick studies, because any NASCAR history fan knows that Ned did indeed win the 1961 championship. It was by a very slim margin, but a win nonetheless.

Ned Jarrett was not just a good race car driver. He was a thinking man's driver and a very fine mechanic in his own right. Bud Allman was also a very formidable opponent too. Together they made for just the right combination of skill, strategy, and a little bit of that good luck for good measure.

The big news for the 1961 NASCAR season was the battle between Curtis Turner and the Teamsters Union vs. Big Bill France and "his" NASCAR. As I remember hearing the situation explained to me, Curtis Turner was in desperate need of a great deal of money to bail the Charlotte Motor Speedway out of a pending bankruptcy. The Teamsters were willing to give him the $800,000 he needed provided he organized the drivers into the union. Needless to say, this would happen over Bill France's dead body. And he was dead serious, too. So Turner made promises to the drivers that they would receive pensions, better race purses, more adequate insurance coverage, a scholarship fund for the children of deceased drivers or mechanic members of the new union. And they would also receive much-needed improvements in the restrooms, showers, and lounge facilities at the larger super speedways. Of course, Big Bill France released his own statement that read: "No known member of this union can compete in a NASCAR race, and I'll use a pistol to enforce it." Curtis Turner and Tim Flock were banned from NASCAR for life for their part in the union plan. The story could go on for quite a while, but I am really here to tell about racing. So, let's go racing 1961 style.

Back during this period of NASCAR, the new season was usually kicked off with a few small dirt track races at the end of the previous year. So race #1 for the '61 season was held on the half-mile dirt track in Charlotte, North Carolina. This would be a 200-lap race at the old Charlotte Fairgrounds track. Twenty cars entered the race and Lee Petty took the pole. Rex White, driving the '59 Chevy with the new body on it, qualified second. Once the green flag waved, Lee Petty led the race for the first 17 circuits. Then Rex took over the lead from lap 18 through 49. Lee got the lead back on lap 50 and held onto it until lap 140, when Rex took it back for another 20 laps. Then, on lap 161, Joe Weatherly took over the lead driving the Wood Brothers '58 Ford and held on to win the race. Weatherly and White were the only cars on the lead lap at the end. Lee Petty, Buck Baker, and David Pearson rounded out the top five positions. Richard Petty finished 11th, Ned Jarrett was 16th and Junior Johnson finished 18th with a broken axle in his 1960 Pontiac. This is just one of those races that I can still remember like it was yesterday. My cousin Gary Clements and I sat beside each other in the front stretch grandstands. We had been told beforehand that this was going to be the final race at this track and the track would be demolished after the race. Well, we were boys and we figured *right* after the race they would mow down the track. We stayed in the stands for a while after the race to watch the graders and bulldozers plow up the track. We didn't realize these things took time.

Anyway, with my dad crew chief for Rex and Gary's dad crew chief for Junior, it was fun for us two sitting in the stands and watching practice with our stopwatches and seeing which one was going to be the fastest. Rex, Joe Weatherly, Lee Petty, Buck Baker, all of them were running pretty well in practice. But Junior Johnson was a rocket! He broke an axle during practice and we could see from our seats that he drove the car into the pits, and Crawford jacked it up and began to swap out that broken axle. They had a spare and Crawford installed it, and Junior went back for just a very few more laps of practice. When qualifying came around, of course, Lee got the pole and Rex was fast enough for second on the grid. But Junior went out and was flying low. He would have surely taken the pole if it were not for breaking another axle. Since we didn't have another spare one, a fan from the infield with a new Pontiac offered to loan his to the cause. Crawford installed it and Junior started shotgun on the field. When the green flag dropped the hammer on this race, the action up front was Lee Petty in the lead with Rex right on him. The two had a great battle going on. But the real excitement for us watching from the stands was seeing Junior come from the tail end of the field to the front in short order. Rex was leading the race at this point when Junior caught him. Just as Junior started around the outside of Rex, that borrowed axle broke too. That took Junior out of the race on lap 35. Both Gary and I said, "Oh man." We couldn't believe it. Gary said, "Man, he sure was fast." And I said, "Yeah, too fast." For him to drive through that field of fine NASCAR racers just like Sherman went through Atlanta, something was amiss. Sure enough, once we all piled into the new 1961 Chevy Parkwood that my dad had bought my mom, my dad told us what had happened. It seems that Rex's car was right behind Junior's car as the two were pushed through pre-race inspection. One of the checks was to jack up the left rear of the car and spin the left rear tire to prove that the car did not have a locked rear end gear. Well, my Uncle Crawford was as cool as a cucumber when it came to stuff like this. As soon as he started jacking up on the left rear of the car he also began to tell the NASCAR official a joke he had heard. While telling the joke to the official, he just continued jacking up the Pontiac's left rear wheel until the right wheel also came off the ground. He then spun the left rear wheel and continued the joke until the car was back on the ground and then finished the joke. The official laughed and said "OK" and let him push the car away. Now Louie, Crawford's brother, was standing right behind this exchange and watched it all unfold. He just smiled and shook his head. What's he going to do? Rat on his brother? Nope. I think he was rather proud of him for the way he handled the ordeal. Crawford had so much charisma that he could tell the Pope a dirty joke and make him laugh. What a day!

So race #2 was conducted at Jacksonville, Florida, this year. This was November 20, 1960. They raced late into the year back then. The big deal about this race is that Lee Petty won it for his 54th and final Grand National victory. An estimated crowd of 5,000 people were on hand to see this milestone. Of course, at the time no one knew it would be Mr. Petty's last victory. Junior Johnson used that potent Poncho again to grab the pole and Buck Baker started outside pole. Baker, Bob Welborn, Tommy Irwin, and Lee Petty were the hard chargers this day and kept their cars up front. Petty won and Tommy Irwin was second, one lap down to Petty's 200 laps. Rex White, still running the '59 Chevy finished third with Richard Petty fourth and Doug Yates fifth in his #23 Plymouth. Ned Jarrett finished 19th with a blown head gasket on the 67th lap. Junior Johnson, still running the Crawford Clements–prepared Pontiac broke a distributor on the fourth lap and ended up with a 22nd-place finish on the day.

Now, if there was an "off season" this would be it. From November 20, 1960, to February 24, 1961, there were no races. Plenty new '61 model race cars were built by many shops and all of them still had to get to Daytona for a test if they could find the time.

What else was going on in 1961? Well Roger Marris hit 61 home runs, Dion had the #1 song, "The Wanderer." "Blue Moon" by the Marcels and "The Lion Sleeps Tonight" by the Tokens were also up on the charts. But my dad's favorite was Jim Reeves singing "Hello Walls." Man, he had a deep smooth voice.

The Daytona 500 for 1961 was advertised to be a real thriller. Much excitement permeated the air around this race. This was now the big one, where everyone got to see the new Detroit iron in racing trim for the first time. I sure miss that aspect of the good old

The 1961 team prior to the Daytona 500: Wes, Rex, Louie and James.

days. Nowadays all we can look forward to is different paint schemes and which 18 year old is cuter than the next. Anyway, once at the track, all cars through inspection and practice, it was time for qualifying and then the two 100-mile races, which were points races at this time.

The first 100-mile qualifier race was started by 34 cars. Fireball got the pole with a speed of 159.709 mph. That was getting the job done in 1961. That familiar black-and-gold #22 Pontiac was a Thoroughbred race horse for sure. On the white-flag lap Fireball was being challenged by Junior Johnson in his new 1961 Holly Farms Pontiac. Crawford Clements was still the crew chief for Junior at this time. Junior was right beside Roberts when the #27 Holly Farms car hit a piece of debris and cut down a tire. Junior's car bumped the new '61 Plymouth of Richard Petty and sent Richard's car into and over the wall, out of the track and almost into the parking lot. Junior's car turned directly head-on into the wall and was virtually destroyed. The engine was shoved up into the passenger compartment, right through the firewall. Junior suffered some cuts and bruises and a cut-up chin. Richard received cuts over both eyes and a cut hand. Jim Paschal finished second driving the #3 '61 Pontiac for Ray Fox. Third place went to Jack Smith, and Buck Baker and Ned Jarrett finished out the top five. Rex finished a very disappointing 21st position, three laps down to the leaders.

The 1960 Pontiac #27 driven by Junior Johnson and maintained by Crawford Clements.

1/24th scale replica of the White and Clements 1961 Chevy Grand National car.

The second 100-mile qualifier was on tap next. This time, Little Joe Weatherly started from the pole in his #8 Pontiac. Starting second was Curtis Turner in his new 1961 Courtesy Ford built by Holman-Moody from Charlotte. I believe the Pontiacs were labeled with a factory rating of 368 hp and the Fords were rated at 375 hp. The '61 Chevys were now enlarged up to 409 cubic inches and rated as having 360 hp. I believe that was a stretch by some marketing manager's pencil, myself. I think the '61 Petty Plymouths were still rated at 325 hp.

Pristine 1961 Chevy arrives for the 1961 Daytona 500.

There were 33 starters in this second of the two qualifying heats. At the end of the prescribed 40 laps, Joe Weatherly brought home the money and Marvin Panch was second in a year-old Smokey Yunick '60 Pontiac #20. Cotton Owens finished third, Banjo Matthews fourth, and Darel Deringer was fifth driving the #32 Ray Nichels '61 Pontiac. There was a very serious accident in this race too. On their 37th lap, Lee Petty and Johnny Beauchamp tangled coming off the fourth corner. The two cars followed each other right up and over the guardrail and out of the track. The cars were total writeoffs, destroyed, and the drivers came very close to the same fate. Lee Petty was gravely injured in the accident, virtually ending his career. He received multiple fractures and many internal injuries. Beauchamp received head injuries and a spectator was severely injured while trying to administer aid to Petty moments after the accident.

One good spotlight on this event was that Mr. Bobby Allison made his first Grand National start in this race driving a white 1960 Chevy #40, and brought home a 20th-place finish, three laps down to the winner.

Two days later, on February 26, 1961, it was race day for the third running of the Daytona 500. Fireball Roberts started from the pole with Joe Weatherly starting outside pole. In third starting position was Jim Paschal in the '61 Pontiac and fourth starter was

Ready to hit the track for practice for the 1961 Daytona 500.

#20, Marvin Panch in Smokey's backup car. The Daytona 500 is a 200-lap race on a 2.5-mile tri-oval super speedway. For the most part, it was the Fireball Roberts Show. He led for 187 laps of the caution-free event. For the third year in a row, Fireball was leading when his Smokey Yunick Pontiac blew an engine in the late stages of the race. Fireball's teammate in this race was the #20 1960 Pontiac driven by Marvin Panch. Marvin took the lead with 13 laps to go and held off a challenge from Joe Weatherly, who finished second. Paul Goldsmith was third, Fred Lorenzen fourth, and #6 Cotton Owens was fifth. Jack Smith, Ned Jarrett, Johnny Allen, Buck Baker and Tom Pistone completed the top 10. At 44 laps into the race, Junior Johnson, driving his 1960 Pontiac backup car, was very fast and in position to challenge Roberts for the lead. In fact, he did lead twice for three laps each. But the tired old backup motor gave up the ghost on lap 44, leaving Junior with a 47th-place finish. Remember, Junior's primary car, a new '61 Pontiac, was destroyed in the first qualifying race. My dad's car with Rex White driving it had a terrible qualifying run and thus started the 500 in the 41st starting position. So when Rex was able to bring the car home 12th, we thought that was a pretty good day. The 12th-place finish paid $500. Marvin's win paid $21,050. Fireball racked up a good bit of lap money while leading the race. His final finish was 20th and that paid him some $4,750. That gave Smokey a total of $25,800 to split up with his drivers and crew. I think Smokey once said that his deal with Panch was for 40 percent of the car's winnings. After the race, Smokey told Marvin that any driver good enough to bring that car home first deserves at least 50

Right-side view of the 1961 Chevy Grand National car.

percent and then paid him that amount, which would have been $10,525. That was more money than most men made in a year at that time. A while after the race was over, my dad was walking through the garage area and saw Smokey about 20 feet from the '61 Pontiac #22 and just lighting his pipe. Louie asked Smokey, "What happened?" Smokey answered with, "The fuel pump fell off." Louie looked under the hood of the Pontiac and said, "I guess it did. That whole corner of the block is gone." Smokey had a pretty good sense of humor too. Buddy Baker ran the entire day and completed 145 laps in the Baker '61 Chrysler #86. That paid him $200.

We loaded up the wagon and headed back home for Spartanburg. If my dad drove all night, we kids could still go to school the next morning. No whining, either! If we hadn't done our homework yet, we'd best get it done on the ride back home. Because, well… the next race was right home in Spartanburg the very next weekend. Ned Jarrett grabbed the pole on the half-mile dirt track but oil pressure problems knocked him out of the race on lap 54 of the scheduled 200. Junior Johnson started second in the Holly Farms '60 Pontiac but a fuel line failure dropped him from the field on the 182nd lap, just 12 laps from the end. Hometown hero Cotton Owens drove the wheels off his '60 Pontiac for the win and was the only car on the lead lap at the end of the race. Richard Petty drove the #43 Plymouth home for the second spot, and another hometown boy, David Pearson, finished third in his Chevrolet. Fourth went to Jimmy Pardue and fifth went to #23, Doug Yates. Rex had qualified fifth but finished seventh, still running at the

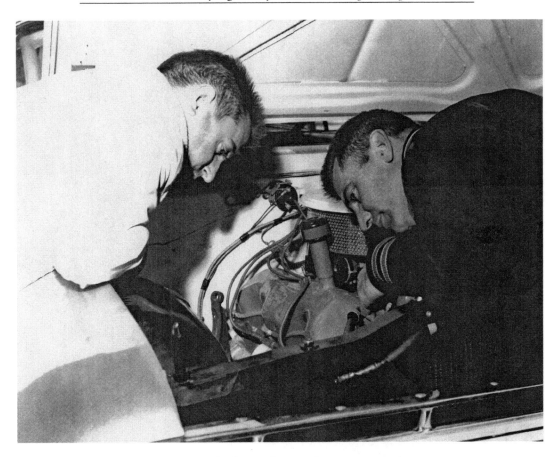

Rex and Louie look over the new-for-1961 409 engine.

end. The #97 of Harry Leake finished ninth, that was the old '59 White and Clements Chevy that had rolled down the mountainside near New Orleans. Wendell Scott had bought the #87 1960 Chevy from Buck Baker and drove it to a 17th-place finish. This was the first time I had seen him race. He may have started some other Grand National races before this one. But this was certainly the first time I had seen him there.

The very next day, Sunday, March 5, 1961, took us all back up the hill to the Asheville-Weaverville Speedway. This was one of those memorable days for our family. Rex qualified fast enough to take the pole at 79.295 mph average speed. Starting second was the #27 Holly Farms Pontiac driven by Junior Johnson. Having my dad as the crew chief on Rex's car and my uncle being crew chief for Junior, it was an all–Clements front row for us. One of my dad's younger sisters was there, and after qualifying was over she said, "Daddy didn't raise no fools." I still laugh when I picture her saying that.

Rex led every lap of the race for a well-deserved win. He was challenged very hard by Junior Johnson until about halfway through the show. That was when the rear end gear gave up on Junior's Pontiac, removing him from the contest. Three cars finished on the lead lap. They were Rex, Cotton and Ned. Richard Petty was fourth, four laps down, and #85, Emanuel Zervakis was fifth. Junior ended up credited with 11th place. The crowd was estimated to be about 8500 spectators.

Rex and Louie pose proudly with their new 1961 Chevy, ready to defend their national championship.

Way out west in California was the site for race #8 on the '61 season. Fireball Roberts flew out to drive the J.D. Braswell 1961 Pontiac. J.D.'s son, Dave Braswell, is about the most popular carburetor builder in NASCAR today. He built one for me a couple of years ago for my super late model that I ran out west on asphalt road courses. Just bolted that carb on and knocked off almost three seconds per lap on a mile-and-a-half road course. The Braswells have always, since I've been around anyway, been engine tuning masters. So we know Fireball had plenty of horsepower on tap for this inaugural Marchbanks 250 race in Hanford, California. Bob Ross took the pole with a 1960 Ford. But Fireball was fast enough to qualify outside front row and win the race. The track was a paved 1.4-mile track and the race commenced for 178 laps. Fireball led the entire way. Rex White and Banjo Matthews were the other two east-coast drivers to fly out for this race. Rex borrowed a '60 Chevy, qualified 14th and finished sixth. Banjo borrowed a '61 Ford, qualified 15th, ran out of brakes and finished 28th. Our good friend Marvin Porter drove a 1960 Oldsmobile and finished 25th. Ron Hornaday, Sr., drove a 1960 Ford, blew an engine early on and was credited with a 31st-place finish. Thirty six cars started this race which paid $2,000 to the winner, Roberts.

In the garage area at Daytona, Rex White and Joe Lee Johnson discuss their new 1961 Chevy race cars.

The ninth Grand National race of the season was contested on March 26 back down in Atlanta. This would be the Atlanta 500, which covered 334 laps on the new 1.5-mile super speedway. Forty-six cars started this race and about half of them finished it. Marvin Panch grabbed the pole away from Fireball this time. Marvin was driving the 1961 Pontiac #3 of Ray Fox. Just my opinion, but I feel Ray Fox was at least Smokey's equal in building horsepower. Panch proved it this day. Fireball did qualify second for the outside front-

Prior to the start of the 1961 500. Left to right: Rex White and Louie Clements have been given the Perfect Circle Piston Ring Championship Award trophy by Gene Stonecipher.

row spot. Starting third was Fred Lorenzen driving the new white #28 Holman and Moody '61 Ford. Outside second row started Rex White in the Louie Clements '61 Chevy #4.

Driving the Roy Burdick–owned 1961 Pontiac #53 was 24-year-old Bob Burdick. During the week and throughout practice, Bob was having problems getting the car to turn and stay where he wanted it. Since Rex was getting around pretty well and their workload was much easier than what Burdick faced, Louie and Rex decided to help Bob get his race car to handle properly. Both Rex and Louie had worked a good bit on their

During the 1961 500, Rex White riding in the draft of Pontiac #49 driven by Bob Welborn.

shock package to get the car to run right through a dip in the first turn. You could waste time by driving around it, or you could spend some time figuring out how to tune the chassis to drive right through it. There was a significant difference in lap times, too. So, after helping Burdick with his Pontiac, he qualified seventh, which excited him and his dad a good bit. They were grateful for the help given to them.

Well, wouldn't you just know that the 500-mile race came right down to the wire with a head-to-head battle between Rex and Bob Burdick? Burdick won this one while under a caution flag. Rex, of course, was right on his bumper for the finish for this one. Our family felt very good about a fine second-place finish and my father never regretted helping Bob Burdick one little bit. First place paid $15,775 and second paid $8,850. That extra seven thousand dollars would have been nice, but still, there were no regrets when helping a fellow racer. However, there was a local radio station DJ who stated on air that Louie Clements was crying after helping Burdick outrun Rex. It took my mom about 10 seconds to pick up the phone, call that DJ and start to give him a piece of her mind. When he answered, Mom asked, "Is this John Cashion?" He answered "Yes." Then she said, "Look here, I am the wife of Louis Clements..." and she didn't even get to finish her sentence. He said, "Look, lady, everybody has their problems." Well, that just poured fuel on her fire! She commenced to read this guy the riot act and ripped him to shreds! Funny thing, after that our families became good friends, and radio DJ John Cashion from Spartanburg station WORD would be a regular visitor around the shop. He enjoyed his spirits, too. He and Louie would share a couple of shots of cherry bounce at lunch time. Cherry bounce is just pure white corn liquor with fresh cherries stored in it for about a year. Do *not* eat the cherries! For that matter, if you're a 10-year-old boy, don't even take a taste of this stuff. I haven't been right since I tried it.

Finishing third was the only other car on the lead lap. This was Ralph Earnhardt, driving Cotton Owens's #6 1961 Pontiac. Nelson Stacy and Ned Jarrett rounded out the top five. Pole sitter Panch ended up sixth, Buck Baker was 15th in his new Chrysler, Jack Smith 21st in his new '61 Pontiac and Junior Johnson brought his Holly Farms '61 Pontiac back with a 27th-place finish after an accident on lap 126. Fred Lorenzen finished 33rd after an accident with his Ford on lap 106. He earned $1,320, which included about $1,100 in lap money. Fireball lost another engine on lap 29, which gave him the 42nd-place finish. Paul Lewis's '61 Chevy blew its engine on the first lap, which gave him the final finishing position of 46th place.

April Fool's Day of 1961 took us about 30 miles west of Spartanburg on Interstate 85. This was the location of the Greenville-Pickens Speedway, which was still dirt at this time. Junior and Crawford had the '60 Pontiac really honkin' on this particular evening. Junior took the pole with a fast time that left outside front-row starter Emanuel Zervakis in the dust when the green flag flew. Junior grabbed the lead and held it for the first 69 laps and was then sidelined by a broken fuel pump. Rex took over the lead for the next 105 laps. Rex was leading with David Pearson right on his rear bumper when they bumped each other after driving through a rough spot in the third turn. Both cars spun and Zervakis found a hole and threaded the needle into first place. Emanuel held onto the lead for the next 24 laps for his first win. Richard Petty came home in the second position and Rex made it all the way back up to finish third. G.C. Spencer and Buck Baker rounded out the top five. The race took just under two hours to complete and Zervakis earned $800 for his first win. Rex earned $475 for his third place. Ned Jarrett fell out at the halfway point with overheating problems for a 14th-place finish. Twenty-one cars started this race.

What I can still remember about Greenville when it was dirt is that the track was always too wet when we got there. The outside groove worked in quicker than the inside. If a driver was caught by lapping traffic that held him to the inside on the straightaways, he was toast until he could get back up in the groove where there was a bit of traction. As the race wore on, the track wore in and by about halfway you had room to run side by side.

Orange Speedway in Hillsboro, North Carolina, was the scene of the 11th race of the season, the very next evening from Greenville. This was a .9-mile dirt track, so the race required 110 laps to complete 99 miles. Twenty race cars and approximately 5,000 spectators came in the gate for this one. Number 11 Ned Jarrett grabbed the pole driving his B.G. Holloway '61 Chevy Bel Air. Second on the grid was Junior Johnson, again in the Holly Farms '60 Pontiac. Starting third and fourth were Cotton Owens and Richard Petty. Considering Richard was only 24 years old when he was basically left in charge of Petty Engineering, he was doing a fantastic job of having the cars race-ready and keeping the family business going. A lot rested on the shoulders of this young man.

At the conclusion of the scheduled 110 laps, Cotton Owens had found victory lane with his '60 Pontiac, white with the bright number 6 on the doors. Richard Petty finished second in the #42 Petty Engineering Plymouth. The #43 Petty Plymouth was driven this night by brother Maurice Petty and he finished 15th. Third and fourth went to Buck Baker and Junior Johnson. Rex brought the gold-and-white #4 Chevy home in fifth spot for another $350 payday. Wendell Scott, driving his own #34 Chevy, was still running at the end and finished in the 13th position. G.C. Spencer was ninth with Zervakis coming in 14th.

Would you believe it? April 3 was Easter Monday and we were back up racing at Winston-Salem, North Carolina, on the quarter-mile flat paved oval. Car #21 with Glen Wood driving took the pole spot for the start of the race. Rex qualified the year-old '60 Chevy for the outside pole. Eighteen cars took the green flag and 16 managed to finish the race. At the start, Rex got the jump on Glen and shot out into the lead. He led every lap for a fine victory for the 150-lapper. That win was worth $700 and many of those nice championship points. Glen Wood finished second, still on the lead lap. Richard Petty was third, three laps down. Fred Harb and Ned Jarrett finished out the top five. Junior Johnson was eighth, G.C. Spencer was 10th, Wendell Scott 11th and Maurice Petty, this time driving the #42, held on for a 14th-place finish. Rex left the track that day with a 782-point lead over Ned Jarrett.

The Virginia 500 at Martinsville Speedway promised to be one of the best races of the year. It was one we always looked forward to. Rex ran very well there and the track was *the* most groomed facility on the circuit. This would be race number 13 of the season and 27 cars started the race. Rex White grabbed up that coveted pole position driving the Louis Clements #4 1961 Chevy. Fred Lorenzen qualified for the outside pole, Glen Wood started third and Reds Cagle started his Café Burgundy '61 Ford from the fourth position. Rex shuffled his Chevy into the lead at the start and led the first 118 laps. After the first round of pit stops, Freddy took over the lead with Rex hot on his heels. At lap 149, the skies opened up and a hard and forceful rain put a stop to the race. It was raining hard enough that Bill France, president of NASCAR, knew they would never get it started again. In a most unusual decision for NASCAR, they called it a complete race way before the 250-lap halfway mark came around. Lorenzen earned $1,150 for winning and Rex was paid $1,275 for second. This was the first time in NASCAR history that the runner-up was paid more than the winner. Glen Wood took third, Zervakis took fourth and Ned Jarrett finished fifth. Junior was sixth, Richard was eighth, and in a rare appearance, Tim Flock finished ninth in the Beau Morgan '61 Ford. G.C. was 15th, Herman Beam was 19th, #34 Wendell finished 24th.

There were a few times that I was right there at my dad's shop when Wendell Scott and his traveling buddy Earl Brooks came by. They were on a budget that was tighter than a banjo string. Any leftover parts that seemed used-up to my dad were still parts that Wendell said he could use. Louie took Wendell into his engine room and would give him a set or two of pistons, rings, rods, etc. Valve springs, rocker arms, valves, anything that had just a couple or three races left on it, he would save and give to Wendell. Thinking he had stocked up Wendell pretty well, Louie was about ready to get back to work. But then Wendell said, "Let's go see what's in the scrap around back." My dad told him that the stuff back there in the weather was sure-enough used up. Wendell picked up an old

Convertible race at Martinsville, Virginia. Rex is shaking hands with Bill France, Sr. Background, left to right: James, Louie, Ken and Wes.

348 Chevy block that had a large portion of one side blown out of it. A piston and rod had come apart and completely blew away that portion of the block. Louie said, "Wendell, you don't want that thing. That's junk." Wendell said, "Shoot, man, I can weld this thing up, put a sleeve in it and race it for 500 miles." Wendell and Earl carried about half of that scrap pile off with them. At one point Wendell said, "See that fender and the hood right over there? That's better than what's on my car right now!" I believe he could do more with less than anybody else in the sport. Wendell was a lot better liked and admired than what many writers have stated. I'm sure he had some rough times with the racial attitudes of the day. But around our shop, he was a racer needing some help. As a young boy, it was kind of like meeting a celebrity the first time Wendell came by the shop. I thought to myself, "Wow, Wendell Scott came to my dad's shop. That's pretty cool."

The five-eighths-mile asphalt oval at North Wilkesboro was the playing field for race number 14 for the '61 season. As I'm sure I've already mentioned, we always liked going to North Wilkesboro Speedway. Up in the mountains of North Carolina it was always nice weather and comfortable. The races there were always a showdown between Rex and usually Junior Johnson. Once in a while someone would come along and challenge them, but not too often. On this day, April 16, 1961, Smokey brought the black-and-gold #22

Dirt short-track convertible race. Rex pits to have a burned rear end gear replaced. Louie is sliding under car while Wes is pouring in fuel. Note Rex smoking cigar.

Pontiac up for a rare short-track appearance with Fireball Roberts driving it. Before qualifying, we were concerned that Fireball just might steal all the thunder this day. But that was not to be. Yes, the Pontiac was always fast, but on this day he had to settle for running behind Junior Johnson and Rex White. Once again, Louie and Crawford had their two cars on the front row. Twenty-five cars entered this 400-lap race and when the green flag dropped, Junior Johnson looked like he was on the run from the Revenuers again. He set sail like a jet on a mission. The Holly Farms Pontiac lost its transmission on lap 62 and that dropped Junior from the field. Fred Lorenzen was right there to capitalize on Junior's misfortune. Lorenzen led for about 60 laps before Rex took the lead for 120 laps. Curtis Turner took the lead for about 50 laps before Rex took it back for good this time. Rex led the final 103 laps to finish a full two laps ahead of second-place Tommy Irwin. Richard Petty finished third, four laps down, and Fireball finished fourth, a full 10 laps off the pace. Fifth place went to #69 Johnny Allen in his B.G. Holloway Chevrolet. Buddy Baker finished seventh, which was a good run for him in the '61 Chrysler #87. Wendell ended up 15th, driving his own 1960 Chevrolet. And points contender Ned Jarrett finished 24th after breaking a piston. The crowd was estimated to be 12,500 spectators.

It was somewhere around this time period that Crawford Clements was still working as Junior's crew chief and he was giving Junior the chalkboard sign to pit. He knew the car was on fumes and could not go much farther. I think it was either North Wilkesboro or Martinsville where this happened. But Junior was so wrapped up in the race that he wasn't watching his pit crew for any sort of signals. After several attempts at trying to get Junior's attention, Crawford walked out to the pit wall and threw a hammer square at Junior to get him to look over toward the pits. Junior didn't have much fear behind the wheel of a race car. But Crawford had no fear of anything under any circumstances. I don't know why NASCAR never did anything about it, either. Maybe they didn't see it.

One other time, the steering wheel broke off in Junior's race car and he held onto a small piece of the steering hub to get the car into the pits. He was so mad, and he wanted to finish the race. He yelled at Crawford, "Just give me a pair of vise grips!" Crawford did and Junior took off. This time NASCAR saw it and black-flagged him. Racing was more fun and less business back then. In another race, Junior's throttle linkage broke. When he pitted, Crawford fixed him up a wire to run from the carburetor up through the driver's window. Junior worked the throttle with his left hand and steered with his right hand. Try that nowadays and see what happens!

Race #15 was set back down in Columbia Speedway in South Carolina. This would be a 200-lap race on a half-mile dirt oval. Twenty-two cars entered this race, just four days after the last race. That didn't leave a lot of time to rebuild engines, brakes, transmissions, and rear end gears, and still get the body work looking good on a crashed car. NASCAR had a rule then that if a driver had damage to his race car at a race, he had one race to run like that, but the second race from the original damage, the car had to look new again. Having the cars look new and having the fans in the bleachers relate with each car was a big drawing card for the Grand National circuit.

So here we were in Columbia for another race. Ned Jarrett was really fast in qualifying trim and easily earned the pole for this race. Cotton Owens's Pontiac was next fastest and he started second. Rex qualified ninth in last year's '60 Chevy. At the start of the race, Ned grabbed the lead and never looked back. This was a 200-lap contest and Ned led the first 196 laps. Then, he ran out of fuel. That pretty much gave the win to Cotton Owens as Ned rolled into the pits for a splash of fuel and get back out for a second-place finish, one lap down to Cotton. Third went to Emanuel Zervakis, fourth was an exceptional run for G.C. Spencer in his #48 1960 Chevy. Rex finished fifth and was glad to get it. Owens earned $950 for his win and Rex made $350 for fifth place. Ned closed the points gap between himself and Rex by 48 points. Richard Petty was sixth, Wendell was 11th, David Pearson came home 14th, Buck Baker 16th, and Jack Smith finished 21st. This was Cotton's third win of the year.

A mere two days later, we were all up in Hickory, North Carolina, for the 16th race of the season. Hickory was a .4-mile dirt track. Tonight's race distance would be 250 laps. Junior Johnson's potent Poncho quickly took the pole position this week. Curtis Turner drove the Holly Farms 1960 Pontiac backup car and qualified it for the outside front row. Watching Junior and Curtis go at it on a short dirt oval in equally prepared equipment was a thrill to behold. Neither of these two men believed in taking prisoners and both would run wide open and sideways all the way around the track. They absolutely used up their equipment whenever they raced. Starting third was Zervakis and fourth was Richard Petty. Ten thousand people were on hand to see Curtis Turner lead the first three laps, then Junior led for a while, then Richard led for about 27 laps until Junior took the lead for good with 151 laps to go. That '61 Pontiac took a beating for 250 laps and was still running at the end.

Junior and Buck Baker took first and second and were the only two cars on the lead laps at the end. Rex finished third in the '60 Chevy, G.C. was fourth, and #54 Jimmy

Pardue finished fifth. Elmo Langley finished sixth in a '59 T-Bird. Out of the 23 starters, 15 were still running at the end. Curtis Turner finished 10th in the backup Holly Farms car. He had some problems that held him in the pits too long, but I don't remember what they were. Jack Smith was 13th and Ned finished 19th with a broken A-frame. Richard finished 20th with a broken radiator. The drivers wore open-faced helmets in those days. I can still remember seeing, while sitting on top of my mom's car inside the fourth turn, Ned drive by with his lips open but his teeth clinched very tightly, just like he was eating dirt and grit. Maybe he was. But to a kid, he looked tough as nails inside that car. It was kind of hard to actually see Rex's face when he was driving. If the gold helmet was still there each lap and it had a cigar hanging out of it, well, he must have been in there too.

The very next night, April 23, 1961, we were in Richmond, Virginia, for a 100-mile race on a half-mile track. Richard Petty took the pole and shared the front row with Ned Jarrett. Seven thousand spectators saw Jarrett take the lead on the start as he led the first 18 laps. Richard took over the lead on lap 19 and was never threatened for the lead again. He was the only racer to complete all 200 laps for the win. Only 12 cars started this race in front of 7,000 paying spectators. Of the starters, only six finished. Rex was credited with 10th place after losing a fuel pump on lap 134.

The Virginia 500 Sweepstakes race was the next one on the schedule. This was one week later and always a crowd pleaser. Rex qualified the '61 Chevy convertible on the pole with Fred Lorenzen taking the outside pole in his white '61 Ford convertible #28. In a recent interview I saw with Fred Lorenzen, he said that without a doubt, Rex White was the best short-track racer NASCAR ever had. Rex was very tenacious and relentless, and still knew how to watch the gauges and do his best to keep the car together. When this race shook out, none other than the wild man from Rhonda, North Carolina, Junior Johnson, walked away with the gold. I believe we have a photo here showing Junior, his wife Flossy, and Crawford in the winner's circle receiving the trophy. Junior won by a whopping four laps after being threatened by his car owner on his last pit stop to back off a bit and save the car. That just wasn't Junior's style. Flat out and belly to the ground was more like it. Zervakis finished second, Fireball was third in his Yunick '61 Pontiac, Tommy Irwin was fourth and Buck Baker's Chrysler brought him home in fifth place. Ned Jarrett started fourth and finished sixth. Rex started on the pole with a new track record but finished ninth. Some problems caused too many pit stops. The Holman-Moody Fords of Nelson Stacy and Fred Lorenzen finished 10th and 11th. Spencer was 13th, Wendell was 15th, Bobby Johns drove his '61 Ford to a 19th-place finish, Glen Wood was 22nd and Richard was 23rd. The race required 3 hours and 46 minutes.

Tim Flock, one of my heroes, finished seventh driving Beau Morgan's '61 Ford Grand National car in one of his final appearances. Rex's ninth-place finish gave him a 1,326 point lead over chief rival Ned Jarrett for the championship points.

The Darlington Rebel 300 was the 19th race for this season. It was run on May 6, 1961. The Rebel was always a crowd favorite because the cars were convertibles and the fans could look right into the cars and see the drivers working in their offices. Three hundred miles on a mile-and-three-eighths track required 219 laps be completed. Starting on the pole was Fred Lorenzen with an average speed of just under 129 mph. Second was Fireball Roberts, third was #94 Banjo Matthews, and fourth starter was #8 Joe Weatherly in another '61 Pontiac. A crowd of 32,000 looked on as 32 cars took the green flag. Loren-

121. Prior to the start of the 1961 Rebel 300 convertible race, James and Louie pose with Rex in their new team uniforms.

zen, Roberts, and Weatherly traded the lead for a while. Then Curtis Turner, Johnny Allen and Banjo Matthews traded off the lead a few times for the next several laps. Richard Petty, Elmo Langley and Tim Flock were the first three cars to leave the race, Richard with a blown engine and the other two with ill-handling cars.

As the day wore on, Rex got to running pretty well and could run with the top five. At one point, though, he challenged Bob Burdick's '61 Pontiac on the low side coming off the fourth corner. This was not a recommended passing spot at Darlington. But hey, they were racing, right? So they bumped side to side and that turned Rex head-on into the front stretch pit wall. His '61 Chevy convertible punched a big hole in that wall, and it knocked the front end clean off that Chevy. Burdick was able to drop low and catch his car right before it crashed. He went on to finish. This accident happened at lap 173 and left Rex with a 24th-place finish. Ned Jarrett finished 10th this day and that cost Rex many valuable points, not to mention the damage to the race car and the banged up chin and sore jaw.

The race resumed and saw Fred Lorenzen beat Curtis Turner, who was driving the #21 Ford for the Wood Brothers. Curtis was leading with 20 laps to go. Each time they entered the first turn, Lorenzen would go high and try to drive around Turner. Each time

Grand National race at Martinsville. While pitting under caution, Louie takes the opportunity to pour two quarts of oil into the 409 Chevy. In the background you can see Crawford Clements fueling Junior Johnson's Pontiac. Note the primitive pit equipment as compared to today.

Freddy did that, Turner would run him up the track and into the guardrail. Lorenzen kept this up until the two-laps-to-go sign. This time, when they got to the first turn, Freddy faked the high move and then drove down low and passed Turner. They traded some paint on this pass but Lorenzen drove off to approximately a five- or six-car length lead. Lorenzen got the checkered flag and won the race. Then Turner drove up beside him and slammed him a good one. Turner said, "If I could have got to him before he got the checkered, I'll guarantee you he would have never finished the race." Johnny Allen was third, Bob Burdick was fourth and Fireball Roberts was fifth. Marvin Panch was sixth, Nelson Stacy was 11th, Joe Weatherly 15th, Spencer was 17th, and Buck Baker was 20th.

With Rex's accident and 24th-place finish combined with Ned's 10th-place finish, Rex lost many points to Ned this day. Rex left the track with a mere 262-point lead.

On May 12, 1961, the racing world lost one of its all time greats. Tony Bettenhausen was asked to make a few laps in Paul Russo's car, which had been the winning car driven by Rodger Ward for the 1959 Indy 500. This car was the #24 Stearly Motor Freight Special Roadster. Russo was having handling problems with the car and had asked his friend

Left to right: Junior Johnson, his wife Flossie, and crew chief Crawford Clements enjoying the victory lane ceremonies.

Tony to please make a few laps in it to see what he felt. Coming wide open down the front stretch, the car dipped a bit on the right front corner, then hit the outside wall and slid on its side until it went over the wall entering turn one. The car, with Bettenhausen still in it, lay on a patch of grass between the track wall and the grandstand seating, engulfed in flames.

Years later, while attending the General Motors training center in Charlotte, North Carolina, I took a lunch break one day and drove over to visit Tiger Tom Pistone at his shop. Tony Bettenhausen, Jr., was there working on his Grand National car. He had a '72 Chevelle sponsored by Vita Fresh Orange Juice. I introduced myself to him and we got along just fine. He remembered that his father had driven my dad's '59 Chevy at Nashville. It was a pleasure meeting him.

Just two weeks later, the wonderful world of NASCAR took us back to the Charlotte Motor Speedway for the second annual World 600. This time, Speedway management figured a way to help themselves try to dig out from under a mountain of financial debt. They decided to put on two qualifying races of 100 miles each. Only the front-row starting positions would be determined by these two races. The first of these two qualifiers was won by #43 Richard Petty, proving his '61 Plymouth was indeed up to the challenge of the new super speedway. Ralph Earnhardt drove Cotton Owens's '61 Pontiac to a second-

At speed during the 1961 Rebel 300. This was the first time Rex had two-way radio communication with the crew.

Pit stop for right-side tires, fuel and one quart of oil during the 1961 Rebel 300.

The crash is underway.

The aftermath of the crash. The car needed a new front frame clip and Rex's jaw and ribs were sore, but fortunately nothing was broken.

place finish and Bob Welborn drove one of Jack Smith's Pontiacs home for a third-place finish. Bobby Johns and Fred Lorenzen rounded out the top five. Fireball was sixth, Banjo was seventh, Ned was eighth, Johnny Allen ninth and #48, G.C. Spencer finished 10th. Of considerable note here is that Bobby Isaac drove Junior Johnson's '61 Pontiac to an 18th-place finish to complete his very first ever Grand National race. Of course, Bobby went on to become the 1970 NASCAR Grand National Champion.

The second qualifier race was actually race number 21 of the season, as these were points-counting races at the time. Junior Johnson started on the pole by virtue of his fastest qualifying time in the '61 Pontiac #3 of Ray Fox. Curtis Turner, in the Wood Brothers Ford, started outside front row. Turner wasted no time in taking the point and driving the wheels off that Ford too. He was clearly in his own ZIP Code when he blew a tire on lap 52, sending him into the wall hard. After that incident, the show was all Pontiac with Joe Weatherly and Junior Johnson. When all the chips had been played, Weatherly won the race with Junior second and Jack Smith third in his other '61 Pontiac. Fourth place went to Nelson Stacy in the #29 Ford from the shops of Holman-Moody. Fifth went to our good friend Marvin Porter, driving the #44 1960 Plymouth. Tim Flock was sixth, Herman Beam was eighth, L.D. Austin 10th, Curtis 11th, Joe Lee Johnson 14th and Cotton Owens 16th. Of the 19 cars entered, only 10 finished.

Races 22 and 23 were both held in California on these same days, so no Southern drivers ventured out there for them. That means for certain I wasn't there either. But I did read about them and I know that Lloyd Dane won the Riverside race on May 21 and Eddie Gray won the 200-lap race at Ascot on May 27.

The World 600 was the longest and most grueling stock car race in the world. This would be race #24 held on May 28 in Charlotte. These 600 miles would require 400 laps on the 1.5-mile tri-oval, high-banked super speedway. Just like it was yesterday, I can still remember being down inside the third corner standing on top of my mom's Chevy wagon. We were right up next to the fence, too. I can still hear the sound of the tire that blew out on the Ford driven by Reds Kagle. I heard the deep BOOM! and right then his Ford ran up the bank and into the guardrail. But the guardrail had been installed backwards. Where the Armco rails overlap, they should be done in such a manner that an oncoming car hitting them at a glancing blow should just glance off and continue to slide to a stop. In this case, the rails were overlapped in such a way as to allow a rail to penetrate an oncoming vehicle, cut the engine block in two and cut a leg off the driver. When his car hit that rail, it impaled itself hard and came to a very fast stop. We could tell that this was not good. The driver lost his left leg above the knee.

Almost 47,000 fans were in attendance to watch this year's race. Fifty-five cars started the race and about 25 of them finished it. Since he had finished 14th in his qualifying heat, we were a little concerned about Rex's chances in the 600-mile grind. As it turned out, he made a very good showing for himself and the entire team. With Junior Johnson back in his own Pontiac, Ray Fox needed a driver. A few people gave the nod to Spartanburg's Little Davy Pearson. That's what they called him before the race. David Pearson was the fastest qualifier for the race at a remarkable 138.381 mph in the Daytona Kennel '61 Pontiac #3. He performed flawlessly, bringing home his first Grand National win, and put himself on the map in doing so. The lead changed hands several times throughout the race, mostly due to pit stops and caution flags. But when the dust settled, David had become the Giant Killer. Pearson won the race in 5 hours and 22 minutes. At the end, even finishing on a blown-out tire, he had a two-lap lead on Fireball Roberts driving Smokey's '61 Pontiac. And our hero, Rex White, finished a very fine third place in the '61 Chevy. Ned Jarrett was fourth and Jim Paschal was fifth in the #14 1961 Pontiac. Rounding out the top 10 were Tiny Lund, Jack Smith, Bob Welborn, Junior Johnson, and Joe Weatherly. Pole sitter Richard Petty lost an engine on lap 332 and wound up in 30th position. Fred Lorenzen broke an A-frame and fell out of the race on lap 274. Tim Flock lost an engine in his '61 Ford on lap 255 and was credited with a 37th-place finish for his final Grand National race. This second annual World 600 actually paid less money to win than the first race a year earlier. I believe Joe Lee Johnson earned over $27,000 in 1960. David Pearson earned just over $24,000 for this race. Rex walked back from the pay window with $7,070 in his pockets! That bought some groceries.

On June 2, 1961, we raced again at the Spartanburg fairgrounds, another 200 laps on a half-mile dirt oval. This time Jim Paschal won the race in the #14 Pontiac. Second was Cotton Owens and third was a fine finish for Maurice Petty in the #42 Plymouth. Herman Beam was fourth and Ned Jarrett was fifth. Rex was fast but the '60 Chevy suffered some rear end suspension problems and he had to settle for a 10th-place finish. Buck Baker was 11th and good old Elmo Henderson finished 12th driving a '59 T-Bird #55. Joe Weatherly and Richard Petty both crashed on lap 70 and finished in 14th and 15th. David Pearson was 17th and Junior Johnson was 19th. Twenty-one cars started the race and Paschal's margin of victory was two full laps over second place.

Two nights later we raced at Birmingham, Alabama. Once again, it was 200 laps on a half-mile dirt track. Only 13 cars entered this one, but there was no lack of racing on the track. Johnny Allen got the pole and Jack Smith took the outside pole. The top five or six cars ran right on top of each other all night. Fourth-place starter Ned Jarrett won the race, followed by Jim Paschal, Jack Smith, and Rex White, once again driving the '60 Chevrolet. Only eight of the thirteen cars finished the race. Ned earned $800 for the win and Rex earned $375 for fourth. This was Ned's only win for the season, but his consistency was paying great dividends. He closed the points gap between himself and Rex to within 198 points. It was getting tough now!

With race #26 in the books, it was time to head back up the road to Greenville for race #27. This was June 8 and again another 200 laps on dirt. Ned grabbed the pole and Junior Johnson's Holly Farms Pontiac was second fastest to start outside front row. Crawford was still crew chief for Junior at this time. Bud Allman was still handling those duties for Ned. Junior lost a fan belt on lap 13 and fell out early. Jack Smith chased Ned Jarrett for 170 laps before getting around him for the lead. Jack drove on for the win with Ned coming in second, one lap down to Smith. Third place went to Zervakis and fourth to Joe Weatherly. Fifth was Jim Paschal, sixth was Elmo Henderson, seventh went to #42 Maurice Petty, and Rex brought the Chevy home eighth. G.C. Spencer was ninth, and Richard Petty had suspension problems and was credited with 16th. David Pearson came in 17th and Junior Johnson was 25th. Interesting thing about the Greenville-Pickens track is that Elmo Henderson was the 1958 track points champion. I believe his name is still painted on the backstretch wall there. Also in the news this same day was the story that Curtis Turner and Bruton Smith resigned from Charlotte Motor Speedway after a board of directors meeting. Taking their place were Allan Nance and Duke Ellington.

We took a couple days off then to drive back up to Winston-Salem for another go at the quarter-mile asphalt flat track. This race would be the annual Myers Brothers Memorial. For this race, Junior Johnson set the fastest time of the evening to take the pole position. Glen Wood from Virginia was second quickest, so he started outside first row. Jim Reed qualified third and Rex was fourth fastest, which let him start outside second row. Twenty-two cars started the race and an estimated crowd of 12,500 paid spectators watched the annual event. Rex White once again won at his favorite track with Jim Reed on the same lap and still in hot pursuit. Third went to Junior Johnson and fourth was #85 Emanuel Zervakis in his Chevy. Fifth place was Richard Petty and sixth was Ned Jarrett. Maurice Petty experienced some handling difficulties and finished 16th. Wendell Scott came to race but suffered from brake problems on lap 78 which relegated him to a 21st-place finish. With Rex having won the race and Ned finishing sixth, Rex opened his points lead slightly to 182 over Jarrett.

One week later saw the same cars in action. But this time we were up in Norwood, Massachusetts, for the Yankee 500. This would be 500 laps on a quarter-mile flat asphalt track. Talk about a tough place to race! Well before the 500 laps were completed, drivers were driving with their left hands and holding their heads up with their right hands. The physical strain was enormous. Rex and Louie took the '60 Chevy up there knowing that 500 laps on a quarter-mile track would certainly do in the body on the race car and they just didn't feel like mistreating the '61 that bad... yet. Rex qualified on the pole and received a beautiful wooden-base trophy with a nice big gold cup on top of it. Very nice for a pole award. When the green flag waved, Rex took off and led the first 125 laps. At the end of the evening, Zervakis won this one with Rex second and Ned third. Fourth was Buck Baker in a '61 Chrysler and fifth went to Jim Reed, a New Yorker driving another '61 Chevy. Four of the top five were Chevys! Wendell finished 10th, and Ed Flemke drove a small Dodge Dart to finish 12th. Eighteen cars started the race.

Zervakis made $2,250 for his win and Rex made $1,000 for second place. This was race number 29 of the season. That leaves us with about 17 more to go.

The Old Pro, Buck Baker, put his 375-hp 1961 Chrysler in victory lane for the 30th race of the season. This time we were down in Hartsville, South Carolina, running 150 laps on a .3-mile dirt oval. Zervakis took the pole but crashed on lap 101. Ned put his #11 Chevy on the outside front row and finished sixth. But it was pretty much Baker's night to shine. That big ol' Chrysler was humming for sure. Jack Smith finished second in a Pontiac and Rex came home with a very fine third-place finish. Pearson was fourth and Junior Johnson was fifth. Wendell Scott brought his Chevy home ninth place for a fine finish and $140. Buck earned $750 for winning and Rex brought back $460. Richard Petty blew his engine on lap 69 and was listed as finishing in the 17th position for $65. This was June 23.

The very next night, June 24, we raced 150 laps at Starkey Speedway in Roanoke, Virginia. This was another happy evening for the Clements family. Rex took the pole with the fast time for the evening. Junior qualified second for an all–Clements front row again. I don't remember Louie and Crawford having any secrets between them. What one learned was shared with the other. It showed up with the on-track performance too. Junior won this round with Rex finishing second. That paid Junior and Crawford $900 and Rex and Louie were paid $750 for second. Third went to Jim Paschal and fourth to Richard Petty.

Zervakis was fifth. Spencer was seventh, Wendell was eighth and Buck Baker finished ninth. Ned finished 11th and Larry Thomas came in 14th. Of the 20 starters, 17 were still running at the end. Rex extended his points lead over Ned to 396 points on this evening.

July 4 was Louie's birthday and he usually had a birthday cake presented to him down at the start/finish line in Daytona. The wife and daughter of one of the NASCAR officials always thought to bring him a cake. He really enjoyed a reputation for his friendliness and willingness to help any and everybody who needed it. Daytona on July 4 meant we were there to see the Firecracker 250. Man, those old truck-motored Chevys had a tough job keeping up with the Pontiacs on the super speedways. Again, Fireball took the pole in Smokey's '61 Pontiac. David Pearson qualified second in another '61 Pontiac and Joe Weatherly took the third spot with his '61 Pontiac. Once the green flag dropped, the cars ran fairly tight for just a few laps. Then those powerful Ponchos began to sprout some long legs and walk away. As a matter of fact, the top 10 finishing cars were seven Pontiacs and three Fords. David Pearson won the race in the Daytona Kennel '61 Pontiac #3. Fred Lorenzen's Ford was second, Jack Smith's Pontiac was third, and fourth went to the '60 Pontiac driven by this year's Daytona 500 winner, Marvin Panch. Fireball drove the '61 Pontiac team car to Panch for a fifth-place finish. Weatherly was sixth in a Pontiac, Nelson Stacy was seventh in a Ford, eighth was Roscoe Thompson driving a Pontiac, ninth was Larry Frank in a '61 Ford and 10th went to Ralph Earnhardt driving Cotton Owens's '61 Pontiac. Ned finished 11th in his Chevy and Rex finished a dismal 23rd after the engine broke a rod on the 63rd lap. The $350 he received from that finish was a far cry from the $8,450 Pearson got for winning. Junior was 17th, and Tiny Lund was 20th driving the west-coast '61 Pontiac of J.D. Braswell. Thirty cars began the race and 20 of them finished it. Of the cars that fell out, eight of them blew engines and two were black-flagged, probably smoking badly enough to signal a soon-to-be-blown engine. Spectators on hand to watch the caution-free event numbered 18,300. The July 4 Daytona was really neat for us kids because it was always hot enough to stay at the motel and swim during the practice and qualifying days. We had a ton of fun. I believe it was this year, 1961, that one of the crew guys showed up at Daytona on his new motorcycle. It was still pretty warm, even at night, and everybody wanted ice cream cones. So I was the designated ice cream holder on the back of that motorcycle. By the time we got back to the motel, the ice cream was half melted away and all over me. One dip in the ocean fixed that issue. Of course, on race day, we came out to the track to cheer on our heroes.

Two big races were less than one week apart. Five days after the Daytona Firecracker 250 we were all down in Atlanta for the July 9 Festival 250 on the 1.5-mile high-banked oval. Atlanta was unique in that being a 1.5-mile track, the straightaways were only a quarter-mile long each. The turns were a half-mile long each. Within the next year, the speed premium would be placed on the handling of the car more so than the horsepower of the car. Oh, the horsepower was still a big deal, but those long sweeping corners helped to act as an equalizer. For this race, 18,000 fans showed up to watch 42 cars take the starter's green flag. On the pole with the fastest qualifying lap was Fireball Roberts driving the familiar black-and-gold '61 Pontiac #22. Starting second was David Pearson driving the Ray Fox '61 Pontiac #3. Starting third was Joe Weatherly and fourth was Nelson Stacy. Three of the quick four were Pontiacs. A first-lap crash took out David Pearson, Herb Tillman, and Roscoe Thompson. That cleanup caution lasted for 12 laps and then we got

Tom Pistone ahead of Rex leaving pit road during the 1961 Firecracker 250 at Daytona.

Bud Moore's 1961 Pontiac driven by Joe Weatherly.

back to racing. The lead changed several times between Roberts, Lorenzen, Joe Weatherly, Jack Smith, Bob Welborn, Nelson Stacy and Junior Johnson. But at the end, it was Fred Lorenzen's day to shine. He won this race by a full lap over second-place #49 Bob Welborn. Finishing third was Richard Petty, fourth was Zervakis, and fifth went to Jack Smith, also in a Pontiac. That set a pretty good variation of race cars for the top positions: Ford, Pontiac, Plymouth, Chevrolet, Pontiac, Chrysler, Chevy, Chrysler, Chevy and Chevy. Having a good mixture of manufactures in the top 10 has always been a goal for NASCAR. In the sixth spot was Buck Baker, followed by Friday Hassler, Buddy Baker, and G.C. Spencer, and 10th went to Rex White. Another top 10 of the season was still a good points day for Rex. Fireball was 12th and Ned was 14th. Of the 42 entrants, 24 finished the race. Nelson Stacy and Bobby Johns fell out early, as did Tiny Lund, Joe Weatherly and Johnny Allen. Although 27th-place Frank Graham's '60 Ford was still running at the end, Ned's '61 Chevy was credited with a 14th-place finish after blowing an engine on lap 153 of the scheduled 167-lap race. Rex made $900 for his 10th-place finish, but Lorenzen earned over $7,000 for his victory. The race took just over two hours to complete. This had been race #33 of the season and Rex regained the very close points battle by a slight margin of 40 points.

Just a week later, the Speedway in Columbia, South Carolina, played host to the next Grand National show on July 20. This would be another 200 laps on the half-mile dirt track. Twenty-one cars qualified for the race, with Cotton Owens snatching the pole away from Little Joe Weatherly. Both men drove Pontiacs and both were from the NASCAR hub city of Spartanburg, South Carolina. Columbia is just 90 miles down the road from Spartanburg, so we kids could hitch a ride in the truck or mom's wagon and go watch the race with no motel bills to raise the cost of going racing. Qualifying third was Ned Jarrett and fourth was Rex White. On the starter's command, they roared into the first turn with Weatherly taking the point. He led for the first 50 laps, and then Jim Paschal, driving Joe Lee Johnson's '61 Chevy, took the lead from lap 51 until Cotton Owens passed him for good on lap 193. Cotton led the race for the last seven laps. This victory paid Cotton $950. Paschal was second with Ned finishing third. Junior Johnson was fourth and Joe Weatherly was fifth. Rex struggled with some mechanical problems and came back with a 14th-place finish. Rex entered the race with the points lead and left the track 136 points behind Ned Jarrett and his team. I still have very vivid memories of Ned's crew lighting a bunch of fireworks to celebrate their points lead after the race. It was kind of a weird feeling for a 10-year-old boy in the pits. Rex and Louie and our whole team were all feeling dejected about losing the points lead. Yet at the same time, another competitor was celebrating his good fortune. Plus, I kind of enjoyed the fireworks. When the firecrackers started popping I was next to my dad's race car but I was helping L.D. Austin load up all of his stuff. He was usually by himself at the track and always nice to us, so lending a hand just seemed natural. L.D. mentioned that he had a real bad toothache and I told him, "My mom has everything. Let me go see what I can find." I ran back to the infield and told my mom and she gave me a couple of aspirin and a coke to give to L.D. He was thankful and I continued to help him.

Two days later, Little Joe Weatherly put a whooping on everybody at Rambi Speedway in Myrtle Beach, South Carolina. Joe qualified on the pole and shot out like a rocket at the green flag and led every lap to earn his paycheck of $950 with his '61 Pontiac. Jim Paschal was second, and Ned "Mr. Consistency" Jarrett was third. Completing the top five were George Green and Emanuel Zervakis. Rex and Louie's '61 Chevy broke a left rear wheel hub and that cost them a lot of necessary traction off the corners. His finish was 10th, which gave Ned a 258-point lead after the 35th race of the season. Richard and Maurice Petty each had mechanical problems and finished 17th and 18th. Fireball Roberts made a very rare appearance to drive Junior Johnson's '61 Pontiac and blew the engine after just 27 laps. Junior drove the '60 Pontiac and broke a ball joint on the 16th lap. They finished 21st and 22nd. The race took about an hour and 45 minutes to complete.

One week later we all loaded up and drove up to Bristol, Tennessee, for the Volunteer 500, which was 500 laps on a high-banked half-mile asphalt track. Just like it happened yesterday, every person in our family remembers this race. At the very top of a huge mountain in Tennessee one of the rear shocks on our new Chevy station wagon rubbed a hole in a brake line. Every time my oldest brother, Lloyd, would use the brakes, more and more brake fluid would squirt out of the system, and it didn't take long until we were coming down the mountain pretty fast with no brakes. Thankfully, he was of age and had enough experience working at the shop with my dad that he knew to drop the car down into low gear and then use the mechanical parking brakes to slow the car down. We kids and especially my mom were a bit concerned. Once down to the bottom of the hill we found a gas station open with a mechanic on duty to help install a new piece of brake line and bleed the brakes. That got us back on the road and headed toward the track. All those prayers the nuns taught us came in handy that day!

I love Bristol. I was fortunate enough to be at the very first ever Bristol race in 1961. At the new track, 25,000 people were on hand to watch this race. The hype was built up that this would be one of the best races of the year. Fred Lorenzen took the pole with Junior Johnson qualifying for the second spot. Jack Smith won the race in his '61 Pontiac with relief driving help from his teammate, Johnny Allen. Fireball was second, Ned third, Richard fourth and Buddy Baker was fifth. Rex was running really well this day and was even leading the race for many laps. This was one of the very few times in NASCAR racing that any of us had to sit in the stands. The newly constructed speedway had a lot of mud and equipment in the infield so my mother, myself and my two-year-old little brother sat in the center of the back stretch grand stands. We never cared for sitting in the stands at a race. It really restricts your mobility and thus ruins about half the fun of the day or weekend. Those bleachers that day were extremely steep. I carried a small cooler and my mom carried my brother, Jeff, and a small blanket to sit on. We were watching the race as it progressed and well after halfway, Rex had put the Chevy out on the point. He was getting through the corners very well. Then, out of the clear blue sky, that 409 engine blew in a million pieces right in front of us. A huge cloud of smoke billowed from underneath the race car. At that instant, the crowd jumped to their feet and roared with approval. I jumped up and said, "What the heck?" My mom quickly put her hand over my mouth and told me to sit down! Then, during the relative quiet of that caution flag she explained that not everyone there was a Rex White fan. Many Ned Jarrett fans were in attendance too, and having Rex fall out gave their favorite driver a chance to finish better. Besides, it could have just been a Ford vs. Chevy thing or a bunch of Pontiac fans, or just a bunch of halfway intoxicated spectators just acting up. It was indeed one of those lessons that stayed with me. Sitting in the grandstands at a few NASCAR races will teach a young kid to never take up drinking or smoking. It sure did for me!

Just ahead of Rex's 25th-place finish was Wendell's 24th-place finish. L.D. Austin was 12th, Bob Welborn was 18th, Junior Johnson was 22nd, Marvin Porter was 28th, David Pearson was 30th, Nelson Stacy, Fred Lorenzen and G.C. Spencer finished 32nd, 33rd, and 34th. Cotton Owens finished 40th. Jack Smith received $3,025 for his win,

1961 champion Ned Jarrett's Grand National car on a trailer at Myrtle Beach Motel.

Ned got $1,125 for third and Rex received $250 for the 25th spot. The main problem for us this day was that Ned opened up his points lead to 918 points over second-place Rex White. The part we didn't yet know was that it was only going to get worse next week.

Race #37 was held back up in Nashville and was scheduled for 403 laps, which would have made up 250 miles on that track. Just a regular as clockwork, Rex qualified with the fastest time again and took the pole position. I think Rex took the pole at least 10 times in a row at Nashville. Richard Petty started on the outside pole. The real fireworks began on lap 15 when Rex blew a right front Firestone tire and drove that '61 Chevy straight up into the wall between the third and fourth turns. The car stood up on the rear bumper and cleaned out about 100 feet of the guardrail and wall. The car was damaged too badly to repair it to get back into the race. So we had another bad week where Rex was fast but finished 23rd and Consistent Ned ran second to winner Jim Paschal. Johnny Allen, Buck Baker, and Zervakis completed the top five. Richard was 14th and Jack Smith was 15th. Junior was 19th. The only car to finish behind Rex was the 24th-place finish of Doug Yates, who lost a transmission on the first lap. Ned's good finish and Rex's poor finish gave Ned a 1,338 points lead.

For some reason that we never figured out and my father really didn't like to discuss, the 1961 tire deal with Rex was a sore point. Rex demanded that the car run every race on Firestones, even if the Goodyears were better. The team had no contract with Firestone, so we never understood Rex's decision to run Firestones exclusively. Rex was a bit more demanding back during this time than Louie was. Louie really just enjoyed racing for a living, hanging with the family, working on the race car and winning races. But not enough to argue over the tire deal with Rex. The two men went through some problems like any driver and crew chief might experience. Even today we see this in modern-day NASCAR. But, several years before Louie passed away in January of '96, he and Rex got back together and carried on their friendship as good as it ever was. I lean on Rex today just like he was my dad. I have thoroughly enjoyed the friends I have made and become reacquainted with while writing this book. You can also add Mr. Ned Jarrett to this list. What a good, decent, Christian man he is! "Gentleman Ned" is more than just a label. It's the honest truth.

We went on home and got tooled up for race number 38 of the season. Back to Bowman Gray, where Rex always ran well. Maybe he could pick up some points there. This race was on August 9, 1961. Junior Johnson took the pole with Glen Wood starting on the outside front row. Rex started third and Ned started fourth. To my knowledge, these two gentlemen never got into a bump and shove during their entire points battle. They kept it to clean, hard racing on the track. After the required 150 laps, Rex found the winner's circle and Glen Wood ran second. But Rex didn't alter the points race much because Ned ran a real fine third position. Emanuel was fourth and Richard was fifth. Our friend G.C. Spencer finished sixth and good ol' Wendell Scott brought his Chevy home seventh, five laps down. Finishing ninth was Harry Leake, driving the old Chevy he had bought from Rex and Louie. Larry Thomas was 10th. On the 44th lap, Junior's accident caused him to be dropped down to 19th in the rundown, and Maurice Petty drove his 6-cylinder Valiant to a 21st-place position. Rex earned $665 for the win. Bill Whitley crashed his 1954 Corvette on lap 39 to finish 20th and brought home $50 for his efforts. The biggest rumor floating around the track that night was that Big Bill France had banned Curtis Turner and Tim Flock from NASCAR for life.

Race number 39 for this season was another one of those that I will never forget. What started out as just another day at the race track turned out to be one of the scariest times of my life. This race was held on the half-mile paved oval at Asheville-Weaverville, North Carolina. This was one of Rex's better tracks and he won several races on this track. On this day, Jim Paschal took the pole driving Julian Petty's '61 Pontiac. Junior Johnson started outside front row driving the 1960 Holly Farms Pontiac. Thirty-eight cars entered the race expecting to run for 500 laps. We're still not sure if we went to a race and fight broke out or we went to a fight and a race broke out. But when the dust settled, it was a pretty scary ordeal for drivers, crews, and families.

On lap 208 there was an accident involving the race car of driver Bunk Moore. At that time, NASCAR officials informed the drivers and teams that the race would continue for another 50 laps and then be halted for good. The track had torn up so bad that flying chunks of asphalt were coming through windshields and things were getting dangerous, not only for the drivers, but spectators too. If I remember correctly, the asphalt was laid over concrete and the two surfaces didn't like each other. Race cars were breaking suspension parts and crashing and dropping out like flies. About 10,000 spectators came out to see the race and ended up getting to see a clash between the drivers and crews vs. the Teamsters Union, who wanted to unionize the NASCAR drivers. When the race resumed and the 50 laps were run, that put the race past the halfway mark, and at that point, under NASCAR rules, the race could be called official. This is exactly what they did. At this point, Junior Johnson was leading, with Joe Weatherly, Rex White and Ned

About 15 laps into the 1961 Nashville 400, Rex blew a right front tire and tore down the guardrail between turns three and four.

Jarrett making up the top four cars. Of the 38 who started, 26 were still running at the halfway point when NASCAR waved the checkers.

Seeing the race was over and done, most spectators did just what spectators do when a race is completed. They headed towards their cars to travel back home. In this case, approximately 4,000 of them hung around for some extra action. A few of them provoked a riot. They pulled a truck and flatbed trailer across the track exit and told the racers to complete the race. Now we had a real problem on our hands. The racers were already packing up to go home and a few hundred alcohol-fueled fans, plus some suspected Teamsters, tried everything they could to cause a huge riot. The drivers, mechanics, etc, mostly stayed with their families for protection. I remember my mother making us kids all lie down flat in the back of our station wagon. The moms were the most scared.

After some time had passed, a few of the team mechanics who were of healthy stature, including Pop Eargle, who was a mountain, walked up to see if they could talk some sense into these people. Pop carried a huge logging chain with him. These chains were normally used to tie the race cars down in their trailers, but for this special occasion, Pop found another use for one of them. One of the protesters standing up on that trailer had a long 2 × 4 piece of wood and he poked Pop in the belly with it. Let's mark this down as a really bad mistake on the part of the protester. Pop grabbed that 2 × 4 from the man and took one swing and cleared off that trailer.

One of the guys who had worked for Cotton Owens was Arthur Coker. He was a tall, white-haired thin man and according to legend he carried a really long switchblade knife with him everywhere he went. The story from some crew guys was that Arthur took that knife and shoved it clear up one rioter's rear end. The entire ordeal was over within about one minute of the crews' taking some logging chains, jack handles, tire irons, and other tools up to talk with the protesters. The crews and teams tried to wait it out for awhile and let the police and sheriff's department get things under control. It became apparent that law enforcement was not in control. It could have taken the National Guard, but in this case, it only needed some tired race mechanics who just wanted to go home.

So, who finished where in the race? Well, pole sitter Paschal finished sixth, Johnny Allen and Jack Smith were eighth and ninth, and Nelson Stacy and Richard Petty finished 10th and 11th. Marvin Porter was 14th, Buddy Baker was 16th, L.D. Austin 17th, Wendell was 24th, and a rare appearance by Fireball Roberts, driving the Lynn Holloway '61 Pontiac normally driven by Tom Pistone, left Fireball back in 31st place after he broke an axle. Junior earned $2,000 for his win and Rex earned $1,100 for third. Junior led all 258 laps.

Just five days later we were up in Richmond, Virginia, at Southside Speedway, which was a quarter-mile paved track, for a race that would run for 150 laps. Again this week, Junior Johnson qualified for the pole. When the green flag waved, he kept his Pontiac on the point for the entire 150 laps. Go or blow was his motto. Completing the top five were Ned Jarrett, Emanuel Zervakis, Rex White, and Jimmy Pardue. Nineteen cars started this race and 15 finished it. Doug Yates was sixth, Elmo Langley was eighth, Richard Petty finished up in the ninth spot, with Buck Baker and Wendell Scott 15th and 16th. About 3,500 people were in attendance. This had been race number 40 for the season.

One week later, Junior Johnson pulled off the hat trick, three in a row. This time he qualified third at South Boston Speedway in Virginia. Cotton Owens qualified for the pole but lost a transmission on lap 75, which left him with a 17th-place score in the rundown. Jim Reed started second and finished second too. Ned Jarrett was third, Zervakis was fourth and Rex finished fifth. Richard lost an engine on lap 32, which left him with a 20th-place finish, and Wendell crashed on lap 114 for a 16th-place payday. Ned raised his points lead over Rex to just over 1,300 points by this time. Now, having Junior Johnson set the fastest qualifying time and win the race three weeks in a row set off somebody in Pontiac Engineering. My dad was very good friends with Frank McGurk, from whom the cartoon "Stroker McGurk" was named. McGurk ground all the camshafts for the 348 and 409 Chevys that Louie put into the engines that Rex drove. Well, that led to another connection between my Uncle Crawford and Frank McGurk. Crawford stopped running the cams that Pontiac Engineering was sending him and started talking with McGurk and together they worked to come up with something better. So just a couple of days after Junior's being the top dog three weeks in a row, Pontiac Engineering had a man show up at Junior's Holly Farms shop and tell Crawford, "We'll take that cam now." Well, you can imagine how that one went over. "Yeah, you and whose Army?" Eventually Crawford gave in and let them have the cam that was in the motor. After that engineer left, Crawford looked over at Junior and said, "Sure glad we pulled the good one out before he got here."

While on the subject of Frank McGurk, it needs to be told that he and Louie became very good friends. They visited as often as their schedules would allow and always enjoyed bench racing and a few brews. On one occasion, McGurk was to fly his small private plane to Spartanburg and pick up Louie to head up to Michigan for a meeting with some Chevy engineers. On the way up to Michigan the two men enjoyed a couple of beers and

Louie wanted to mess with the air fuel mixture control knob in the plane. Any pilot reading this knows fully well that as the plane gains altitude he has to adjust the air-fuel mix for the thinner air. And, as the plane begins your descent back down, the pilot has to richen the mixture so as to avoid burning a piston and blowing the engine. This is no joke at 20,000 feet! Today, they have electronic devices that do this automatically. But at this time, no such device existed.

So Louie said to Frank, "I'll bet we can lean this thing so much that it can't burn the piston." Frank said, "You know that running it lean *will* burn a piston." Then Louie said, "If I lean it so much that it doesn't have enough fuel to even make a fire, it *can't* burn a piston." Frank said give it a try. Now they are still quite high at this point. (No, I mean above the ground!) So, Louie watched the exhaust temperature gauge and leaned the motor right past the danger zone and down so low that it still ran but could not burn a piston at the temperature where he stopped. This let both men know that better fuel economy for our cars would be just a matter of Detroit catching up with what they had just tested and proven. Yep, men were still men back then.

This next race would be race #42 of the season and it would be contested at the granddaddy of all stock car tracks, Darlington, South Carolina. The '61 Southern 500 is an interesting story in itself. Driving Smokey Yunick's '61 Pontiac, Fireball easily earned the pole position from any other contenders. Fred Lorenzen's '61 Ford #28 started from the outside of the front row. Third on the grid went to David Pearson driving Ray Fox's '61 Pontiac and fourth starter was Joe Weatherly in another '61 Pontiac. Five hundred miles on a mile-and-three-eighths track called for 364 laps. Both Rex and Louie had mapped out a strategy that they felt gave them a real shot at winning this race. The car qualified well and ran well in practice. They felt that they had come so close to winning last year, that this was sure enough their year to win the big one! But it was not to be.

Now right here is where the story starts to get convoluted. Here we were, about 30 to 45 minutes before the largest race of the year, the Labor Day Southern 500 at Darlington. Big money, famous names, tradition, excitement, etc. Everything was up for grabs. During this time period in NASCAR, even if one guy won the championship, another guy could say, "Yea, but I won the Southern 500!" It was that big of a deal. So right before the race, NASCAR inspector Norris Friel came down to the #4 Chevy and told Rex and Louie that the car had been protested and it was not going to compete in today's race. They asked, "Who protested?" and received no answer. Then they asked, "What is wrong with the car?" Mr. Friel told them that he had been tipped off the engine was slid back in the car from its original location. Well, yes, it had been. However, the rule book stated that the motor mount bolt holes in the frame could not be altered in such a way as to allow the engine to be set back. This particular frame and body style came from the Chevrolet factory with one of four different engines in it. And that's not counting the assortment of transmissions that were possible in these cars. The car could have come with a 235-cubic-inch straight 6-cylinder, a 283-cubic-inch small-block V8, the 348 W block, or the 360-hp 409 Big Block engine. Using the existing holes in the frame, without any modification to them, they merely loosened up the motor mounts, slid the engine back three-quarters of an inch and then tightened everything up. Of course, that required them to shorten up the drive shaft by three quarters of an inch also. Louie and James started grabbing the tools to quickly move the engine back forward the three-quarters of an inch. Then Norris Friel said to them, "You don't understand. These orders just came down from Daytona. This car is *not* going to race today!" That was the end of that. So, with 20 to 30 minutes before the race started, Rex and Louie ran over to the back stretch pits and "borrowed" Jack Smith's backup car for Rex to drive in the race. Actually, that's what they requested, but the backup car was #46, and Larry Frank was already scheduled to drive that car. So Jack gave up his own race car #47 for Rex to run to help keep him in the championship hunt. Jack was about 6'3" and 250 pounds. Rex is about 5'4" and 135 pounds. It took a lot of scrambling to get the seat adjusted for Rex to somewhat fit that Pontiac. The seating arrangement, the chassis setup — nothing like this had Rex ever driven before. It was a major accomplishment that they were able to scramble to get this done in time to start the race. But they did. The rest of the crew loaded up the pit equipment and dragged it over to the back stretch pits. It was a definite hindrance to have to pit on the back stretch then, too. But they held their heads up and went on with the race.

When the race started, Fireball took off with the lead and pretty well put on a driving clinic for the other guys. Nelson Stacy stayed right there with him for most of the day. On one of Roberts's pit stops, he had signaled for a relief driver. Marvin Panch was available because his car, the #42 Petty Plymouth, had lost an engine on the 94th lap. Marvin had driven for Smokey before and they could communicate well. Fireball had terrible neck cramps and needed to get out of the car. Panch got in and took off after the win. The average pit stops this afternoon were taking over 46 seconds. When the checkers fell on this 500 miles, Nelson Stacy had passed the '61 Pontiac of Roberts/Panch and led the final six laps. His yellow #29 Holman-Moody Ford won the 12th Southern 500 in style. Panch finished second, which is credited to Fireball. Third and fourth were David Pearson and Jim Paschal in Pontiacs and fifth was Zervakis in his '61 Chevrolet. Rounding out the top 10 were Ned Jarrett, Johnny Allen, Roscoe Thompson, Ralph Earnhardt and Rex White driving the big old Pontiac. All things considered, 10th place was not a bad finish for Rex with the Pontiac. He was sure whipped after this one, though. One reason was because many racers were pretty good-sized people with big strong arms. Not that Rex wasn't strong, but he was 5'4" and small-framed. Early on, a couple of years earlier to be exact, Rex and Louie were to our knowledge the first to figure out the split stagger and split caster in the front end. Most of the guys ran a lot of positive caster in the front wheels to make the car very positive on corner entry when they steer into the corner. Through testing, Rex and Louie came up with running much less positive caster and running variable caster from side to side to help the car steer into the corner. That took a ton of load off the driver with a setup like this. Rex's Chevy that they intended to race was set like this. The Pontiac he ended up driving was set up for the 6'3", 250-pound man with huge arms. Yep, Rex earned every bit of his pay this day.

So who else finished where? Bobby Johns was 11th and Junior was 14th. Tiny was 15th and Larry Frank was 20th. The #8 Pontiac of Bud Moore and Joe Weatherly broke a right front hub and finished 22nd. Jim Reed, the 1959 winner of this race, lost his brakes on lap 228 and finished 23rd. Richard Petty and Buck Baker finished 26th and 27th. Fred Lorenzen and Cale Yarborough finished 29th and 30th. Marvin Panch, who was actually driving the winning car, was credited with a 31st-place finish because the car he started the race in broke and fell out of competition early in the race. Banjo Matthews lost an engine and finished 36th. If you wonder why I mention Banjo as often as I do, well, that's because I got to watch him race a lot. And when he raced on short tracks, he displayed no fear at all. Big thick glasses and all, this man would flat-out stand on the gas. You just have to love a guy like that! Of the 43 cars that started this 500-miler, only 17 were actually running at the end. Over 80,000 people were in attendance this day.

Now, let's talk about who had protested Rex's '61 Chevy so as to prevent it from being raced this day. After the race, Rex and Louie and the team kind of figured that Emanuel Zervakis had to be the culprit. First, because White and Clements, Inc., had built a car for him to race the year before and while changing engines, he surely noticed this and kept it in his back pocket. But he was not actually in competition to win the points championship, so why would he do such a thing? Though some study and research to write this book, I notice that just two weeks before this '61 Southern 500, NASCAR was up north in Massachusetts at the Norwood Arena for the Yankee 500. Rex took the pole but at the end of 500 laps on the quarter-mile track, Zervakis took the win with Rex finishing second. Ned Jarrett was third. Rex felt Zervakis had made an illegal pit stop and protested him after the race. NASCAR checked the score cards and the win remained with Zervakis with Rex second. So, nowadays, we sort of think that the Darlington protest was just payback for the protest Rex made against Emanuel two weeks earlier.

Now, step back in time with me to 1989. A super young man and NASCAR historian by the name of Greg Fielden put a lot of work and effort into writing his book titled *Forty Years of Stock Car Racing*. In Greg's book, he tells the story that points contender Ned Jarrett and his crew chief Bud Allman filed the protest. Remember that Ned and Rex were involved in a very tight points battle for this season. Also, Rex and Louie had invited Ned and Bud to visit their shop to show them everything they could about making the Chevy run. So, I'm reasonably certain that Ned and Bud knew about the engine placement adjustment. So, from 1961 until 1989, Rex and Louie thought Zervakis filed that protest and that pretty much ended their friendship. However, from the time that Greg's book came out until just recently, we all felt that Ned had been the protester. Recently I got to meet Ned Jarrett in person and learn that he is above board and a fine person. I inquired about the Darlington incident and he told me straight out, "I'll guarantee you, I had nothing to do with it." He said, "I can't say for sure about Bud, but I don't think that sounds like something he would do either." So, after speaking with Mr. Jarrett, I can personally feel in my heart that this is a man of God, and that if he had been involved, he would have told me. I simply do not believe that Ned had anything to do with it. Then, I sat down beside Rex and spoke with him about it. It is his feeling that, without a doubt, the protest was filed by Emanuel Zervakis. Rex is over it and it didn't seem to bother him one bit to talk about it.

Now to the real question that still digs at me today. You tell me. Why in the world did NASCAR officials wait until 30 minutes before the race to lay this on the Rex White team? To me, that is the much larger question. And here is what I think about it. Any NASCAR historian can go back to the beginning of NASCAR and name out loud the times through the course of each season when NASCAR tried to manipulate who the victor would be. They have an inside group of officials, maybe only three or four people in the real know. These folks do whatever they are told from the top down to help control the circumstances of a race. Now, to just outright manipulate a race to determine a winner would be really tough to get away with. Too many people would have to have knowledge of it and that makes it not likely. But if a very few key players in the NASCAR officiating game were on the *real* inside, you can see how slight manipulations of a race could easily be pulled off. If we need to, just to prove the point, we can write a complete book on this very subject. I know of many, many cases where I feel this is exactly what happened to determine a winner. I am now pounding on my keyboard about as hard as it is going to stand. I think we'll change subjects and get back to some more racing.

Just a mere four days after the '61 Southern 500, we were back up in Hickory, North Carolina, for the Buddy Shuman memorial race. This would be another 250 laps on a .4-mile track. Ten thousand five hundred people came out to watch this race. And whatever they paid to get in, I am reasonably certain they got their money's worth. Rex White qualified fast enough to grab the pole position with the same '61 Chevy that he didn't get to run at Darlington. The engine had been moved back to NASCAR's liking and we were set to go. Junior Johnson, driving my Uncle Crawford's '61 Pontiac, sat second quick for outside pole. I think this make four times for the season that they did this. Sure was fun for my cousin Gary and me. When the green flag waved, Junior shot out to lead the first 58 laps. Then, while showing a superb skill of racing sideways, Junior went for a hole between Ned Jarrett and Cotton Owens while attempting to lap them. By the time Junior got to the hole, it had closed down a bit and he crashed his car while trying to regain control of it. This took him from the race for a 20th-place finish. Rex and Ned traded the lead back and forth a few times for several laps before Rex grabbed the lead for good on lap 240. He led the final 10 laps for the win. This was Rex's sixth win for the year. Second went to Jack Smith in his Pontiac, third was Buck Baker in his big ol' Chrysler, fourth to Cotton Owens driving his '60 Pontiac, and fifth went to Zervakis in his '60 Chevrolet. G.C. Spencer came home in sixth and Ned finished eighth in his #11 Chevy. L.D. Austin was ninth, Herman Beam finished 13th, Joe Weatherly 15th, Richard Petty 17th, and #23 Plymouth of Doug Yates was 19th. Rex White was the only car on the lead lap at the end of the 100-mile race.

Race #44 this year carried us back up to Richmond, Virginia. But this time it would be on the half-mile Fairgrounds dirt track. Junior Johnson wasted no sweat or energy in setting fast time for the pole position. Ned qualified outside front row. The race was scheduled for 250 laps, and the noise lasted for just over two hours. When it all shook out, Joe Weatherly had won the race in his '61 Pontiac and Junior Johnson drove home second in the Holly Farms '60 Pontiac. Rex brought the Louie Clements '61 Chevy home for a fine third-place finish. Didn't gain many points, though, because "Mr. Consistency," Ned Jarrett, followed him home for the fourth position. Fifth went to Jim Paschal driving the Julian Petty '61 Pontiac #44. Wendell Scott finished 14th with Buck Baker in 15th and Cotton Owens in 17th. Richard was credited with 18th place because of a blown engine on lap 157. Twenty-five cars started the race and only 15 finished it.

Sacramento, California, played host to race #45 for the season. This was the same day as the race at Richmond that we just finished, so no east-coast drivers went out for this one. The race was a 100-lap contest over a one-mile dirt oval. Eddie Gray won it with his '61 Ford and our half-crazy buddy Frank Secrist finished fourth in his '60 Ford. Eddie Pagan ran 10th and Ron Hornaday finished 24th. Number 44 Lloyd Dane was the west-coast short-track champion and on this day he finished 26th in a '61 Chevy with a broken sway bar. Thirty-two cars started this race, which was led to the green flag by pole sitter

Bill Amick. I mentioned Frank Secrist because I still remember him bringing his USAC Sprint Car to our home in Mesa, Arizona, when I was a senior in high school. We changed the heads on the small-block Chevy and then rolled the car out to the street. Several of us hand-pushed the car and it lit off and he drove it around the neighborhood block. Man, that thing sounded really good! And by the time the police arrived, the car was back up and under our carport with several guys standing around it. The officers asked a few questions, said, "Well then, enjoy your afternoon," and then left. Just pure fun. Frank was there for a USAC race on the half-mile dirt track at Manzanita Speedway in Phoenix. This would have been around 1969.

One week after the Richmond race we were all back down in Atlanta for the '61 edition of the Dixie 400. This would require 267 laps on the 1.5-mile super speedway. All things considered, it was a pretty good race, but it was way less than what Rex and Louie went after. They struggled all day. Once again, Fireball grabbed the pole in Smokey's '61 Pontiac as Nelson Stacy qualified second, driving his yellow #29 Holman-Moody Ford. The race ran fairly smooth except for the accident involving Fred Lorenzen on lap 52. The '61 Ford engine erupted like a grenade and Fred spun in the oil. He hit the wall rear end–first and he hit it hard. He crawled out of the car OK. Roberts, Stacy, Pearson, Mathews, and Johnson all swapped the lead back and forth through pit stop cycles and good hard racing. Banjo had a 15-second lead with five laps to go when smoke poured from underneath his #94 Ford. He looked sure to win his first race, but it wasn't in the cards for him this day. Banjo suffered fatal engine problems, which left the door open for Fireball to cruise right into the lead. Then, when his fuel tank went dry with only two laps to go, Fireball coasted down pit road to get a splash of fuel to finish the race. Bunkie Blackburn, driving in relief of Junior Johnson, then inherited the lead. His pit crew was jumping for joy. Then lady luck struck again. Bunkie slowed while driving down the back stretch and entered the third turn very slowly. Blackburn was also out of fuel but he coasted by the flagman at about 50 mph. David Pearson was driving the Ray Fox '61 Pontiac sponsored by Daytona Kennel Club. He passed Blackburn at full speed coming through the fourth turn. Blackburn was flagged the winner, but Pearson immediately filed a protest and it took the NASCAR officials about an hour to figure out who actually won the race. David Pearson had just won another super speedway race in front of 30,000 spectators. This win paid him $9,330. Junior Johnson, Fireball, Jack Smith, and Richard Petty completed the top five. Ned Jarrett finished a fine seventh place, and much to our emotional pain, Rex finished a dismal 18th, still running at the end. Banjo finished 11th, Tiny Lund was 15th, Joe Weatherly 16th, Nelson Stacy was 19th, Buck Baker 25th, T.C. Hunt was 30th in his '61 Dodge, G.C. Spencer was 31st in his Chevrolet, Ralph Earnhardt was 35th, and Herb Tillman drove Baker's second Chrysler to a 39th-place finish. Of the 42 cars that started this race, only 21 were still running at the end. With Ned finishing seventh and Rex finishing 18th, this all but killed our chances for a repeat championship. Ned left the track with a 2,182 points lead over Rex.

The next weekend we were back up in Martinsville, Virginia, for the 48th race of the season. This was the Old Dominion 500 on the flat half-mile paper-clip track that taxed every piece of the race car and even some drivers' tempers, just like it does today. Fred Lorenzen qualified for the pole this time in his '61 H-M Ford. Outside pole would be Rex White in the '61 Chevrolet. Although Rex did lead the race in its late stages for

57 laps, when push came to shove, Joe Weatherly got the lead and drove on to victory lane. Rex finished second as he and Joe were the only two cars on the lead lap. Junior Johnson, Fireball and Ken Rush completed the top five this week. Drag racer Art Malone drove the second Petty Plymouth for an eighth-place finish. Ned Jarrett finished 13th with a blown motor on lap 407. Richard finished 17th with a blown engine and Fred Lorenzen finished 18th with rear end gear failure. Glen Wood finished 20th with a rear gear failure and Buck Baker fell out on lap 214 with a broken rocker arm. Wendell Scott was knocked out of the race on the second lap when broadsided by another car. With Rex finishing second and Ned finishing 13th, that narrowed the points gap from 2,182 down to 1,852. That brought a glimmer of hope back to the team.

Race #48 for the 1961 season was battled out back up in Wilkes County, North Carolina. North Wilkesboro Speedway would be the site for the Wilkes 200. Two hundred miles on a five-eighths-mile track required 320 laps be run. Again, this was an asphalt track that required a smooth driver, plenty of horsepower, and an excellent handling race car. This was Junior Johnson country and his fans came out in droves to watch him race. He was called the "Wild Man from Rhonda." He used his Pontiac horsepower and his big arms to wrestle that big Indian to a qualifying lap quick enough to sit that car on the pole. Second fastest was Banjo Matthews driving the Wood Brothers #21 1961 Ford. Rex started third and Jim Paschal started fourth. Thirty cars qualified for this race. Approximately 9,000 people showed up to watch Johnson, Weatherly and White trade the lead four times during the 320-lap contest. Rex won the race, with Fireball second and Richard third.

Charlotte Motor Speedway was only about an hour from our home in Spartanburg, so my mom and us kids didn't usually go until the night before the race or way early on race day. October 15, 1961, was the 49th race of the season and Rex normally ran pretty well at Charlotte. This race was titled the National 400, and would call for 267 laps on a 1.5-mile super speedway. Charlotte's World 600 winner, David Pearson, was fast enough to take pole position honors. Fireball Roberts, driving the black-and-gold Smokey Yunick '61 Pontiac, qualified for the second starting spot. Third and fourth starting spots were won by Banjo Matthews and Fred Lorenzen, both driving 1961 Fords. There was the usual razzle-dazzle before the race, which naturally involved Miss Linda Vaughn. Only by now she was no longer "Miss Pure Firebird," representing the racing gasoline; she was now "Miss Pontiac." Little did she know before the race that it would be Joe Weatherly she would kiss in victory lane for winning this race.

Once the race got underway, Pearson and Roberts traded the lead a few times and then Junior Johnson came into the picture and gave them both all they could handle. Junior led on five different occasions during the race. Bob Welborn was leading the race in the closing stages with Richard Petty and Joe Weatherly right on top of him. With just four laps to go, Little Joe took the lead from Welborn for good and drove to his victory in the '61 edition of the National 400. Coming in second was Richard Petty, third was Bob Welborn, Cotton Owens finished fourth, and fifth was our guy Rex White, driving the '61 Chevy #4. Weatherly won $9,510 for his victory. Rex brought back $1,800 for the team's fifth-place effort. We felt good about that finish. Joe Lee Johnson and Junior Johnson finished eighth and ninth. Tiny Lund came in 15th and Buck Baker was 17th. Points leader Ned Jarrett blew an engine on lap 233 and was still credited with an 18th-place finish. What did that do to the points total for the season to this point? Well, just a couple of weeks earlier Ned had had over a 2,000-point lead over Rex. After this race, his lead was shortened to 1,062 points. That glimmer of hope for the championship repeat began to brighten.

David Pearson lost a fuel pump and finished 21st with Wendell Scott right behind him in 22nd position. Elmo Langley was 24th and Spartanburg's Elmo Henderson finished 27th, still running at the end. Second-place starter Fireball Roberts was involved in a vicious accident on lap #113. His car spun and stalled sideways in the middle of the track. Fireball was hit in the passenger-side door by a wide-open-throttle Bill Morgan driving a Ford. Roberts was credited with a 29th-place finish, which didn't pay very well, but he did receive over $1,000 in lap money for leading those early race laps. Even as a young kid, I knew a fair amount about race cars and how they were built. I walked over to the '61 Pontiac that Fireball had crashed and got a real good look at it. After all, some day I was going to be a big-time NASCAR star and I needed to know this stuff, right? Well, the car was crashed bad enough to strike fear into me. I looked down at the Pontiac frame rail that I could see, and I could recognize exactly where the main hoop of the roll cage was welded to that frame rail. The impact had sheared that weld clean off and the paint from Morgan's Ford was clearly visible on the side of Roberts's seat. The car was literally bent in half. It was a total writeoff. Roberts stated later that he had to pick glass from his neck and back for two weeks. Bill Morgan was hospitalized with broken ribs and facial cuts.

Following Roberts, Fred Lorenzen was 31st after losing a head gasket, and #72 Bobby Johns was 32nd after falling out due to another accident. Third-place starter Banjo Matthews finished 33rd after his '61 Ford blew an engine on lap 54. Jack Smith was 37th and Nelson Stacy was 41st after losing his engine due to an overheating problem. It took approximately 3 hours and 20 minutes to finish the race. Forty-three cars had started this contest and 20 cars were still running at the end. These numbers attest to the fact that these were truly stock cars the way they were intended to be. These were nowhere near the purebred, full-tube chassis, wind-tunnel tested, multimillion-dollar stuff that races today. At this time, a race fan sitting in the stands didn't have to read the name on the front bumper to know what type of car his hero was driving. I, among many friends, am truly sorry the sport has lost this aspect.

Race #50 took us back to Bristol, Tennessee, for the second Bristol race of the season. This was a new track for this season and it was high time to test it out again. The Southeastern 500 was the race title. This would be a 500-lap race on a half-mile paved oval. The Bristol track was actually built between two mountains. The track is down in the valley and those two mountains made for sort of natural grandstand seating. Qualifying for the pole was Bobby Johns driving Jack Smith's Pontiac #47. Jack himself drove his #46 Pontiac and did not qualify well or finish well either. Second quick time went to #8, Joe Weatherly. Seventeen thousand people came out to watch a race that saw the leaders trade positions for about three and a half hours. Bobby led the first 30 laps and then Junior took over the point for almost 200 laps. Johns got the lead back for the next 100+ laps and then Fireball Roberts led for the next 50 laps. Junior grabbed the lead for the next 111 laps and then Rex White led for the next 23 laps. When Joe Weatherly took over the lead on lap 419, it was for good this time. Weatherly won the race for his second in a row.

Rex White finished a very welcome second place and Nelson Stacy finished third. They were the only cars on the lead lap at the end. Jim Paschal was fourth in a Pontiac and Emanuel Zervakis was fifth in a '61 Chevy. Points leader Ned Jarrett finished in sixth position, a full 19 laps off the pace. It made no difference, though. Sixth is still sixth even if he had finished 90 laps off the pace. He still received the same number of points. So Rex gained a little ground on him in the championship standings, but it was all for naught once we counted up the next two races. Rex had brought Ned's points lead down to 894 points. But the next two races only paid out a total of 800 points even if Rex won both of them. So the fact is, Ned Jarrett clinched his first NASCAR Grand National championship at this race on this day. Congratulations to the new champion!

Tenth, 11th and 12th places went to Bob Welborn, Buck Baker and G.C. Spencer. Wendell finished 16th and Bobby Johns finished 17th, still running at the end. Thirty-eight cars started this race and only 19 were running at the end. Nineteenth place and still running was Bill Latham driving a 1960 Chevy, and he was a full 60 laps down to the leaders. Among the half of the field that failed to finish were drivers Jack Smith, Tiny Lund, Richard Petty, Junior Johnson, Fireball Roberts, Johnny Allen, Bunkie Blackburn, Paul Lewis, Larry Thomas, Friday Hassler and Doug Yates. Of interest is the fact that one 1959 Nash Studebaker Lark entered the race and was black-flagged after three laps for being "too slow." That car was #88 and driven by Allen Franklin.

The half-mile dirt track over at Greenville-Pickens Speedway was the battlefield for the 51st race of the season. I remember this race as plain as day. My Uncle Crawford prepared two of Junior's Holly Farms Pontiacs for this race. They brought them both down to the track and invited Fireball to come up and run a dirt race. Roberts accepted the invitation and Junior told him to go practice both cars and choose the one he liked best. "I'm gonna outrun ya anyway," were Juniors words. So, on October 29, 1961, Fireball chose the '60 Pontiac, which was a little more to his liking. Surprising everyone there, Buck Baker got that '61 Chrysler barge around the track fast enough to take the pole starting spot. To no one's surprise, Joe Weatherly, who was on a hot streak, qualified for the outside front row. Junior qualified third and Jimmy Pardue qualified fourth. The condition of this dirt track had a lot to do with who qualified where for this race. During the race, the track "came to" the drivers and everyone picked up their pace a bit. At the end of the 200 laps, which required just over an hour and a half to complete, Junior Johnson took home the gold, driving the 1961 Holly Farms Pontiac. Another win for the Clements family! Second place went to Joe Weatherly in a '61 Pontiac and Rex finished third in my dad's '61 Chevy 409. Richard finished fourth in the #42 Petty Plymouth. Fifth went to Curtis Crider in a '61 Mercury and sixth was points leader Ned Jarrett. Maurice Petty drove the number 43 Petty "Mayflower" to a fine seventh-place finish. Wendell Scott finished eighth driving his own 1960 Chevy. Jack Smith, Fireball Roberts and Buck Baker all fell out with mechanical problems. Junior won $950 for his first-place finish and Rex won $435 for his third-place finish. Eighteen cars had started this race.

It was late that night when we got back to the shop to unload the cars. My cousin Gary was there too, and Fireball stopped by to have a drink and shoot the breeze before going home for the evening. We had a couple of gloves there and a baseball. So Gary and I asked Fireball, "Hey, come on outside and show us where you got that nickname." He obliged. My hand and Gary's hand must have stung for a week. And I'm pretty sure that

Fireball was taking it easy on us rookies. I can still hear the sound of the ball as it hit the pocket in my glove. BAM! It had a little sting on it too. We told Fireball it was probably too dark to be throwing the ball outdoors and we should probably get back in the shop. The memories we share when thinking back make this a perfect childhood.

The very next evening we were back down in Hillsboro, North Carolina, for race #52, the final race of the season. A really long season too.

This race was scheduled for 165 laps on a .9-mile track. Qualifying for the pole was Joe Weatherly in his #8 '61 Pontiac. Second fast time went to Rex White driving the 1961 Chevy 409. For this race, Junior and Fireball traded cars. Junior drove the '60 Holly Farms Pontiac and Fireball took the newer '61 Pontiac. Well, Junior qualified third and Fireball qualified fourth. We figured this was going to be a real barn burner. But once the green flag waved, Weatherly took off and led the first 100 laps. Then Junior led for two laps and then Weatherly took over the lead again and went the distance for a win of one lap over the entire field. Rex started second and finished second in his Louie Clements–prepared Chevrolet. Third went to Ned Jarrett in his '61 Chevrolet and fourth was a great finish for Maurice Petty. Fireball finished fifth in the '61 Holly Farms Pontiac. Richard finished 10th, Junior was 12th, Wendell was 15th and Buck Baker finished 17th. Only 20 cars started the race and eight of them were still running at the end. Rex trimmed Ned's points lead from 894 the week before, down to 830 at the end of the season. When you look at the final points tally for the season, you can only figure that some of the bad luck that Rex suffered from during the year played right into Ned's hands. Ned even told me himself that after Rex and Louie had given Chevrolet the recommendation for him to be given a Chevrolet deal for the season, he feels like he flat lucked into the points victory. Well, nowadays we define luck as when preparation meets opportunity. Ned and Bud were prepared for the right opportunity. So once again, we held our glasses high to the new NASCAR champion. Now, let's examine the final scoreboard.

Ned won *one* race and Rex won seven races. Ned had 23 top fives and Rex had 29 top fives. Ned had 34 top tens and Rex had 38 top tens. Ned won a total of $41,055. Rex won $56,394. So what happened? The points system has changed many times over the years in NASCAR. Under the system they ran in 1961, "consistency" paid better than winning. That's pretty much all there is to it. I do remember, though, that Ned made a vow to himself that he would come back and win a championship the way he wanted to win it: by winning races and being the top dog. He made good on the vow to himself during the 1965 NASCAR Grand National season, a good happy ending for a well-deserving champion.

Finishing third in the '61 points chase was Emanuel Zervakis (probably another reason for that Darlington protest), fourth in the points went to Joe Weatherly, and fifth went to Fireball Roberts. Crawford's car with Junior driving finished sixth in the points this year. Richard Petty finished eighth and Buck Baker, two-time national champion himself, finished 10th this year. Wendell Scott entered and competed in 23 races in his first year of racing in the Grand National division. He scored five top-10 finishes and won a total of $3,240. Doug Yates finished 27th in the points, scored two top-10 finishes and won $1,090, the least amount of money paid out at the banquet.

I have recently completed a restoration of the '61 Rex White Chevy and hope to have it in a museum in Myrtle Beach, South Carolina, very soon.

CHAPTER 7

1962: She's Real Fine, My 409

We were excited going into the 1962 season with a new and slicker body style and the new, more refined 409 engine rated at 380 hp with one 4-barrel carb. That is, until my dad and Rex got out to the Arizona proving grounds and actually ran that engine. It was a slug just like last year's engine was. It *may* have made a few more horsepower, but it was way out of the Pontiac and Ford league. And the Plymouths even came out with their wedge engine rated at 385 hp. They ran pretty well, too. But the Pontiacs were stout enough to just pull out of the draft and go on by themselves. I have seen recent magazine articles on the buildups of the engines of that period and run on today's computerized

The restored 1961 White and Clements Chevy Grand National Car.

engine dynos. The best blueprinted 409 Chevy was just over 400 hp in NASCAR trim. The Pontiacs and Fords were easily over 450 hp in legal NASCAR trim. Fifty hp is a huge deficit to overcome on the race track. But we marched on. Throughout the year, Duntov would send cylinder heads, intake and exhaust manifolds and dump tubes with variable tapers to them. Camshaft development was an ongoing struggle. The 409 made good torque but just no horsepower for stock car racing. The basic design with the combustion chamber in the cylinder instead of the head was not working well with the port layout. The air had to turn too many directions, too many times. Pontiacs and Fords had them covered. Ford's problem was the Galaxie body style with that blunt rear window. That was hurting them on super speedways. However, on at least one occasion, Ford got one car, the #28 Ford for Fred Lorenzen, into the Atlanta 500 with what they called their "Starlift" roofline. I even heard they had one passenger car built and placed inside a Ford dealership in Atlanta in case NASCAR officials wanted to actually see a production version of it. It was discovered to be a one-off and NASCAR outlawed it after that one race. That car did make a trip to the Bonneville Salt Flats, though. Ford was pleased with the results.

Something really cool occurred when Rex and Louie went back down to Rathmann's Chevrolet dealership to pick up the new '62 Bel Air bubble top with the 409 and a 4-speed. They also picked up a new spare 409 too. All this was given to them from Chevrolet, in an under-the-table fashion. While at Jim Rathmann's, they noticed a gold anodized, aluminum monocoque racing kart with light blue leather upholstery and a McCulloch engine on it. They brought it home and put it up on a high shelf where everybody who entered that shop could see it. When I first saw it, I knew that somehow, I had to have it. That kart remained up on that same shelf for one year. Then, for Christmas of '62, my dad got it down one day and got it to running and race-ready. He brought it home and told me merry Christmas. Rex donated a brand-new McCall helmet and a new clear bubble shield too. I was set to go racing. Once I got mine, my Uncle Crawford went and got a family friend and team race mechanic to go find one for Gary. Dickie Caldwell came back with a twin-engine, dual-railed Simplex racing kart with two modified West Bend 710s on alcohol and nitro. With both motors hooked up, his kart was a monster! More on that later.

The Big Three auto builders were on the verge of jumping back into racing with both feet. The AMA ban on auto manufacturers from 1957 had been skirted around for years by the manufacturers giving "marine" speed equipment to special dealers to dole out to a select few racers. Winning races on Sunday still amounted to selling cars on Monday and everybody wanted back in the deal. So demand slowly built up until the manufacturers came out and told the AMA that they were going racing and that was that. Well… it wasn't quite that simple. But in essence, that is sort of what happened. Little by little, better parts became available. And, little by little, cash money started to show up in some shops' bank accounts.

Race number one for the '62 season was actually run on November 5, 1961, at the half-mile dirt track in Concord, North Carolina. Twenty-six cars and 3,000 spectators showed up for the 200-lap race. Joe Weatherly and Jack Smith grabbed the front-row starting spots with some pretty quick qualifying laps. Junior Johnson and Rex White took over the second row. Once the green flag waved, Weatherly took the point and paced

Louie Clements and Bradley Dennis (accepting for Smokey Yunick) receiving the Master Mechanics of the Year Awards.

the field for the largest portion of the race. After receiving the white flag and heading down into the first turn, Jack got his right front under Joe and they bumped. Joe spun out and Jack led the final lap, which of course is the one we all want to lead. The difference in their payday was $800 to Smith and $525 to Weatherly. There were some harsh words exchanged between the two after the race but the NASCAR official in charge said all he saw was two racers racing very hard. Cotton Owens finished third, giving Pontiac a 1-2-3 sweep. Fourth place went to our car with Rex White at the wheel. Ned Jarrett finished fifth. Richard was 13th, Wendell was 14th, Buck Baker 15th, and Junior Johnson was 20th due to a blown engine on lap 42. Maurice Petty finished 26th driving the number 43 Petty Plymouth. I don't know why he and Richard traded car numbers back and forth. Maybe it had to do with the points system in place at that time. Sixteen of the 26 cars finished the race.

November 12, the very next weekend, we were back up at Weaverville, North Carolina, for a 200-lap race on the half-mile paved oval. Again, Weatherly took the pole with Junior Johnson on the outside pole. Tommy Irwin and Ned Jarrett started on the second row. On a positive note for this race, it was named the Rain Check 200 as most of the 6,500 spectators were admitted free if they had their ticket stub from the last race there when the track tore up and the race had to be shortened. This was the track promoters' way of trying to make it up to them.

At the start of the race, Joe Weatherly took the lead for 16 laps before Rex White passed him and led for the next 15 laps. Then Jim Paschal, driving the "Neil Pontiac" #44, took the lead for about 30 laps. Buck Baker then put his big Chrysler on the point for the next five laps before allowing Paschal back by for 23 laps. On lap 94, Rex White took the lead for good this time and was never really contested for the lead again. Rex won the race, which paid $800 and required almost one and a half hours to complete. Buck Baker was second, Joe Weatherly third, Jack Smith fourth, and Ned Jarrett fifth. Richard was seventh in the #43 this week and Paschal finished eighth. G.C. Spencer finished 22nd, still running at the end. Junior Johnson and Joe Lee Johnson finished 26th and 27th.

Couldn't help but notice that the '61 Lynn Holloway Pontiac driven by Tom Pistone at the start of the '61 season was being driven by a different driver almost each week for the last portion of the '61 season and starting out the '62 season too. This week it was driven by Fred Harb, who fell out due to a loss of brakes on lap 60. At the end of this race we actually had a three-way deadlock for the points lead. Rex White, Jack Smith and Joe Weatherly each had a total of 752 points.

Finally, race #3 took us kids out of school for speed weeks at Daytona. Man, life just didn't get any better. We got out of school for a week and got to go the races too! Man, this was Heaven! Both

Closeup of the NASCAR logo on Louie's Master Mechanics Award.

Full-length view of the Master Mechanics Award.

Rex posing with the 1962 Jim Rathmann–sponsored Chevrolet.

of the 100-mile qualifier races were held on the same day. That was February 16, 1962. This would be the first time the new 1962 cars would be shown in competition. After these two races, pretty much everybody knew what you had. And it didn't take long for the Pontiac dominance to shine through. As a matter of fact, the car that Fireball Roberts drove was the black-and-gold 1962 Pontiac #22 built by Smokey Yunick. This car was so dominant that it became known as the "Daytona Dominator." I looked inside this car and was truly shocked at just how rudimentary the roll cage was. The bars were just plain ugly. The main hoops in the car didn't position like any other car there. The one hoop ran from the right front corner to the left rear corner. Then, the other hoop ran from the left front corner to the right rear corner. The bends looked sloppy and by the time the secondary bars were added, I could see no advantage to doing the bars like that at all. This is of course my personal opinion, although I have certainly heard this same thing from just about anyone who speaks of this car. But the one thing we can all agree on, this sucker would flat out tote the mail! Fireball qualified for the pole at 158.744 mph. That was indeed getting it done in 1962.

For the first 100-mile qualifier this year, Fireball had the pole with Junior on his bumper starting third. The two Pontiacs broke away from the field and set sail for no-man's land. They traded off the lead back and forth, neither wanting to use all of his fuel

White and Clements crew prior to 1962 Daytona 500. Left to right: unknown, James Hylton, Ken Miller, Louie Clements, Rex White, Wes Roarke, Buddy Payne and Slick Owens.

to "tow" the other car. Sure enough, Junior ran out of fuel on the last lap and coasted home fifth while Fireball won the caution-free race in record time. Second was Jack Smith in a Pontiac and third was Cotton Owens in another Pontiac. The first Ford was fourth-place finisher Dan Gurney, driving the Holman-Moody '62 Ford #0. Fifth went to a coasting Junior Johnson. Fred Lorenzen's new '62 Ford #28 blew an engine on the eighth lap, which gave him a 24th-place finish. I'm sure Fred doesn't know me, but he is still one of my heroes today and will always be. He was smart, smooth, and fast.

The second qualifying race started with Darel Dieringer on the pole driving Ray Fox's '62 Pontiac #39 with Banjo Matthews outside in his own '62 Pontiac, white with the number 94 emblazoned on it. Dieringer was involved in an early race crash which took out six cars from the field of 25 starters. After that, all the action up front came down to one Pontiac, one Ford and one Chevy. That's the stuff real NASCAR races are made of. Joe Weatherly held the point for the win and Nelson Stacy drove his new H-M '62 Ford home second. Third place had us all jumping up and down on my mom's Chevy wagon. Rex White brought that beautiful Venus gold-and-white #4 Chevy 409 home in third spot. Those were the only three cars on the lead lap at the conclusion of this race. Richard Petty and Johnny Allen rounded out the top five. Indy car driver Wally Dallenbach's #37 Ford finished sixth, one lap down. Ned Jarrett finished 16th because of a broken rocker arm in his 409 Chevy.

All things considered, anyone who was there would have to admit that this was for certain the Fireball Roberts Show. Over 58,000 spectators showed up for this race. That was a fantastic crowd for those days. The Daytona 500 had started to really catch on as *the* race to win by this time. The Darlington Southern 500 was still a very relished crown jewel, but Daytona had made its place in history by now. The lead changed hands several times among the top five cars throughout the race. Fireball and Smokey had stated that they intended to go or blow. So Fireball was the right man for the job. He put the pedal down and ran the #22 Pontiac wide open the entire way. Doing so caused him to run dry on fuel twice. Luckily, he was within coasting distance from his pits each time and got right back into the hunt. Richard Petty finished second with his new '62 Plymouth, which had considerably more horsepower than his '61 Plymouth displayed. Third place went to Joe Weatherly in a '62 Pontiac, and fourth went to third-place starter Jack Smith, also driving a '62 Pontiac. With a new engine bolted in his '62 Ford, Freddy Lorenzen finished fifth and David Pearson drove the #39 Pontiac for Ray Fox in the 500 to bring it home in sixth place. That favorite race car of mine, the #4 Louie Clements Chevy driven by Rex White, finished seventh in the '62 Daytona 500. Not a scratch on it, just as pretty and fine-sounding as when the race started. Eighth was Banjo Matthews and ninth went to Ned Jarrett with Bob Welborn 10th.

Rookie Billy Wade drove a '62 Ford to finish 18th and Dan Gurney's H-M '62 Ford #0 blew an engine, which relegated him to a 27th-place finish. Buck and Buddy Baker finished 29th and 30th in their new red '62 Chryslers. Junior Johnson blew his Pontiac's engine for a 34th-place finish and soon-to-be NASCAR superstar Cale Yarbrough finished 48th and last place due to a blown engine in his '61 Ford on lap 4. The race took just over 3 hours and 10 minutes and Fireball's pole speed was 156.999 mph! The win was worth $24,190 for Roberts and Yunick. Rex's seventh-place finish brought in $1,550. All of the cars from 20th to 48th received $400 each. This was already race number five on a season which felt like it had just started.

One thing I really liked about the '62 Chevys were those 409 engines. They had their problems, which I was learning to understand at the time. But to just look at them, they looked like monsters! I still build engines for a living and I still like that look of the Chevy orange block and heads with the silver valve covers. The '62 got a new intake manifold that was a bit taller than the '61 engine. If you have a good 409 today or a rebuildable one, you can bore it .060" over and install the crankshaft from a 454 Chevy and get 474 cubic inches. It's not too hard to pull about 550 hp at 6,000 rpms with the new parts available today. There is a guy in Atlanta by the name of Llamar Walden who has built up some aluminum heads for the 409 blocks. They are about a $10,000 option on the engines he builds. But he is cranking out some serious horsepower today too! Man, just to take a ride in a time machine and carry one of those engines back to my dad in 1962 would have put a smile of the face of the Chevy fans.

Concord, North Carolina, held the sixth race of the season on its half-mile dirt track on February 25. It was scheduled for 200 laps but a terrific downpour came and about washed us away. The race had already been washed out once before. So, at the 78-lap mark, NASCAR threw the checkered flag and called it a day. Rex was a contender for the win but was caught up in an accident with Fred Lorenzen and Stick Elliot. That left Joe Weatherly in the lead for the win. Richard was second, Ralph Earnhardt was third, Jack

Crawford Clements (left) and Bill Ellis, mechanics for Junior Johnson Holly Farms Poultry Pontiac.

Smith fourth and Buddy Baker was fifth. The accident left Rex and Fred in 15th and 16th positions. Ned was the first car out of the race with a blown engine on lap 17. About 8,000 people came out to watch a race that became a mudfest.

It was on to race #7 at Weaverville, North Carolina. This was another 200-lap race on the half-mile paved track. Rex always got around Weaverville well. This day he took the pole and set sail at the drop of the green flag. He led for the first 119 before Tommy Irwin took the lead for 10 laps. Then Rex took the lead again until lap 143, when he blew the right front tire and popped the wall. Joe Weatherly held on to win this one, with Jim Paschal, Buddy Baker, Maurice Petty and Jack Smith rounding out the top five. Richard finished eighth with Wendell 12th, Ned was 16th, Rex was 18th and Junior Johnson was 20th, having crashed by himself on the eighth lap.

Two weeks later we went to Savannah, Georgia, for the St. Patrick's Day 200. Two hundred laps on a half-mile dirt track was today's challenge. Rex White quickly qualified the 1961 Louie Clements Chevy for the pole position. Darel Dieringer took the outside pole. At the start, Joe Weatherly used that famous Pontiac horsepower to jump out into the lead on the first lap. He led the first 36 laps before Ned Jarrett took the lead for the next 80 laps. Cotton Owens led for about 34 laps, and then on lap 153, Jack Smith took the lead for good. Jack won the race and Cotton finished second. They were the only cars on the lead lap at the end. Joe Weatherly was third and Curtis Crider came in fifth. Rex dropped out with 17 laps remaining but still managed to be credited with a fourth-place finish. The Chevy broke an axle and ruined what was shaping up to be another win for the team. Wendell was seventh, Buddy Baker was eighth, Spencer was 12th and Ned was credited with 13th. Richard lost a ball joint and that scored him a 14th-place finish. Approximately 7,000 spectators came out to see this race on St. Patty's Day.

The very next night we drove to Hillsboro, North Carolina, and Rex and Louie again put the '61 Chevy back into action. Hillsboro was a .9-mile dirt track and the race was to be run over 110 laps. Joe Weatherly took the pole with his '61 Pontiac and Richard Petty took the outside pole with the new '62 Plymouth sporting the new 385-hp Wedge engine. Rex qualified third with Cotton starting fourth. When the race started, Joe took the point for the first 24 laps. Then Richard took over for about 23 laps. Weatherly took the lead again on lap 48 and led until lap 102. But Richard was coming on strong right then. Petty took the point from laps 103 to 105 when Rex decided to make his move. He led the final four laps for a very sweet victory and a $1,000 payday. Petty was second, Paschal third, Jack Smith fourth, and Buddy Baker came in fifth. Maurice Petty finished sixth driving the number 41 Plymouth. Together, the Pettys brought home $840. Ned finished 10th in his '62 Chevy. By this time Wendell had bought Ned's '61 championship-winning car and finished 12th with it. About 9,000 fans came out to watch the 21 starters take the green flag. Only 14 finished the race. Tommy Irwin crashed the Monroe Shook Chevy on the first lap and received $50 for competing in race number nine of the season.

April Fool's Day was just two weeks later and Rex was no fool on this day. Neither was Louie. We towed the '61 Chevy back up the road to the Richmond Fairgrounds Speedway. The Richmond 250 would be a 250-lap race over a half-mile dirt track. Mother Nature had had her way with the speedway the night before with a torrential downpour. The track was a virtual mud pit when the racers arrived to prepare for the race. Road graders and passenger cars were used to help run in the track a bit so the race could proceed. As it turned out, the race didn't start until after 5 P.M., which was two hours later than planned. There was no qualifying so they all had to draw from a hat for their starting positions. Wouldn't you just know that good ol' Herman Beam would draw the pole. During the pace lap, he drove into the pits and let every other car go on by. Afterward he stated that he was just not comfortable starting in front of all the hot dogs. Twenty-five cars started the race and when the green flag said "go," Richard Petty was listening. He set sail to lead the first 34 laps. Then it was Ned's turn to lead for six laps and then Junior took a turn at the point for about 10 laps. Marvin Panch took the lead for about 15 laps when he was sidelined by overheating problems. Next, Jim Paschal took his turn up front for 15 laps, driving the Cliff Stewart '62 Pontiac #2. On the 84th lap, Ned Jarrett put his '62 Chevy up front and held on for 88 laps. That was the most dominant performance to that point in the race. With just seven laps to go, Rex White drove the Louie Clements '61 Chevy into the lead for good. After drawing for starting positions due to the problems drying the track out, Rex had to start 20th this week. He had a lot of hard work to do to climb that rope to the top. We didn't know it at that moment, but NASCAR had made the decision to throw the checkered flag on lap 180 of the scheduled 250 because of darkness. So Rex brought home the win and the $1,850 that went with it. Louie received a very nice wall plaque for the Outstanding Winning Mechanical Performance of the race. This award was given by the Wynn Oil Company and signed by Carl E. Wynn. It was welcomed as a nice classy touch for the weekend. Finishing second, one lap down, was Ned Jarrett in his '62 Chevy 409. Third went to Junior Johnson in the Holly Farms '61 Pontiac tuned by good ol' Uncle Crawford! Fourth place was Joe Weatherly driving the Bud Moore '61 Pontiac and fifth went to NASCAR's first superstar, Fireball Roberts, in another rare short-track appearance. He was driving the other Crawford Clements–tuned 1961 Holly Farms Pontiac. G.C. Spencer was eighth and Jim Bray finished 13th. Jack Smith was 14th with Jim Paschal running 16th. Marvin Panch was 17th and Wendell Scott finished 18th. Richard Petty lost a radiator on lap 34, which left him with a 20th-place finish. Buck Baker ran out of brakes and settled for 24th position. Ralph Moody came out of retirement to run this race but an overheating problem took him out early for the 25th and final position. The race ran for about an hour and 45 minutes.

Race number 11 took us all back down to Columbia, South Carolina, and Ned Jarrett was known to get around this track as fast as anybody, and tonight would be no different. Joe Weatherly took the pole in the '61 Pontiac #8 and Jack Smith started outside front row in another '61 Pontiac. Once the green flag waved, the Arclite 200 saw some good racing up front between Joe Weatherly, Jack Smith, Ralph Earnhardt and Rex White. They were pretty much all in a wad and fighting for land. As the race wore on and they started to become separated from each other, Ned was sure enough back up front. He kept the point for the win with Joe Weatherly running second. They were the only two cars on the lead lap at the end. Third place went to Jack Smith and fourth to Jim Paschal. Fifth place was brought home by #48 G.C. Spencer in his 1960 Chevy. Spencer was a dirt specialist from his modified days. Sixth place went to Rex White driving the '61 Chevy #4, while Richard Petty and Buck Baker came home on seventh and eighth positions. Buddy Baker was 13th and Wendell came back in 16th spot. Of the 19 starters, 16 were still running at the end. Jarrett earned $1,200 for his victory.

The Gwyn Staley 400 was the next race on the schedule. This was held up in North Wilkesboro, North Carolina, where the fans usually got to see an excellent race. This race required 400 laps on the five-eighths-mile paved track. Junior Johnson qualified for the pole again. And Joe Weatherly was fast enough for second starting spot. Third-place qualifier was rookie Billy Wade and fourth-place starter was none other than Fireball Roberts driving the Banjo Matthews '62 Pontiac #22. Legend has it that Smokey and Fireball broke up their team just after Fireball won the Daytona 500 this same season. I have read Smokey's book, and in it he clearly states that he really didn't like Fireball much. Seems that Smokey pretty much said whatever was on his mind, whenever he felt like it.

The green flag waved and the roar of 35 NASCAR Grand National stock cars filled the air around North Wilkesboro. Over 9,200 people came out to watch Junior lead the first 19 laps. Then Fireball took the point for the next 94 laps. Weatherly took his turn in the lead and held it for 110 laps. Next, Richard Petty and Ned Jarrett traded the lead back and forth for the next 118 laps. Petty walked away with the victory this day with Fred Lorenzen the only other driver on the lead lap with him. Pole sitter Junior Johnson finished third, and fourth place went to Fireball Roberts, who was two laps down because of a problem in the pits that cost him three laps. He was the fastest car in the second half of the race and that allowed him to make up one of those laps under the green. There was no "lucky dog" in those days. If you wanted it, you had to race for it. Darel Dieringer and Buck Baker were fifth and sixth. Rex White ran very strong and kept the car in the top five, just biding his time like he always did. But this week that didn't work. After 162 laps the oil pressure on the 409 went to zero. He pulled it in and parked it. That gave him a final position for the day of 31st. Wow, he was paid a whopping sum of $25 for that, too. Man, have things changed.

Rookie Billy Wade brought his Pontiac home for a fine 10th-place finish and in a very rare appearance, Herb Thomas drove his '62 Chevy home for a 14th-place finish. What a treat it was to see a man who was already a legend driving that day! Bobby Johns was 16th and Tommy Irwin was 18th. Ned lost his 409 engine on lap 318 for a 24th-place finish and Ford man Nelson Stacy lost a transmission on lap 289 for a 25th-place finish. Wendell finished 27th place, still running at the end of the day. And there really were cars that had a worse day than Rex. Marvin Panch, driving the Wood Brothers Ford, lost the rear end gear and finished 32nd, with David Pearson right behind him having lost oil pressure in his '62 Pontiac. Doug Yates and Bobby Waddell completed the field.

One rather strange thing happened during the course of this race. The fuel trucks ran out of fuel and some mechanics were actually out in the infield siphoning gas from their passenger cars to finish the race. The caution flag was thrown on lap 250 to allow the fuel truck out to go get some more fuel. It did not make it back in time. Some crew members were actually running with buckets and hoses pulling gas from the first car they came to. The race took the better part of three hours to complete.

Race number 13 proved to be an unlucky number for our team. This race was held back over at the Greenville-Pickens half-mile dirt track. It was scheduled for 200 laps on April 19, 1962. Ned Jarrett qualified on the pole with his B.G. Holloway '62 Chevy 409. Second fastest time was set by Richard Petty in his '62 Plymouth. Third fastest was Jack Smith with his '61 Pontiac and fourth quickest went to Rex White in the Louie Clements '61 Chevy. When the green flag gave the start to this contest, Ned, Rex, Richard, and Jack all headed for parts unknown. They were all chasing the proverbial rabbit, and fast too. But on lap 41, the darned old 409 in Rex's car gave up the ghost and laid down for the final time. It was used up and needed a real serious makeover. Ned, Jim Paschal and Joe Weatherly soldiered on to put on a good race for the fans. Ned brought home the win in fine fashion, bringing home $1,200 too. Paschal was second in a '62 Pontiac, and third went to Joe Weatherly in his '61 Pontiac. They were the only three on the lead lap. Fourth was a great finish for Wendell Scott and a good payday for him too. Spencer was 10th and Richard was 11th after losing a ball joint on lap 139. Third-place qualifier Jack Smith fell out on lap 89 for a 13th-place finish. Buck Baker lost a read end gear for 16th spot, Rex was 17th, and George Green and George Alsobrook experienced engine problems, relegating them to 18th and 19th positions.

Two days later the race was held at Myrtle Beach, South Carolina, on the half-mile dirt track for 200 laps. After experiencing engine problems two races in a row, Rex and Louie decided to pass this one up. The race went right on without them, just as does life. Jack Smith won the race with Richard Petty second and Ned Jarrett third. Tom Cox and Curtis Crider rounded out the top five. Wendell finished ninth with Neil Castles in 10th. Joe Weatherly was 13th and Buck Baker and G.C. Spencer were 16th and 17th.

Rex and Louie on the cover of the North Wilkesboro program, April 15, 1962.

The race required about one-and-a-half hours to complete, and Smith earned $1,000 for his victory.

Race number 15 brought us all together again up in Martinsville, Virginia. This would be the Virginia 500 which was 500 laps on a half-mile paved oval track. The track is more of a paper-clip design where the mechanics have to install new brake linings right before every race. And they run a pretty deep gear, which helps the engine's compression to slow the car down for the corners to help save on the brakes. That very low gear also helps the cars accelerate off the corners but it's very hard on the gear itself. In those days, we didn't yet have the inner axle seals we have now. Nor did we have the internal lube pumps for the rear gear we have now. The gear lubricant is also much improved over the old 90/140 lube with the smell of iodine in it.

Qualifying for the pole was Fred Lorenzen with his teammate Nelson Stacy on the outside pole for an all–Ford front row. Third starter was Marvin Panch in the Wood Brothers Ford #21 and fourth was Bobby Johns driving his dad's '62 Pontiac. The lead changed hands several times between Fred Lorenzen, Nelson Stacy, Rex White, Junior Johnson, Richard Petty and Fireball Roberts. But in the end, it was Richard Petty who found victory lane. He and second-place Joe Weatherly were the only two cars on the lead lap at the finish. Rex White brought the '62 Louie Clements Chevy home for a well-deserved third-place finish. Fourth went to Fred Lorenzen and fifth was credited to Lee Petty, who competed for the first time since his near debilitating accident the year before while qualifying for the '61 Daytona 500. Lee received relief from Jim Paschal for this race. Paschal was a long time friend of the Pettys and often drove one of their cars. Marvin Panch was sixth with Jack Smith seventh. Billy Wade was eighth, with Larry Frank ninth, and Darel Dieringer 10th driving the Bob Osiecki '62 Dodge. Ned finished 13th with Wendell 14th and Fireball 18th due to a rear gear failure. Johnny Allen, Nelson Stacy and Junior all fell out with rear gear failures. They were credited with 20th, 21st and 22nd positions. Of the 32 cars that entered this race, only 14 were running at the end. Fourteen thousand five hundred came out to this race, probably just to watch me jump up and down and turn in circles in the back of the tow truck, cheering Rex on every lap.

As was quickly becoming tradition, we raced again on Easter Monday at Bowman Gray Stadium in Winston-Salem, North Carolina. If I didn't say it before, this track has that Roman coliseum feel to it. The concrete grandstands surround about 80 percent of the track itself. The track is a flat quarter-mile paved oval around a football field. The track is still run today and is the site of some very good stock car racing. This day, April 23, 1962, was the 16th race for the season and Rex wasted no time in qualifying his '62 Chevy on the pole. Qualifying outside front row was once again my uncle's car with Junior Johnson. I believe this was the fifth time they had done this. With our family sitting right with my uncle's family, my cousins, we always enjoyed the races where our dads' cars were on the front row together. As long as either car was in first or second, it really didn't matter. This is where the winning spirit was instilled into all of us kids.

Third starter was Joe Weatherly and fourth qualifier was Ned Jarrett with his 409 Chevy. Johnny Bruner waved the green flag and the house came alive again. The cars sounded awesome with their open exhaust pipes blaring and the roar bouncing off the concrete walls in such close quarters. Rex took the point at the start and never looked back. He won this one in fine fashion, although the record books do show that the race was shortened and halted on lap 108 due to a very hard downpour of rain. Junior was in the pits getting two new tires when the caution came out and that dropped him to a 15th-place finish. Second place went to Jack Smith, third was Joe Weatherly and fourth was George Dunn. Richard brought the Petty Plymouth home for fifth place. Ned was seventh and Spencer was ninth. Wendell was 16th, Neil Castles was 17th, rookie Billy Wade finished 19th because of an overheating problem on lap 3. Rex was paid $565 for the victory and the top four cars were on the lead lap at the end. This race required about 38 minutes to complete with its abbreviated format. Heck, I take longer naps than that nowadays during the Cup races on Sunday afternoons!

So, what else was going on in 1962 besides NASCAR Grand National races and the infamous Cuban missile crisis? Well, for one thing, Sam Cooke had a #1 hit with "Bring It on Home to Me." The Four Seasons had a hit with their song "Sherry" and the Beach Boys sang "She's Real Fine My 409" and also "Surfin' Safari." The most famous death of 1962 would have to be that of Marilyn Monroe. Also, Walter Cronkite took over the nightly news on CBS. Johnny Carson began hosting *The Tonight Show* on NBC and stayed as host for 30 years. Television premieres for 1962 were *The Jetsons* on ABC, *The Beverly Hillbillies* on CBS, *McHale's Navy* on ABC, *The Match Game* on NBC and the five-day afternoon version of *To Tell the Truth* on CBS.

Feast or famine: Just an expression? Sometimes it seems to hold true in sports as well as life. Such was the case this year with the Chevy 409. Race #17 took us back up the hill to Bristol, Tennessee, for the Volunteer 500. This would be 500 laps on a half-mile paved track. Fireball Roberts took the pole with a one-lap average speed of 81.374 mph. Starting second would be Fred Lorenzen in the 1962 H-M Ford #28. Marvin Panch was third with Nelson Stacy fourth. When the green flag started this race, Fireball took off and led the first 61 laps and pretty much had the field covered. Then the ignition coil failed on his Banjo Matthews Pontiac and he lost 12 laps in the pits due to the lengthy repairs. Once back on the track, Fireball put on a racing clinic for everyone else. He made up six of those laps under green flag conditions. That was surely a show of dominance if there ever was one! At the end of the 500 laps, Our friend Bobby Johns had won the race driving his father's blue-and-white #72 Pontiac. Bobby was still six laps ahead of second-place Fireball Roberts. Third place went to Jack Smith in a '62 Pontiac and fourth place went to Gentleman Ned Jarrett driving his #11 Chevy. Fifth spot was secured by Tom Cox driving a '60 Plymouth. Of the 36 cars that started this race, only 11 were still running at the end. Maurice Petty and Nelson Stacy were the only two cars involved in an accident. Twenty-three cars fell out with mechanical failures. Top contenders such as Rex White, Junior Johnson, Fred Lorenzen, David Pearson, Joe Weatherly, Buck Baker, Marvin Panch, Richard Petty, and many more just plain had a bad day.

Rex's '62 Chevy 409 broke a rocker arm, as was fairly common with those engines. Lorenzen, Richard Petty, Johnny Allen, Joe Lee Johnson, G.C. Spencer and Larry Thomas all blew engines. The fifth-place car of Tom Cox was 30 laps down to the winner, Johns. Bobby collected $4,405 for his win and Fireball brought back $2,500 for second place. Rex broke the rocker arm on lap 109 which landed him in the 29th position and paid a mere $125. This was one of the "famine" races. And, it didn't get much better the next week either.

Southside Speedway in Richmond, Virginia, was the site chosen for the 18th race of the season. Rex got around this little track very well and wasted no time in setting the fast time of the day which gave him the pole position. Once the race got underway, Rex took off and led the first 134 laps unchallenged. It looked to us like he was on a Sunday stroll and due for another win. But as they say, it ain't over till it's over. On lap 134, the 409 Chevy scattered and left Rex to coast into the pits and park his ride for the evening. Jimmy Pardue took over the point and held onto it for the duration of the race. This was Pardue's first-ever Grand National victory. Jimmy was a likable 31-year-old driver and everyone was happy to see him win his first victory in the toughest stock car series in the world. Second place went to Jack Smith and third to Richard Petty, this week driving a '60 Petty Plymouth. Fourth was Joe Weatherly and fifth went to Jim Paschal, driving Cliff Stewart's '62 Pontiac. Approximately 4,500 people came out to watch 16 cars start the race and 12 of them finish.

The very next night we cruised up to Hickory, North Carolina, again for the Hickory 250. Race #19 called for 250 laps on a .4-mile dirt track. Jack Smith's '62 Pontiac #47 qualified for the pole with Jack at the wheel. Junior Johnson drove his '61 Pontiac #27 to start outside front row. Louie got the '62 put back together by working through the night on the blown 409 engine. Must have done a good job because Rex qualified third with it. When the green flag signaled the start of the Race, Jack Smith took off on a mission and was never seriously threatened. He won this race handily. Rex drove an exceptionally good race for a second-place finish. A good finish had eluded this team for the past couple of weeks. Joe Weatherly was third and Jim Paschal was fourth. Ralph Earnhardt drove a '61 Pontiac home in fifth place, just ahead of Richard Petty's '62 Plymouth in sixth. Johnny Allen was 10th, Ned Jarrett finished 13th, Junior Johnson 14th, G.C. Spencer was 15th, and Wendell finished 16th. The race lasted just shy of an hour and a half in front of a crowd estimated to be around 10,000 people strong.

On the next evening we were over in Concord, North Carolina, for the 200-lap dirt race on the half-mile oval. The track was in terrible shape. The dust was so thick you couldn't see anything going on and the racing surface was full of potholes. It was a total and complete disaster. Some racers chose to stick it out, but Ned Jarrett, the reigning champion, retired from the race on the first lap in disgust with track conditions. Rex and Louie had the '62 Chevy very fast in practice and qualifying, but an electrical fire on the first lap took Rex out of the race. Approximately 8,000 people turned out to see a pathetic race in which only seven of the twenty entries finished. Only two cars were on the lead lap. They were the winner, Joe Weatherly, and second-place Cotton Owens. Wendell Scott had a very good finish at third spot, even if he was eight laps down. Fourth was Jack Smith, nine laps down, and fifth went to Maurice Petty, 12 laps down to the leaders. Richard Petty broke an axle, Ralph Earnhardt ran out of brakes, Johnny Allen and Jim Paschal both just pulled into the pits and withdrew from the race after 33 laps. G.C. Spencer's car also broke an axle. Everyone was happy to see this carnage come to an end. Richard Petty led the first 134 laps and Joe Weatherly led from there to the 200-lap finish line. He earned $1,000 for his efforts this evening.

Darlington's Rebel 300 was the brainchild of track promoter Bob Colvin. And Bob was very good at what he did. The day after the 1960 race at Darlington, Mr. Colvin took my mom and dad and all of us kids for a tour of the track and explained many things we didn't know about the facility. He had an office just outside the entrance to the first turn. He sat there listening to the race on the radio and typing on his teleprompter typewriter which gave up-to-the-minute results to the Associated Press as to the progress of the race. He was a very gracious host to us all.

The Rebel 300 this year would take the 21st billing of the season. Fred Lorenzen put the #28 H-M Ford on the pole with Fireball on the outside front row driving the Banjo Matthews '62 Pontiac #22. Starting third would be #29 Nelson Stacy in a Ford and fourth was Joe Weatherly in the #8 Bud Moore '62 Pontiac. Once the race started, Fireball shot out to a lead for the first lap. Then on the second lap, Freddy took the lead back and held it to lap 52. Then Bobby Johns, driving the Shorty Johns '62 Pontiac #7, took over the point for two laps. Next it was David Pearson's turn to lead the pack. Pearson, who became famous for his abilities at the "Track Too Tough to Tame," led for the next 55 laps. Darel Dieringer took the lead for 16 laps before Lorenzen took it back for another 20 laps. There was a good bit of fighting for the lead in this race. But there was also some unfortunate action going on elsewhere around the track. First, Fireball crashed on the fourth lap, which dropped him to the 32nd position. Then the motor let go in the #39 Pontiac driven by Junior Johnson and built by Ray Nichels. Lee Roy Yarbrough lost his engine on lap 23, right before Zervakis called it a day on lap 28. G.C. Spencer and Rex White tangled on lap 48, which took them both from the race. Cars were dropping like flies. But back up front, Nelson Stacy was making things tough on everyone. Stacy led from lap 148 to 161 before Marvin Panch mounted a charge and led the race from lap 162 to 218. Nelson Stacy once again grabbed the lead on the 219th and final lap, and held it to take the checkered flag for the 1962 Rebel 300 Convertible race. I have looked at every photo I can find and have not been able to come up with a photo of Rex and Louie's '62 Chevy with the roof cut from it. That's the car they ran. I just don't have a photo of it.

Stacy brought home $7,900 for the win and Panch made $4,890 for second. Lorenzen was third, Jack Smith fourth and Cotton Owens was fifth. David Pearson was seventh and Ned Jarrett was ninth. Cale Yarborough brought his '62 Ford home in 13th and Richard Petty finished 15th. Of the 32 cars that started the Rebel 300, only 17 finished. Curtis Crider finished the race in the 21st position, still running at the end. He was 41 laps down to the winner.

The track at Darlington was built out in the middle of a farmer's field and miles from any real civilization. Just one little narrow two-lane highway led to it from town. So there was no need to panic about getting things loaded up and ready to go home. Once we had the wagon loaded and headed home, we would usually find a drive-in restaurant, order outside, eat in the car and swap stories from the day. We had some very good family moments rerunning the race: What caused the crash? Who hit who? Man, that Ford was fast! (Yeah, that one went over real well with my dad.) But then the food came and all our little starving mouths were occupied for a while. Then we would fall asleep on the ride home. School came early the next morning.

The next race for the NASCAR Grand National cars was race number 22 for the season and it was held right in our home town of Spartanburg. Even though the race was right in our own back yard, the team members were suffering from a bit of burnout. So at the team meeting Monday morning they all elected to just skip this race at the half-mile track at Spartanburg. It was a 200-lap race and 15 cars showed up to take the green flag. Ned Jarrett took home all the gold by himself this night. He won the race in fine fashion. Pole sitter Cotton Owens set a new track record to take the pole. Ned qualified second quickest. Jim Paschal started third, Cotton blew his Pontiac engine on lap 20 and David Pearson blew up his Ray Fox Pontiac engine on lap 30. Richard finished third and Spencer finished fourth.

The Charlotte Motor Speedway was the place to be on May 27, 1962. This was the 1962 version of the World 600 NASCAR Grand National Race. Six hundred miles on the 1.5-mile paved tri-oval called for 400 laps from real stock cars. Yes, they were beefed up in places to help them finish the race, but any kid in the stands could tell his daddy which one was a Ford and which one was a Chevy, Pontiac, Dodge, Buick, Oldsmobile, Chrysler or whatever they were. In those days, a team went to the auto dealership and picked out a car, took it home and built it into a race car. We won't even get started into what is required today. Anyway, the fastest car for the World 600 qualifying was Fireball Roberts, driving the Banjo Matthews '62 Pontiac #22. His average lap of 140.150 mph set the record for that time. Second fastest was the '62 Pontiac #3 built by Ray Fox and driven by David Pearson. Third spot went to Banjo himself driving his #94 Pontiac, and fourth went to Joe Weatherly driving the #8 Bud Moore 1962 Pontiac. Fifth-place starter was Bobby Johns driving a '62 Pontiac, and sixth went to Johnny Allen, making his first appearance driving for the Holly Farms Pontiac team. Seventh position on the starting grid was ready for Jimmy Pardue driving the #54 1962 Pontiac. Ninth starting spot went to Junior Johnson, and the only non–Pontiac car to start in the top 10 was Rex White in the '62 Chevrolet Bel Air 409. Seems that Junior Johnson had complained to Rex and Fred Lovette that his Holly Farms Pontiacs were not being prepared up to his standards. So he quit the team and went to driving for Cotton Owens in the #6 white Pontiac. Meanwhile, the new Pontiac pilot for Holly Farms was hard-luck Johnny Allen, and his Crawford Clements and Bill Ellis–prepared #46 Pontiac outqualified Junior by three positions. Now, to add insult to injury, Junior's new ride lost a clutch 72 laps into the race and he was credited with a 38th-place finish. Over in the Holly Farms pits, Johnny was doing a fine job clicking off laps and finished the day with a 15th finishing spot. Not too shabby for the first effort with the new team. When the 600 long and stressful miles were completed, Nelson Stacy had won the race in a pretty fine fashion. Just about seven laps from the end, David Pearson was driving around Stacy to take the lead for the win when his Ray Fox engine expired all over everything. Stacy stated in victory lane that he just couldn't believe it. He said that David had everybody covered and was a sure-fire winner and then BOOM! That blown motor dropped Pearson down to seventh place in the same race he had won just one year ago. Stacy's Ford was not adorned in the familiar yellow as was usual for his ride. This time his Holman-Moody Ford came to the track painted red and still carried the familiar #29 with Ron's Ford Sales as the sponsor. Joe Weatherly's Pontiac finished second and Fred Lorenzen's Ford #0 finished third. Fourth went to a well-deserving Richard Petty and fifth was #66 Larry Frank driving the Café' Burgundy '62 Ford. Larry had a surprise in his pocket for everyone and he pulled it out when we got to Darlington this year. Sixth was Ned Jarrett, driving the highest-placing Chevrolet, and seventh went to Pearson in the Pontiac. Marvin Panch brought the Wood Brothers #21 Ford home in eighth, while pole sitter Fireball Roberts drove his Banjo Pontiac for a fine ninth-place finish. Tenth went to Bunkie Blackburn driving the #41 for the Petty Engineering team. And still chewing on his "Have-A-Tampa" and driving hard for that 11th-place finish was Rex White in his Louie Clements '62 Chevy #4. Larry Thomas and Darel Dieringer each drove '62 Dodges and finished in 16th and 23rd respectively. Spencer finished 21st and Jack Smith finished 24th in his '62 Pontiac, which ran out of brakes on lap 355. Wendell's Chevy blew an engine on lap 277 for a 30th position in the rundown. Third-place starter Banjo Matthews crashed on lap 13 and was credited with 43rd position. Ralph Earnhardt crashed on lap 11 and was credited with a 45th position with his '61 Pontiac. Forty-eight cars started the race and 23 cars completed the grind. Approximately 46,000 spectators came out to see the World 600 this year and they got a pretty good race, which required just short of five hours to complete.

One thing that the Chevy boys were unaware of at this point was that the new Chevy-engineered MKII 427 was already starting to go from drawing board to prototype components. The blocks were completed and the heads were being worked on right then. They would not get to enjoy this new-found horsepower for another nine months yet. The Chevy day was coming…

About 55,000 people came out to see the Atlanta 500 this year. This was the 24th race of the season and was held on June 10, 1962. Qualifying for this race was a big deal for our family. The excitement was electrifying for all of us. Many of the Pontiac, Plymouth and Ford drivers just shook their heads in amazement. Banjo Matthews took the pole with his '62 Pontiac #02. Fireball Roberts took the #22 Pontiac out to qualify and he had earlier run a couple of laps above 139 mph. Banjo's pole speed was 137.640. My dad had mentioned that when Fireball came off the fourth corner while qualifying, everything was smoking, including the steering wheel. The car was pushing badly. Smokey was there and I don't remember how much he had to do with that car at the time, but Fireball qualified 14th. Very unusual for him. Next out was Rex White in the gold-and-white #4 Chevy 409. The Chevy engine was just not up to snuff with the Fords and Pontiacs, but Rex and Louie had worked a lot on their shock package and got the car through the corners wide-open and clean. Rex qualified second fastest to put him on the outside pole. To do this on a super speedway was a victory in itself for our family. A certain mechanic from Florida threw his black hat down and stomped on it, he was so mad. Third quick was David Pearson and fourth quick was Bobby Johns, both driving Pontiacs.

The race was scheduled for 334 laps but was shortened to 218 laps because of a downpour of rain. Many of the teams knew the rain was coming. Some bet that it would be a race-ending torrential rain, and some were betting that it just might be a short shower and racing would resume. Rex pitted around lap 205 for fuel and tires. He was set to go had the rains passed and the race restarted. But that would not be the case this time. Freddy Lorenzen stayed out on the track and within just a few more laps under the caution flag, NASCAR threw the checkered flag, ending the Atlanta 500 114 laps early. Several drivers were in the catbird seat and made the right decision. Several, like Rex and Louie, chose the wrong path. Lorenzen won the race on lap 218 with Banjo Matthews a close second. Bobby Johns was third and Fireball was fourth. Troy Ruttman, driving a Bill Stroppe '62 Mercury, finished fifth. Finishing sixth through 10th were Goldsmith, Pearson, Panch, Johnson and Paschal. Joe Weatherly, Rex White and Richard all made the decision to pit before the rain hit and that left them back in the pack when the rains fell harder than we anticipated. Joe was 18th, Rex was 21st and Richard was 23rd. Nelson Stacy had some mechanical problems and was credited with a 45th-place finish. Ned Jarrett lost an engine on lap 114 and was credited with a 39th-place finish. Of the 46 cars that started, 31 were still running at the end. There were 23 lead changes and our beloved second-place qualifying run was short-lived.

Rex always wore the open-faced McCall helmet of that period. He also wore bubble goggles over the helmet to protect his eyes. Once seated in the race car he would normally stuff that soft clean tissue paper that came wrapped around those goggles right between his legs so he could use it during the race to wipe the goggles clean if they needed it. Right as the field came down for the start of the race, that piece of paper flew up right in front of Rex's face and completely blocked his vision. Just that momentary stutter of having to grab that paper away from his face before accelerating made Rex look like the only car there in reverse gear. He dropped through the field like a chunk of lead. He finally settled in somewhere around eighth or ninth. But the damage was done by that point. I can only imagine his disappointment when that happened. But this kid was standing up in the back of the truck in the garage area and when I saw him backing up, it just crushed me. I so badly wanted the Chevy to run with the Pontiacs and Fords on this day. But we would have our turn. It was just put on hold a couple of months.

One very bright note was notched into the belts of the White and Clements Team this weekend, though. On June 9, 1962, the day before the 500, the Prestolite Company sponsored the first-ever NASCAR Grand National Pit Crew Challenge. Each car had to enter the pits and come to a stop, and then the crew jumped over the wall and went into action. They needed to change just the two outside tires and take on one 11-gallon can of fuel. Now during this period of NASCAR, each lug nut still had to be hand-threaded onto its lug stud. That meant that each particular tire changer carried over the wall with him spare lug nuts either in his mouth, on a rubber hose clinched between his teeth, or maybe on the wire hook on his belt. The jacks were still the 75-pound service station issue. The quick aluminum jacks had not yet been invented. Also, there was still a gas cap that had

Left is Louie Clements, right is Crawford Clements, at Atlanta Motor Speedway.

to be removed and replaced securely. The Chevys had six lugs to change, and the Fords, Pontiacs and Plymouths had only five lugs on each wheel. Rex White's team won this competition and were rewarded $200 from the Prestolite Company. Each team member also got a new shiny white Prestolite T-shirt to wear for the photo after the competition. The winning trophy was a gold-plated, 4-way lug wrench affixed to a hard wooden plaque with the inscription, "Winner Prestolite Championship Pit Crew Contest, June 9, 1962, Atlanta Motor Speedway." I still have the trophy in my own trophy room today along with a few others I have collected over the years. How fast *was* their pit stop? Well, you could change 12 tires and add 66 gallons of fuel in today's numbers. In 1962, the winning time was 36 seconds for two tires and 11 gallons of fuel. For the Atlanta 500 in '62, I believe most teams averaged around 46 seconds for a two-tire stop and almost 90 seconds for a full 4-tire stop with two cans of fuel. Usually that also included pouring one quart of oil into the engine. Winning that contest is something that can never be taken away. I have the trophy and the photos to go with it and I am fortunate enough to get to look right at it every day. It seems to instill the winning spirit in me every time I see it.

Then, one race night in 1962, we went back to Bowman Gray Stadium for Rex to try for six in a row. He ran very well and should have won. But one of the other drivers had a different idea. Rex was spun out and went a lap down. When the green flag flew again, there were about 50 laps left in the race. Rex drove his tail off and wore out that '62 Chevy with the 409 engine. In the lead was the #46 Pontiac driven by Johnny Allen. It just happened that my Uncle Crawford was the crew chief on that car. To make it more interesting, my cousin Gary Clements and I were sitting up in the scoring stand together with my brother Lloyd, who was scoring Rex, watching this mess unfold. My dad took us with him to the race and Uncle Crawford took Gary to the race. I think they gave us each a couple of dollars and told us to stay out of the pit, go up in the stands, and come back down here after the race. We had enough money to buy a couple of Pepsis, a hot dog and maybe some popcorn. But we were there for the racing. And that race came right down to the wire. Rex got around everybody to make up his lap. Then he started passing cars to get back to the lead. As Johnny Allen came off the fourth turn headed for the checkered flag, George Green in his '60 Chevy was down on the inside and right in Rex's way. Johnny drove around the outside of George and Rex drove up onto the grass and drove up beside Johnny's Pontiac and just missed winning by what Morris Metcalf said was "about 6." Then, when Johnny got down to turn one, after the race was already over, he hit the wall so hard he went over it and tore up the bottom side of that race car really bad. It made no difference to him, though. He had just won his first Grand National race. That stopped Rex White's stranglehold on Bowman Gray's quarter-mile track. Johnny was paid $580 for his win. Rex made $500 for running second. Richard was third, four laps down, and Larry Thomas was fourth, five laps down. Weatherly was fifth and Wendell was sixth. George Green ended up 15th, a full 55 laps down to the leaders. He had broken a control arm near the start of the race on his Jess Potter '60 Chevy. They replaced the broken A-frame and he came back into the battle. It certainly made for an exciting finish.

The half-mile dirt track in Augusta, Georgia, was the battleground for race number 26 this season. Rex and Louie decided to let them run this race without the gold-and-white #4 Chevy. I was not at the race, obviously. But here is what I read about it. Joe Weatherly qualified for the pole, took the lead at the start and was never challenged for the win. He led the entire 200 laps. Ned Jarrett brought his #11 Chevy home in second spot, one lap down. Richard was third and Jim Paschal was fourth. G.C. Spencer drove his 1960 Chevy to a fifth-place finish for $275. Joe earned $1,000 for his victory. Sixteen cars started the race and eleven were still running at the end.

Race #27 this year was a different story. Rex and Louie did go to this one. Rex liked the third-of-a-mile paved track called Southside Speedway in Richmond, Virginia, and he wasted no time in qualifying for the pole position on this evening. Richard Petty qualified second quick to start on the outside pole. Approximately 5,000 people came out to watch this 300-lap race. At the drop of the green flag, Rex jumped right into the battle in taking the lead and ran off with the show for the first 276 of the scheduled 300 laps. They were trying to make the whole race on one tank of fuel. But on lap 277, the Louie Clements–prepared 409 Chevy ran out of fuel and coasted into the pits. James Hylton and Jerry Donald quickly poured in a splash of fuel and Rex went back into the contest. But he had lost precious time in the pits and coasting to get there. Jimmy Pardue took over the lead when Rex pitted and it looked like he was going to be tonight's victor. But he blew a tire on the 291st lap and drove to the pits to get a replacement tire. That cost him two laps. At that point, Jim Paschal took the lead with his '62 Pontiac and held onto it for the final eight laps. Rex finished a strong second place. Pardue was third and Johnny Allen, driving the Crawford Clements–tuned Pontiac, finished fourth. Fifth went to Jim Reed and sixth to Ned Jarrett in his Chevy. Weatherly, Jack Smith, Tommy Irwin and Buck Baker rounded out the top 10. Buddy Baker and Larry Thomas crashed together on the 41st lap, taking both cars out of the race. Richard was credited with a 19th-place position after burning up the rear end gear in his Plymouth. This had been the 30th time in Rex's career that he had earned the right to start from the inside front row.

The very next night we raced in South Boston, Virginia, on the .375-mile paved short track. Again, this was just the type of racing that suited Rex's style. But on this night, Spartanburg racer Jack Smith would set his big tin Indian on the pole. Rex qualified fast enough for the outside pole. One hundred miles on this track required 267 laps be run. Under normal conditions, Rex would size up the competition and either take off and lead the entire distance or let the faster car lead till he wore out his tires. Just after halfway, Rex would see the crossed flags signaling the race was halfway complete, and then he would begin his climb to the front. At the start, Jack's Pontiac had the ponies to pull away for the lead. Rex followed him closely while Jack led the first 152 laps. Then Rex poured the fuel to it and drove under Jack for the lead. He never looked back and won the race by about one-half of a lap. That win paid $1,000. So the White and Clements team had earned $1,650 over two nights of racing and the race car was still in one piece. Hard to beat a deal like that. This was Rex's fifth win of the year and it had also been the 28th race of the season. Third was Richard Petty and fourth was Johnny Allen in the Holly Farms Pontiac. Larry Thomas brought his '62 Dodge home in fifth place and Ned Jarrett would finish sixth after starting fourth. Tommy Irwin, Buck Baker, and Wendell Scott finished eighth, ninth, and 10th. Buddy Baker drove his father's '61 Chrysler #86 and finished 15th. Jim Reed was 17th after an accident on lap 210, and G.C. Spencer was credited with 19th position after losing the rear end gear in his '60 Chevy. Twenty-four cars started this race and 17 were still running at the end. Another win on this season felt real good!

July 4 saw all of NASCAR back down in Daytona for the '62 edition of the Firecracker 250. This would require 100 laps on the 2.5-mile tri-oval super speedway. This Daytona summer race was always a favorite for us kids. We would stay pumped up for this trip for weeks leading up to it. It was warm in Daytona, we could hang out at the motel for the practice days and swim in the motel pools or in the ocean. Sunburns were pretty common for us then. We wouldn't dare slow down for a little lotion to keep us from getting burned. My cousin Gary and I both learned to swim at the motel pool in Daytona. Every night we went out to a nice restaurant for a fine dinner, too. There was one restaurant that almost all the teams would go to. It was called Tettors Steak House. I don't know if it's still there or not. But I do remember some of the outlandish things we saw there. For example, Crawford and Buck Baker were always pretty good friends. Even if Crawford wasn't working for Baker, they would still do dinner together. They both had dinner this one night and that included a few adult beverages, probably enough to make either one of them think they could tug on Superman's cape. So, when they got up to visit the men's room, there was a double swinging western-style door on this restroom. Just as Baker pushed on the door to open it, someone on the inside pushed to get out. That stopped everything in its tracks momentarily. Then Buck put his hand back to keep Crawford out of the way and he reared back and kicked that door down. The guy standing behind the door also went down. Since he was out of it, they went ahead and did their business and then left the restaurant.

Then there was the time that A.J. Foyt was down there at this same restaurant and when he went to leave, there was a policeman in the parking lot who asked him, "Say, you aren't going to drive like that, are you?" To which Foyt replied, "Well, I'm in no condition to walk." Then the policeman asked, "Sir, are you drunk?" And Foyt said, "I had better be, I spent enough money trying to get this way." I never learned the total outcome of that encounter.

For the July 4 Firecracker 250 at Daytona in '62, Louie worked extra special hard and put in many nights on a new 409 engine for the gold-and-white Chevy. He took special care and performed several modifications, all legal, that he normally never had time to make. He wanted for Rex to break the 160 mph barrier at that race. Each team member had a new pair of shoes and uniform for that race, and they had their sign painter come to the shop and paint 160 on the right shoes and MPH on the left shoes. If you stood face to face with one of them, you could look down and see 160 MPH on his shoes. They were so determined to be the first NASCAR stock car to get to that magic 160-mph mark. They knew they could do it.

Well, you know what they say about the "best laid plans of mice and men." We got to Daytona and that Chevy wouldn't fall out of a tree in a high wind. It was terribly disappointing to my dad, Rex and the entire crew. All of us felt that hurt. I think they finally ran around 157 mph with it. But that was over three mph slower than Banjo's qualifying time.

They worked on the car right up to race time and finally put in just a little higher rear end gear and decided to draft all they could. With the higher gear, when Rex caught the draft, he could run faster than the lower gear in the draft. This way, he could run with those incredibly fast Pontiacs. Rex qualified a dismal 21st for the 33-car field. He drafted those fast Pontiacs all day and brought the Chevy home with an 11th-place finish, still running at the end of the race. Pole sitter Banjo Matthews was driving his 1962 Pontiac #02 and blew an engine after 73 laps. That gave him the 21st finishing position. Fireball won the race in Banjo's #22 Pontiac and Junior Johnson drove a '62 Pontiac to second spot. Johnny Allen, driving the '62 Holly Farms Pontiac, tuned by Crawford Clements, qualified third for the race but lost the transmission and ended up with a disappointing 27th-place finish. Marvin Panch, Jack Smith and Jimmy Pardue rounded out the top five this day. Ned Jarrett finished seventh in his '62 Chevy 409, which made him the highest-finishing Chevrolet in the race. Good job, Ned and Bud!

Pole winner Banjo Matthews, driving his own '62 Pontiac, actually did break that 160-mph barrier. He was the only car to accomplish this with a qualifying speed of 160.499 miles per hour!

David Pearson, driving the #3 Ray Fox Pontiac, qualified fifth and finished eighth. Drag racer Art Malone drove another '62 Pontiac to finish 10th, one position in front of Rex in his Chevy. Malone was also the driver of the famous Mad Dog IV. This was an Indy roadster that Bob Osiecki put together with a Chrysler Hemi engine in it with a supercharger on top of the engine. They also fabricated an airplane-style wing to bolt onto the car to try to hold it down to the track. Bill France put up a sizable chunk of money for the first car to break the 180-mph mark at his new Daytona super speedway. Malone did it with a speed of 181.561 mph in August 1961.

In the Firecracker 250, second-place qualifier Bobby Johns lost a transmission on lap 82 and was credited with a 19th-place finish. Buck Baker finished 12th with that big Chrysler, and good old Herman Beam ran all day, steady as she goes, and finished 13th in his '62 Ford. Ralph Earnhardt was 17th with #86, Buddy Baker finishing 18th. Three cars, Joe Weatherly, Fred Lorenzen and Lee Roy Yarbrough, were all three tangled up in the same crash on lap 34. That inflicted enough damage to remove them all from competition. Nelson Stacy crashed his Holman-Moody '62 Ford on lap 32, which completed his race day for a 26th-place finish. Richard Petty crashed on lap six and it was serious enough to park his racer for the rest of the day. Finishing 31st was Tiger Tom Pistone, who crashed on the second lap, ending his day too. Four engines were blown during the race and six cars were involved in accidents. Two cars lost transmissions and two lost oil pressure. One car, driven by Bob Welborn, fell out of the race due to loosening lug bolts. Twenty-two thousand six hundred spectators saw Fireball cross the finish line 12 seconds ahead of second-place Junior Johnson. Joe Weatherly and Jack Smith were heavily involved in this year's points battle. With Jack's fourth-place finish and Joe's accident for a 23rd position, Joe's point lead was cut to 1,272 over Smith.

In 1962, we also had a brand new '62 Chevy Bel Air bubble top that was solid white with a red interior, a 409 single 4-barrel engine and a 4-speed transmission. Chevy gave that car to White and Clements racing to build a new '62 race car with. But, before building a new race car with it, my dad drove us around in it for a few weeks. We were really a hot dog on the streets with that car. One Saturday morning on the way to the shop with my dad, we were driving down a frontage road next to the freeway. I said, "Stand on it!" That is racer talk for "Let's see what this thing will do." So he did, and it pinned me back against the seat. Right then I asked him, "What is downshifting?" So he shoved it up into third gear and let out the clutch. The motor sounded like a jet engine at that point and it felt like he put the brakes on. When I said that to him, he said, "Very good." I guess

In the pits following the July 1962 Daytona race, Louie Clements in center of photograph talking with race fans. The little boy in the foreground is Tony Clements, the father of current Nationwide driver Jeremy Clements.

The 1962 Chevy 409 loaded and ready to leave after the Firecracker 250 Daytona race in July of 1962.

my description was fairly accurate. I built a model of that car recently to go alongside the model of the #4 Gold Thunder car.

Just three days after the summer shootout at Daytona we were loading up the family wagon again and headed down the road to race #30 at Columbia Speedway. Tonight called for another 200 laps on the half-mile dirt. This was one track where Ralph Earnhardt could really shine. But he was a no-show this evening. It wouldn't have mattered anyway because this evening belonged to Rex and Louie and their team. Jack Smith qualified on the pole with his potent Pontiac. Richard put his '62 Plymouth on the outside of the front row. Starting in the second row were Joe Weatherly on the inside and Rex White on the outside. Ned qualified fifth in his '62 Chevy. When the 200 laps were completed, Rex White came home victorious in the Chevy and almost one lap back was second-place Joe Weatherly. Jack Smith, Cotton Owens and Ned Jarrett finished out the top five, all one lap down to the winner. Second-place qualifier Richard Petty ran just 20 laps before losing the engine in his Plymouth. This left Richard with that non-coveted last-place spot in the field. Larry Thomas crashed his Dodge on lap 60, which gave him a final finish of 19th position. Wendell blew a tire just a couple of laps from the end and finished ninth place. Rex won $1,000 for the victory and it was his sixth win of the season. This was more than any other driver to this point in this season. It was his 26th career victory and we were all jumping up and down on top of that Chevy wagon. Yes sir, that wagon earned its keep!

But alas, all good things come to an end. Racing is a fickle thing like that. On July 13, 1962, we were all up at what they called the New Asheville Speedway. This was to be a 250-lap race on a .4-mile track. Race number 31 for this season saw Rex White qualify on the pole in track record time. Approximately 5,000 spectators were there to see it. Outside pole would be Richard Petty in his Plymouth again and third starting spot went to Jack Smith driving that '62 Pontiac #47 again. Fourth starter was Ned Jarrett. Rex wasted no time in taking the lead at the start. He led the race for the first 118 laps and then a couple of shock mounts broke. That took him from the race and dropped him to a 17th-place finish. At that point, Jack Smith took over the lead and was really never challenged afterward. Jack was the only car on the lead lap at the end of the 250 laps. Weatherly finished second, one lap down, and Richard was third, two laps down. Buck Baker and Ned Jarrett finished out the top five. Wendell Scott and his traveling buddy Earl Brooks finished ninth and 10th, still running at the end. Pardue was 11th and Stick Elliot finished 13th, driving a 1960 Ford for Toy Bolton. Nineteen cars started the race and 14 were still running at the end. Smith earned $1,000 for his win and Rex earned a whopping $65 for leading 118 laps and finishing 17th.

The very next evening we were all packed up and back over to Greenville, South Carolina, for 200 laps on Greenville's half-mile dirt track. Rex did his job and put that 409 Chevy on the pole again. That had us all smiles. Jack Smith qualified his Pontiac second quick. Tommy Irwin was third fast in his '62 Chevy, and qualifying fourth fastest was 25-year-old Richard Petty. The top five all ran well at the start of the race. But it was Richard's night in the spotlight. He picked off one car at a time until he took the lead and then pretty much ran away with the show. Weatherly lost an engine on lap 45 and then Ned lost his engine on lap 118. Ned received $285 for his 15th-place finish. I believe $85 of that was the purse for the 15th-place finish and $200 was a guaranteed fee to the current champion for entering and competing in the race. That's the way the old entry blanks used to state that rule, anyway. By the completion of the race, Richard Petty had won by a full three laps over second-place Jack Smith. Third went to Wendell Scott in his best run of the season. He really ran well this week. Fourth was #27 Tommy Irwin and fifth was Rex White in the '62 Chevy Bel Air. Twenty-one cars started the race, which concluded in just over an hour and a half. This had been race number 32 for the season.

Tommy Irwin was a short racer from up in Inman, South Carolina. During his racing days, G.C. Spencer was also living and racing from Inman. Later, James Hylton settled his shop and race team in Inman. It is just about 12 miles up the old Asheville Highway from Spartanburg. And after the race and qualifying position Tommy had at Greenville, I thought it might be a good time to talk a little about the engine he had built. First, when he started the '62 season, his red '62 Chevy was #85 and owned by Monroe Shook, who had Emanuel Zervakis driving his cars for 1960 and '61. For whatever reasons, he chose Tommy to drive for him in '62. Then, about halfway through the season, Tommy showed up with the number 27 on his car. This was after Junior had left Holly Farms and no longer ran that number. Tommy Irwin was a pretty nice guy as I remember him. He bought a few parts from White and Clements Racing, and on one occasion he asked for some help with a "special" motor. He really wanted to go fast and stipulated that he didn't mind stepping out of bounds to get there. Louie ran Rex's engine close to the edge, but wouldn't go over, with the exception of that one race at Asheville-Weaverville in 1960. But for this engine, Tommy and Louie worked together and built up a '62 Chevy 409 and they bored the right side bank of cylinders .060" over stock, which was not legal. Then they had Jahns Pistons make them a set of high-compression pistons that fit both the right bank and the left bank of the engine. That is all I was told. I don't know if they had a roller cam, ported heads, big carburetor or what else. But we do know that this particular 409 was a hoss! My dad told me that he could hear the difference in Tommy Irwin's engine while it was going down the back stretch at Daytona while he was standing in the pits. That had to sound good! Now, this is in no way an attempt to embarrass anyone today. But as far as I know, none of the drivers from that time period eventually found out about that engine. Just another racing story of interest.

Races number 33, 34, and 35 on this season were held at Augusta, Georgia; Savannah, Georgia; and Myrtle Beach, South Carolina; all within a four-day span. White and Clements decided to stay home and prepare the car for the upcoming Bristol race, which would be held one week later. Not running for points this season, the guys enjoyed more family time at home. For me, well, it gave me a chance to catch up on some of my model car building and hang around the shop on the weekends.

Joe Weatherly won both Augusta and Savannah with Richard Petty and Tommy Irwin right up there with him. All three races were 200-lap contests on half-mile dirt ovals. Ned Jarrett won at Myrtle Beach with points chaser Joe Weatherly finishing second. In the Savannah race, Wendell put on a fine display of driving during qualifying trials and set fast time to put himself on the pole that night. I really wish I had been there to see that. Wendell faded back but still finished eighth which proved him to be a real hard charger when his equipment held up. At Myrtle Beach, Wendell finished seventh and Tommy Irwin's big motor finally blew up, leaving him back in 18th position. Richard experienced suspension problems and fell out of the race and was credited with 16th position.

July 29, 1962, brought with it race number 36 for this NASCAR season. This was the second annual Southeastern 500 held at Bristol Motor Speedway. Today, tickets for the Bristol night race are the most difficult in all of NASCAR to obtain. That is just how good the racing is there. I believe today this track will hold approximately 150,000 spectators. For this 1962 race, 15,000 paid to watch their heroes do battle for 500 laps. Taking the pole was Fireball Roberts driving the Smokey Yunick and Jim Stephens '62 Pontiac. Outside pole went to Junior Johnson driving the #6 Cotton Owens '62 Pontiac. Third starter was Floridian Bobby Johns driving his father's '62 Pontiac. Fourth-place qualifier was Fred Lorenzen in his Holman-Moody '62 Ford. Joe Weatherly qualified for the 13th starting spot but refused to pull his car into that starting position because of an extreme phobia of bad luck associated with the number 13. So the race promoter used that as another selling feature. He let Joe start in position 12A. Same position on the track, just a new "official" name.

The top three cars completed all 500 laps. Winning the race, driving for Petty Engineering, was Jim Paschal in the #42 Petty Plymouth. Second place went to Fred Lorenzen in his Ford and third place belonged to Richard Petty driving the #43 Petty Plymouth. The Pettys also entered a third car with Bunkie Blackburn doing the driving. Bunkie finished eighth in the #41 Petty Plymouth. So while the winner Jim Paschal, driving for Petty, won $3,930, Richard brought home $1,540 for third and Bunkie brought home $550 for his eighth-place finish. The Petty team made $6,020 for this race. That was real good money for the first team to figure out how to make a living from stock car racing. Johnny Allen, driving the Pontiac prepared by Crawford Clements, finished fourth, which must have been due to superior preparation of race cars, since Junior Johnson finished 29th driving the car he chose over the Holly Farms car.

Nelson Stacy, Joe Weatherly and Rex White finished in the fifth, sixth, and seventh positions. With 44 cars having started this race, we felt a seventh-place finish in this crowd was not too bad. Heck, just about anytime you could get a 409 to complete 500 miles you were having a good day. Ned Jarrett was ninth and Jimmy Pardue was 10th. Marvin Panch drove the Wood Brothers '62 Ford #21 to finish 11th and Wendell finished 19th, still running at the end. Modified standout Ray Hendricks finished 22nd driving a '61 Pontiac for Rebel Racing. Bobby Johns, Fireball Roberts, Stick Elliot, Reb Wickersham and T.C. Hunt all lost engines and did not finish. Seven cars lost rear end gears and two more lost axles and wheel bearings. As is plain to see from the final rundowns in these races, competition improves the breed. The cars we all drive on the streets today are much better because of early stock car racing.

I was not in attendance for the next two races, but here is what the record books say happened. On August 3, 1962, NASCAR ran a 200-lap Grand National race in Chattanooga, Tennessee. This race was titled the Confederate 200. I doubt we'll be seeing this name applied to a NASCAR race anytime in the near future. Anyway, 21 cars came to do battle and Richard Petty took the pole. Ned Jarrett qualified for the outside pole with his '62 Chevy. Once the race started, Ned grabbed the lead for the first nine laps and was then passed by Richard Petty on the 10th lap. Petty would lead until late in the race. On lap 181 Petty's car sputtered like it might be running out of fuel. Weatherly slipped by Richard and led the final 18 laps for his eighth win on this season. Fireball Roberts drove the Jim Stephens '62 Pontiac to finish second place on the same lap with Joe Weatherly. Third went to Jim Paschal in a '62 Pontiac belonging to Cliff Stewart. Richard steadily lost ground but still managed to finish fourth. Then a '62 Ford, car #61, came in fifth with Sherman Utsman at the wheel. Spencer was sixth, Jarrett was eighth, Buck Baker was ninth and Jack Smith finished 10th. Coming home with the 17th finishing position was Junior Johnson, who was standing in line to take over the #3 Pontiac ride from David Pearson after Ray Fox reportedly "dismissed" him. After this deal, David went over and started driving for Cotton Owens. They had a real good run together for a few years. I think Mr. Pearson even drove a couple of Cotton's drag cars around '64 and '65. Finishing in the 21st position in this race was a driver I had never heard of until I began to do some research for this book. Nero Steptoe was the first car to fall out on this evening, driving a 1960 Chevrolet #39. His name will come up again.

Two days later everybody, except our family, was back up in Nashville. Even today it's cool to know that Rex qualified on the pole every time he ran Nashville. I guess that's why I get a kick out of knowing that for the one Nashville race Rex did not go to, my Uncle Crawford's Pontiac, with Johnny Allen driving, did take the pole. So we kept it in the family.

Richard was second quick and Jim Paschal, again driving a Petty Plymouth, was third fastest. Once the Nashville 500 got underway, #46 Johnny Allen took the lead and held it for the first 46 laps before releasing it to Richard Petty for the next 130 laps. At that point, the other Petty Plymouth, with Paschal driving it, took over for about eight laps in the lead. Buck Baker took the point for about 12 laps before Jim Paschal took over for good on lap 203. He led the following 297 laps for a very fine and well-deserved victory. Paschal won the race over second-place Richard Petty by a margin of 11 laps. He pretty much had his way with the field. Baker was third, Weatherly fourth, and #2 Tom Cox drove the Cliff Stewart car home to fifth. Out of the 25 cars that entered this race, only 10 were running at the end. Ned Jarrett blew his engine with 113 laps to go. He finished ninth, and there were still two cars running that finished behind Ned! Johnny Allen was involved in an accident on lap 179 and was relegated to 17th finishing position. Fireball Roberts's '62 Pontiac broke on lap 78 for a 19th-place finish and our mystery driver, Nero Steptoe, was involved in an accident, also on lap 78, and was credited with 20th place. This week he was driving a '61 Pontiac #49 as compared to his ride last week, which was a '60 Chevy #39.

NASCAR scheduled Huntsville, Alabama, for race #39 of the season. We didn't go to this race, but I know what happened. It was basically a Richard Petty benefit show. Richard qualified for the pole, the race started and he took the lead and held it for the entire 200 laps. That is pretty much a full house, a royal flush, and a one-armed bandit spilling silver dollars all over your feet at the same time. You can't win a race better than that. So what happened to everybody else? Well, Bob Welborn ran second and Jim Paschal ran third with Buck Baker and Ned Jarrett completing the top five. Petty was the only car to complete the full 200 laps. G.C. Spencer qualified his '62 Chevy 409 for the third-place starting spot, which was a pretty good showing for him. He raced very much underfunded and just never had the money to get the equipment he needed to support his driving talent. What appeared to be a good night fixing to go his way died a quick death in the second lap when his Chevy broke a timing chain. That left him in dead last with a $75 payday. Not much money to fix a broken race car, feed and house a family, and get to the next race. Buddy Baker was eighth and Herman Beam finished 12th, still running at the end.

Asheville-Weaverville was the next race on the list and you can bet your last box of Wheaties we went to this one. Race #40 this year would be the Western North Carolina 500 on the half-mile paved oval up in Asheville. Rex always ran well on this track and it was high time for us to get nomadic again and hit the road! So Mom said, "Load the wagon," and we did. I can still remember my mother staying up late the night before we would drive to a race. She would fry up a bunch of chicken, make biscuits, fry up sausage patties for the morning trip to the track, pack up all sorts of food, supplies, and about everything you could think of. That Chevy wagon was loaded when we pulled out of the driveway. I believe this was the time that we pulled up to the gate right behind Rex and James, who were driving the truck and trailer with the race car loaded on it. We had all of our credentials with us, but for some weird reason, the guard at the track entrance was determined to let Rex cross the track with the truck and trailer but didn't want to let us in the infield. When he held his hand in front of our car Louie quickly told him that apparently he didn't understand the situation. He said, "When that race car goes across this track, we are going too." The guard got all shook up. Then Rex pulled into the track and down into the pits. The guard stood in front of us and my dad just hit the throttle and the guard suddenly found the urge to move out of the way. Once we got parked down inside the fourth turn, where we always parked, there were guards and a policeman running to get my dad. He stopped real quick and told them, "Don't even start with me. That's my race car, we have all our credentials and you will not keep me from walking right over to the pits. Are we clear?" And honestly, that is all there was to it.

Once again, Jack Smith qualified his Pontiac for the pole. Jim Paschal drove his Petty Plymouth for second quick time and Jimmy Pardue and Tommy Irwin started third and fourth. Rex qualified fifth for this race. About 6,000 people came out to watch the 500-lap race on this day. If you remember, this same race last year in '61 was the race where we had the riot at the end of it all. That would not be the case today. Once qualifying was over, it was time for me to get a piece of that fried chicken and a Pepsi and take my spot on top of the Chevy wagon. This was going to be a good race and I wasn't going to miss one bit of it. Once the green flag waved, Jack Smith took the point and led the race for the first 163 laps. Then, on lap 164, Jim Paschal took over the lead and held it for the remaining 336 laps for the win. Paschal finished a full three laps ahead of second- and third-place finishers Joe Weatherly and Rex White. Ned Jarrett and Jack Smith completed the top five. Jimmy Pardue, Richard Petty, George Green, Tom Cox and Larry Thomas rounded out the top 10. Wendell finished 14th and Eddie Pagan was back in action and finished 15th driving the #00 Chevrolet. Fifteen of the 25 entries were running at the end of the Western Carolina 500 this year. Paschal earned $2,350 for his win and Rex earned $1,150 for third place. Just got enough time to find me one more piece of chicken before loading up the wagon with five kids, Mom and Dad and the little dog.

Roanoke, Virginia, played host to NASCAR's 41st race this year. James Hylton had come down from the Roanoke area with his wife and son when he came to work for White and Clements. But I never made the trip to that track. I believe Rex had run there a few times, though. This week, they would have to put on the circus without the Clements Clan. We stayed home and worked and played.

At the Roanoke Speedway, Jack Smith took the pole for the 200-lapper and Richard Petty qualified second fastest. This track was a small paved and flat quarter-mile oval. Two hundred laps on a tiny little paved oval and Richard pretty well kicked butt and took names. Although the top five cars did finish on the lead lap, nobody had anything for Richard. Joe Weatherly ran second and Ned ran third. Bob Welborn and Jack Smith finished fourth and fifth. Rookie of the Year candidate Tom Cox finished sixth in the Cliff Stewart Pontiac. Spencer finished 10th and Wendell was 12th. Eighteen cars entered this race.

The International 200 was the next race on the schedule, and this week it would be held at that fine little quarter-mile paved oval in Winston-Salem, North Carolina. Bowman Gray Stadium was a track we all really enjoyed, but by this time Rex and Louie were involved with the new MKII 427 Chevy Mystery engine that was hidden within the walls of Chevrolet Engineering in Michigan. They had been given the word that this new, "race only" engine was coming together and they were busy making plans for a more successful '63 season. So with all of that on the table, we missed a few of the smaller races toward the end of '62. This was one of them. According to records, 24 cars started this 200-lap race and 10 of them were sports cars from the SCCA ranks. Fourteen Grand National cars competed in the race. It was pretty much little cars being led to slaughter by the big American iron. Jack Smith took the pole, Joe Weatherly took second and Richard Petty qualified third. Approximately 13,000 people came out to see how the sports cars would fare against the big heavy Detroit iron. When the green flag dropped, Jack Smith jumped out to a lead and held it for 138 laps. Then, Richard took the point for eight laps. On lap 148, Smith took the lead again for about eight more laps. Then, on lap 156, Richard pulled the trigger on his Plymouth and took over the lead for good. He led the remaining 46 laps to take the win and the $600 that went with it. Second-place Jack Smith and third-place Joe Weatherly both finished one lap down to Petty. And they both immediately filed an official protest against the engine in Petty's car. Norris Friel, the chief inspector, was not in attendance. So in his absence, Dick Beatty took charge of the situation and had Richard give him the manifold which was in question. He took it to Charlotte, where it was ruled legal the next day. I personally don't understand what made them believe the Pettys would have cheated in such a blatant manner in an area that is so easy to see. Besides that, both Lee Petty and Richard got around Bowman Gray as well as Rex White and Glen Wood. Neither of those two principals could say that they were as good at that track.

Jimmy Pardue and G.C. Spencer finished out the top five. Wendell ran ninth and the highest-finishing sports car was the 6-cylinder Corvette driven by Bill Whitely who finished 12th. In addition to Chevrolets, Fords, Pontiacs, Plymouths, Mercurys, and Dodges, there were also the one Corvette as well as a few MG's, Austin Healeys, Sprites, MGA's, and one lone Alfa Romeo in the field.

Three days later brought the crowd back to the Hub City Speedway in Spartanburg, South Carolina. There were a few times when even if we were not racing there, we would go out and spectate anyway. At least a couple of times we went out just to watch Little Davey drive the modifieds before he came into Grand National racing. But on this evening, David Pearson didn't even enter the race. He had just switched over to driving for Cotton Owens instead of Ray Fox. In the lineup for this 200-lap dirt race would be Richard Petty on the pole and Cotton Owens in his older Pontiac starting second. Third starting spot went to Ned Jarrett in his '62 Chevy and fourth starter was G.C. Spencer in his new Floyd Powell '62 Chevy. Richard Petty took the lead at the start and held it for the entire race. Ned ran well for most of the race until he popped a tire and hit the old wooden guardrail on lap 158. Joe Weatherly, the only car on the lead lap with Richard finished second about half a lap back. Jack Smith and Cotton Owens finished third and fourth, both three laps down to Petty. Fifth spot went to Spencer. Wendell finished 11th and Tommy Irwin crashed on lap 123 for a 13th-place finish. Eighteen cars started this race. Joe Weatherly was soundly in control of the championship points by now.

Valdosta, Georgia, brought us the 44th race of the season. Rex and Louie opted to stay home to prepare for the upcoming Southern 500 at Darlington. Many of their counterparts elected to compete down in Georgia for another 200-lap, half-mile dirt contest. Richard once again grabbed up the pole starting spot with Little Joe Weatherly starting second. When the race started, it became apparent that 29-year-old Ned Jarrett was running very well and in control. The lead swapped a few times, but when the checkers flew, it was last year's champion, Ned Jarrett, taking home the gold and putting an end to Petty's three-race winning streak. Richard finished second, one lap down to Ned. Third went to Joe Weatherly and fourth was the property of our friend, G.C. Spencer. In a rare appearance, Lee Roy Yarbrough finished fifth in a '62 Chevy. Sam McQuagg lost an engine and finished 12th in the 13-car field. Ned brought home $1,200 for this win.

September 3, Labor Day, 1962: We were all down in Darlington for what was still the most prestigious stock car race in the country. Daytona was getting there, but Darlington had already built up so much tradition, everybody who ever climbed into a race car wanted to win there. About 60,000 spectators came out to watch the 44 entrants take the green flag and wage battle for over four hours in the sweltering Carolina heat. Fireball was quick to lay claim to the pole position in the Smokey/Jim Stephens #22 Pontiac. Second quick in qualifying would be Junior Johnson driving the white '62 Pontiac #3. Third starting position went to Fred Lorenzen driving the white #28 Holman-Moody '62 Ford. And fourth starter would be Floridian Bobby Johns driving the blue-and-white #72 Shorty Johns '62 Pontiac. Bobby and his father Socrates, aka "Shorty," were a good team to be reckoned with. The race was a long, drawn-out and grueling affair. When the checkered flag waved signaling the end, it actually started the war over who really won this race. This was the 45th race of the season and a scoring snafu was all that was needed to create chaos at this point in the season. Junior Johnson was originally flagged the winner. But protests came in shortly from a few directions. Lee Petty was the first to officially file a protest. After a couple of hours, it was discovered that ex–Marine Larry Frank had indeed won the Southern 500 in style. The top six cars were shuffled around to their rightful finishing order. Larry Frank had already left the track for his motel room. He was dehydrated and blistered from the heat and the physical toll during the 500-mile war. NASCAR official Joe Epton made a statement that Frank had indeed won the race and that Junior Johnson was second, Marvin Panch third, David Pearson driving Cotton Owens's Pontiac was fourth and Richard Petty had finished fifth, one lap down to the top four cars. Petty's teammate car, driven by Jim Paschal, had finished sixth and Nelson Stacy brought his H-M Ford home in the seventh position. Finishing eighth was Ned Jarrett in a '62 Chevy, and our hero, Rex White, finished ninth driving my father's '62 Chevy 409. Joe Weatherly completed the top 10.

Crashes and blown engines were the order of the day, it seemed. My uncle's #46 Pontiac was driven again this week by Johnny Allen. His Holly Farms Poultry–sponsored car bounced off the first turn guardrail, slid on the driver's side for quite a ways and then flipped over onto its roof. The fuel tank was ruptured when he rode on top of the guardrail momentarily and the car caught fire as it slid down the track. This was a huge fire with high billowing black clouds of smoke from the exposed burning fuel. Johnny crawled out of the car when it came to a stop and was very lucky not to be run over at that point. We certainly all held our breath for a few minutes. A collective sigh of relief came to us all when we received word that he would be OK. My personal relationship with Johnny was one of respect because he was a Grand National driver. What I remember most about him was that his wife was always the sweetest and kindest person you could hope to meet. She was very soft spoken and seemed to genuinely care for people.

Of the 44 entries, only 23 cars were still running at the end of the race. A few notable finishing credits are as follows. Pole sitter Fireball Roberts crashed on lap 74 for a 36th-place finish. Fourth-place starter Bobby Johns was taken out in an accident with Darel Dieringer on lap 184. Bunkie Blackburn's #41 Petty Plymouth was also involved in this accident, while Dieringer's car went up in flames. These were the days before the invention of the safety fuel cells. Jack Smith and Roscoe Thompson were also involved in accidents and taken out of the race. The '62 Ford driven by Darel Dieringer was owned by a young lady named Mamie Reynolds. She was the daughter of a U.S. Senator and a racing fan for sure. I believe she became the first female owner of a winning car.

Buck Baker was 11th, Elmo Langley finished 16th, Tiny Lund was 19th and Fred

Lorenzen was credited with a finishing position of 24th. Nearby home town racer Cale Yarborough fell out of the race on lap 39 with an overheating problem. He received credit for 38th position. For us kids, we were fully aware that just to finish, to be running at the end of the race, was a great achievement. To know the race car was coming home with all its fenders, doors, and bumpers still intact and the engine still running, meant that we would get to see our daddy a little more through the next week. And again, as always, on the ride home from Darlington we would seek out that little drive-in restaurant and get our fill of fresh hamburgers and Pepsis. It was a wonderful life!

Hickory Speedway in Hickory, North Carolina, was the site of the next race. This was on September 7, just four days after Darlington. I can still remember this race like it was yesterday. Hickory Speedway is paved nowadays, but it was a little dirt bullring back then. Junior Johnson took the pole and G.C. Spencer took the outside pole in his '62 Chevy. Rex qualified third and Jimmy Pardue started fourth. Once the race started, Rex just kind of fell back and let the crowd go. The track was still quite wet and muddy in several places. Several guys trying to lead the race had their radiators clog up and then had to pit to cool down those steaming hot race engines. Rex was always a very patient driver and knew how to watch the gauges and take care of the car the best he could. On this night, it just seemed that everything went our way and everybody else had problems. As the mud started to dry up and Rex began to throttle up for the win, he was already in the lead and pulling away. At the end of the 250 laps, Rex had won by a huge margin of nine full laps over the field. What a deal! This was our seventh win of the season, too. There were about 12,000 fans that came out to watch this race and hopefully some of them were Chevy fans! Jimmy Pardue finished second in a Pontiac and Buck Baker was third in a Chrysler. Fourth was owned by the '62 Dodge driven by Larry Thomas, and fifth was credited to season championship contender Joe Weatherly. Spencer finished seventh and Richard finished 10th. Bob Welborn was 12th and Wendell was 15th. Ned Jarrett burned a piston in his Chevy and finished 17th. Fred Lorenzen made a rare short-dirt-track appearance and drove the '62 Ford owned by Mamie Reynolds. That radiator clogged up on lap 106 and knocked Freddy out of the race for the 20th position. Pole sitter Junior Johnson got a dose of the clogged radiator blues on lap 72 and that ended his night. Jack Smith also fell out with overheating issues on lap 62.

About an hour after the race was completed, Joe Weatherly walked over to our family station wagon and just stood around and talked with us for a while. Kind of seemed like he just needed a friend and someone to talk to. I remember him telling my dad, "Louie, this stuff just ain't like it used to be. It's getting so expensive." For a kid like me, who idolized these drivers and mechanics, it was awesome when Joe or Fireball or Fred would come around and interact with us. They were all heroes to me. Jack Smith was always coming over and raggin' on my little brother. Jeff was about four at the time that Jack was teasing him so much. I don't know which one had more fun.

September 9, we were back at Richmond, Virginia, for the Capital City 300, which was scheduled for 300 laps on a half-mile dirt track. This was race #47 of the season. Thirty-three cars came out for the night's race, and it was a good one, too. Rex qualified for the pole. Second quick time went to Joe Weatherly driving Bud Moore's #8 1962 Pontiac. A scoring snafu was in the works, though. As happened often during this period of NASCAR, manual scoring by persons in the scoring stand was just nowhere near as accurate as the electronic scoring transponders we have today. Years ago, after the winner took the checkered flag, he often ran at least one more safety lap, if not two. You don't see that nowadays.

Approximately 13,000 people came out on this evening to watch the 33 entries go at it tooth and nail. When the 300 laps were completed, that is when the scoring snafu came to the surface. It took a while to figure out, but chief scorer Joe Epton found an error in Weatherly's score cards. His scorers somehow missed over 10 laps that Joe had completed. So the finishing rundown was Joe Weatherly in first place, second was Jim Paschal, and third was the property of Fred Lorenzen, driving for Holman-Moody in their '62 Ford. Fourth-place finish belonged to Richard Petty driving the #42 Petty Plymouth. Our hero, pole sitter Rex White, came across the finish line in fifth place with that '62 Chevy 409 engine still singing a tune. Sixth tonight went to Mr. Consistent, Ned Jarrett. Driving home in seventh was Mel Bradley in a '62 Chevy, and eighth went to #49 Bob Welborn, driving another '62 Pontiac. Ninth and 10th belonged to Dick Getty and Jimmy Pardue.

Modified standout Ray Hendrick finished 11th and our friend G.C. Spencer finished 14th after starting third. In a rare short-track appearance, Fireball Roberts finished 17th,

Louie Clements (far left) and Rex White (far right) having brake drums machined at the Grey-Rock trailer.

driving his Jim Stephens '62 Pontiac #22. Wendell was 21st and Canadian Jim Bray finished 23rd, driving a 1960 Holman-Moody Ford that he still owns today. Last I spoke with him he had it about halfway restored.

Jack Smith crashed completely through the guardrail on the 50th lap and was unhurt, but out of the race for a final credit of 29th position. Buck Baker, Bill Champion, Elmo Langley, and Larry Frank all suffered from mechanical failures and finished in the final four positions.

Getting down to the end of the '62 season now, race #48 was next in line. This race was held at Dog Track Speedway in Moyock, North Carolina. It was scheduled for 250 laps on the quarter-mile dirt track. We were not present for this one but the records show that Ned Jarrett took the pole and won the race. Ned was the only car on the lead lap at the end of the contest. Finishing second was Joe Weatherly, third went to Curtis Crider, fourth was Mel Bradley and fifth went to George Green. Richard Petty broke an axle on lap 151 and was credited with the 11th-place finish. Bob Welborn, Larry Frank, Runt Harris, and Larry Thomas completed the field of 15 starters.

Just two days later NASCAR ran the 49th race of the season at Augusta Speedway. This would be a 200-lap race on a half-mile dirt track. This turned out to be a very special night of sorts. Fred Lorenzen made a rare appearance on the short tracks and he drove the #26 Mamie Reynolds–owned '62 Ford to victory, giving the lady her first Grand National win. It was also Fred's first Grand National dirt-track win. Second spot went to Richard Petty as third position was held down by pole sitter Joe Weatherly. Fourth position went to Ned Jarrett and fifth went to Wendell Scott. On down the field, positions 11, 12, and 13 went to finishers Buck Baker, Jack Smith, and soon-to-be superstar Cale Yarborough. A total of 16 cars entered and started this race.

Race #50 for the season carried us all back up to Martinsville, Virginia, for the Old Dominion 500. Martinsville was always fun to visit. We usually went to church there the morning of the race. We would try to make it to the earliest service they had. We had already run into a priest there who didn't have much empathy for my younger brother crying in the middle of the service. And they had that "Women wear dresses" thing going on. One of the greeters saw my mother heading into the church with a pair of long slacks under her big winter overcoat (it was cold that morning) and he stopped her and told her that women must wear a dress at this church. She handed off my baby brother to my sister and said, "I'll be right back." Then she walked around the side of the church building and pulled up the legs on her long pants so that they didn't show. With the big overcoat on, it looked like she was wearing a dress. She then entered without a problem.

Fireball Roberts took the pole position driving for Banjo Matthews in his '62 Pontiac. Second quick was Joe Weatherly. Third and fourth fastest in qualifying were Nelson Stacy and Fred Lorenzen. At the start of the race, Fireball took the lead with Stacy running second. Lorenzen was running in third and gave a couple of taps to the rear bumper of his teammate Nelson Stacy, who then let him by. Then, after a short caution period, Lorenzen began to tap on Robert's rear bumper. Fireball waved Lorenzen off in a manner explaining to him to knock it off. But then the bumping became more pronounced. So Fireball reached into his bag of tricks and pulled out an old one. Coming off the second turn with Lorenzen chasing him, Roberts gave a quick park and stop move and Lorenzen hit him wide open. This shoved Freddy's radiator back into the fan and pretty much killed his

Left to right: Crawford Clements, with NASCAR officials Pat Purcell and Joe Littlejohn.

chances for the day. Car owner for Fireball was Banjo Matthews, who was quite upset about the "unnecessary tactics" displayed by Lorenzen. Fireball still finished the race a respectable seventh. Ford Team driver Nelson Stacy made an excellent drive to win the race, three full laps ahead of second-place Richard Petty. Third went to Ned Jarrett and fourth was owned by Jack Smith. This was as good as it gets in NASCAR. The first four cars were: Ford, Plymouth, Chevrolet, and Pontiac. Every fan there rooting for a particular brand name of car had at least one good finish. Fifth place went to Joe Weatherly and sixth was the #26 Ford driven by Darel Dieringer and owned by Mamie Reynolds. Completing the top 10 were #22 Fireball, #54 Jimmy Pardue, #41 Jim Paschal, and 10th was #49 Bob Welborn.

     Our day didn't go all that well. It looked in the early stages like Rex was going to be able to ride for a while and then pick up his pace when he needed to for a good finish. All of that was foiled on lap 203 when my dad's 409 Chevy scattered all over the place. Back during this era, these were still wet oil sump cars and engines. When one of these babies came apart, everyone knew about it. But hey, the sheet metal was still good and there was a fresh engine back at the shop. We'd just go home and freshen up for the next race. Rex was credited with a 27th-place finish this day. It would likely be a quiet ride back home this evening.

Victory ceremonies following the win at the Richmond Fairgrounds. Louie and Rex are shown with the track promoter and the speedway announcer.

Junior Johnson broke an axle in the Ray Fox Pontiac and finished 17th. Wendell was 19th, Larry Frank was 22nd, Paul Lewis was just in front of Rex in 26th place and Lorenzen was just behind Rex in the 28th spot. G.C. Spencer was 30th following an accident in which he was not injured. Johnny Allen crashed the #46 Holly Farms Poultry on lap 84 to finish 32nd and Marvin Panch, driving the Wood Brothers Ford #21, ran out of brakes on lap 83 for a 33rd-place finish. A crowd of about 11,500 watched the 37 cars take the green flag.

There were only three more races left in this season and Rex and Louie were well aware of the new mystery 427 coming their way for the next season. So they patched up what they had for the 409s and saved the best engine for the last race at Atlanta. Race #51 came on September 30 in North Wilkesboro, North Carolina, back up in Junior Johnson country. For this race, the Wilkes 320, Fred Lorenzen qualified for the pole and his #29 Ford teammate qualified second quick to start on the outside pole. An all–Ford front row! Starting third was Marvin Panch, driving the Wood Brothers Ford, and fourth went to Jim Paschal driving the #41 Petty Plymouth. Approximately 11,000 fans came in the watch the 31 cars start this race. Shortly into the race, around lap 75, Fireball's '62 Pontiac pushed out a head gasket and overheating took him out of the race for a final position of

29th. Not exactly what he came to town to accomplish. The winner? Well, that honor went to #43 Richard Petty in his '62 Plymouth. Second place went to Marvin Panch in his Ford and third was Joe Weatherly in his Bud Moore–prepped Pontiac. Fourth-place finish was another Pontiac with Junior Johnson driving. Fifth place found its way to Jim Paschal driving the second Petty entry. Sixth and seventh were taken by Fred Lorenzen and his teammate Nelson Stacy with their duo of Holman-Moody Fords. Finishing in the eighth position was the Louie Clements–prepared '62 Chevy with Rex White at the wheel. Rex usually ran much better than this at Wilkesboro. Still, eighth place? We'll take it and go home.

Ninth and 10th were credited to Johnny Allen in the Holly Farms '62 Pontiac #46 and Jimmy Pardue, also driving a Pontiac. Ned was 11th and Jack Smith was 13th. Bob Welborn was 15th and Larry Thomas finished 16th driving Bob Osiecki's '62 Dodge. Buddy Baker was 23rd, Tiny Lund was 25th, Buck Baker was 27th, and Wendell finished 28th. The 31-car field required about two and a half hours to complete the race.

Two weeks later, the championship trail took us all back over to the Charlotte Motor Speedway. This was race #52 and the one they called the National 400. Four hundred miles would require 267 laps around this 1.5-mile, paved super speedway. Fireball started the week out right by qualifying his Jim Stephens '62 Pontiac on the pole at a speed of 140.287 mph. I just watched this year's edition of this same race. The cars were hitting 200 mph down the straights and I believe the pole average speed was around 192 mph. Horsepower and traction, that's where it's at!

Second quick for this race was David Pearson driving the white #6 Pontiac of Cotton Owens. Third fastest qualifier was Junior Johnson driving the #3 Ray Fox Pontiac, and fourth fastest was Johnny Allen driving the '62 Holly Farms Pontiac vacated by Junior Johnson. Fifth fastest was Marvin Panch driving the Wood Brothers Ford again. Once the green flag waved, Pearson led a couple of laps and then Junior Johnson drove his Pontiac into the lead until lap 70, when Bobby Johns took over the point for about five laps. Panch then pulled his Ford into the first-place spot for about 23 laps before Junior regained the point for another 26 laps. The heat was on. The battle raged. On lap 184, Panch once again took the lead and held it until lap 196, when Junior grabbed that top spot for good this time. Junior led the final 71 laps for a well-deserved victory. Second place went to Fireball Roberts in Banjo's '62 Pontiac, and third went to Fred Lorenzen in his H-M Ford. Bunkie Blackburn and Joe Weatherly finished fourth and fifth. Paschal's Petty Plymouth was sixth. Of the 44 starters, only 21 were still running at the end of the race. Rex White ran very well until we scattered another engine on lap 178. That left us with a 30th-place finish and a payday of $350. Ned was 11th and Richard was 16th. Panch finished 15th and Buck Baker finished 18th. David Pearson wound up 23rd with Jack Smith 24th, and Cale Yarbrough was 25th. Bobby Johns was 28th and Nelson Stacy, as a result of an accident, finished 31st. Buddy Baker was 33rd due to a blown engine. Mamie Reynolds's '62 Ford also blew an engine with Darel Dieringer at the wheel for a 38th-place finale. T.C. Hunt and Doug Yates were 39th and 40th, with Holly Farms #46 Johnny Allen completing the field as he blew a head gasket on the eighth lap.

Over 40,000 people turned out to see this one. Junior collected $11,365 for the win and Fireball brought in $5,420 for second.

The very last race of the season was the best race of the season, too, with excitement throughout. This was October 8, 1962, and Rex and Louie had already done a good bit of testing just a month earlier at this Atlanta Motor Speedway. They were testing with Zora Duntov and driving Rex's '62 Chevy along with one of Ray Fox's '62 Pontiacs that Chevy bought from Ray just for the test. More on that testing later. Right now, let's do the race. This would be the 53rd and last race on the 1962 schedule.

Qualifying on the pole was the #22 Pontiac with Fireball Roberts at the wheel. His speed was just a tick under 139 mph. And yes, the RF tire was smoking and blistered after qualifying. But nonetheless, he was the quickest and deserved the spoils of the pole victory. Second fastest was Fred Lorenzen in his '62 Ford. Third on the starting grid went to Marvin Panch in the Wood Brothers Ford, with Junior Johnson qualifying fourth in Ray Fox's '62 Pontiac. Fifth fastest this day belonged to the Rex White 409 Chevy. By this time, Nelson Stacy's Ford was back in its original Ford yellow with the familiar "Ron's Ford Sales" sponsorship down the sides. My dad's Chevy was the gold-and-white #4, and this week it had the rear quarter panels painted to reflect local sponsorship from Atlanta's Nally Chevrolet and the Nally/Nichelson Dyno Shop. Drag racer Dyno Don Nichelson was working with Nally Chevrolet in Atlanta trying to squeeze a few more ponies from the 409 engines for drag racing. The #4 Chevy never went anywhere near the Nichelson Dyno Shop, but the sponsorship dollars sure came in handy. Rex and Louie had tested for this very race. They worked very hard and long hours trying to get just the perfect combination of shock package, springs and sway bars too. They lowered the front of the car a bit and did everything they could to help them stay in the lead draft all day. The strategy was mapped out before the race and they stuck to their guns.

When the green flag flew over Atlanta Speedway this day, Fireball set sail. But then again, so did Bobby Johns, Richard Petty, Marvin Panch, and Junior Johnson. Rex stayed right in the slipstream of those fast Pontiacs and held on all day. When the race was nearing its final stages, we knew that Rex had made his final stop and could go the distance. But Marvin was leading in the final stages with Rex right on his bumper. Marvin would have to pit for at least a splash of fuel if he wanted to finish the race. Mom, my sister, my little brother and I were all standing up in the back of our stake bed tow truck watching this race from start to finish. Those last few laps had my stomach in knots. With two laps to go, Marvin Panch brought the Woods Brothers Ford down pit road for a splash of fuel. That left Rex in the lead with two laps to go. I thought I was absolutely going to explode with excitement. For those last two laps, I must have prayed every prayer I knew. Probably even made up a few. But Rex held on for the win. As the race car came down the home stretch for the win, Louie held up the chalk board real tall. He had written on it "Giddy Up 409" real big and showed it to Rex as he came by. The fans loved it and the Atlanta crowd went into an uproar. They were cheering, screaming, whistling, and yelling because the underdog Chevrolet had defeated the Pontiacs, Fords and Plymouths on the super speedway. This was the only super speedway victory for the Chevy 409 engine in NASCAR history. I am very proud of my dad and Rex for getting their only super speedway victory this day. In the winner's circle with them was country music star Faron Young, who was the Grand Marshal, along with the lovely Miss Atlanta 500. Rex stated clearly during the live post-race interview, "We didn't outrun anybody today. We just ran with them. We mapped out a strategy and held to it." First place for this race was $10,315, which was very nice to receive right as we were going into the off season.

Victory lane ceremonies after 1962 Atlanta win, left to right: Country music star Faron Young, Louie Clements, Rex White, "Miss Atlanta Speedway," and a NASCAR track official.

Only moments before the race started — I believe the cars were actually starting their pace laps— my dad came down inside the fourth corner were our family was parked. He told us that we could all come into the garage area to watch the race but we had to go right this second. We did. We closed up the car and ran with him just inside the gate, and Dad showed us where the truck was. While it was really cool to have a much better viewing point for the race, we ran off and left all of our food, drinks and supplies locked up in the station wagon. No food made for a very long day. Only a few families elected to go to the garage area for the race. Or maybe only a few had the chance. But my little brother went to every person in that garage asking if anyone had even just a slice of plain old bread to eat. He was three years old and very hungry at that point. Eventually, the food found its way to us.

Joe Weatherly was officially crowned the new champion after this race, too. Joe finished the race in second position, just about half a lap back. Marvin Panch finished third. These and Rex were the only three cars on the lead lap. Richard Petty was fourth and Fred Lorenzen was fifth. Buck Baker drove Jack Smith's #47 Pontiac to an eighth-place finish and Jack Smith drove his backup car to a ninth-place finish. Fireball finished the race in 10th position, five laps down to the winner. Pearson was 11th in the Bud Moore

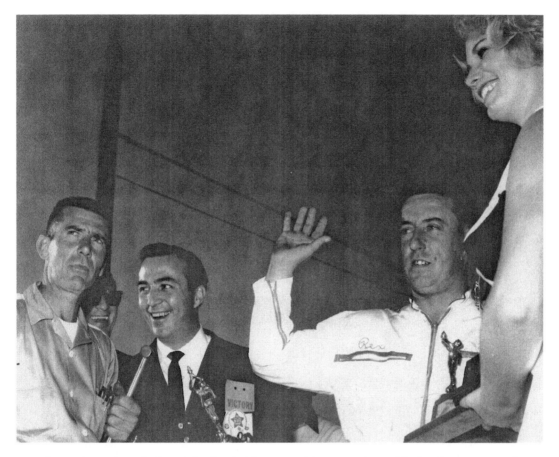

Atlanta victory lane. Left to right: Louie Clements with yet another gold-plated torque wrench for 1962 Mechanic of the Year, Faron Young presenting another trophy, Rex White, and the race queen.

backup car #08. Tiny Lund finished 19th driving the 1962 Cliff Stewart Pontiac. Johnny Allen started eighth and finished 20th in the Holly Farms Pontiac. Cale finished 33rd and Nelson Stacy came in 35th after an accident. Junior crashed his Ray Fox Pontiac for a 36th-place finish, and #81 Mercury with Lee Roy at the wheel finished 37th after an accident on lap 62. Ned Jarrett finished 40th after losing an engine on lap 12. About 25,000 people came out to watch the Chevy win this one.

The top 10 in the points championship for 1962 were: First, Joe Weatherly; second, Richard Petty; third, Ned Jarrett. All of the top three points finishers competed in 52 races each. Fourth went to Jack Smith, while Rex White finished fifth in the points, having competed in only 37 of the 53 races. Finishing sixth was Jim Paschal and seventh went to Fred Lorenzen. Eighth was Fireball Roberts and ninth went to Marvin Panch, with David Pearson finishing in 10th place in the '62 final points standings. Weatherly won a total of nine races, Richard won a total of eight races and Rex won a total of eight races for this season. Weatherly earned a total of $70,742 for the championship.

Several of the Spartanburg NASCAR drivers drove their race cars down Main Street as part of the city's 1962 Christmas parade. I remember Rex in the Gold Thunder '62

Commemorative award for outstanding mechanical performance given to Louie by Wynn Oil Company.

Louie receives Golden Lug Wrench trophy from the Atlanta Speedway announcer after the White and Clements race team won the first NASCAR Pit Crew Competition.

Chevy 409. As he got up beside where my mom, my sister, my little brother and I were standing, we could see Rex's daughter Brenda inside the car with him. Jeff and Brenda were about the same age. So, right through the crowd, Jeff went running out to meet the race car. Rex reached down and picked him up and put him inside the race car for the duration of the parade. Also in the parade were Bud Moore in the '62 Pontiac that Joe Weatherly drove, Cotton Owens in his white #6 Pontiac and Jack Smith in his red-and-black #47 Pontiac. Man, those were the days! Have I said that yet?

Now we come to the off season between racing in '62 and racing in '63. Some big changes were on the horizon. It couldn't have been but just a few nights after this Atlanta victory that my dad, after dinner with the family, asked if we would like to go for a ride down to the shop and see what next year's cars were going to look like. For those who remember, cars looked different each year in those days. When the new cars came out each year, it was a big deal. So sign me up. Let's load the wagon.

We all rode down to the shop and my dad opened it up and flipped on the lights. There sat two of the most beautiful cars I had ever seen. They were amazing to say the least. These were 1963 Chevy Impala SS 4-speed cars with the 409s, bucket seats, consoles with floor shifters, stereo radios, nice flipper-style hubcaps, etc. Absolutely amazing! One

Left to right: James Hylton, Ken Miller, Louie Clements, a Prestolite representative, Slick Owens, unknown, and Jerry Donald. Note the $200 cash being presented to Louie by the Prestolite rep.

was a solid-white car with red interior and one had a red exterior with red interior. Both cars had that engine-turned aluminum or stainless steel inside the side moldings and across the rear body panels. My dad explained to us that this all had to stay quiet. We were instructed not to talk to anyone about it. And we didn't.

White and Clements Inc. were to build up two complete race-ready cars for testing the new 427 engines out at the Mesa, Arizona, proving grounds. Both Rex and Louie had already been up to Michigan to see the engines and they were going to be receiving two of them. Louie did the buildup on the engines. With the expert help from team members James Hylton, Ken Miller, Buddy Payne, and Slick Owens, they got the two cars built and trailered them out to Arizona for the testing. Both Rex and Louie were astounded. Chevrolet engineer Dick Kieneth was the engineer who designed this engine from a clean sheet of paper. And it was a hoss. Louie built the first two engines that ran in the tests and they were rocket ships! On the perfectly round 5-mile circular track at GM, they ran a best lap of 188 mph in stock '63 Chevy body trim. Rex and Louie were hired by Vince Piggens, Bill Howell and Paul Prior to build two new '63 Chevys for this test to be conducted out at the Mesa GM desert proving grounds.

The first tests they ran, towards the end of the '62 season, were down in Atlanta with

The Golden Lug Wrench award resides in my office today.

This photograph shows the inscription.

Louie "Hollywood" Clements (in shades) prepares to show Rex the pit board inscribed with "Giddy Up 409" on the last lap of the 1962 Atlanta Dixie 400. Seated to the left is James Hylton.

the newer 409 parts that were "above board" and all of Chevrolet knew about them. They took the '62 Chevy down there with the 409 in it and compared it to a '62 Pontiac they bought from Ray Fox with one of his good Pontiac engines in it. To no one's surprise, the Pontiac was faster. So they modified the two cars so as to allow them to swap the Chevy engine into the Pontiac and the Pontiac 389 or 421 engine into the Chevy. In the tests, the Pontiac body was faster with both engines, and the Pontiac engine was faster in both bodies. That meant the Pontiac went faster with the 409 than the Chevy went with the 409, and the Chevy went faster with the Pontiac engine than it ran with the 409. Also, the Pontiac was faster with the Pontiac engine than the Chevy was with the Pontiac engine. Bottom line: the Pontiacs had more horsepower than the Chevys. That was just a plain old hard fact of life. Nothing we didn't already know.

Then, Paul Prior and Louie went over to the Chevy and lowered down the front end to the height of the Pontiac and raised the rear end up to the height of the Pontiac, and things began to change. One thing they learned from that test was that the lean to the left that Rex was running on the Chevy was fast on the short tracks, but having the front end higher than the rear hurt the car's performance on the big tracks. The Pontiac engine still had considerably more horsepower than the Chevy engine, but they all learned that the

1/24th scale model of the 1962 Chevy 409 as it appeared in victory lane after the Atlanta Dixie 400, October 1962.

The victorious 1962 Chevy 409 impounded, awaiting post–race technical inspection.

coefficient of air friction drag was greater going under the car than it was going over the car. They did a lot of exhaust header testing those days. Zora Duntov was there and he had some trick-engineered pipes and headers for the 409 that picked it up a bit. They also ran some other 409 parts that Mr. Duntov had brought down with him. He was knee-deep in the development of the new Z-11 427-cubic-inch "W" motor which looked like a 409 but was built for drag racing only. That engine came standard at 427 cubic inches, had a two-piece high-rise aluminum manifold and twin 4-barrel carburetors. They ran well, but nowhere near the new MK-II Mystery Motor.

One really cool thing that came out of this particular test session was that Louie and Chevy engineer Paul Prior got to talking about the heat under the hood of the race car. So, with the 409 back in the Chevy, they installed several thermocouples (heat sensors) under the hood of the Chevy. They had Rex make some laps and then pulled in and read the data they recovered. The temperature was even higher than they had thought it might be. Louie suggested that maybe instead of trying to get fresh air from the radiator area or the grille area, they try picking up air from the base of the windshield. Prior agreed and the two men then took some sheet metal and fabricated the first "cowl induction" ever run in a NASCAR race car. They installed some more thermocouples as well as a few magnahelic gauges, which told them that there was about three or more inches of water pressure right at the base of the windshield. So by the time the Daytona 500 rolled around, Chevrolet Engineering had built up some very nice factory-looking air cleaners that just happened to pull cool, clean outside air in from the base of the front windshield. And that is where the "cowl induction" system came from. They say competition improves the breed.

Back at the proving grounds for some more testing, they proved that they had the horsepower to outrun everybody when they got to Daytona. The problems began to set in when they discovered the core shift in the block castings. Some cylinders were not correctly aligned with the proper bore spacing and that left some cylinders thin on one side and thick on the other. Keeping the engine cool was another problem. The biggest obstacles they had were, first, parts were few and far between, and second, upper management at GM and Chevrolet division knew nothing about this program. It was every bit "top secret" and kept under wraps till the end.

Of the two new cars that Rex and Louie built and took out there to Arizona, the white one was left there to be used for tire testing. It lived its life out running tire tests every day for about three years. The red car was left there, too, but plans for it weren't spoken about much. What we later found out was that the Chevy engineers that had ordered these two new cars and paid White and Clements to build them into racers shipped the red one down to Smokey Yunick to entice him to leave Pontiac and come over to Chevrolet. So the fact is, the black-and-gold #13 that Smokey took to the speedway for Johnny Rutherford to drive was actually built by Rex and Louie. Now there is some racing trivia for you!

It soon came about during a press meeting that some reporters blindsided some GM corporate execs about how fast the Chevys were testing at Daytona. The GM top bosses knew nothing about this and they were embarrassed. Note to self: Never embarrass the boss!

When the corporate management got hold of the engineers running this program,

Promotional shot of 1963 Chevy inside White and Clements garage, Spartanburg, South Carolina.

The November 1962 test at the General Motors Proving Grounds, Mesa, Arizona. Rex in car, Louie standing beside car. The first "Mystery 427" Chevy propelled this new 1963 Impala Super Sport to speeds in excess of 180 mph.

all heck broke loose. It was a real bad stink, too. They came and told Rex and Louie, as well as Smokey, Ray Fox, and Junior Johnson, that as soon as this Daytona 500 was over, the program was over. All players were allowed to keep whatever they had, but nobody got anything new. Because the engineers knew that Daytona was going to be their one shot, they set up shop at Smokey's "Best Damn Garage In Town" in Daytona. All parts they had were shipped to Smokey and he was to give out the parts to Rex and Louie and Ray Fox for their cars. Ray Fox built two cars, both painted white. He got Junior Johnson to drive the #3 car, and he hired G.C. Spencer to drive his #03 car. Smokey hired a USAC dirt champ car driver out of Texas. His name was Johnny Rutherford and he did a fine job indeed. Of course, Rex and Louie built themselves another new '63 Chevy when they came home from the Arizona tests.

Once down in Daytona for speed weeks they started to have some durability problems with the engines. Overheating was the main problem. Also, these were not yet four-bolt blocks. Looking at the bottom of the block, it looked just like the 409 engine. These new Mystery Motors had the same bore spacing as the 409s. The tops of the blocks were cut much differently, which allowed the combustion chambers to be located in the heads instead of the cylinders like the 348s and 409s. The heads and intake manifold were major improvements over what was built into the Beach Boys' 409s. These new 427 MK-II heads had splayed valves. The valve angles greatly enhanced their ability to let air flow through the ports and into the new four-tube cast iron headers that bolted to the heads. After the engine was installed into the car, there were very nice 4-tube pipes that bolted to those cast iron headers. Rex ran some laps and blew a head gasket. There were no more head gaskets, but there were a few spare complete engines at Smokey's shop. So Louie went over to Smokey's shop and stayed up all night rebuilding the engine for Rex's car. As soon as he finished it, it was time to put it on the dyno and see what it had. Now entered Mr. Yunick's personality. Smokey could be your best buddy or your worst nightmare. Since the engine was just completed right before the sun came up, Smokey was not in his best of moods. He flat-out told Louie, "I will dyno that motor for you, but you are not coming into my dyno room to watch." Nobody understood his reasoning. Louie had built several of these engines before Smokey even laid his eyes on one. But nonetheless, Louie responded with, "Do you mind if I lie down on this sofa and take a nap?" And that seemed to be a good answer. For whatever reason, after getting some sleep himself, Smokey came back and told Louie, "By the way, your motor pulled 540+ hp on my dyno." Now, I don't know that any one of those three men, Smokey, Ray Fox, or Louie Clements, had any more horsepower than the next. By watching the race, it appeared that they were all very even and all of them outran everything else at the track. Each of those cars led the race at one time or another. Junior Johnson led the first portion of the race. He in fact led the first 26 laps until his Mystery Motor failed him. G.C. Spencer was driving Ray's other car and he traded the lead back and forth with Rex White and A.J. Foyt a few times before blowing his #03 Mystery Motor. Rex and Johnny Rutherford both finished the race, but they were not without problems.

CHAPTER 8

1963: The Chevy 427
Mystery Engine

In 1963 NASCAR had a whale of a year. The year before, Joe Weatherly won the Grand National championship and set an all-time high-water mark for money won during a season. Joe earned just about $71,000 for his 1962 championship. But this year would see a new superstar by the name of Lorenzen become the first-ever driver in the history of NASCAR to win over $100,000 in a single season. In fact, Lorenzen won $122,587.28 during the '63 season. He was the Golden Boy, Fearless Freddy, Fast Freddy; he was the Man! And the Man was chased all season by the Mountain Man, Junior Johnson. The Ford vs. Chevy battle raged on for the entire season.

The 1963 NASCAR Grand National season started off with its first race at Birmingham, Alabama, on their half-mile dirt track. Two hundred laps on the half-mile track were slated for November 4, 1962. Rex and Louie towed the '62 Chevy 409 down there for this one as they could not run the new '63 Chevy until they got to Daytona in February. Jim Paschal took the pole this day driving the #41 Plymouth for the Pettys. Jack Smith started outside pole with his '62 Pontiac #47 and Mamie Reynolds's Ford #26 started third with Darel Dieringer at the wheel. Rex qualified the Chevy fourth quickest to start outside second row. A crowd of 5,000 people came out to watch the 21 drivers battle it out for the 200-lapper. At the green, Paschal took the point for the first 146 laps. Richard Petty took over the lead and held it for about seven laps before Jim Paschal retook the lead for good on lap 155. With Paschal the winner and collecting the $1,000 first-place prize, Richard finished second, one lap down to Jim. Second paid him $600. Third place went to #87 Buck Baker driving his '62 Chrysler. Fourth-place finisher was #54 Jimmy Pardue with Dieringer fifth. Driving home in sixth was Jack Smith and seventh went to Rex White. Joe Weatherly finished eighth, making his first drive toward his desired second championship. Ned Jarrett was 11th and Maurice Petty finished 14th in the #42 Plymouth. Petty Engineering came away from the pay window with $1,700 for this race. That was good money in 1962. The race lasted for almost an hour and a half. Five of the 21 starters failed to finish.

One week later, on November 11, all the fun was down in Tampa, Florida. This time it was Rex White who qualified quickest for the pole position. An audience of 6,000 people watched as Rex set fast time at just over 60 mph average on the slick, muddy one-third-mile track. Outside pole went to last week's winner, Jim Paschal, in his #41 Petty Ply-

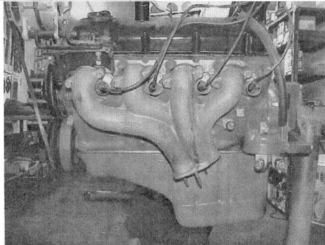

Various photographs of the original 1963 427 MKII Mystery Engine.

mouth. Third on the grid was won by Buck Baker and fourth quickest was Fireball Roberts driving Banjo's '62 Pontiac. As I stated, when the green flag waved, Rex White took the point for the first 41 laps before settling down to a more comfortable pace. Richard then took advantage of that opportunity to jump out front and lay down some lead laps. Richard pretty much controlled the race the rest of the way with heat on his tail from his own teammate, Jim Paschal. Joe Weatherly was third in the Bud Moore '62 Pontiac. These were the only cars on the lead lap at the conclusion of the contest. Finishing fourth was Jimmy Pardue and fifth went to the '62 Pontiac #54 of Jimmy Pardue. Rex had some over-heating problems and came home 13th, still running at the end. Tommy Irwin was fifth and Maurice Petty gave an excellent effort for a fine sixth-place finish. Possum Jones, Sherman Utsman, George Green and Buzzie Reutiman finished seventh through 10th. Buzzie is the father of today's Cup series racer, David Reutiman. Baker was 12th, Herman Beam 16th, Ned and Fireball were 19th and 20th. Spencer came home 21st after losing a rear end gear on lap 83. Twenty-four cars began the race and only five failed to finish. This had been win number 14 for the future king of stock car racing.

The Turkey Day 200 was held on November 22, 1962. Who could have known that day that exactly one year later, our American commander in chief, President John F. Kennedy, would be gunned down in the streets of Dallas?

This race, #3 on the '63 season, was held at Tar Heel Speedway in Randleman, North Carolina, right in the Pettys' back yard, so to speak. The race came to them this time. Rex and Louie did not compete in this one because they needed the time to stay home and prepare for the long haul across country to the Riverside Speedway next week. The record books show that this was a quarter-mile dirt track and Glen Wood sat his Ford on the pole for this one. Jim Paschal started outside pole with third starting spot going to Jimmy Pardue and fourth to #11 Ned Jarrett. Ned dropped out after just six laps with handling issues. Glen Wood led the first 173 laps in front of a crowd of 3500 spectators and appeared to be on his way to a complete shutout. Then he blew a tire with 27 laps remaining. Paschal then took over the lead and went on to win by a margin of two full laps over second-place Joe Weatherly, again driving the '62 Pontiac. Third went to Tommy Irwin, driving a Ford this week, and fourth was the soon-to-be superstar David Pearson, driving the #6 1962 Dodge of Cotton Owens. Fifth went to hometowner Maurice Petty in the family Plymouth. Wendell was 10th and Richard finished 11th. Glen Wood was credited with a 15th-place finish and awarded $125 for taking the pole and leading the first 173 laps. Life ain't fair! Our Canadian friend Jim Bray finished 16th, driving his 1960 H-M Ford #5. Spencer was 18th and Ned ended up 24th. This had been race #3 for the season.

Race #4 for the '63 season turned out to be a six-hour marathon for all 44 cars and drivers entered, a tough, long, grueling drive in 4,000 pound stock cars shifting gears about 20 times per lap. This race was held on January 20, 1963, at the Riverside Raceway in Riverside, California. It was a long haul out there for the east-coast boys too. Five hundred miles of racing on this track came out to be 185 laps on the 2.7-mile paved road course. I have some film of this race and just as clear as I could want, I can see Rex and Louie with the '62 Chevy jacked up on four stands, sitting on the wheels and sanding the insides of the brake drums to scuff them up a bit to allow the new shoes to wear in during the race. Rex is still chomping away at that Tampa Nugget Sublime cigar. I know that because I used to run up to the little store and buy them for him. This track was really hard on brakes… unless your name was Dan Gurney. Over 52,000 spectators came out to see this spectacle on wheels. Car #01 was a '63 Pontiac driven by Paul Goldsmith and he set fast time for the pole position. Second fastest went to #02 A.J. Foyt, who was also driving a Nichels Engineering '63 Pontiac. Third- and fourth-place starters were #22 Fireball Roberts, driving Banjo's '63 Pontiac, and #07, another Nichels '63 Pontiac. The Pontiacs were strong here, no doubt. Richard Petty brought out his new '63 Plymouth #43 with a new experimental automatic transmission in it. The idea was to lessen the work load on the driver and let this automatic transmission do some of that work. Well, that lasted for 27 laps, until his transmission went up in smoke. Also falling out early were fourth-place starter Len Sutton and pole starter Paul Goldsmith. Both cars blew engines and were out of the race by the 59th lap. Jim Paschal crashed his '63 Petty Plymouth on lap 81, and west-coast drivers Parnelli Jones and Marvin Porter both lost rear end gears and transmissions early on. David Pearson fell out on lap 113 when the engine in his '63 Cotton Owens Dodge let go. He was credited with a 33rd-place finish. USAC Indy car racer Jim Hurtubise finished 27th after blowing the engine in his Pontiac on lap 142. Joe Weatherly started fifth but an off-track excursion tore a hole in his '63 Pontiac's oil pan, leaving him with a 24th-place finish. Finishing in the 22nd spot, after the engine let go on lap 158, was Fred Lorenzen driving the Wood Brothers Ford. The crowd was starting to thin down a bit, but the action was still all over the track.

Wendell Scott posted an 18th-place finish after starting the race in his new '62 Chevy 409 that he had just purchased from Ned Jarrett. Ned of course had switched over to the Ford camp for the '63 season.

My mom and James Hylton's wife, Evelyn, were in the scoring stand for this race. Each of them stayed glued to the track and that big NASCAR clock that flips over the numbers right in front of the scoring stand. They had heard all the scoring nightmares they cared to hear and there was no way they intended to be a part of it.

To no one's surprise, Dan Gurney and A.J. Foyt finished in the lead lap with Gurney taking the win for $14,400 in his #28 Holman-Moody '63 Ford with the new 427 engine aboard. Foyt's '63 Pontiac was a Nichels Engineering–built race car and well deserving of the ride A.J. gave it this day. Third place, one lap down, went to Troy Ruttman, driving a Bill Stroppe–built '63 Mercury with the same 427 Ford engine. Fourth-place finisher was Fireball Roberts in the Banjo Matthews '63 Pontiac, which was red and white instead of his familiar black and gold like his cars from Daytona. Bobby Johns and Ned Jarrett finished fifth and sixth with rookie Billy Wade placing, coming home seventh in the #5 1963 Dodge of Cotton Owens. Billy was really very good at Riverside. Eighth, ninth, and 10th belonged to Jimmy Pardue, Danny Letner, and #98 Joe Ruttman, driving a Bill Stroppe Mercury too. Ron Hornaday, Sr., was 11th, with Dave MacDonald finishing 12th in another Holman-Moody car. Rex White was running up close to the front when the 409 engine departed this life on lap 173. Not completing the last 12 laps, he was still credited with a 15th-place finish. Had the engine remained intact, he would have finished fifth. Of the 44 starters, only 21 were still running at the completion of this endurance contest.

Time to load up and go to Daytona. We had one month to be there and be on our game!

The 1963 NASCAR Daytona 500 was a Cinderella event if there ever was one. The whole story of Marvin Panch being hurt and burned in a birdcage Maserati with a big block Ford 427 power plant in it, and then NASCAR's biggest kid, Tiny Lund, coming to his rescue and pulling him from the fiery wreckage, was a pretty strong story in itself. But when Marvin asked, from his hospital bedside, if Tiny could drive his car for him, that just made the story so much better. And who would believe a storybook ending could actually come true and the Big Kid would actually win the Daytona 500? Well, that is *the* race, in my mind at least, that put the Daytona 500 on the map. That race had everything Mr. France could have hoped for. The Chevrolets were dominant and fast during practice, qualifying as they never had before. The Nichels Engineering Pontiacs were fast too. The Fords held their own and proved their long-run durability. The race had everything!

There were several new cars that showed up for the 500 this year. Jack Smith was in a brand-new Chrysler 300, red with the bright white #47 on the doors. Who would have figured Jack to build a Chrysler? There were also several one-lap exhibition runs and even a 100-lap, 250-mile championship called the first annual American Challenge Cup Grand Touring Race on the oval at Daytona. This race sported Corvettes built and brought in by Mickey Thompson with modified 327 small block Chevy engines and 4-speed Muncie transmissions. Rex White was asked to drive one and accepted. He grabbed up the pole with a one-lap average of 162.264 mph! And that was with the small block! Paul Goldsmith drove a Pontiac Tempest with a Grand National Pontiac V8 on board. There were Ferraris, AC Cobras, Porsches, Jaguars, Alfa Romeos, Lotus Elites, Triumphs, MGA's, and one Abarth Simca. The race started out pretty good, but out of the sky came a torrential rain and that greatly slowed the pace. The Corvettes began to fill up with water inside and also had no defrost mechanism or wipers. This Thompson team was not prepared for the possibility of rain. Rex pitted one time and showed Louie all the water inside the car. Louie jumped into the car with a big hammer and a punch and began knocking holes all into the floor pan to let the water out. The doors were also full of water, so he punched holes from the outside the let the water out of the doors. They even stuffed shop rags up into the fender wells where the water was coming from. It was to no avail. The windows were so fogged up, Rex couldn't see where he was going, and it all turned out pretty disappointing for the #4 Corvette. Goldsmith won the race in the Tempest, and Fireball finished fourth in a Ferrari GTO. Rex dropped out after 38 laps and did not finish.

There were more races that preceded the 500, including a sports car race which ran for three hours and was called the Daytona Continental Grand Touring Road Race. This race was won by Mexican road racer and champion Pedro Rodrigues. Rodrigues was driving a new Ferrari which was owned by socialite Mamie Reynolds, who was the daughter of an American senator and lived in Asheville, North Carolina. This was Pedro's first start since his brother Ricardo was killed in a race in Mexico the year before. Winning this race paid him $11,000. Of course, the other race which ran before the 500 was the NASCAR modified-sportsman race which was a thriller in its own right. These cars came to race with aerodynamic body enhancements, really big engines with multiple carburetion, fuel injection, supercharging, etc. They were built using a much more tolerable and lenient rule book than the Grand National cars were held to. The race was 100 laps on the 2.5-mile tri-oval.

What about the two Grand National qualifying races? For the first race, February 22, the scheduled distance was 100 miles or 40 laps. Fireball Roberts #22 was driving the new '63 Pontiac built by Banjo Matthews. Outside front row was Junior Johnson driving the Holly Farms '63 Mystery Motor Chevy. Starting third would be the #03 Chevy driven by G.C. Spencer. It was sponsored by Cottrell Bakery. Fourth-place starter was #06, a 1963 Holman-Moody Ford driven by ex–Marine Larry Frank. At the start of the race it was quickly apparent that the Pontiacs were not up to speed with the Chevys this year. Teammates Johnson and Spencer drafted most of the way and led the race to the checkered flag in first and second place. Spencer was docked two laps by NASCAR for failure to acknowledge a black flag for his misplaced fuel cap. He was credited with an 11th-place finish. Johnson was given the win with #01 Paul Goldsmith second, #02 A.J. Foyt in third, #06 Larry Frank fourth, and #0 Dan Gurney fifth. Of the 31 starters, 23 were still running at the end of the 100 miles.

For the second 100-mile qualifier, race #6 for the season, it was an all–Ford front row with Fred Lorenzen on the pole in the Holman-Moody #28 Ford and Tiny Lund, subbing for the injured Marvin Panch, starting second. Lining up third on the grid was #11 Ned Jarrett driving a '63 Ford this year. Fourth-place starter was Jimmy Pardue driving a Pontiac. Rex White and Johnny Rutherford started the race in their new Chevrolets from the eighth and ninth positions. Once this second race got underway, Lorenzen took the point for the first eight laps. Rex White passed him and led from lap 9 through lap 32. The gold-and-white #4 Chevy was fast this year and we all felt real good about running in the lead with a Chevrolet on a super speedway. There was such a feeling of pride seeing that #4 up front at Daytona. Rutherford led lap #33, then Rex led for laps 34 and 35. Then Rutherford grabbed the lead for good and held onto it for the remaining four laps for his first-ever NASCAR victory. Rex White finished a very close second, with the Fords of

1963 Mickey Thompson–prepared Corvette race car driven by Rex White in the 100-lap Daytona Continental.

Lorenzen, Jarrett and Nelson Stacy finishing third, fourth and fifth. Of the 31 cars starting this race, only 20 finished. Over 27,000 spectators came out this day to watch these two qualifying races.

Just two days later, February 24, brought us the 1963 Daytona 500. This year our vantage point was not down inside turn four as we would normally be at most tracks. We were just past the start/finish line on top of my mom's station wagon in the infield. We could see the cars coming through the tri-oval much better this year. There was a television crew scaffolding set up just behind the pit areas and barely to the right of our vantage point. Below it was a parked car and a chain-link fence very close to it. During the TV filming of the race, one of the cameramen fell from at least twenty feet high and landed most of his body on the roof of the parked car. It caved in the roof of the car pretty bad. But his neck hit the top of that fence and it killed him right there on the spot. My dad and Rex's pit was just in front of where this happened.

For the 500 itself, the pole sitter was Fireball Roberts in the #22 Pontiac. This was determined nearly one week earlier during a special 25-mile event. Don't ask me. I didn't get it either. Starting second was the #28 Ford driven by Fred Lorenzen. Again, I didn't get it. Neither one of these cars qualified fast enough to be there nor did they win either of the qualifying races. It must have been "New Math." Starting third was Junior Johnson in the white #3 Chevy and fourth was Johnny Rutherford in the black-and-gold #13 Chevrolet. Now those two spots made sense. Starting fifth was Paul Goldsmith and sixth-place starter was Rex White in the #4 Chevrolet.

The Chevrolet teams knew very well by this time that they were in trouble. How they handled that problem would determine their fate this day. The core shift in the new engine blocks, the lack of spare parts, the lack of time to conduct any durability tests, and so on greatly hampered their efforts to win the Big One.

When the race started, Fireball took the lead and held it for about 10 laps before Bobby Johns took over for a few laps. Then Paul Goldsmith, driving about the fastest Pontiac there, took the point for a while. A.J. Foyt's #02 Nichels Pontiac was also a strong horse and he led from lap 34 to lap 38. By this time, the Chevys started to turn up the heat and take the ride up front. G.C. Spencer led for two laps and then Rex White led for two laps. Then they traded off, leading a few more laps each. This went back and forth several times until those pesky overheating problems reared their ugly heads. Junior's Chevy blew its engine on lap 26, which gave him a finishing position of 42nd. Next, that fast Pontiac that Goldsmith was driving lost its engine on lap 39. By this time, David Pearson, Billy Wade, Ralph Earnhardt, and Bunkie Blackburn were already out of the race with mechanical problems. An interesting point here is that Bunkie Blackburn was driving the previous year's "Daytona Dominator" '62 Pontiac that belonged to Smokey Yunick. They changed the #22 to the #10 and let Bunkie drive it in the 500. As the three remaining Chevys had to pit for fuel as well as water for cooling, Lorenzen's Ford grabbed the lead on lap 70 and held it until lap 105, when Bobby Johns Pontiac took the point for one lap. Lorenzen, Johns, Jarrett, and Roberts traded the lead back and forth among themselves for several laps. Just before the halfway point in the race, both Spencer's Chevrolet and Len Sutton's Nichels Pontiac blew their engines and fell out of the battle. Then there were two. The Chevys of Rex White and Johnny Rutherford were left to try to salvage something of the day for the "Stove Bolt Gang." Stove bolt was an early nickname given to any Chevrolet because of some of the hardware they were assembled with during their early years. I believe Rex pitted at least twice just for coolant to save the engine. Rutherford must have been doing about the same thing. But one thing was for certain by this point: neither the Chevys, the Pontiacs, the Petty Plymouths, the Dodges, nor the Stroppe Mercurys had anything for those Fords running up front. By watching the last thirty laps, we just knew the winner was going to be Lorenzen, Jarrett or Lund. But we really hadn't considered a top-five sweep by the Fords. That was a major feat back then. These were real Fords. They were not carbon copies of every other tube chassis out there with just a decal to set them apart. This was real stock car racing the way it is supposed to be.

At the end of the race, Ford Motor Co. had indeed swept the top five positions. Tiny Lund won the biggest race of his career for the Wood Brothers. Lorenzen, Jarrett, Stacy and Gurney rounded out the top five. The first non–Ford was sixth-place Richard Petty driving his #43 1963 Plymouth. Bobby Johns finished seventh even after a short pit fire had slowed him for a while in the pits. Eighth place went to Joe Weatherly driving Bud Moore's '63 Pontiac and ninth-place finisher was the black and gold #13 of Johnny Rutherford in his Chevy. The 10th and 11th places went to Tommy Irwin and Larry Frank, both driving Fords. Twelfth position went to #14 Troy Ruttman driving a Bill Stroppe Mercury. Leroy Yarbrough finished 13th driving a Pontiac, and Rex White's #4 Chevy finished the race in 14th position. Finishing 15th was west-coast Indy car driver Parnelli Jones, driving another one of Bill Stroppe's '63 Mercs.

Fireball lost an engine and was credited with 21st spot. Foyt crashed his Nichels Pontiac and finished 27th with another Indy car driver, Jim Hurtubise, driving a Petty Plymouth, finishing 28th.

Fifty cars started this race in front of 71,000 spectators. Of those 50 entries, 24 actually finished the race, still running at the end of the day. Rex's 14th-place finish was a full six laps down to the winner Tiny Lund. After a long pit stop to cool the engine down, my dad looked back toward our station wagon and motioned for my mom. She carried our 8mm movie camera over to him and he stood up on top of his toolbox in the pits and made some home movies of the cars coming through the tri-oval. What a treat to still have those old home movies almost 50 years after the race!

The next morning after the race, we all packed up and pulled out from the motel on the beach and rode back out to the track. My dad got out and went inside NASCAR headquarters with Rex and there was a meeting with Mr. France and the Chevrolet engineers. I can still remember the look on Rex and Louie's faces when they came out. They were terribly disappointed and feeling dejected about what they'd heard. Chevy had pulled the plug on racing and they couldn't even discuss it any more. It hurt Rex more than it hurt my dad. My father had a very strong work ethic and always did whatever was necessary to keep a roof over our heads and food on the table. So together, they soldiered on as long as they could with the parts they had. Obviously, with only one engine and not even one spare part for it, their racing would be greatly curtailed this season. They stuck it out racing with the one Chevy 427 Mystery Motor they had until it was just a fruitless effort from their standpoint.

They had some very good runs with the '63 Chevy that year. Rex ran very well at Bristol and finished third in the World 600 at Charlotte. The Atlanta 500 was held in March of '63 and Rex had a very good run going there but was overcome by carbon

Louie Clements and Dean Hall installing fresh Mystery Engine into the #4 Chevy prior to the Daytona 500. Man in center with his back to camera is mechanic Bud Moore.

Louie Clements revving up the 427 "Mystery Engine," with James Hylton listening intently.

monoxide fumes and had to get relief driving help from G.C. Spencer during a pit stop. When the car stopped in the pit stall, Louie jumped over the wall and lifted Rex from the car. They had a paramedic standing by with fresh oxygen for him and a wet cloth to cool him down. The rest of the crew serviced the car with right-side tires and two cans of fuel. Spencer still brought the car home with a fine sixth-place finish. Spencer was kind of a tall man and I still remember watching him sit in the race car with his knees up pretty high. Rex is a short man and when Spencer sat in the seat of that race car he looked kind of like a 7-foot-tall man driving a Go Kart. It would have been funny if we hadn't been worried about Rex at that point.

Fred Lorenzen won that Atlanta race, by the way. Junior Johnson had quick time for the pole but blew his 427 Chevy on lap #65 for a 42nd-place finish. Junior had set a new track record during qualifying too. A.J. Foyt was driving the #13 Chevy for Smokey Yunick at this race, but he blew on lap 126. Fifth-place starter was Buck Baker driving the #87 Pontiac maintained by my uncle, Crawford Clements. Baker was fast but fell victim to a blown engine on lap 157 and was credited with a 33rd-place finish.

I was too young at the time to realize the entire story going on here. And that is without a doubt a good thing. If this same scenario played out today, I would likely raise a very loud stink that would hit all the radio and TV stations on the sports news. If we NASCAR historians look a little further back, we see that while Smokey and Ray Fox

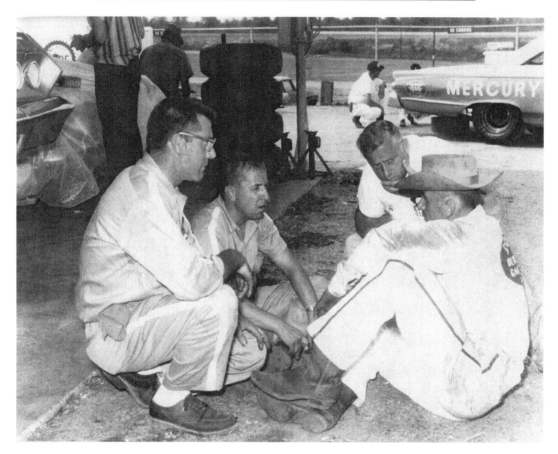

Discussing race strategies before the big race. Left to right: Louie Clements, Rex White, Chuck Warren and Smokey Yunick.

were running Pontiacs or Fords, Rex and Louie were running the Chevys, even when the Chevrolets didn't have a chance to run with the faster cars. From 1956 through mid-season of '63, Rex drove Chevrolets. He and Louie were even both members of the 1957 Chevy Factory racing team. In 1960 they won the Grand National championship for Chevrolet and finished second in '61. They even helped out and recommended Ned Jarrett to Chevrolet for the '61 season, in which he won the championship. What ever happened to loyalty? Chevrolet dumps off a truck load of Mystery Motors in Smokey's shop so Smokey and Ray Fox can run their Chevys all year. Both of those two cars blew engines several times through the year. As a matter of fact, at one time, Ray Fox had three '63 Chevys at the same time. Where did those extra engines come from? For the October National 400 in Charlotte, North Carolina, in '63, Fox came with three white Chevys. The #3 was driven by Junior Johnson, the #03 by Jim Paschal, and the #33 by Buck Baker. And guess what? When they had motor problems, they just reached into Smokey's storage shed and pulled out another motor. But Rex and Louie, who had remained loyal to Chevrolet through the years *and* did all of the pre-race testing for Chevrolet *and* built the car that Smokey now owned, could not even get so much as a new pair of head gaskets or a can of orange spray paint to paint the engine with. During the races Rex did get to

Left to right, James Hylton, Dean "Goat" Hall, Ken Miller, Slick Owens and NASCAR Official inspect 427 "Mystery Engine."

run the Chevy 427, my dad had to set up the carburetor on the rich side to reduce the chances of burning a piston. Of course this made the engine consume more fuel and that ultimately caused them to have to make an extra pit stop during each race. Of course, Smokey and Ray didn't have to worry about that. If they needed parts, Smokey had a floor full of them, and he was *not* willing to share with Rex or Louie. The very least Chevrolet engineers could have done was divide the engines equally between the four cars they had in the Daytona 500.

Now there has been talk that there was a fifth '63 Chevy in the '63 Daytona 500 with a Mystery Motor. People have said that the Chevrolet #71, driven by Bubba Farr, had a Mystery Motor in it too. I have spoken with many people during the course of interviews for this book and most of them feel that engine was the Zora Duntov Z-11 427-cubic-inch version of the old Chevy "W" motor. Farr's car certainly didn't run like it had a Mystery engine in it. To my knowledge, he never got anywhere near the front of the pack during the race. He qualified 31st and fell out of the race on lap 22, listed in the record book as having lost a fuel pump. He was credited with a 43rd-place finish. However, after a lengthy conversation with Rex, he assured me that one of the two engines Chevrolet was forced to sell to Holman-Moody, Inc., was loaned to Bubba Farr for the race, and he had to return it right after the race. Junior ran just about every race there was this season with his Holly Farms '63 Mystery Motor Chevrolet and although he did win some races, he also blew a ton of those 427 engines doing it. Seems there were plenty of spare parts for that #3 car, the #03, #33, and #13. But, there were no spare parts for the #4 car. Anybody else smell a fish?

The next big race after Daytona was the Atlanta 500, which we just spoke of. Think of this: The highest finishing Chevrolet in this race was the sixth-place finish by Rex White. If we hadn't lost that extra lap in the pits swapping drivers, Rex would have finished second. After Rex and Louie's #4 Chevy, the next highest finishing Chevrolet was A.J. Foyt's 37th place in Smokey's #13, which blew an engine. The next highest finishing Chevrolet was the #3 of Junior Johnson and Ray Fox, who reportedly burned the pistons and finished 42nd. Conspiracy theory? Maybe. But any way you look at it, there was definitely a frog in the mayonnaise.

A week after the Atlanta race, NASCAR ran a 250-lap race on the .4-mile dirt track in Hickory. Like manna from Heaven, a new 427 Mystery Motor must have fallen from the sky and right into the chassis of the #3 Chevy for Junior to win this race. Winning that race paid $1,150. That was nowhere near the $25,000 they were racing for in Daytona. Why risk a million-dollar engine on a small dirt track for very little publicity gain for Chevrolet and very little monetary gain had the normal blown-engine scenario played out? There were three other Chevys in the race, but they had the old 409 motors in them.

March 31, 1963, brought about the Bristol Southeastern 500, which was a 500-lap race on a high-banked half-mile paved oval. This week, Fred Lorenzen put his '63 Ford on the pole and Tiny set the Wood Brothers Ford #21 on the outside pole. The big NASCAR news this week was that Fireball Roberts had made the switch over to the Holman-Moody Ford camp and was set to drive the new lavender Ford #22. Fireball qualified that Ford for the third starting position. Starting fourth this week was Junior Johnson in the '63 Chevy. Starting fifth would be Darel Dieringer in a new '63 Bill Stroppe Mercury, and sixth was a surprise effort by Bobby Isaac driving the Bondy Long Ford #99. Qualifying seventh this week was Rex White with the new sponsorship from Sherwood Chevrolet in Johnson City, Tennessee. Eighth-place starter was #6 David Pearson driving a Dodge for Cotton Owens. The race turned out to be a very fierce battle between teammates Roberts and Lorenzen. Fords and Pontiacs led this race the entire way. The closest Chevy was Junior, who finished third. Rex's Chevy again experienced overheating problems. He got to running very well for quite a while and was holding his own inside the top five. But the heating gremlins bit again on lap 291. He finally parked the car for the day to avoid further risk to the engine. Crawford's Pontiac with Buck Baker at the wheel lost its engine eight laps after Rex dropped out. He finished 23rd.

Fireball won this race with Lorenzen finishing second. There was quite a bit of discussion as to how and why Fireball's car got so much better fuel mileage than Fred's car. Lorenzen mentioned that his car ran 110 miles on its first tank of fuel and only 85 miles on its second tank. The general consensus again was "conspiracy theory." Seems that some folks felt that Fireball was supposed to win this race and not Lorenzen. I don't know that the real facts ever come out when something like this occurs.

Junior finished third with Richard Petty fourth and Stroppe's Mercury fifth with Lee Roy Yarbrough driving it.

One really cool memory from this race was that before it began, my cousin Gary and I were inside the infield where we could watch the races in those days. They had a huge tent set up with a couple of folks in there blowing up balloons with helium to be released right before the race started. We thought this was the coolest thing a kid could mess with. The man doing the balloons put us to work. We enjoyed playing with this job for a while and then said, "Well, 'bye, mister." And we headed back towards our cars to hang out for the rest of the day. There were about 28,000 people there that day and the race lasted for about 3 hours and 15 minutes.

We skipped over race #14, which was won by Ned Jarrett in Augusta, and prepared the old '62 Chevy for battle in the April 7 race at the Richmond Fairgrounds. A scheduled 250 laps on a half-mile dirt track, Richmond always provided plenty of excitement for the fans. Rex took the old '62 Chevy with the 409 and quickly established quick time for the night by placing Louie's Chevy on the pole. Fifteen thousand spectators were there to watch Rex qualify the Chevy on the pole in the still-damp dirt track. Starting second was David Pearson in the #6 Dodge and third would be Joe Weatherly in the '63 Pontiac. Fourth quick was Buck Baker back in the '63 Pontiac #87. Pearson grabbed the lead at the start and held on for just four laps before Weatherly took the point for four more laps. By this time, Junior Johnson took over and led for the next 60 laps, providing a fine display of sideways driving. Joe Weatherly, Jim Paschal, and Junior Johnson traded the lead back and forth several times before Weatherly took over for good on lap 208. He led the remaining 42 laps for a one-lap victory over Ned Jarrett in second and Rex White in third. Billy Wade finished fourth, driving the #5 Dodge for Cotton Owens. Johnson was fifth with Richard sixth. Junior Johnson blew another Mystery engine with just eight laps remaining. Seems to me the "mystery" was where do all these new motors keep coming from? Spartanburg's David Pearson broke a spindle and finished 14th. Baker suffered more mechanical problems and came away with a 16th-place payday. The #03 Chevy driven by G.C. Spencer blew its 427 Mystery engine on lap 166 and dropped out. Both Fred Lorenzen and Fireball Roberts blew their engines well before halfway and finished 22nd and 23rd respectively. Zervakis was 24th and Larry Manning blew his 409 on the 35th lap for a 25th-place finish. Rex earned the team $900 for the third-place finish. This had been race number 15 for the season. Ray Fox had just lost two more 427 Chevys in the same night.

The next race we saw was over at Greenville-Pickens Speedway in Greenville. This was race #16 and was held on April 13. Rex and Louie were not going to compete, but since our friend G.C. Spencer was going to be running the #03 Chevy for Ray Fox, we decided to drive over and spectate. Besides, Crawford's Pontiac was racing this evening and he could use some help in the pits. This race would be a 200-lap contest on a half-mile dirt track. Jimmy Pardue put his new '63 Ford on the pole and Fred Lorenzen borrowed another '63 Ford #44 and qualified it for the outside front row. Starting third was Richard Petty and fourth was Ned Jarrett. Spencer qualified fifth with Bobby Isaac starting sixth. Jimmy Pardue held the lead for the first lap before Richard Petty took over for the next 45 laps. Then Ned Jarrett and David Pearson traded the lead until lap 91, when Baker put his #87 Pontiac out front for the next 60 laps. Ned took the lead back for the next 47 laps, but he blew a tire with two laps remaining. Buck Baker was right there in his Crawford Clements–tuned Pontiac to snatch his first win in two years. Ned limped around for a second-place finish and Spencer drove the 427 Chevy home for a fine third-place finish.

Petty was fourth and Pearson was fifth. Lorenzen crashed the borrowed Ford on lap 158 for 19th place in the final rundown. Points contender Joe Weatherly fell out early for a 24th-place finish. There were approximately 9,000 spectators on hand to view this race. White and Clements elected to skip over the next two small races in favor of preparing for the upcoming Martinsville Virginia 500 coming up in one week.

Race number 17 saw Richard Petty win his fourth race of the year at South Boston Speedway. Paschal was second with Ned Jarrett third. The very next evening, Richard took top qualifying honors at Bowman Gray Stadium, but fell out of the race on lap 146 due to a faulty fuel pump. Jim Paschal won this race driving a Petty Plymouth and Fred Harb ran second in a '62 Pontiac. Larry Thomas was third, Buck Baker fourth and Ned Jarrett fifth. G.C. Spencer was back in the Holly Farms Chevy #03 and qualified it for the fourth starting spot. But a first-lap accident took him out of the race. Joe Weatherly drove the Cliff Stewart '62 Pontiac to a 10th-place finish in an effort to score more of those valuable season points.

As previously stated, Rex and Louie had decided to run the next two races as they were a little more money and a bit more prestigious. April 21 saw Rex White set the Louie Clements '63 Chevy on the pole for the Virginia 500 at Martinsville, Virginia. Qualified for the outside front row was Fireball Roberts in his new lavender #22 Ford. Junior Johnson qualified third with Tiny Lund, still driving the Wood Brothers Ford, starting fourth. Old Man Baker still got around Martinsville pretty darned well, as was evidenced by his sixth-place qualifying effort in the #87 Pontiac. Rex told me recently that he and my dad had spoken about race strategy and they knew they could run hard for just a few laps and be OK. But there was no way they wanted to risk the only engine they had for the entire 500 laps. So at the drop of the green flag, Rex drove with caution and let Fireball take the lead. Roberts held that lead for the first 177 laps. At that point, Fearless Freddy took the point for the next 281 laps. Lorenzen was flying during that period of the race. Rex kept the Chevy in the top five, hoping for a shot at victory in the closing stages of the race. Richard Petty grabbed the lead on lap 460 and led to the end. This would be Richard's fifth win of this season. On lap 484, just 16 laps from the end of the race, Rex was coming off the fourth corner when he was tapped in the left rear quarter panel, spun completely and hit the inside wall. He had a solid top five going until that ruined it for him. He was done for the day right there. We finished the race on the wrecker's hook in 11th position and messed up a good payday.

Tiny Lund finished second and we were all naturally very happy for him. Tiny was a family friend and that's what friends do: they feel good for each other when good things happen. Third place went to #26 Darel Dieringer in his '63 Stroppe Mercury, and fourth went to Ned Jarrett in his #11 Ford. Fifth spot was reeled in by Fred Lorenzen driving the #28 H-M Ford. Driver Jim Paschal was overcome by heat exhaustion and drove into the pits on lap 218, got out of the car and collapsed. Daddy Lee Petty jumped over the wall, helmet in hand, and got into the car to finish the race. The old man surprised everyone with a fine drive and an eighth-place finish. Good for him! That must have felt good for the leader of the Petty Dynasty. Fireball Roberts crashed his new Ford on lap 223 for a 28th-place finish. The Chevy driven by Junior Johnson once again blew an engine, spun in its own oil, and hit the wall very hard on lap 23 for a 33rd-place finish. Bobby Isaac lost an engine and was credited with 21st place. Wendell Scott ran his '62 Chevy and

Prior to the Martinsville 500, the crew posed for this shot. Left to right: James Hylton, Buddy Payne, Dean Hall, Rex White, Louie Clements, Slick Owens, Jerry Donald and Ken Miller.

burned down a rear end gear for a 25th-place finish. Buck Baker finished 24th and Sgt. Roy Mayne, still running at the end, brought his '62 Chevy home in 15th spot. Rex White's pole speed was an average of 72.000 mph. Approximately 18,500 paid spectators saw this one go down in the history books. By the way, I still have the pole trophy Rex received for qualifying up there. It sits in a place of honor, right here in my office every day.

Just one week later, April 28th, Louie had beat the dents out of the Chevy and got it back in race shape with the help of James and Ken. We towed it up to North Wilkesboro, North Carolina, for the Gwyn Staley Memorial 400. This is a five-eighths-mile paved oval and it is right in Junior Johnson's back yard. It paid more money than Martinsville, so it was a good place to carry the '63 Chevy with the "Unobtanium Engine." Fred Lorenzen qualified on the pole just a tick over 96 mph average. Second quickest was the #21 Ford with Tiny Lund doing the driving. Third fastest went to Joe Weatherly in the '63 Bud Moore Pontiac, with fourth quick time taken by Junior Johnson driving the Holly Farms '63 Chevy again. Buck Baker qualified fifth driving the '63 Pontiac #87 tuned by Crawford Clements, and sixth on the grid went to Rex driving the #4 gold-and-white Chevy. G.C. Spencer was in a borrowed ride this week, which was a '62 Chevy with the old 409 engine. This race, though promoted as a 400, was actually scheduled for 257 laps over the five-eighths-mile track. At the green flag, Lorenzen took the point for the first 19 laps. Then that massive Chevy horsepower carried Junior Johnson past Lorenzen's Ford to lead the next 78 laps, at which time Junior blew up yet another Chevy 427 Mystery engine, spun in his own oil again and crashed. I'm telling you, someone must have planted an engine tree down in Florida. Fox went through engines like my dog goes through beef jerky! Freddy took over the lead again on lap 99 and held it until Tiny Lund took over on lap 103. Richard Petty was coming on very strong at this point, and he passed Tiny on lap 128 and never looked back. Richard had won yet another race on this season. Lorenzen and Lund finished second and third, both one lap down to Richard. Fourth place went to Jim Paschal driving the other Petty Plymouth, and fifth was the Baker/Clements #87 Pontiac. David Pearson brought the Dodge home sixth and Rex was the highest-finishing Chevrolet, coming home seventh. Normally they would jet the carb so the engine would lean out on the top end as the car drove up the back straightaway. With no available spare parts, that was not an option this year. Louie played it safe, left the carb rich and took the extra pit stop for fuel.

Bobby Isaac was eighth, Billy Wade ninth and Jack Smith finished 10th driving a '63 Plymouth #47. I wonder whatever became of that '63 Chrysler he built and raced at Daytona? Twenty-two of the 31 cars finished the race, still running at the end. Joe Weatherly, a championship contender, was the first non-finisher with his Pontiac due to a burned-up ring and pinion gear. Ned lost an engine too and finished 25th. Junior's Holly Farms Chevy ended up in 27th place. The paid attendance was estimated to be 13,500. Richard earned $3,575 for his win.

Race number 21 this year was a 200-lapper in Columbia, South Carolina. On May 2, 1963, the racers were ready to place their bets on the half-mile dirt again. Richard took the pole with an average speed of 68+ mph. Second quick went to the Buck Baker Pontiac, and Ned Jarrett qualified third. Fourth quick went to Spencer, back in the #03 Chevy again this week. Once the race started, the lead pack stayed very close in formation and traded the point back and forth between each other. When the 200 laps had ended, the top five cars were still on the lead lap. That was fairly uncommon during this period of NASCAR. Richard Petty won for his third straight victory. Buck Baker passed Ned on the last lap for the second spot. Ned was third, Buddy Baker drove a very fine race for fourth, and Jack Smith finished fifth in his Plymouth. Jimmy Massey, Joe Weatherly, Maurice Petty and Bobby Isaac all crashed but were not injured. Spencer's 427 Chevy burned a piston on lap 54 and he was credited with a 22nd-place finish. Having Crawford's work rewarded with a second-place finish was a fine moment for us. Rex did not enter this one.

Just three days later, fifteen cars showed up to do battle at the Randleman Tar Heel Speedway, another 200 laps on a quarter-mile dirt track. Ned Jarrett was the fastest qualifier this evening and Richard took second spot on the grid. Starting third was Jim Paschal and fourth was Larry Thomas. About four thousand people turned out to watch Ned lead the first 130 laps. Paschal took over the point on lap 131 and held onto it for the victory. Joe Weatherly finished second with Ned coming back third. Fourth went to Jimmy Pardue and fifth to the #36 Dodge of Larry Thomas. Spencer ran his '62 Chevy and finished seventh and Wendell finished eighth driving his older '61 Chevy this week. Richard was the last car still running at the end and that netted him a 13th-place finish.

The 1963 version of the Darlington Rebel 300 was up next. Race #23 would be held on May 11, 1963. One of my more fond memories of this race was that this was during the 100th anniversary of the Civil War, or War between the States. As usual on a Sunday morning before the race, we went together as a family to the earliest Mass on the schedule for the local Catholic church. When we arrived, it was almost full, but we found a pew near the back of the church. More and more people were still coming. I sat at the end of our bench, closest to the right side outer church wall and window. Within just a few minutes, people were coming up past me and standing along that outer wall. Yep, standing room only for the Sunday morning church service. Right then, Fred Lorenzen came up and stood right beside me! He stayed for the entire church service right there, up against that wall. For a while, I forgot that I was in the presence of God, our Lord. Instead I felt as though I were in the presence of royalty.

After the Mass, Louie and Fred exchanged pleasantries and wished each other good luck today. Well, it didn't exactly work out that way. See, Lorenzen had qualified for the pole at a shade under 132 mph average speed. Tiny Lund was second quick driving the Wood Brothers '63 Ford, and Rex White qualified his Louie Clements–prepared '63 Chevy for the third starting spot on the grid. Fourth quickest time went to Junior Johnson driving the Holly Farms '63 Chevy #3, and fifth went to Fireball with Little Joe starting sixth. I was up in the scoring stand which was just inside the fourth corner at that time.

Bench racing during a break. Left to right: Louie Clements, Rex White, Nelson Stacey, Fred Lorenzen and John Holman.

I could see the race very well from there. Never in my life were my hopes and dreams shattered so bad as on this day. It had started off so nice. But as soon as the green flag waved, things got out of shape really quick.

First, this would be the first time that this race was not run with convertible race cars. To add a bit of spice to it, promoter Bob Colvin changed the format to include two separate heats of 110 laps each. Then, when the day was over, they would tally up the points each driver scored in each race to determine just who the winner would be. It was confusing to the fans, and a few of the 12-year-old boys had a problem with it too. Anyway, when the first race started, I could clearly see the field accelerate down the front stretch. I could hear them roaring down the back stretch and then they appeared right in front of me. I saw the pole sitter Fred Lorenzen get all crossed up coming out of turn four. His car headed down toward the pit wall, hit it and bounced right back out in the track. Rex tried to squeeze between the concrete outside wall and Fred's crashing car. Fred's car backed into the rear end section of Rex's Chevy so as to pinch him between the concrete wall and the Ford's rear bumper. The Chevy was hit so hard that the rear end housing was bent and not repairable. So our race went up in flames on the second lap. Afterwards, Lorenzen explained that he got a bit overanxious, and he accepted blame for the accident. Never had I gone from such a high to such a low in such a short period of time. I think I'm still in shock when I picture that in my mind. Fred was credited with a 30th-place finish and Rex was listed as 31st spot.

I was ready to go home right then. The race was over for me. I sat and watched the rest of the race just sulking for the longest time. Then I thought, it's probably all for the best. That is one thing our parents taught us to understand. Usually, when something seemingly horrible comes into your life, there will also be a silver lining to that cloud.

Once both heat races were completed and the points scores tallied, Joe Weatherly came out on top. Second went to Fireball in his Ford, and third was #42 Richard Petty. Fourth place was property of Tiny Lund in the Ford and fifth went to Bobby Johns driving his dad's Pontiac #7. Buck Baker finished eighth in his #87 Pontiac, and Billy Wade and David Pearson both finished well, driving Cotton Owens team cars this day. G.C. Spencer also had a good finish this day. Stick Elliot drove Jack Smith's #47 to a 15th-place finish, while #11 Ned Jarrett was credited with a 20th-place finish, still running at the end. Bobby Isaac was listed as 21st position while driving his #99 Bondy Long Ford. Junior Johnson was credited with 25th, Neil Castles and Johnny Allen finishing 26th and 27th. Petty overtook Jarrett in the points chase by a total of 652 points. Approximately 25,000 people came out to watch the race and most left there confused over the whole "twin race" concept. It would take a call from NASCAR to convince Bob Colvin and the Darlington Raceway officials to come up with a new format that made more sense. We just can't have people leaving the track and not knowing who finished where. By the way, I still have one of those 33⅓ rpm record albums with all of the recorded sounds of this race. I don't believe I ever played it after the first day I got it, which was a few weeks after that race.

The next two races, the 24th and 25th of the season, were held on small tracks with low payouts. So Rex and Louie decided to sit them out in favor of the big-money race coming up in Charlotte called the World 600. On May 18, Richard Petty won the 300-lap race at Manassas, Virginia, with Ned Jarrett right on his rear bumper for second. Then on May 19, Ned Jarrett won the 300-lapper at Southside Speedway in Richmond, Virginia.

Mechanic Slick Owens prepping a fresh engine for the #4 Chevy prior to the 1963 World 600 at Charlotte, North Carolina.

Richard Petty finished second place, two laps down to the winner Jarrett. Larry Manning scored a sixth-place finish in his '62 Chevy 409, still running at the end.

To help you with the timeline, here are a few other things that were going on during 1963. The Beatles had a hit song with "She Loves You," Jan and Dean had a hit song with "Surf City," and Bob Dylan was singing his brand of folk music with "Blowin' in the Wind."

June 2, 1963, brought us all together again for the World 600 in Charlotte, North Carolina. This was shaping up to be as great a battle as it did turn out to be. It ended up a split decision for the Clements family, though. Buck Baker was again driving the #87 Pontiac with Crawford as crew chief when on the 23rd lap he collided with Larry Frank and Jim Paschal. For a few months after that crash, that white '63 Pontiac sat crashed and messed up pretty bad inside Crawford's shop, which was just down the street from our homes out in the Fairforest portion of Spartanburg County. Gary and I would look at the race car every day and either sit in it and pretend to be crashing or ask my uncle when this thing was ever going to get back on the race track. I loved that old Poncho.

In qualifying for the race, it wasn't really a surprise that Junior Johnson took the pole. He was brave and had plenty of horsepower on tap. Ford Motor Company must

Ken Miller and James Hylton putting the final touches on engine swap.

have spent millions of dollars trying to outrun the Chevys this year. Qualifying second quick was Freddy Lorenzen in the H-M '63 Ford Fastback. Third-place qualifier was Marvin Panch, which was his first time back in the seat since the fiery accident back in February at Daytona. He was, of course, driving the #21 Wood Brothers Ford. Starting fourth would be Fireball Roberts in that lavender #22 H-M Ford, and fifth-place starter was Nelson Stacy driving another H-M Ford. Sixth quickest of the 44 starters was Rex White in Louie's '63 Chevy #4. Tiny Lund was then given the ride in the #44 H-M Ford owned by S. McKinney. This just happens to be one of those races I remember very well and I also have a filmed copy of it on VHS tape. Once the race got underway, Junior ran hard, very hard. Lorenzen worked very hard just to stay with him. At one point, around the 100-lap mark, Rex kind of got tired of riding behind both of them and just flat-out drove by them both down the back stretch. When he came around that lap, Louie gave him the "Think" sign, meaning, "I understand you want to lead, but we need to conserve fuel and hold down the heat in the engine." Rex was easily very fast but the plan was to take it easy until the end was in sight, *then* we'd go for it. So Junior, Fireball and Fred took over again, trading the lead until around lap 130, when G.C. Spencer, this week driving a new Bill Stroppe Mercury #25, passed them all for the lead. Panch got to lead a few laps too, and then, after that round of pit stops was completed, Fireball, Junior and Fred were back up on top. Rex would make a run up to second and draft for a while and then back off to save the best for last. It must have taken every bit of self-control a racer can muster to hold back when he knows he can go right up there and get it done. By lap 111, all three of the Petty Plymouths had fallen from the race. This was indeed a rarity in NASCAR racing, even in those times. Of the 44 starters, only 20 were still running at the end of the day. There were 14 blown engines, two burned-down differential gears, six cars crashed and two withdrew early.

The final stages of the race came down to Lorenzen, Johnson and White. Junior was leading when he blew a right rear tire with just three laps to go. At that point, Junior held a 16-second lead over Freddy when Lorenzen took the point and looked like a sure-fire winner. Then, coming off the fourth corner and heading for the checkers, the #28 Ford ran out of fuel and had to coast. Rex had a full head of steam and was coming in a hurry. But Lorenzen crossed the finish line around 40 mph and then turned his car across the tri-oval dirt area to roll into victory lane. Junior got back out with a new tire in time to finish second and White finished third. Having two of the Chevys in the top three was a good day for the Bowtie Brigade. The other 427 Mystery engine was inside of Smokey's car, which was driven this week by Banjo Matthews. It blew on lap 358 for a 17th-place finish. Finishing fourth was Joe Weatherly and fifth was David Pearson. Nelson Stacy and Marvin Panch drove their Fords to finish sixth and seventh, while Darel Dieringer and G.C. Spencer drove their Stroppe Mercurys to finish eighth and ninth. Fireball Roberts brought the pretty new Ford home in 10th place, nine laps down to the leaders. Points chaser Richard Petty fell out on lap 90 with a blown engine and was credited with a 36th-place finish. The future king of stock car racing was still in waiting at this point. By finishing so far back he lost his point lead to Joe Weatherly by a margin of 1,338 points. Lorenzen earned almost $28,000 for his victory, with Johnson bringing home $17,460 and third-place Rex White earning $8,310. Rex and Louie accepted that with a smile and a sigh of relief, knowing the worn-out engine was still running at the end of the world's longest stock-car race. Almost 59,000 spectators came out to the Charlotte Motor Speedway to watch the greatest show on Earth.

Race number 27 was held on June 9 at Birmingham Raceway in Alabama. It was another 200-lap contest on a half-mile of dirt. White and Clements stayed home for this one and spent the time preparing for the upcoming Dixie 400 in Atlanta. Down in Birmingham, sixteen Grand National cars made the 200-lap race. Jack Smith took the pole in his Plymouth #47. Richard qualified second in his Plymouth #41 and Junior Johnson was back in action with another fresh Mystery Motor. When the laps ran out, Petty was again the winner. He was racking up quite the win column this year. Johnson's Chevrolet was the only other car on the lead lap with Richard. Third went to Buck Baker in a new '63 Pontiac, and fourth place was taken by #11 Ned Jarrett in his '63 Ford. The fifth spot was won by the pole sitter, Jack Smith. Wendell finished seventh in his '62 Chevy, and David Pearson's Cotton Owens Dodge fell victim to a faulty fuel system on lap 162 for a 13th-place finish. Joe Weatherly was back driving the Cliff Stewart '62 Pontiac this week, and a broken wheel on lap 71 left him with a 15th-place finish. His point lead over Petty fell to only 938 points.

On June 30, 1963, we were all back down in "Hotlanta," Georgia, for the Dixie 400. Four hundred miles here called for 267 laps. All the big players came loaded for bear. Marvin Panch silenced his critics by qualifying the Wood Brothers Ford on the pole at a speed of 140.743 mph. Second quickest time went to Junior Johnson in his Holly Farms '63 Chevy, with third spot on the grid being #22 Fireball Roberts, driving his Holman-Moody Ford. Fourth on the grid was #28 Fred Lorenzen. Thirty-six cars started this race and 23 were still running at the end. These were pretty good numbers for this period in the sport. However, there was one certain '63 Chevy, the black-and-gold #13 that Smokey Yunick prepared for Lee Roy Yarbrough to drive, that was pulled from the lineup before qualifying. Smokey said, "It will just clog up the track," and "It's too hard for anyone to drive that car," so he withdrew his entry. Of note here is the fact that Smokey's Chevy was built exactly like the one Rex drove. Rex was a polio victim in his childhood and was short and small of frame, yet he had no problems driving the Chevy. Also, when G.C. Spencer had to step in as a relief driver when Rex was overcome by carbon monoxide fumes at the earlier Atlanta race, Spencer said after the race, "This is the easiest car to drive there ever has been." That front end caster split, lower caster numbers, and having the bump steer figured out before the other mechanics gave Rex a distinct advantage over some larger drivers. Once Smokey received the car that Rex and Louie had built, he didn't care for the Chevy half-ton truck rear axle assembly they had installed. Of course, Smokey had been running Pontiacs for several years before this so it only made sense that he swapped out the Chevy rear axle for the Pontiac equipment. Those rear end gear assemblies don't come cheap. But who knows what he did with the control arms and rear Watts link setup that was on the car? That car pushed so bad coming off turn four at Atlanta that everybody there could see the tire smoke coming from the front wheels. I guess it was better to withdraw from the race than destroy a good race car. That had to hurt.

While I'm on the subject of Smokey, I'll say this: I read his book and even bought the book on CD, read by John DeLorean. I loved riding down the road listening to Smokey's stories. But to me, the very best part of the book was probably the most sad for him to write. When he spoke of losing his dogs and having to bury them, you could tell he let his heart show. Otherwise, he was a pretty gruff man to a lot of people. But he could not hide the fact that he really loved his dogs. He scores big credits with me for that one.

At the drop of the green, Junior grabbed the lead for the first 33 laps before 18th-place starter Billy Wade passed him for a couple of laps. Then Junior took the lead back and Billy took it right back again. The two waged a pretty exciting battle for several laps before Panch snatched up the lead for about 122 laps. Nelson Stacy and Darel Dieringer also led for a few laps each. Junior took the lead for good on lap 235 and led the final 32 laps for the victory over Fred Lorenzen and Marvin Panch. Lorenzen and Panch were the only other cars still on the lead lap at the conclusion of the race. Finishing fourth was Dieringer in his Stroppe Mercury, and fifth went to points leader Joe Weatherly in his '63 Pontiac. Rex White brought the '63 Chevy 427 home in a fine sixth place. Again, because of having to jet the engine rich and consume too much fuel to save the engine, Rex made an extra pit stop and finished one lap down to the three leaders. You do what you have to do in these situations. Finishing seventh was Nelson Stacy and eighth went to #5 Hard Chargin' Billy Wade. Ninth place was Buck Baker in Crawford's Pontiac, and 10th went to #11 Ned Jarrett driving the Burton-Robinson '63 Ford. Bobby Isaac was 11th and Richard Petty was 12th. Finishing 13th was our good friend G.C. Spencer, driving another Bill Stroppe Mercury. Wendell finished 20th driving his '62 409 Chevy. He must have had a boneyard full of those engines by that time. Ed Livingston drove Mamie Reynolds's #56 Ford home to a 22nd-place finish. In 23rd place was the last car still running at the end. That was Herman Beam driving his own Ford #19. Tiny Lund drove the #0 H-M Ford and suffered from a broken tie rod for a 27th-place finish. The #22 Ford of Fireball Roberts blew an engine and was credited with finishing 31st. Johnny Allen, driving the #66 Ford of Ratus Walters, blew a right front tire, hit the guardrail extremely hard and destroyed the car, but walked away unhurt. The engine was ripped from the chassis and landed some 100 feet from the crumpled race car. Finishing last was David Pearson, who lost the engine in his Cotton Owens #6 Dodge for a 34th-place finish. A crowd of over 20,000 people came out to watch this race for over three and a half hours. Johnson earned over $12,435 for his victory.

This had been race number 28 of the season, and it was the very last time that Rex and Louie ran the '63 Chevy. After this race, they pulled out the engine and gave it to Junior, thinking that might help him through the end of the season. The '63 Chevy sat around the shop for a while with no motor or transmission in it and just collected dust. Then G.C. Spencer stepped up and bought it and tried to campaign it for part of the '64 season with a 409 in it. He finally gave up on it and sold it. I think Roy Mayne drove that car for a while after that.

On to Daytona for the July 4 Firecracker 400. This was always one of the best trips of the year for us kids. Hanging out on the beach every day, swimming in the motel pool and then playing on the beach, just walking up and down the beach strip was entertainment for us. Of course, on race day, we all came out in force. But the beach lifestyle definitely took hold of each of us kids.

When we all left the shop on the way to the beach for this race, the Chevy stayed home. It was kind of strange to be hauling an empty truck down there. Mercury Division of Ford had made a deal to get Rex and Louie to campaign a new Bill Stroppe–built Mercury for the remainder of the year. I'll say one thing for the Mercury guys, they were very nice to work with and they took every opportunity to take my folks out to dinner and treated them very well. They made us feel like family right away. When we got to Daytona, Stroppe already had one of his red, white and blue '63 Mercurys prepared for Rex to drive. It even had the #4s painted on it with Rex's name on it and was signed in under the owner's name, Louie Clements. As soon as Rex made just a few laps in it, he came in and reported, "This thing is a dog!" It had about 50 hp more than the old 409s, but was about 75 to 80 hp shy of the Chevy Mystery Motors. He and Louie knew something was wrong. They had stood by all year and watched as the 427 Ford boys got closer and closer to the Chevys. So, why wouldn't their new 427 Ford motor do the same thing? Well, I think I remember that back when Richard Petty took ownership of a '69 Ford from H-M because Plymouth would not let him run a Plymouth with the wing like the Dodge had, he stated that his new 427 Ford wouldn't keep up with the other Fords either. I guess these horsepower tricks were a closely guarded secret.

On qualifying day, Junior Johnson qualified faster than any stock car in Daytona history up to that point. His run of 166.005 mph sat him squarely on the pole. Chevrolet teammate Jim Paschal drove the #03 Fox Chevy to qualify second fastest. An all–Chevy front row! You have to believe that Big Bill France was thinking to himself, "Well, *that* ought to fill the stands." Third quick time went to Fireball in a Ford, and fourth went to Fred Lorenzen in another H-M Ford. Darel Dieringer was fifth quick in his Stroppe Mercury and Paul Goldsmith was sixth in his #01 Ray Nichels '63 Pontiac. That car was very fast while in the draft of any one of the Chevys. Starting seventh fastest was Rex White in the new red, white, and blue '63 Stroppe Mercury.

At the start of this race, the Chevys of Paschal and Johnson swapped the lead back and forth a few times. Then Roberts, Lorenzen and Johnson began playing a game of cat and mouse at 166 mph! That had to be fun! Paschal got up there to lead a few more times also. By lap #61, Paschal's Chevy Mystery Motor had expired and left him with a 23rd-place finish. Shortly after that, the 427 Ford motor in dad and Rex's new Mercury blew on lap 79. Rex received credit for finishing in 21st place. Joe Weatherly blew his Pontiac engine on lap 102, and within about nine more laps, the rocket ship #3 blew its engine, leaving Junior Johnson in 17th position. It also left the Fords of Roberts and Lorenzen to battle it out between themselves for the $12,100 first prize. Fred was leading in the final stages and slowed down to try to get Fireball to go on by. But Roberts would not take the bait. Lorenzen led the white flag lap and Roberts used the famous "slingshot" pass to drive by for the victory in the fifth edition of the July 4 Daytona tradition. Marvin Panch was third, Darel Dieringer was fourth and Ned Jarrett finished fifth. Richard Petty, G.C. Spencer and Tiny Lund finished eighth, ninth, and 10th. The #13 Chevy of Smokey Yunick's was driven this week by Super Tex A.J. Foyt, who blew the engine on lap 145 for an 11th-place finish. Wendell Scott was still running at the end and came home with a 14th-place finish. Buck Baker and Bobby Isaac both lost engines for 15th and 16th places. Joe Weatherly blew his Pontiac motor for an 18th finishing spot and Pedro Rodrigues blew his Pontiac Nichels Engineering engine for a final position of 25th. Troy Ruttman

Rex White driving the new red, white and blue 1963 Mercury for the first time in practice for the July 4 Daytona Firecracker 400.

drove his Stroppe Mercury and finished 26th due to an accident on lap 50 on the front-stretch wall. I saw that accident as I was looking right at the spot when he bounced off the wall. Nelson Stacy was 33rd-place finisher after blowing the Ford engine in his H-M ride on lap 11. About 27,000 people came out to see this race.

Just in case you are counting, this was two more blown engines for the Ray Fox cars and one more blown engine for Yunick's car. These were engines that could not be replaced and had no possibility of spare parts availability. Yep, almost 50 years later we are still not too pleased with the way that mess went down. The new boys got all the engines they wanted but Rex and Louie got *one*. Kind of like shaking someone's hand and spitting on him at the same time. That is ultimately what took Rex away from the sport. They both, Rex and Louie, tried hard to just flip that page and go on to the next adventure. There was just too much lying, backstabbing, and jerking around going on in the Chevrolet engineering department. In my adult life, I worked for GM Engineering staff myself for twelve years. I saw the same lying and backstabbing from a personal perspective and know that it exists.

Rex and Louie skipped the next five races so as to just get away a bit, learn their way around the new Mercury and test it some. I'll fill you in on what I know about the races they didn't run. The first one was actually race number 30 for the season and it was run down in Myrtle Beach, South Carolina, at Rambi Speedway. This would be a 200-lap race on another half-mile dirt track. Ned Jarrett came home with the win. Not that this would surprise anyone. Ned always ran well there. Second went to Buck Baker in the Pontiac, seven laps down to Jarrett. Third place was taken over by Joe Weatherly driving the '62 Pontiac again for Cliff Stewart. Fourth and fifth went to Neil Castles and Cale Yarborough. Richard qualified for the pole but crashed on lap 60 for a 15th-place finish. Wendell was 16th and Bobby Isaac finished 18th after losing an engine on lap 30. About 4,000 people came out for this race. On this very night, J.D. McDuffie drove his very first Grand National race and came home with a 12th-place finish driving a '61 Ford.

Just three days later, the boys were in Savannah, Georgia, for a 200-lapper on another half-mile dirt oval. Again this night, Richard would take the pole and then crash on lap 38 for a final position of 38th. Also on this night, Ned Jarrett would repeat as the winner. This time, David Pearson finished second to Ned and on the same lap too. Third place went to Jimmy Pardue and fourth went to Jack Smith. Cale Yarborough drove Herman Beam's Ford to a fine fifth-place finish. Baker finished ninth, still running at the end, and Joe Weatherly finished 14th after an accident on lap 57. This race, number 31 for the season, required about an hour and forty minutes to complete.

The quarter-mile dirt track in Moyock, North Carolina, was the stage for race #32 this year. This was scheduled for 250 laps and it only paid $550 to win. So once again, you have to ask yourself: Why did Ray and Junior risk another million-dollar Mystery Motor on such a small stage? Junior qualified on the pole with little effort. But an over-heating and blowing engine dropped him from the race on lap 179 for a 10th-place finish out of a total of 14 cars entered. Jimmy Pardue won this one with Ned Jarrett a very close second place. Third went to Buck Baker in the '63 Pontiac again. Richard burned down a ring and pinion rear gear on lap 114 for an 11th-place finish and Joe Weatherly lost an engine on lap 19 to finish in the 13th spot. I wonder if his paycheck said position 12A for this race?

Two nights later, on July 13, the guys were all over at Bowman Gray Stadium again for race number 33. This was a quarter-mile flat paved oval around a football field in a stadium atmosphere. It was always one of our favorite tracks to visit. On this night, Glen Wood took the pole driving his own '63 Ford, which had supplied Tiny Lund and Marvin Panch with some nice rides this year. Qualifying second quick was Junior Johnson driving the #3 Chevy. Starting third was Richard Petty and fourth was Ned Jarrett. When they took the green, Glen Wood led the first lap. Then Junior took over the point for the next 80 laps. Ned Jarrett and Glen Wood traded the lead for the remainder of the race. Junior again suffered from an overheating engine, but then was fortunate enough to blow a tire and hit the wall before blowing another engine. He finished 17th in the field of 23 starters. Glen Wood won the race and Ned Jarrett came home second. Third went to Buck Baker and·fourth went to the old man himself, Lee Petty. Lee got around the track in Winston-Salem as well as anyone. Fifth place went to Jack Smith, and points contender Joe Weatherly finished seventh this week driving an older '62 Pontiac again. Richard finished eighth and David Pearson was 11th. Wendell was 13th and Spencer was 18th. Billy Wade lost oil pressure on the first lap and parked it for the 23rd spot. There were approximately 15,000 spectators in attendance for this race.

The New Asheville Speedway was the site for race number 34 this year. This track, sometimes referred to as the "River Bottom," was a one-third-mile paved oval. This race was just the next night after the Bowman Gray race. David Pearson took the pole and Junior Johnson qualified second quick. Third quick was Richard Petty and fourth spot was taken by Jimmy Pardue in his '63 Ford. As the race got underway, Pearson led the first lap and then Junior Johnson drove on by to lead the next 31 laps. Pearson led for two more laps and then Richard and Ned traded the lead back and forth for the remainder of the race. Jarrett led the final 19 laps to take the victory. Richard was second and Pearson was third. Finishing fourth was Joe Weatherly, who had hitched a ride in the #41 Plymouth of Petty Engineering. Fifth place went to Buck Baker again in the Pontiac. Junior Johnson is listed as falling out of the race because of "handling" problems on lap 90. (He qualified second fastest, led 31 laps, then pulled in due to "handling" problems? I'm just a bit suspicious about what went on under the hood. Just maybe it wasn't "handling" too well down the straightaway.) About 4,500 spectators came out to watch the 20 entries do battle. And a battle was almost what they got to see. Seems there were some hard feelings after the race between Ned and Richard and they began scuffling in victory lane. As Ned and Richard were about to start into a wrestling match, Ned's crew chief, Bud Allman, stepped in to stop it. Maurice Petty felt differently and restrained Allman until NASCAR officials could gain control. The fight was over just a little "rubbin'" during the final laps.

Race #35 was upon us and it's about time. This week, the gold-and-white '63 Mercury #4 with Rex White at the wheel got back into the game. And a good game it was, too. It was July 19 at Old Bridge, New Jersey, which was a half-mile paved track. Rex was having problems adapting to the rear leaf springs and what he called the rear "overhang" on the car. But in spite of the circumstances, he did an excellent job. Joe Weatherly took the pole in Bud Moore's Pontiac with second fast time going to #28 Fred Lorenzen. Third on the grid went to Marvin Panch and fourth quick was #43 Richard Petty. Fireball qualified fifth and Rex qualified sixth. The race would run for 200 laps. There were 5,400 people who came out to watch the 20 NASCAR Grand National cars take the green flag. At the

Buck Baker's 1963 Pontiac, maintained by Crawford Clements, pictured before the start of the Bristol, Tennessee, Volunteer 500.

start, Joe Weatherly jumped on the lead and held it for the first 179 laps. With just 21 laps to go, Joe's crew couldn't get his car restarted after fueling it and he lost six laps in the pits. Fireball went on to win the race in his lavender Ford, with Mercury driver Rex White finishing second, the only other car on the lead lap and just about two seconds behind Roberts. That was a great confidence-booster for the new Mercury team. The Mercury engineers gave my dad a diamond-studded gold Mercury-head tie tac for that finish, and they gave my mom a gold with diamond-studded lapel pin. They were very appreciative of the effort put in by the team. Fred Lorenzen brought home third place with Ned Jarrett in fourth. Bobby Isaac was fifth with Marvin Panch sixth. Weatherly finished seventh and Fred Harb ended up eighth. Wendell was ninth and Neil Castles was 10th. Buck Baker was 14th and Richard finished 16th after losing his brakes on lap 83. Poppa Lee Petty, still attempting his comeback, drove well until lap 59, when an oil line broke. New York's Jim Reed finished 19th after losing a rear end gear on lap 29.

It was a very good day for the White and Clements team.

Just two days later, the teams were all up in Bridgehampton, New York, for a 100-mile race on a 2.85-mile road course. This was still kind of new stuff for these guys. Some of them caught on pretty quick, though. Race #36 would take the cars for 35 laps to make up the 100 miles. A crowd of 11,200 spectators came out to watch 17 Grand Nationals race on the twisting road course. Richard took the pole at an average speed of 86.301 mph. Fred Lorenzen qualified second, and third on the grid went to David Pearson driving the #6 Cotton Owens Dodge. Once the green flag waved, Lorenzen took off and led the first two laps. Then Richard took the lead on the third lap and never looked back. He led the rest of the way for a fine victory on a road course. Lorenzen was second, Panch was third and Pearson was fourth. Fifth went to Ford's Fireball Roberts and sixth was taken by #41 Lee Petty. Rex White drove the new Mercury to a fine seventh-place finish, still on the

Junior Johnson's #3 Ray Fox Chevrolet.

lead lap with Richard. Eighth place went to Ned Jarrett and ninth was Bobby Isaac. Tenth place belonged to Buck Baker driving the Crawford Clements–tuned Pontiac. Billy Wade was 12th and Joe Weatherly had a heartbreaking 13th-place finish. Wendell was 16th, still running his 409 Chevy at the end of the day.

July 28th was the next race, which carried us all back up the hill to Bristol. This just happens to be another one of those races that I have on 8mm home movie film. Once again, during the race and well between scheduled pit stops, Louie took the home movie camera and stood on top of his toolbox in the pits and filmed about the full three minutes that one roll of film had to give. This race was the Volunteer 500, which called for 500 laps on the half-mile paved track. Fred Lorenzen took the pole with an average speed of just over 82 mph. Fred's teammate Fireball Roberts qualified fast enough for the second starting spot, placing him on the outside of the front row, right beside Lorenzen. Starting third was Junior Johnson driving the #3 Chevrolet, and fourth was Marvin Panch in the #21 Ford. Lorenzen led the first lap and then Junior led the next 161 laps. That was the lap that Junior began suffering from engine problems that would eventually take him out of the race. Lorenzen led for the next 80 laps before Paschal carried the stick for one lap. Then, Fred went right back up front. He led for the next 74 laps until Richard got by and held the point for just two laps. When Lorenzen took the lead again on lap 320, he never looked back and held on for a sweet victory. He must have felt at least a little redeemed from the race earlier in the year at this same track. Richard finished second, on the same lap with Freddy. Finishing one lap down to the leaders was Jim Paschal, Marvin Panch and David Pearson. Joe Weatherly brought that Pontiac home in sixth place and Tiny Lund drove the #0 H-M Ford to a seventh-place finish. Darel Dieringer drove his Bill Stroppe Mercury home for the eighth spot and Rex finished ninth with the gold-and-white #4 Mercury. Tenth place went to Tommy Irwin driving the H-M #44 Ford. Junior

Johnson blew another engine on lap 407 and was credited with the 22nd finishing position. The #22 Ford of Fireball Roberts crashed on lap 312 after slamming the wall hard and rolling side over side about four times for a final spot of 29th. Buck Baker finished 32nd after losing an ignition on lap 62. Nelson Stacy crashed his #29 H-M Ford on lap 47 for a 34th-place finish. The #03 Chevrolet driven by G.C. Spencer lost a fuel pump on lap 11 and was credited with a 35th-place finish. Over 23,000 fans came out to watch this showdown between the Holly Farms Chevy and the #28 Lorenzen Ford.

There was another Grand National race just two days later over at the Greenville-Pickens Speedway on their half-mile dirt track. We did not enter this race, electing instead to prepare for the Nashville 400 coming up the next week.

At Greenville, Ned Jarrett took the pole, with rookie Billy Wade qualifying for the outside front row spot in his '63 Cotton Owens Dodge. However, that Dodge burned up its rear end gear on the 23rd lap and Billy finished in the 18th position.

Ned Jarrett led the first 69 laps before David Pearson took the lead for 35 laps. When Ned took the lead again on lap 106, he led until lap 148, when Richard Petty kicked his Plymouth into high gear and took over the show. Richard led the final 51 laps for a fine victory with only himself and Ned on the lead lap. Third went to Buck Baker driving the #87 Pontiac, and fourth was the property of Fred Harb driving the '62 Cliff Stewart Pontiac. Fifth place went to #99 Bobby Isaac driving the Bondy Long Ford. Pearson was sixth with Tiny seventh and Joe Weatherly eighth. Frank Warren and Wendell Scott rounded out the top 10. Twenty-one cars started this race and 14 finished it. This had been race number 38 of the season. This had also been Richard Petty's 24th career win.

On August 4 we were all back up in Nashville, Tennessee, for the Nashville 400. Let me tell you, it is *hot* in Nashville in August! They said it was 102 degrees in the shade. Some of our Kentucky relatives drove the two-hour trip from Owensboro down to watch this Nashville race. It was always fun getting to mix racing with family gatherings. In my research I noticed one NASCAR history book showing Richard as being on the pole for this race, but that was not the case. Rex White set that '63 Mercury on the pole just as he did every time he ever ran at Nashville, and I have the photos to prove it. There was never a time, in seven years of racing at Nashville, that Rex did not have the field covered and either win the race or get involved in an accident of some description.

When the 350 laps were completed (the race was shortened due to darkness), Jim Paschal had brought home the gold. Billy Wade had finished second and Joe Weatherly had finished third. Fourth spot went to Richard Petty and fifth went to Crawford's Pontiac with Buck Baker at the wheel. Ned Jarrett was seventh and Cale Yarborough finished eighth. Ninth and 10th went to Jimmy Pardue and Larry Thomas. The #03 driven by G.C. Spencer burned a piston on the first lap and was shown as finishing 21st. Fred Lorenzen lost an engine on lap 158 and finished 18th. Tiny Lund, David Pearson and Rex White were all involved in a horrific accident on lap 194. The #32 was a '63 Ford of Tiny Lund. Tiny blew an engine and spun in his own oil. His Ford struck the fence and was hit hard by David Pearson, who had just run through the oil from the blown engine. Right then, Rex White came along, leading the race in his gold-and-white '63 Mercury, and drove right under Tiny's car, which had climbed high up and into the wooden fencing behind the metal guardrail. The right rear tire and wheel of Tiny's Ford left a big black mark down the right side of the hood on Rex's Mercury. Then that RR wheel ripped the roll

David Pearson driving the Cotton Owens Dodge collides with Rex White during the course of the accident at Nashville.

cage right out of that Mercury. The Mercury caused the fuel tank on Tiny's car to erupt in flames. It was a very scary sight to see. My dad's younger sister, my aunt Helen Payne, just happened to have our 8mm movie camera in her hands and she managed to get most of the flaming aftermath of the crash on film. It was a very hot and humid day in Nashville anyway. These flames didn't do anything to cool things down one bit.

After this Nashville crash, the Mercury was repaired again and raced a few more times. But this time, when the new roof and roll bars went in, there were two additional bars added that ran from the upper corners of the main cage hoop to the lower corners of the frame where it kicks up for rear axle clearance. After the other drivers and mechanics in the garage area saw the damage done to this Mercury, I heard a few claim that Bill Stroppe didn't know how to build race cars. I also heard my father correct them and tell them that no other car at the track that day could have withstood the hit that Rex took. Almost all of the other teams installed those new bars after that weekend. There were no hard feelings toward Mr. Stroppe at all. We were all very thrilled that Rex and Tiny escaped the flames. It was one of the nastier crashes I have ever seen.

One thing about the old Nashville Fairgrounds speedway that must be a record of some sort: Rex sat on the pole every time he raced there. He first ran there in 1957 with the '57 Chevy Black Widow racing team. He sat on the pole and was driving away when

Photograph snapped just after Rex White's 1963 Mercury collided with the rear of Tiny Lund's Ford. Note half of roof and roll cage is torn away.

Wrecker crews removing Tiny Lund's car from the accident scene.

the RF wheel broke. Again in '58, Rex was on the pole. Same thing again in '59, '60, '61, '62 and '63. Seven years in a row, Rex set fast time and got the pole at Nashville. He was no doubt the master of that track. The 1960 Nashville 400 is posted on You-Tube nowadays. If you log on to watch it, you will see Rex starting on the pole and running away with the race. He clearly had the field covered again that day. Wins at Nashville were hard to come by, though. Right about the time they had to pit for their final pit stop for tires and fuel during the 1960 race, Rex pitted and got right back out. That left Johnny Beauchamp's #73 Chevy in the lead. Right as Beauchamp started down pit road, his crew chief, Dale Swanson, noticed a few raindrops. He flagged Johnny to keep going and maintain the lead. He did and within a couple of minutes, the heavens opened up and that was that. Johnny won on fuel mileage in a rainshortened race and Rex had to settle for second. Well, it was still a good points position and still paid fairly well. After all, Rex and Louie were indeed in the points chase to win it that year.

With the new gold-and-white '63 Mercury all but destroyed in the accident at Nashville, it was apparent that Rex and Louie would have to miss a few races to rebuild the entire car. By this time, they had sold the '62 Chevy, complete with the best 409s they had, to Canadian Jim Bray. Jim still remains a family friend to this day.

What happened at the races we missed? Well, we didn't miss all of them from a spectator's point of view. But we didn't get to race in any of them either. The next one, race #40 of the season, was held in Columbia, South Carolina, and was titled the Sandlapper 200. Richard Petty set quick time for the pole and Joe Weatherly's Pontiac was second quick for the outside front row. Third on the grid went to Bobby Isaac in a '63 Ford, and fourth-place starter was the #3 Chevy of Junior Johnson. The #03 of G.C. Spencer qualified fifth for this race. Once underway, Richard Petty and David Pearson traded the lead back and forth a few times. Junior Johnson was right up front racing in close quarters with Petty and Pearson when, on the 102nd lap, his Chevy sailed over the banking and landed bottoms-up in the late night sky. He was credited with a 17th-place finish. Richard led the final 34 laps for a well-deserved victory in front of about 8,500 people. Pearson drove the #6 Dodge to a second-place finish, and Isaac finished third with Jarrett fourth. The top four cars were still on the lead lap. Finishing fifth was G.C. Spencer in the Chevy #03. Billy Wade was sixth and Jack Smith was seventh. Weatherly finished 11th and Baker was 15th, both having suffered suspension problems. Twenty-two cars started this race.

Three nights later the big show was back up in North Carolina at the Asheville-Weaverville Speedway. Fourteen thousand five hundred spectators came out to watch 27 drivers take the green flag for this 500-lap race on the half-mile paved track. There was no qualifying this day and the cars started the race in the order in which they showed up at the gate. This put Ned Jarrett on the pole with #28 Fred Lorenzen on the outside front row. Third was #44 Ford of Tommy Irwin, and starting fourth was G.C. Spencer driving the #48 Plymouth for Jack Smith. Once the green waved, Ned led the first 13 laps before Lorenzen took the point for the next 174 laps. Fast Freddy was indeed earning his nickname today. When Lorenzen pitted, Petty took the point for 34 laps. Lorenzen regained the lead and drove away for a one-lap victory over second-place Richard Petty. Third place went to Jim Paschal driving for the Petty team, and fourth spot was taken by #6 David Pearson. Finishing fifth was Billy Wade, Pearson's teammate driving the other Cotton Owens Dodge. Jack Smith, Buck Baker, Joe Weatherly, Ned Jarrett and Buddy Baker rounded out the top 10 today. Lorenzen earned $2,550 for his win.

Our hometown track in Spartanburg, South Carolina, played host to race number 42 for the '63 season. Again, this would be 200 laps on a half-mile track. Hometown car owner Cotton Owens came out of retirement for this one. This was one of Cotton's favorite tracks and his shop was within walking distance from it. Joe Weatherly took the pole in Bud Moore's Pontiac. Second fastest was Ned Jarrett and third quick was Richard

Petty. David Pearson started the Owens #6 Dodge in the fourth position. Owens ran all three of his cars this evening as Billy Wade drove the #5 Dodge to start seventh and Cotton qualified 10th on the grid. Once the race started, Weatherly led the first 33 laps before his Bud Moore Pontiac engine scattered, leaving him with a 17th-place finish. Jarrett, Buck Baker, and Richard Petty swapped the lead until around the final lap when Jarrett emerged victorious in his #11 1963 Ford 427. Finishing second was Richard with Buck Baker in third. The top three were still in the lead lap. Fourth went to the #5 Dodge driven by Billy Wade and fifth was taken by Cale Yarborough driving the #19 Ford for Herman Beam. Spencer finished seventh with Cotton finishing eighth. Roy Mayne was 13th in his '62 Chevy and Wendell was 15th in his '62 Chevy. Pearson finished 16th after losing oil pressure on lap 43.

Race #43 this year was another International 200 held at Bowman Gray Stadium. Tonight would be a bit different, though. Junior Johnson started the 427 Mystery engine Chevy on the pole and actually finished the race with a nice victory. He was the only car on the lead lap at the end. Only two sports cars started this race. One was an MG and the other was a Corvette. They fell out early for 17th and 19th places respectively. Finishing second was Richard Petty and third went to #21 Glen Wood. I have been told that the Wood Brothers can still be seen in the stands at Bowman Gray Stadium on Saturday nights during the present-day racing seasons. That was always a successful track for them and it has a certain allure all its own. David Pearson was fourth and Ned Jarrett came home fifth. G.C. Spencer brought the #03 Chevrolet back in sixth spot. Weatherly drove a borrowed '62 Dodge and finished ninth. Buck Baker was 10th and Wendell was 11th. Junior Johnson won $580 in front of 11,500 people.

The Mountaineer 300 was the 44th race for this season. This race was held on a .375-mile paved oval in Huntington, West Virginia. Starting from the pole would be Fred Lorenzen, and outside pole would be Jack Smith in his #47 Plymouth. Third place on the grid went to Richard Petty and fourth-place starter was Junior Johnson driving the Holly Farms #3 Chevrolet. Fred Lorenzen led the first 62 laps before Richard Petty took over for the next 52 laps. At that point, Jim Paschal led for 12 laps, and then Weatherly led from lap 133 to lap 197. Lorenzen passed Joe for good on lap 198 and held the lead to the conclusion of the 300 laps. He won $1,600 for his efforts in this race. Finishing second was Joe Weatherly, this week back in Bud Moore's Pontiac. Third went to Jim Paschal in the #42 Petty Plymouth, and fourth and fifth went to Ned Jarrett and Buck Baker. G.C. Spencer brought his #03 Chevy home sixth, with #29 Nelson Stacy coming home seventh driving the yellow Holman-Moody Ford. Panch was ninth and Richard was 10th. Our friend Jim Bray brought his '62 Chevy #14 home for an 18th-place finish, still running at the end. The #3 of Junior Johnson reportedly ran out of brakes on lap 90 for a 20th-place finish. Joe Weatherly retook the points lead by a slim margin of 112 points over Richard Petty.

It was about time *we* got to race again. The Merc was all fixed up with a new face and fresh makeup and we were loaded for Darlington and the 1963 Southern 500. This would be race number 45 for this season.

When they unloaded the newly rebuilt '63 Mercury, ran it through inspection and began practice, they were fairly content with the car. Rex was really good with chassis and he and Louie both had learned a lot from their chassis mentor, Frankie Schneider. Those '57 Chevys had leaf-spring rears, so they reverted back to some of what they knew from the past. Plus, setting up the front end in the Mercury and reducing the "bump steer" also helped them a great deal. I don't believe too many guys were onto bump steer in these days. I know for a fact that Ray Nichels wasn't. That's because he learned it from Louie and Crawford when they went to work for him during the '64 season. We'll talk about that shortly.

The car ran well during practice and the engine even picked up a bit from some of the Chevy knowledge Louie put into it. The H-M Fords still had the horsepower edge over the Mercurys at this point, though. Not a lot, but just enough. Fred Lorenzen qualified on the pole at a speed of 133.6 mph. Second quick went to the #3 Mystery Motor Chevy of Junior Johnson. Third and fourth fastest went to Joe Weatherly and Darel Dieringer, both in new Mercurys. Darlington is a 1.375-mile, high-banked paved oval.

G.C. Spencer poses outside the shop with the #03 Ray Fox Chevrolet.

Turns one and two were pretty tight at this time. Turns three and four were not as tight, but only one lane could get through them. Nobody with any level of sanity ran two wide through turns three and four. Getting a good run off turn four made for a good passing zone as you entered turn one. Rex qualified the gold-and-white #4 Mercury in 10th place for a fair starting position. Forty-one cars started this race in front of 62,000 paying spectators. Fireball Roberts was the fastest qualifier for the race at 133.819. However, since he didn't qualify on the opening day, he started at the head of the second-day qualifiers. That put him ninth on the grid with Rex just outside of him. They were the first and second quickest cars on the second-day time trials.

Once the race began, Lorenzen led the first lap, and then Johnson led the next 72 laps. Pit stops began to cycle through, so Panch led one lap and then Lorenzen led another one. Marvin Panch then led laps 76 through 143 until Junior Johnson took the point from lap 144 until lap 234. At that point, Johnson's Chevy began overheating, so he backed off to try to cool the engine down. After about twenty more laps, he pulled in with yet another blown engine and was credited with a 20th-place finish. During this period of NASCAR, the sanctioning body paid extra money to the leader of each lap. And it was good money that added up at the end of the day. In this case, the car that finished 19th

Freshly painted 1963 Mercury ready to be loaded for the Southern 500. Red truck in background was used as a 1957 Chevy factory team tow truck. By this time it was relegated to use as Louie's daily driver, which he used to take us kids to school.

1963 Mercury, with a fresh coat of gold-and-white paint, loaded up and heading off to the Southern 500 in Darlington.

Rex White on the hook after first-lap accident in 1963 Rebel 300 at Darlington.

earned $500. For his 20th-place finish, Junior earned $4,705. That was the fourth-highest paycheck for the day. On lap 235, Marvin Panch, driving the #21 Wood Brothers Ford, regained the lead for the next 33 tours of the speedway. Fireball passed him on lap 289 and led through lap 313. Fred Lorenzen again took the point for a few laps before Fireball grabbed the lead and drove away for the remainder of the race. He received the winner's checkered flag on lap 364 for an excellent job of winning a caution-free race and a paycheck of $22,150. Roberts had set an average race speed of 129.784, which was not only a new record for the race, but many believed at the time it would never be broken. Marvin Panch and Fred Lorenzen finished second and third. They were the only three cars on the lead lap at the conclusion of the event. Nelson Stacy and Darel Dieringer finished fourth and fifth, with our hero Rex White bringing the #4 Mercury home sixth. Finishing sixth paid the team $2,155 and left us all feeling relieved that both Rex and the race car came back safe. All of that brand-new Mercury sheet metal did indeed receive the infamous "Darlington Stripe," as evidenced by the photographs. Joe Weatherly finished seventh with Tiny Lund finishing eighth. Coming home ninth was Bobby Johns driving the blue-and-white Pontiac #7. Finishing 10th was the #13 Chevy 427 driven this week by Buck Baker.

The Pettys had entered three of their Plymouths in this race. Credited with 12th

My dad and mom, Louis and Magdalene Clements, stand in front of the 1963 Mercury.

place was Richard Petty driving the number 43. However, there was a bunch of commotion going on in the Pettys' pit area. Jim Paschal was driving the #41 car and Bob James was driving the #42 Plymouth. During one pit stop, Papa Lee Petty ordered Paschal out of the #41 and put Richard in it because he felt that car was the quickest of the three. Then Paschal got into the #43 car. The #42 car, driven by Bob James, broke a spindle on lap 59 and fell out of competition. He was credited with finishing 27th. After that, the engine in the #41 that Richard was now driving blew to pieces and he fell out. So when Paschal pitted for his last stop, Petty ordered him out of the car and put Richard back in the same car he started the race in. Are you keeping up here? I'm getting confused. Richard is credited with a 12th-place finish and Paschal gets credit for the 22nd-place finish. This way, the Pettys only have to share 30 percent of $500 instead of 30 percent of $1,030. Now I get it. That wasn't so hard now, was it? The Petty team was about the lowest-paying team to drive for in those days. While they paid 30 percent, other teams paid 40 percent of the winnings to the driver.

Of the 41 starters, only 16 were still running at the end of the race. Our friend G.C. Spencer was driving the #47 Plymouth for Jack Smith. Jack never cared too much for the Darlington after crashing over the wall and outside the track during the '58 Southern 500. Spencer finished 24th. Buddy Baker finished 23rd after being given the ride in his dad's '63 Pontiac #87 when Smokey offered Buck Baker the ride in the #13 Chevy. Funny how some things turn out. Buck was getting older and most race car owners didn't think much about having Buck drive their cars until it came to Darlington. Baker was a master of that track, and given the right equipment, he could still get it done. A couple of smart mechanics figured this out. Just wait till next year! Oh yeah, for those of you watching Lorenzen's checkbook, this was the race that put him over the $100,000 season winnings total. Most racers felt this amount would be unobtainable in a single season. Fred knew otherwise and the season wasn't over yet.

Just four days later, we towed the Mercury over to the .4-mile dirt track in Hickory, North Carolina, for race #46 of the season. This would be a 250-lap race, and some fast cars came out for this one. Junior was there with the #3 Chevy and Spencer was there with the #03 Chevy. They *must* have been breeding those engines down in Florida! Anyway, David Pearson grabbed the pole in Cotton Owens's '63 Dodge. Fred Lorenzen brought the #28 H-M Ford out for a rare short dirt track race and he qualified second quick. Starting third was Joe Weatherly and fourth was Jack Smith back behind the wheel of his own '63 Plymouth. Fifth and sixth starting spots went to Richard Petty and Rex White.

We had our family Chevy station wagon parked about midway down the back stretch in the infield. During practice, I was watching Junior Johnson putting on a display of "sideways" driving. Junior had a lot of flair on the dirt tracks but on this particular lap, he slid a little too high entering turn one. Right between turns one and two, Junior high-centered the car on the dirt embankment and the car rolled over, kind of gently, but still crumpled things a bit. The wrecker came out and right-sided the car and pushed it back into the pits. Ray Fox and his crew went over the car and got it ready for the race anyway. Junior started in the seventh spot on the grid.

Once the race got underway, both Pearson and Weatherly traded the lead back and forth several times. It was some real good racing up front. Jack Smith and Ned Jarrett also joined the hunt for the lead during the first half of the race. Both Rex White and Joe Weatherly crashed their Mercurys on lap 58. I honestly don't remember if they hit each other or what really happened. In any case, on lap 125, the exact halfway point in the race, Johnson took the lead and never looked back. He led the final 125 laps for a fine victory. Amazingly, his teammate G.C. Spencer, driving the #03 Chevy, finished in second place, right behind Junior. I can only imagine the number of hose clamps and tie wraps, how much bailing wire and duct tape, it took to hold those Chevys together for the entire race. Bob Welborn finished third in a Pontiac and Jimmy Massey finished fourth in a '61 Chevy 409. Fifth place went to Larry Thomas driving Wade Younts's '62 Dodge. Buck Baker and Neil Castles finished sixth and seventh. Fred Lorenzen finished ninth, 32 laps down to the winner. Ned was 14th and Richard was 15th. Pole sitter Pearson blew an engine on lap 123 for an 18th-place finish. Rex was credited with 22nd place, which paid $50 and a wrecked race car. Yes, racing for a living was very tough during this time. If you were not directly connected to a factory ride, you had to live off your earnings at the track. We ate a lot of baloney sandwiches and never went hungry even once. We usually got a new pair of shoes at the start of the new school year, and about six months later we had new soles and heels sewn onto them. Like I said earlier, if we were poor, we didn't know it. Nobody bothered to tell us. That big box of fried chicken my mom made for every race would feed a bunch of friends after the race.

Once back at the shop Louie knocked the dents out of the fenders and straightened

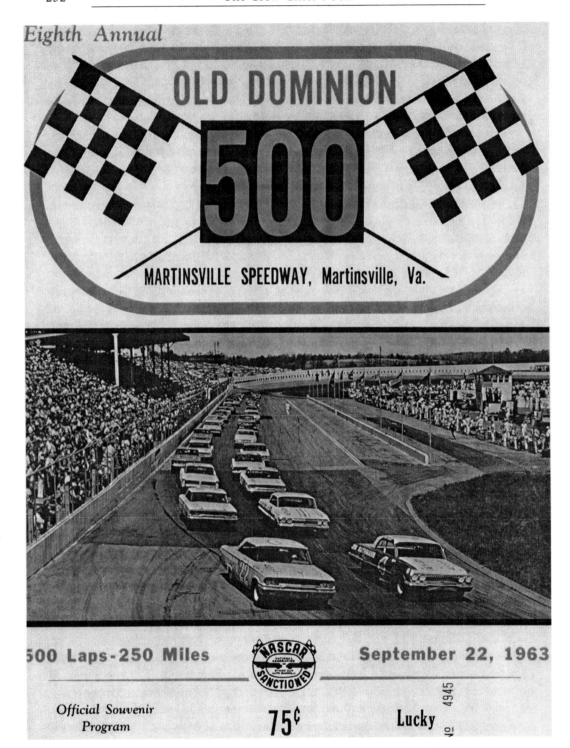

A souvenir program from Martinsville Speedway showing Rex White on the pole and Fireball Roberts outside pole.

things out. Rex and James and Ken would usually take care of changing the gear and springs and shocks, etc. It was up to Louie to determine if the motor had to come out and also do all the body and paint work. With just two days to put things back together, the engine was good to go another round. It was off to Richmond, Virginia, again for the Capital City 300, which was scheduled for 300 laps on a half-mile dirt oval.

The Richmond Fairgrounds always provided a good race. The surface from one dirt track to the next was nowhere near as consistent as it is today. Drivers raced on what was there, and different teams and drivers had a handle on various types of surfaces. For this race, 15,000 people came out to watch Joe Weatherly take the pole and Jack Smith take the outside pole. Third quick went to #41 Richard Petty, and fourth spot on the grid went to David Pearson in the Dodge. Rex qualified the Mercury fast enough to start fifth place, inside third row. Crawford's Pontiac, with Buck Baker driving, qualified sixth, which put him just outside of Rex at the start. That was a sure-fire recipe for my cousin Gary and me to climb to the highest spot we could find to watch the fireworks. This was going to get good. Grab your Pepsi and some chicken and let's go climb a pole or something.

At the green, Weatherly led the first 98 laps, and then Ned took over for around 20 laps. Joe retook the lead from lap 119 until lap 165, when Rex grabbed the top spot. Rex led the next 100 circuits to lap 263, when Ned Jarrett got by and held on for the next 36 laps for the win. Rex finished second, which paid $1,475, a far superior sum to the one received just two days earlier. Larry Frank brought the Bondy Long Ford home in third, with Spencer driving the #03 home for the fourth spot. Fred Lorenzen finished fifth in the H-M Ford and Richard finished sixth. Modified standout driver Ray Hendrick drove a '61 Pontiac home for the seventh position. Tiny Lund was ninth, Wendell was 14th, and Pearson finished 15th. Weatherly lost an engine on lap 175 and finished 21st. Baker finished 22nd. Junior Johnson dropped out after 62 laps and was credited with a 25th-place finish in the '63 Chevrolet.

We had two weeks to get things back in shape for the Old Dominion 500 back up in Martinsville, Virginia. Five hundred laps on this half-mile paved oval was a true test of man and machine, just as it remains today. It is very hard on engines, brakes, tires, sheet metal and patience. September 22 was race day and we were there in full force. I still remember that my older brothers and I had our ball gloves with us and one baseball. We were in the motel parking lot and started out just stretching and playing gently. Pretty soon, my oldest brother Lloyd threw one pretty hard and it snapped into my glove with that nice *pop* sound that we like to hear at a ball game. We all got to throwing pretty hard, and right before we broke something, the motel manager came outside and requested that we take the game elsewhere. Probably a good thing.

Once at the track, Junior Johnson set fast time for the pole and Fred Lorenzen set his Ford on the outside pole. Third quick went to Fireball Roberts driving his lavender #22 H-M Ford. Fourth fastest was Rex White driving the gold-and-white #4 Mercury. Anytime we could start in the top five, we felt good about our chances. Thirty-six cars started the race in front of a crowd of 20,000 spectators. At the wave of the green flag, Junior put the Chevy out front for the first 51 laps. Then Fred put a bumper to him and moved him just enough to get by. One lap later, Junior drove around Lorenzen's Ford and led for the next 30 laps. Lorenzen took the point for good on lap 81 and was never really threatened for the lead again. After qualifying fourth for the race, Rex crashed the

Rex White leading the 1963 Old Dominion 500.

car on lap 183. After that, Johnson kept hounding Lorenzen and literally drove the tires off his Chevy. He blew a tire and crashed on lap 296 for a 21st-place finish. Rex was credited with 25th place. Lorenzen went on to win by one lap over second-place Marvin Panch in the #21 Ford. Third spot went to Joe Weatherly and fourth was David Pearson in the Dodge. Fifth went to Richard Petty, four laps down to Lorenzen. Billy Wade, Fireball Roberts, Nelson Stacy, Jack Smith and Buck Baker rounded out the top 10 finishers. Of the 36 starters, 16 were still running at the end of the day. Lorenzen earned another $3,800 for his checkbook.

Martinsville was the prettiest track we visited all year. Clay Earls was the owner and promoter there and he kept the track very well groomed and always very neat and clean. It was not at all the stereotypical race track for that era.

Two days after the Martinsville race, NASCAR held another 300-lap race at Dog Track Speedway in Moyock, North Carolina. It didn't pay much money, so unless you were racing for points, it just didn't make much sense to go. So we didn't.

Joe Weatherly and Ned Jarrett took the front row, with Tiny Lund and David Pearson taking up the second row. Jarrett and Weatherly finished first and second, on the same lap. Third went to David Pearson, nine laps down to the leaders. Fourth spot belonged to Richard Petty with Fred Lorenzen fifth. Cale Yarborough and Buck Baker finished sixth and seventh. Wendell finished 11th, still running at the end. Only 15 cars started the race and 10 finished it. This had been race number 49 for this season.

Just one week after the Martinsville race the guys had the '63 Mercury ready to race again. This weekend we traveled back up to North Wilkesboro, North Carolina, for the Wilkes 250. This required 400 laps on the five-eighths-mile paved oval. Qualifying on the pole for race #50 this season was Fred Lorenzen, back in his '63 H-M Ford #28. Starting second was Fireball in the lavender #22 Ford. Third on the grid went to Marvin Panch in the Wood Brothers Ford #21, and fourth-place starter was Nelson Stacy, driving the yellow #29 H-M Ford. The Chevy with Junior Johnson at the wheel qualified ninth, and Rex qualified 13th on the grid. Fourteen thousand spectators came out to watch this race. Lorenzen's pole speed was 96.566 mph. Once the race started, The roar of the crowd could be heard above the roar of the 28 Grand National engines. The people had come out to watch the expected duel between Lorenzen's Ford and Johnson's Chevy. But it was not to happen this day. Junior's Chevy broke a brake cylinder on the fourth lap to take him out of the race. The fans still got a good treat, though. Marvin Panch and Fred Lorenzen drove all over each other all day long. Nelson Stacy and Fireball Roberts led a few laps during the pit stop cycles. But it was mostly a Lorenzen and Panch show. Panch won the race with Freddy second. They were the only cars on the lead lap. Stacy was third, Roberts fourth and Jarrett was fifth. Finishing sixth was Joe Weatherly, and coming home seventh was Rex White in the gold-and-white Mercury. David Pearson, Tiny Lund and Larry Thomas rounded out the top 10. Wendell Scott, Larry Manning and Roy Mayne brought their older 409 Chevys home, still running at the end, for the 15th, 17th, and 18th positions. Jimmy Massey and Richard Petty both blew engines in their Petty Plymouths for respective finishes of 25th and 26th place. Eighteen of the 28 cars were still running at the end.

We didn't take the Mercury to the next race, either. The guys in the shop enjoyed some time at home with their families and it took a bit to get the car back in race shape again. Race #51 was held at Tar Heel Speedway in Randleman, North Carolina. This race would run 200 laps on a quarter-mile paved track. Lorenzen took the pole with Richard the hometown boy starting second. Third quick was Joe Weatherly and fourth was Ned Jarrett in his '63 Ford. David Pearson started sixth in the white '63 Dodge with the red roof and the big red #6s on its doors.

When the race started, 3,000 paying fans watched as Lorenzen led for the first 159 laps. Then Richard with the #43 Plymouth took the lead on lap 160 and held on for forty laps to win his 13th race of this season. Car #8 with Joe Weatherly at the wheel finished second and was the only other car on the lead lap at the end. Third spot went to #42 Bob Welborn driving a Petty Plymouth, and fourth position was taken by Darel Dieringer in a Ford. Finishing fifth was Lorenzen, who fell out of the race with four laps to go with a burned up rear end gear. Eight of the 19 entries fell out of the race. Richard brought in $580 for his win and his other Plymouth, driven by Bob Welborn, was paid $380.

Eight days later we were scheduled to be in attendance for the 1963 edition of the Charlotte National 400 event, which was always a good race. Rex had a history of running in the top three at this race. Well, things just didn't turn out that well for the entire Clements family for this race. My sister and I and our baby brother had all gone to bed Friday night. My mother and oldest brother had stayed up to watch the late news to see who qualified where. Instead of that, what they saw when the sports news came on was that the crew of driver Rex White had been wiped out in a traffic accident that evening. It was shocking at best for my mother. She came and woke us up and our phone started to ring off the hook. What a way to find this stuff out — over the TV late night news!

My dad, Uncle Crawford, Wilbur Hayden from Owensboro, and Berlin McBee from Spartanburg were all four riding in a new '63 Oldsmobile Coupe, on their way back to their motel after having a nice dinner out. While they were traveling down a straight road at about 45 to 50 mph, an approaching car turned head-on into them. This was before the days of seat belts, which which were not universally found in American cars until 1968. The steering wheel broke Crawford's ribs and one of them punctured a lung. He was in very bad shape. Louie was riding in the front passenger seat and was thrown through the windshield. At the moment he cleared the glass, his head hit the hood of the car, which was now bent straight up in the air. Both cars were totaled. Wilbur Hayden was right behind my father and was just leaning forward to ask a question when the collision occurred. His head went top first right into a steel dash. This car did not have a padded dash. Wilbur's head never regained its normal status. Berlin was taking a nap and had a pillow in his lap with his head laid down and was not injured. Before passing out, Crawford grabbed Louis and pulled him back through the broken windshield and saw that his face had been cut off from the tip of his nose all the way up to his hairline. Crawford reached over and pulled the skin and nose back down over my dad's face. At that point he blacked out.

An ambulance took them all to Cabarrus County Memorial Hospital in Concord, North Carolina. Within minutes after being brought into the ER, the doctors pronounced my father D.O.A. They covered him up with a sheet and went to work on Crawford and Wilbur. After maybe 30 minutes or so, someone in the ER heard my dad make a noise and went and pulled that sheet back and yelled, "This man is still alive!" They went to work on him right away. In the meantime, a personal friend and a man who had worked at the shop off and on, Dickie Caldwell, called and volunteered to take my mother and my Aunt Dottie from Spartanburg over to the hospital in Concord. That ride is about an hour and 20 minutes. Louie and Crawford were both medicated very heavily and didn't know what had happened.

On Sunday morning, while the Charlotte race was preparing to start, my mother was driving all of us kids to go see my dad in that hospital. At that point, the doctors really didn't know if he would live or not. Crawford was conscious and asking for some medication for really bad gas that he had. That gas made his ribs extremely sore and nobody seemed to be doing anything about it. Just as clear as a bell, I can still hear Crawford saying to his nurse, "If you don't get me something real good for this gas, when I heal up I am coming back here just to kick your chest in and pray that you get gas!" Nope, even sedated, my uncle Crawford had no fear of anything.

I still remember my mom taking each of us kids in one at a time to see dad. When she took me in, he tried to sit up and couldn't. He asked me, "Weren't you hurt too?" He held my hand tight and my mother explained to him that I was not in the accident with him. He fell back asleep at that point. This was a very scary time for all of us. All of the kids in my family worshiped my father. We loved him to no end and were praying all we could just for his survival. Friends and neighbors were bringing over prepared foods for all of us kids. Crawford and Dottie and their four kids lived just about four houses up the street from us. Mario Rossi and his wife, Janie, and their two kids lived just across the street from us. My cousins came down to stay with us while our moms were staying at the hospital. The Spartanburg NASCAR community came together and treated us very well and made sure we had everything we needed.

But, there was still a race to be run that day. I asked Rex and James Hylton if they did anything different for the race, like appoint a crew chief. Rex said, "No, we just carried on just like Louie was there. We ran the race we would have normally run and luckily, the car held together." Marvin Panch took the pole and Junior Johnson's Chevy set second quick time for the front row outside position. Third on the grid went to Fireball in his Ford and fourth quick time was set by Ned Jarrett in his '63 Ford. Another Chevy, this time Smokey's car, with Bobby Isaac driving it, qualified for the fifth position. When the race started, Panch led one lap before Junior took over and led the next 49 laps. Panch, Darel Dieringer, Roberts, Lorenzen and Johnson traded the lead around for the most of the day. Rex qualified the Mercury 12th fastest while Louie was still in the Intensive Care Unit of the Cabarrus County Hospital. When the race was over, Rex had brought the Mercury back in one nice clean piece with a ninth-place finish. Junior ran wide open all day just to prove that he could outrun the Fords. There had been some talk about how the Ford guys had caught up to the Chevy guys and Junior said in victory lane that he just wanted everyone to know that was not the case. He stated, "I don't guess Freddy will be doing anymore bragging about outrunning me. He had his chance today and he couldn't do it." The Detroit battle waged on. Lorenzen was second and Panch was third. Fourth went to Fireball Roberts and fifth was taken by Joe Weatherly in his Pontiac. Sixth place went to Richard Petty in his Plymouth and seventh was captured by G.C. Spencer driving this week again for Jack Smith in his #48 Plymouth. In eighth place was Darel Dieringer in a Mercury and ninth spot was won by Rex White and the team without the help of Louie this day. Tenth was Nelson Stacy driving another H-M Ford. Junior won the race in the Chevy with 46,500 fans watching. Finishing 22nd and 27th were the other two Chevys of Ray Fox with Jim Paschal and Buck Baker driving. Both cars blew engines with around 100 laps remaining. Smokey's Chevy with Bobby Isaac driving it this day slammed the wall on lap 57 for a 31st-place finished. Bob Welborn and Bob James each drove a Petty Plymouth and each blew his engine before the halfway point in this race. Bob James was 23rd and Welborn finished 26th. Aside from Junior's victory, Wendell Scott was the next highest finishing Chevy in 16th place, still running at the end. Socialite Mamie Reynolds entered her H-M Ford with the #56 painted on it for Ed Livingston to drive. He finished 17th, still running at the end.

My mother spent most of that day in the hospital with my dad. We kids rode back home to Spartanburg. About two hours after the race was completed, my father heard some commotion going on in the hallway and heard a nurse say, "You can't go in there, he's knocked out and won't know you anyway." Then Louie spoke up and said, "Yes, I do know him, that's Junior Johnson." Junior and his wife Flossy came to visit my dad in the hospital just a couple of hours after victory lane ceremonies. That one memory of Junior coming to visit after the race meant more to Louie than anyone will ever know. For Junior to take time away from a huge celebration to visit a fallen fellow NASCAR member in the hospital spoke volumes to all of us. Unfortunately, there was already some terminal friction starting between the team members and not even one of Rex and Louie's team members had the time to make a hospital visit. It didn't go unnoticed, either.

With Louie being a 50 percent owner of the team and still hospitalized, Rex did not enter the next two races. Race #53 was held at South Boston, Virginia, at the South Boston Speedway for 400 laps on a three-eighths-mile paved oval. Richard Petty won it with a two-lap lead over second-place David Pearson. Third went to Joe Weatherly and fourth was Bob Welborn in a Petty Plymouth. Fifth place went to Larry Thomas in a '62 Dodge. Junior Johnson qualified his #3 Chevy third and fell out on lap 208. About 5,500 were in attendance.

Race #54 would be 150 miles on the Hillsboro, North Carolina, .9-mile dirt track. Joe Weatherly started on the pole and won the race too. He was the only car on the lead lap. Second position went to #41 Bob Welborn in a Petty Plymouth and third was #02 Doug Cooper driving Banjo's old '62 red-and-white Pontiac. Buck Baker took fourth with Curtis Crider fifth and Richard Petty sixth. Junior Johnson had qualified his #3 Chevrolet second quick for the outside starting spot. He led about five laps then blew an engine on lap 104. Twenty-four cars entered this race in front of approximately 6,800 fans. Spencer lost an engine for the 17th spot and Ned Jarrett and Billy Wade both lost engines and were credited with 20th and 21st. Of the 24 starters, only 9 finished the race.

At last, the final race of this season was upon us. My dad was still recovering, but had been transferred from the Concord hospital to Mary Black Hospital which was in the center of Spartanburg. Mary was Dr. Black's mother, and they were from a very prominent family in the area.

This race was number 55 for the long and grueling season and it required all of the east-coast guys to tow out west to the road course in Riverside, California. Rex and James took the Mercury out there for the race and qualified very well for the fifth spot on the grid. Running against some USAC and road course ringers, they were in an excellent starting spot. Marvin Panch took the pole with an average speed of just over 101 mph. Starting second was #22 Fireball Roberts in the H-M Ford, and third quick was Darel Dieringer in the Stroppe Mercury. Fourth starter was #28 Fred Lorenzen, fifth was Rex White, and sixth went to Panch's teammate Dave McDonald in the #21 Ford. Panch carried the #121 on his car.

There was a 5-car pileup on the first lap. As I remember, Rex dropped a wheel off through the esses, which stirred up a bunch of dust. He spun around and most of the field missed him. But four cars didn't miss him. Short day; small paycheck, too. Very long ride back home.

Dieringer won the race in his '63 Mercury with Dave McDonald second and Marvin

Panch third. Fireball was fourth and Junior Johnson, driving a new Stroppe Mercury #26, finished fifth. Forty-one cars started the race in front of 32,500 racing fans that had come from all over the country to watch the stock cars race on the famous road course. Of the 41 starters, only 22 were still running at the end of this one. I also have this race on a nice VHS tape and it even shows racing school owner Bob Bondurant crashing his '62 Chevy hard into the concrete wall at speed. He was not injured. Dieringer earned $7,875 for his win. The next two cars were Wood Brothers Fords, and they totaled $7,515 for those next two positions. Joe Weatherly finished seventh and that sewed up his NASCAR Grand National championship for the second year in a row. Lorenzen's total money earned for the season was over $122,000. That was a phenomenal feat for that period. That made Lorenzen a superstar, with big bucks, good looks, and fast cars—and he was single. He probably did OK with the ladies! Pete Brock, Augie Pabst, and Ken Miles were all considered to be road course ringers for their time. Ken Miles did finish the race in 11th position driving a new '63 Ford.

The official points rundown for the season had Joe Weatherly at the head table with earnings of $74,623. Second went to Richard Petty with earnings of $55,964, and third in the points standings belonged to Fred Lorenzen with a dollar total of $122,587. Weatherly and Petty both ran 54 of the races and finished only 1,128 points apart. Lorenzen had started only 29 of the 55 races. Weatherly won three races and Petty won 14 races. Lorenzen won six times. Rex White finished ninth in the points, having only started 25 races. He won about half the amount of money he had won during the 1960 season when he had won the championship. Junior Johnson started in 33 races and finished 12th in the final points count. At $67,350, Junior won the fourth highest amount for that season. He won seven races, one more than Lorenzen, but he blew up over 20 of those Mystery engines in doing so. I guess we have to think of this kind of like the parable of the loaves and the fishes. They just kept reaching into that basket and pulling out a new engine whenever they needed it. I think Spencer blew about five of those engines, and Smokey's car blew about five engines too. It would have been nice to have had access to enough engines to have run the Chevy all season.

After a lengthy conversation with Rex White today, we found the numbers of Mystery Motors to be even more of a mystery. We know that Rex and Louie were definitely the first to ever assemble them in race configuration and they were also the first to actually run them in test cars that they had built. But after that, things start to get fuzzy. I have read accounts from Smokey's book and several other writers saying that there were over 40 of these engines built and shipped to Smokey's shop right before the '63 Daytona 500. Rex tells me that he and Louie were right there when the big truck delivered those engines to Smokey's shop and there were exactly 14 of them. Of the 14 engines delivered, they were forced to sell two of them to Holman-Moody.

Speaking of Holman and Moody, I was fortunate enough to get to visit H-M shops a few times when my dad went up there. As a kid I thought their shops were huge and really cool. Now, at my age and frame of reference, I have to think it is a wonder that anyone *ever* beat them. They were so far ahead of everyone else in terms of money to spend, number of employees, and space to work, their resources seemed unlimited. Just my opinion, but to me, Ralph Moody has never received the credit he rightfully deserved/deserves. He was *the* man who convinced Big Bill to allow larger and stronger suspension pieces. He explained to Bill that if no one actually "finishes" the race, pretty soon you won't be able to sell tickets. Big Bill understood well.

Rex says for certain that H-M had to allow Bubba Farr to use one of the Mystery Motors for the 500. As soon as the 500 was over, he had to return it. So, Ray Fox's third car could have been the car built by Bubba Farr. Of the twelve remaining engines, Rex and Louie received only the one that was in the car when the race was over. Fox was supposed to have two engines, one for each of his cars, but both of his cars blew up during the race. That leaves 11 engines in Smokey's floor, not counting the one he had in his own car. I have heard stories that H-M actually sold their Chevy motor back to Junior Johnson. So, it is really left up to guesswork as to where and how all those blown engines got replaced throughout the season.

Very much worthy of mention for the 1963 NASCAR season was that this was the year that my mother, Magdalene Clements, invited over several drivers' wives to our home in Spartanburg, South Carolina, for a meeting to draw up the bylaws for the newly formed Grand National Racing Wives auxiliary. I believe the idea to start this organization was actually thought up by Bettie Panch, wife of Marvin Panch. In attendance during this meeting in our kitchen and around our dinner table were Betty Smith, wife of driver Jack Smith; Coleen Baker, wife of driver Buddy Baker; Betty Baker, wife of driver Buck Baker; and Linda Petty, wife of driver Richard Petty. Together, these women put together an organization that was charged with providing assistance in the unfortunate event of a serious injury or death of the mechanic or driver. This organization has grown today into a multimillion-dollar group that volunteers to help many charitable organizations across our country. I am very proud to say that I was actually there at the very beginning of this group, and to see my mother take part in such an awesome undertaking. What a historical moment for NASCAR!

CHAPTER 9

1964: Working on the Hemi Engines

Simply put, the 1964 NASCAR season was one of the toughest seasons ever for the racers and fans alike. The Grand National series alone lost four drivers in this one season. Joe Weatherly was killed during the opening race at Riverside, California. Then, NASCAR's first real superstar, Fireball Roberts, was severely burned in an accident shortly after the start of the '64 World 600 in Charlotte. He died in the hospital in Daytona about a month later from complications of pneumonia. Next, Jimmy Pardue, a regular on the circuit driving a Nichels Engineering '64 Plymouth, was killed during tire testing at the Charlotte Motor Speedway. Driver Larry Thomas, who had finished 22nd in the 1963 points championship, was killed in a highway accident in 1964. Then, shortly before the '65 season could get up and running, Joe Weatherly's replacement, Billy Wade, was killed while tire testing at Daytona. Bud Moore Engineering had lost two drivers in one year.

The speeds were getting much higher due to the introduction of the newly redesigned Chrysler Hemi engine and the Ford effort to improve in order to catch it. The Mercury teams were also catching up with the H-M Ford in the horsepower race with the same engine. Bud Moore, despite the terrible emotional setbacks he must have felt after losing Joe and Billy, worked very hard to produce even more horsepower for his Mercurys. The entire atmosphere around White and Clements, Inc., in Spartanburg began to feel heavy. With Louie injured so badly in the highway accident, it was a sure-fire miracle that his good physical conditioning and extremely strong will to live kept him going. All of the good wishes and prayers from family and friends certainly didn't hurt anything either. James Hylton had said from his first day at work with Rex and Louie that his intentions were to become a Grand National driver himself as soon as the opportunity presented itself. For the '64 season, Ned Jarrett hired James to be his crew chief, and that certainly helped James climb one more step up the ladder. At the end of the '64 season, Ned even let James start a couple of races in his backup car for a little driving experience as well as extra cash for the team going into the end of the season. James did a good job, which gave him the confidence to go out on his own as soon as he could arrange it.

At times like this, right here, it can be lonely writing a book. Some things need to be said so that you, the reader, can get a true grasp of what really went down. But to do that means throwing someone under the bus, and I am not willing to do that right here. What I can say that is fair game is that Rex and his wife, Edith, were going through a divorce. Rex had a new lady friend who lived down in Atlanta. Once Louie began to feel well enough to get out of the house and start to try to get back to work, Rex was well involved with this new person in his life.

The first race of 1964 was held at Concord, North Carolina, and was called the Textile 250. This race would be 250 laps on a half-mile dirt track. Rex was out of town and the car was not race ready, and Louie wasn't feeling up to working yet anyway. But just exactly one month from the accident that had the E.R. doctor declare Louie DOA, he and Crawford were both standing up on the tailgate of my mom's Chevy wagon watching this dirt race at Concord. I was for certain watching my dad more than I watched the race that day. He was still moving very slowly and was still bandaged up pretty good. Nothing would do for Crawford but to climb up and on the top of that station wagon for a better view of the race. This was a man with several broken ribs and one punctured lung. He held his left side for the entire race. But he didn't miss one bit of it.

Funny thing is, I remember seeing Junior roll his Chevy over during qualifying for this race too. He didn't do much damage to it so they made repairs in the pits and he started the race outside the front row. David Pearson had the pole. Ned Jarrett won that race with Joe Weatherly finishing second. Richard was third, two laps down, and David Pearson was fourth, nine laps down. Fifth went to Maurice Petty in the #41 Plymouth. Tiny Lund ended up in the 10th position after a severe metal-bashing contest with Joe Weatherly. They exchanged a few words, but knowing them both, I would say Joe knew when to walk away and did so. Tiny was about four times the size of Joe. Wendell crashed his Chevy on lap 134 and finished 17th. Junior Johnson lost another engine on lap 109 and finished 19th. Don't even bother counting those Mystery Motors anymore. You could do permanent damage to an otherwise good brain trying to figure out how two engines turned into 26 engines without any parts availability. I'm kind of thinking it was smoke, mirrors, a rabbit's foot, one clove of garlic and a chicken leg bone on a necklace. I saw it in an old western movie, so it must be true!

The second race of the '64 season was run on November 17, 1963, in Augusta, Georgia, on a 3-mile paved road course. The Mercury was ready to race so Rex and Louie and Ken Miller took the car down there for the 417-mile event. This was the only time that the NASCAR Grand National cars would compete on this track. Fred Lorenzen took the pole with Fireball Roberts starting outside front row. Starting third was Marvin Panch and fourth was David Pearson driving the #6 Dodge. Thirty-six cars qualified for this race and Rex qualified the Mercury for the 13th spot on the grid. Once the race started, he made a pretty good charge to get into the top five, but on the 17th lap, that 427 Mercury gave up the ghost. Rex said the he accidentally over-revved the engine, causing it to blow. That left us with a 26th-place finish and $575 to carry back home. Several cars took a shot at the lead during the 139-lap race. Mostly it was between Fireball and Freddy, but Junior got the Chevy out front on a couple of occasions too. On lap 52, Junior broke the transmission and finished 21st. Fireball won the race with Dave McDonald finishing second in another H-M Ford #29. Billy Wade drove the '63 Dodge home third and Joe Weatherly drove a Bill Stroppe Mercury #26 for a fourth-place finish. Coming home fifth was Ned Jarrett in his '63 Ford. Atlanta businessman and sports car racer Graham Shaw drove his Ford home for an 11th-place finish, still running at the end. Tiny Lund drove the #32 Ford home for the 12th finishing position. These two names would be of increased impor-

After the 427 "Mystery Engine" is given to Junior Johnson, the White and Clements 1963 Chevy rests comfortably outside the shop in Spartanburg, South Carolina.

tance over the course of the next few races. David Pearson and Richard Petty both blew engines for finishes of 17th and 19th. Spencer lost the engine in his Pontiac for the 24th spot. Darel Dieringer, Fred Lorenzen, Buck Baker, Jack Smith and Ed Livingston all lost engines and dropped to the bottom of the field. Jim Bray, who was driving the old White and Clements '62 Chevy 409, lost his transmission on lap seven for a 30th-place finish. Fifteen thousand spectators came out for this road course event and to watch Buck Baker set the fastest qualifying time of 89.545 mph average lap speed.

Race #3 for the 1964 NASCAR season was history in the making and I wasn't there. I have heard a million and one stories about it… enough to know that when time travel becomes an option, I will book a flight on the trip back to this race. That is because the race, held at Jacksonville, Florida, was a scheduled 200-lap race, but the winner had to run 202 laps to actually get credit for his win. It took NASCAR officials four hours to go through the scoring cards to determine that Wendell Scott had actually won this race and the $1,000 first-place prize that went with it. It was Wendell's only Grand National victory and it was surrounded by conspiracy theories. Buck Baker had been flagged the winner but Wendell was actually shorted a couple of laps on the score cards. By the time NASCAR announced that the winner was Wendell Scott, most all of the 5,000+ spectators had already left the track. I don't think Wendell ever got the trophy that was due him. He even made a statement after receiving the win officially: "I wasn't going to kiss the queen anyway." Racial tensions were very high in America at this time and it is entirely possible that this had something to do with the officials' requiring four hours to determine a winner. Jack Smith was third, Ed Livingston fourth and Richard Petty fifth. Twenty-two cars started and only 10 finished the race.

The Sunshine 200 was the fourth race of the season and it was run at Savannah, Georgia, for 200 laps on a half-mile dirt track. We did not make this race either as Louie was still not up to speed to put in a full day's work, the car was not ready and Rex was still in Atlanta. Ned Jarrett and Jack Smith took the front row starting spots in front of 3,500 spectators. Maurice Petty qualified third and Lee Roy Yarbrough started fourth. When the race started, the noise level grew as did the competition for the #1 position. Ned Jarrett, Jack Smith and Richard Petty all ran very strong up front and put on a good show for the fans. Richard won the race and Jack Smith was second. Third went to Tiny Lund and fourth to Maurice Petty. Fifth place was won by Curtis Crider in a '63 Ford. Of the 22 starters, exactly half of them were still running at the end. Richard won $1,000 for his victory.

This next race is one that all NASCAR historians will remember and never forget. This was race #5 for the season and it was titled the Motor Trend 500 at Riverside, California. As I am writing this, I am just about without words to describe my feelings on this day. The race was held on January 19, 1964. This was a Sunday and we kids had school on Monday morning. It was too long of a haul for us to make from California back to South Carolina and stay in good standing with the deal my folks had made with the teachers at our school. I sat by the radio and listened to the entire race.

To start with, my dad and Ken Miller got the Mercury all rebuilt and a fresh engine, trans and rear gear too. They had also installed all-new brakes and shocks. The Merc had had body work and was repainted and looking right. I remember being at the shop when Wes, our sign painter, came in to letter the car. Louie told him not to paint a name on this car yet. Louie had no idea if Rex would go to the race or not. When it came time to leave for California, Louie called Rex down in Atlanta and said, "We have the car ready to go to Riverside. Are you going to be there?" Rex said "No." So Louie said, "Well, I'm taking it out there and I'm going to have Billy Wade drive it." Rex then stated, "Well, if he crashes it, *you* have to fix it." Louie said, "Hey, if *you* crash it I have to fix it. What's the difference?"

Louie struck up a deal with my Uncle Crawford to go with him to Riverside. Crawford was to be the crew chief on the gold-and-white #4 Mercury for Billy Wade to drive. This guy in Atlanta, Graham Shaw, was supposedly a big-dollar guy who really liked road course racing and he wanted to hire my dad to be the crew chief for the #32 Ford for Tiny Lund to drive. He was willing to pay enough to make the entire trip worth the effort.

So they towed all the way out there for the race and began to practice. Billy was very fast in the Mercury and he must have run 5 or 10 laps before he figured out the esses were paved. Once he kept the car on the track, he was very quick indeed. He showed no fear at all. Tiny wasn't doing too bad in his '63 Ford, either. Tiny was always without fear. He was one of those guys who could drive a race car even if it had no wheels on it. A few times he proved it. There were certainly some road course ringers in the race just as we have in today's NASCAR road racing. Several west-coast drivers had much more experience on this track than the visitors from the east. Once the race was started, pole sitter Fred Lorenzen led the first seven laps before Richard Petty took the point for the next 10 laps. Then, as usual, Dan Gurney took the lead for the next nine laps. Parnelli Jones then began to flex his muscle over the next 10 laps. Richard took the point over again for the next 15 circuits before Gurney took the lead for good on lap 54. From that point until the final lap, #185 Gurney was in his own zone. Lorenzen even stated after the race that there is just no sense in even trying to run down Gurney at Riverside when his car is right.

At the end of the five-and-a-half-hour marathon, Dan Gurney was victorious driving his #121 Wood Brothers Ford. Second place went to Marvin Panch driving the second Wood Brothers Ford. The Woods had a decent payday of $19,520 for the combined efforts of both cars. Third spot went to Fireball Roberts driving his H-M '64 Ford #22. Finishing fourth was west-coast driver and Indy car driver Bill Amick, driving a new Bill Stroppe Mercury. Fifth spot went to Ned Jarrett driving the new Bondy Long '64 Ford. David Pearson was sixth in the Dodge and our west-coast friend Marvin Porter finished a fine seventh place in his '63 Ford.

At one point during the race, Billy Wade dropped a wheel in the dirt, which caused him to spin and hit a dirt embankment front end first. That knocked the oil filter off the engine. By the time he righted the car, got it refired and drove slowly around the track, Crawford was waiting to find out what had happened. Once under the hood he knew what he had to do. The slow time on the track and replacing the oil and filter in the pits cost Billy a total of six laps. Had it not been for that, he would have finished fifth. But if a frog had longer legs, he wouldn't bump his butt when he jumped! Billy finished the race, still running at the end, and came back with a 13th-place finish and $625 for the Louie Clements '63 Mercury. The Ford that Tiny was driving was encountering problems staying on the paved portion of the track too. This was pretty common during this period of NASCAR. Tiny finished, still running at the end, with a 15th-place spot and $575. I believe the deal was that Graham Shaw paid Tiny to drive the car and Louie got to keep whatever the car won plus the fee offered to him for taking on the job anyway. Even though my father was still not up to 100 percent physically and emotionally from that highway accident, I know it gave him some confidence to bring home both cars in one piece and a pocket full of cash.

The worst thing about this race was sitting right beside the radio in our living room and hearing the radio announcer broadcast that Little Joe Weatherly had lost his life in an accident on lap #86 of this race. Bud Moore said that a front-wheel cylinder had come apart and that let the brake pedal go to the floor as Joe was entering turn number five. Joe hit the concrete wall with the driver's side of the car and was not wearing a shoulder harness. His head came outside the window and also hit that concrete wall. As far as I ever heard, he was killed instantly. He was a hero to many of us and it was really hard to take that sort of news. It is shocking, it's painful, then you get angry at the situation, and then you come to acceptance. We will always remember Joe Weatherly as a flat-out race car driver and a ton of laughs in the garage area. He was one of a kind.

Forty-four cars started this race in front of over 58,000 spectators. Twenty-one cars were still running at the end.

This Riverside race marked the end of White and Clements, Inc. Once Rex came back to the shop they agreed that Rex would buy out Louie's portion of the business and that is what happened. There were some hard feelings for a little while. But really true friends don't stay angry at each other for long. As you will see, there will come another time when Rex and Louie team up again. However, right after splitting up the team, both my dad and my Uncle Crawford took jobs up in Highland, Indiana, working for Ray Nichels Engineering. Nichels had struck up a deal with Larry Rathgab, an engineer at Chrysler, that allowed Nichels to have access to cars, engines, and engineering assistance from the Chrysler Corporation. Louie was going to be the chief mechanic for Bobby Isaac's Dodge #26 and Crawford would do the same for the '64 Plymouth driven by Paul Goldsmith.

There were a few weeks in December when my dad was just not yet up to doing a full hard day's work as he had done all of his life. He felt the responsibility to be the stable provider for our family, but had to deal with the rehab that comes with living through a big accident. He never let us down, though. After he and Rex split up their business, there were a few weeks before he went up to Indiana to work for Nichels. One morning he got up and drove over to Bud Moore's new shop and spoke with Bud. Bud Moore was a longtime family friend and as good a man as you could hope to meet. Louie asked Bud if he had any work and Bud immediately gave him a job. My dad told me years later that Bud knew he wasn't up to speed yet, but pretty much employed him as a gesture of friendship.

The first job he did there was to fabricate the new fuel inlet for refueling the car and blend it into the rear quarter panel. That job stuck in his mind. Bud told him to take all the time he needed and not to worry about anything. I called Bud a few weeks ago and spoke with him a while about this as well as other things we shared from the past. Bud said, "Well, we were all family back in those days. If one of us needed help, the others would chip in." As soon as Louie and Crawford were released from their doctors and given a clean bill of health, they both drove up to Highland, Indiana, to work for Nichels Engineering. It was ironic that the car Louie built the fuel receiver for would turn out to be numbered 4 and that Rex would drive it for four races for Bud before Bud had to cut back to just one car. Rex sat on the pole in Atlanta for Bud and he finished third in the '64 World 600 in Bud's Mercury too. He did a good job for Bud.

The first race we would see with Louie working for Nichels Engineering turned out to be a good one. Louie was assigned by Ray Nichels to serve as crew chief and chief mechanic for the '64 Dodge that Bobby Isaac would be driving. Crawford was asked if he would handle the same chores for the '64 Plymouth for Paul Goldsmith to drive. Isaac carried the #26 and Goldsmith ran the #25. The cars were absolutely beautiful when they rolled out into the sunlight. We used to keep a little transistor radio in our shirt pocket with an earphone so we could hear the radio broadcast while watching the race. I can still remember hearing the announcers calling the race and making reference to those gorgeous red cars with the golden numbers on them.

For the first 100-mile qualifying race, Goldsmith set fast time for the pole at 174.910 mph. This was 10 miles per hour faster than those ferocious Chevys were last year. This new Hemi was a serious machine, although it was really no more legal than those unobtainable Chevys were. There were no Hemis on the street yet, just as there were no 427 Chevys on the street back then either. Even the folks working out in the Nevada desert at Area 51 didn't know about those Chevys. With Goldsmith on the pole with a '64 Plymouth Hemi, and #3 Junior Johnson driving a '64 Dodge Hemi for Ray Fox, the front row was set for the first 100-miler. Twenty-three cars started the first qualifier. At the green flag, Paul Goldsmith grabbed the lead for the first 17 laps. Then, Buck Baker, this year driving the #41 Plymouth for Petty Engineering, took the point for three laps. Paul led another lap and then Baker took over again from lap 23 to lap 39. Since it was a 40-lap race, when Junior Johnson passed Baker on the last lap, that settled the race with Johnson as the victor. That race was #6 of the season and paid Junior and Ray $1,100. Baker was second with David Pearson third and Marvin Panch fourth. Darel Dieringer finished fifth driving a new Bill Stroppe '64 Mercury. Paul Goldsmith and Johnny Rutherford both blew engines and finished 17th and 18th. Rutherford was driving a second Bud Moore Mercury for this race. Jim Bray drove the old Rex White '62 Chevy to finish 23rd.

The second Daytona qualifier was race #7 of the season and shaped up with a fine lineup of very fast race cars. Again, 23 cars would start this race with #43 Richard Petty taking the pole position at 174.418 mph. That was about .5 mph slower than Goldsmith's qualifying time. At the start of the race, Petty seemed to have been blasted from a race car cannon. His blue Plymouth drove away from the field and was looking very strong and flexing its muscles. I remember Richard saying that he could run with almost anyone in practice but he was sliding around in the seat. He brought the car into the garage area and they took a 2 × 4 piece of wood and wrapped it with a piece of a blanket and then bolted it to the right side of the driver's seat. This held Richard's ribs in place so he could hold the throttle wide open through the corners. It proved to be a pretty good piece of wood, too! However, all that speed came at a price. And the price this day was using too much fuel. Petty ran out of fuel in the middle of the fourth turn as he was headed for the checkered flag and the win. Bobby Isaac and Jimmy Pardue were drafting each other right behind Richard and they passed him right before he got to the finish line. Bad news for Richard, but good news for Louie Clements and Bobby Isaac. They had won their first race together.

Jubilation ran rampant through our family at that moment. Many people had stated that Isaac was a troublemaker, difficult to get along with, and so forth. My dad loved Bobby Isaac. They got along well and had great respect for each other. Finishing second was #54 Jimmy Pardue, who was also in a '64 Plymouth with the Hemi motor, and third was Richard Petty in his out-of-fuel Hemi Plymouth. Fourth place went to car #00 A.J. Foyt, driving a Banjo Matthews '64 Ford. Fifth spot was the #5 Dodge of Cotton Owens, which was driven by Jim Paschal. Dan Gurney finished 10th in a Wood Brothers '64 Ford #12. After starting fifth, Fred Lorenzen finished 17th due to a blown tire on lap 31. Only 15 cars were still running at the end of the 100-mile race.

The 1964 Daytona 500 was a spectacle to behold. Being NASCAR race #8 for the season, it started with 46 racers lined up to give it their all. On the pole was the red #25 Plymouth of Paul Goldsmith. With Crawford tuning on this car, we were very proud. Outside front row went to Richard Petty in his new Hemi Plymouth. Starting third was the #3 white '64 Dodge with Junior Johnson at the wheel. Fourth starter would be the car Louie was working on, the #26 Hemi Dodge driven by Bobby Isaac. We were feeling pretty good about our chances.

So it was time for Gary and me to grab another piece of chicken and a Pepsi and climb up on the roof of that station wagon. We were about to see that nobody was tougher than our daddies' race cars. The only drawback to that theory was that no one had bothered to mention this to Richard Petty. Seventy thousand spectators came out to watch this 500-mile contest, and when the green flag waved, they got the show they paid for. Goldy led the first lap with the red Plymouth #25. Man, that was a pretty sight! Richard was right on him when they came across the line. Richard then took the point and led laps 2 through 6. At that point, Isaac flexed his muscle and led for three laps. Petty then retook the lead for the next thirty laps. At that point, they were starting pit stops, mostly for fuel. Foyt led for two laps and then Goldsmith led for another 10 laps. Petty blasted out front again on lap 52, and this time he never looked back. Richard led from lap 52 to the final 200th lap for a one-lap victory over Jimmy Pardue and Paul Goldsmith. Fourth place went to Marvin Panch in a Ford and fifth went to Jim Paschal in the white Dodge #5. Petty mentioned after the race that it really wasn't any fun out there. He said he had to stay right with the car every second and hang onto it. The cars had reached the point of having some very serious horsepower on tap. They had horsepower numbers like 400 hp painted on their hoods, but in actual engine dyno tests the engines were closer to 600 hp. The cars were still racing on narrow tires, no fuel cells, and no rear spoilers or front air dams. They were actually running too fast for the aerodynamic stage they were in at the time.

Billy Wade, Darel Dieringer, Larry Frank, Junior Johnson and Dave McDonald completed the top 10. Bobby Isaac had an excellent run going until they tried to squeeze just one more lap from that tank of fuel. He ran out and coasted into his pit, and by the time they refueled it and primed the carb and got him back on track, he had dropped to 15th position. He had a top-five car pretty easy. Just a miscalculation on fuel mileage. Foyt's Banjo Mathews Ford blew its 427 engine on lap 127 for a final position of 24th. Jim McElreath crashed his #14 Bill Stroppe Mercury on lap 126 for a 25th-place finish.

Texan Johnny Rutherford was driving the #01 Mercury for Bud Moore and crashed while going down the back stretch. He hit the guardrail and spun, and the air rushing under the rear of the car picked it up and flipped it onto its roof. The car slid for about 800 feet. Rutherford said two things that I remember about that crash. First was that he kept mashing on the brake pedal but the brakes didn't seem to be working. Maybe he was joking when he stated that. But he also stated that he held his arm up in front of his face because of the grinding hot sparks that were flying at him. That crash was on lap 107.

Ned Jarrett crashed his '64 Bondy Long Ford on lap 106 for a final spot of 27th. Parnelli Jones was driving the Bill Stroppe '64 Mercury #15 and blew an engine on lap 77, which gave him the 28th final position. Seventh-place starter was the #6 Dodge driven by David Pearson, and he crashed on lap 52 for the 30th position. Fred Lorenzen's #28 Ford blew its engine on lap 49, and he was credited with the 31st-place spot. The Holman-Moody Ford #22 driven by Fireball Roberts locked up its transmission on lap 13 and he was listed as finishing 37th.

Forty-six cars began the great American race and only 20 were still running at the end. Richard Petty won $33,300 for his victory. This was the largest sum of money ever paid to a NASCAR race winner to this date. The previous record was the 1960 World 600 won by Joe Lee Johnson, which paid him $27,150.

Since Ray Nichels Engineering only concentrated on the larger races and not the points championship, we did not attend nearly as many races as we had become accustomed to traveling to. That saved some mileage on our Chevy wagon. But we still listened to every race on the radio. My mother is in her late 80s as I write this, but she is still with the program and is right in front of that TV for every NASCAR truck race, nationwide race and cup race. One of us calls the other as soon as it's over.

The next race for us was the March 22 race at Bristol. This would be 500 laps on the half-mile, banked, paved oval track. Marvin Panch grabbed the pole position driving the '64 Wood Brothers Ford #21. Second fastest was Fred Lorenzen driving his #28 H-M Ford. Third quick went to Fireball Roberts and fourth fastest was Richard Petty in his Hemi Plymouth. The Old Master, Buck Baker, got around very well this day too. He was driving the #41 Petty Plymouth. It still sounds strange for me to think of Baker driving for the Pettys. I guess money can heal some wounds. I remember back in 1958 and '59 when those two guys, Buck Baker and Lee Petty, would have killed each other had it been required to win the race. And on this day, they were working together. I guess that's the "family" part of racing. Like the way you can yell at your brother, but you won't let anyone else do it.

To help you with the proper time frame here, let me tell you a few other things going on at this time. The Drifters had a #1 hit with "Under the Boardwalk," the Temptations had a hit song called "My Girl," and the British Invasion hit America's music industry really hard with the Beatles, the Rolling Stones, the Dave Clark Five, and others.

Ray Nichels was not really interested in the smaller short-track races, so he mostly ran the larger races with greater spectator appeal and larger audiences. Our next race was the Southeastern 500 at Bristol. This was run on March 22, 1964. Marvin Panch set the fastest qualifying lap to grab the pole position in the Wood Brothers Ford. Lorenzen was second quick and Fireball qualified third fastest. Richard Petty would start fourth. Once the race started and the cars began to string out, both Isaac and Goldsmith drove well into the top 10 and were just riding and biding their time. Marvin Panch led the first six laps before Fred Lorenzen drove by him with seemingly little effort. After that, Lorenzen led the 494 remaining laps. The real excitement came with about 24 laps remaining. Freddy's Ford began to smoke and it was obvious to the crowd that he was experiencing engine-related problems. He had to slow down for the last few laps, and that let his team-mate Fireball Roberts close the big gap down some. Lorenzen crossed the finish line at approximately 40 mph, still one-half lap ahead of Fireball. Paul Goldsmith drove the red #25 Hemi Plymouth to finish a fine third place. Buck Baker drove the #41 Petty Plymouth to finish fourth and pole sitter Marvin Panch finished fifth. Sixth through 10th were Ned Jarrett, Jim Paschal, Richard Petty, #4 Rex White driving Bud Moore's Mercury, and #1 Billy Wade driving Bud's primary Mercury. As I stated earlier, Bobby Isaac was running very well through the first 100 laps. But fate intervened on lap 110 when the rear end gears welded themselves together. He was credited with a 27th-place finish. A capacity crowd of 26,500 people came out to watch the 36 starters race for three and a half hours.

The next two races were short-track races that we did not attend. Our next event would be the Atlanta 500 on April 5. Again, Fred Lorenzen smoked everyone in time trials to grab the pole for this race. Starting on the outside front row was A.J. Foyt driving the '64 Ford #00 of Banjo Matthews. Third quick was Paul Goldsmith driving the Nichels Plymouth tuned by Crawford Clements. Fourth quick went to Fireball Roberts in the #22 H-M Ford. Fifth fastest was Billy Wade in the #1 Bud Moore Mercury, and sixth fastest

Bud Moore's Mercury #1 driven by Billy Wade, loaded on the transporter after the Atlanta 500. A couple months later, after Billy's death, I trimmed down this photograph and carried it in my wallet.

1964 Plymouth #25 driven by Paul Goldsmith loaded on the Nichels transporter after the Atlanta 500.

was Bobby Isaac driving the Nichels Engineering #26 Dodge tuned by my dad, Louie Clements. Hours before the race, Goldsmith had complained to Nichels that Isaac's car seemed to handle better than the Plymouth he was driving. At that point, Ray Nichels asked my father what had he done differently from what might be in the car Crawford was working on. Louie told Ray that the front end settings were different on the cars and that Isaac could drive his car deeper into the corners and get back into the throttle sooner. This was something they had figured out after qualifying was over. So Louie and Crawford

Just a split second after blowing a right front tire, Goldsmith slams the wall and flips onto his roof. Fred Lorenzen barely missed contact with the sliding car of Goldsmith.

went to the Plymouth that Goldy was going to drive and reset the front alignment on his car just like Isaac's car. As soon as the green flag waved, Goldsmith shot out like a rocket. Everyone had expected Lorenzen to take off and not look back, but Goldsmith led the first 55 laps. Louie gave Bobby the pit board to bring him in for the first stop of the day just a few laps earlier. Once fueled and supplied with four new tires, Bobby ran back into the fray. Louie looked over the tires that came off the #26 Dodge and noticed the RF tire was gone. Bare cords were showing all the way around it. He ran down to Goldsmith's pit to tell Ray Nichels about it, and Ray had no sooner said, "Aw, he'll be OK," when *kabloom!* The right front tire on Goldsmith's Plymouth blew out, and that sent him up the hill and straight into the turn one guardrail. The car climbed up on top of the railing, then flipped onto its side and then rolled over onto its roof and slid down the embankment. Lorenzen had a full head of steam and just barely drove under Paul without touching him. It was a spectacular type of accident, the kind that makes the newsreels. From there on in, they pulled Isaac in to pit in plenty of time to keep that problem from occurring again. The teams had choices of compounds during this period of NASCAR. Choosing the softest compound tire for a 500-mile race might not have been the best decision. It's all hindsight now.

Fireball Roberts, Lorenzen, Isaac, Jim Hurtubise (relief driving for Junior Johnson), and Marvin Panch traded the lead many times throughout the race. When the checkered flag waved, it was Fred Lorenzen right there to take it home with him. He was indeed "Fearless Freddy" on this day. Bobby Isaac drove the Dodge home for a well-deserved second-place finish. Ned Jarrett was third in his Ford. The first Chevy in this race was 25th-place G.C. Spencer driving the old White and Clements '63 Chevy with a '64 body on it and an older 409 engine in it. He fell out early with a broken rocker arm. Only 10 cars from the starting field of 39 were still running at the end. Yes, it was a pretty good feat back then just to complete a race. Dan Gurney and Parnelli Jones crashed together on the 17th lap and were credited with finishing 36th and 37th. Of note here is that A.J. Foyt set a record of sorts when he qualified his '64 Ford with three laps of identical speeds of 145.945 mph.

Our next visit to a race track as a family would be the Darlington Rebel 300 on May 9, 1964. The Ray Nichels team had two of the big Dodge crew cab trucks with the bed and tire tracks on the back. Many of the guys rode together from Indiana down to Dar-

lington. Both Louie and Crawford would come home first and pick up their families. We all learned a lot from being on the road and going to the races together. We learned about fair play, about keeping families together, about how sometimes you win and sometimes you don't. We learned that you win with humility and you lose with gracefulness. Some days you're the windshield and someday you're the bug.

Crew member "Jimbo" loading Bobby Isaac's 1964 Dodge on the transporter after the Atlanta 500.

Ray Fox's #3 Dodge driven by Junior Johnson loaded on transport after the Atlanta 500. This race was won by "Gentleman" Ned Jarrett driving his blue 1964 Ford.

On this race day, we learned something we already knew: that Fearless Freddy was on a winning streak. He qualified on the pole with Richard Petty on the outside pole. Third-place starter was #54 Jimmy Pardue in another Hemi Plymouth. Fourth quick was #27 Junior Johnson driving a new Banjo Mathews '64 Ford. He quit the Ray Fox Dodge team because he said they were not getting the same good engines and stuff like the Pettys and Nichels were getting. He had certainly changed his tune from the '63 season when he got everything handed to him on a silver platter!

Lorenzen won this race with teammate Fireball Roberts second and Johnson third. Ned Jarrett finished fourth, making this a 1-2-3-4 sweep for Ford Motor Company. Fifth place went to Jimmy Pardue in the Plymouth Hemi. Paul Goldsmith finished this race in the ninth position, still running at the end. Bobby Isaac was credited with 27th position after being involved in an accident on lap 35. Finishing 16th and 17th were the first two finishing Chevys this week. Ironically, 16th went to G.C. Spencer, driving the old '63 Chevy he had bought from Rex and Louie. In the 17th spot was J.T. Putney, who would later find a big spot in our family. He was driving an older, worn-out '62 Chevy 409. Curtis Crider finished 28th driving the '63 Mercury he had bought from Rex after the breakup of White and Clements, Inc. Twenty-six-year-old Bobby Allison was slated to drive the team car from Ray Fox's shop, which was a '64 Hemi Dodge. After the first few practice laps, he came in and told Ray that he was not quite ready to take on the Track Too Tough to Tame. Lee Roy Yarbrough took over the driving duties on that car and gave it a fine eighth-place finish. This victory for Lorenzen had been his fifth straight win. Not bad!

The '64 World 600 in Charlotte, North Carolina, was the next race on our schedule. I remember this race like it was yesterday. We were again parked inside the fourth corner and I was standing on top of my mom's Chevy station wagon and prepared to watch every lap of this thing. I had my little Brownie 126 camera with me and it was loaded with a fresh roll of black-and-white film. With the roar of the engines, the race got underway with speeds we hadn't seen at Charlotte yet. Jimmy Pardue, Bobby Isaac and Paul Goldsmith took off with the show.

On lap #7, Junior and Ned tangled coming off turn two and Fireball hit them running wide-open. His car flipped and erupted in enormous flames and black smoke. From my vantage point, I could not tell who was involved in the crash. Standing right down beside our family car was my mother, having a conversation with Ned's wife, Martha Jarrett. At this point, she didn't know that Ned was involved in this accident either. I snapped a couple of shots from my position, but about all you can see are all the cars and people in the infield, with two giant plumes of black smoke rising to the heavens in the distance. The cars were covered up with tarps once towed to the pits, but I looked under them after the race was over. It was pretty obvious the superstar Fireball Roberts would be in terrible shape after this one. Like I said, Pardue, Isaac and Goldsmith took command of the race after that long caution and were all driving away fast. But once again, Lady Luck interrupted the party. Goldsmith blew an engine on lap 253 for the 19th position. Jimmy Pardue blew an engine on lap 195 for the 24th-place spot. And Bobby Isaac's Dodge broke a motor mount bad enough that it couldn't be repaired and he was credited with the 25th position.

Jim Paschal came back to the Petty Engineering ride after almost a year away from

I snapped this shot moments after Fireball Roberts, Ned Jarrett and Junior Johnson collided on the back stretch of Charlotte Motor Speedway during the 1964 World 600.

it. This time he made the agreement that he would drive the car as long as he wanted and no relief drivers would be forced on him. Richard Petty finished second in his own Petty Engineering Plymouth, which gave Petty Engineering a phenomenal payday of $35,240 for just this one race. That was a huge chunk of change at this time. Rex White finished third, driving Bud Moore's '64 Mercury #4. Fourth was Fred Lorenzen in the Ford #28, and fifth went to Billy Wade, driving the other Bud Moore Mercury. Bud had a good day too with a payout of $12,145. That was more than Richard earned for second spot. Finishing in the sixth position was a spectacular run for G.C. Spencer, still wheeling that old Chevy 409. Luck was with him on this day. He earned $2,950, which was more than he had earned for the entire season just two years earlier! Finishing 12th this day was J.T. Putney driving the '62 Chevy owned by Walter Hunter of Asheville. It was the #46, which was indeed the same old Rex White '62 Chevy. Good for him. By lap 11, fourteen of the cars had already fallen out of the race. Of the 44 starters, only 16 were running at the end. There were 63,300 spectators in the grandstands and infield for this race.

June 7 was the date set for the Dixie 400 in Atlanta. This is also a race we attended. And again, I was on hand with my little Brownie 126 camera, playing "Racing Photographer" for the day. Forty thousand spectators came out to watch this race on this day. Rex White was the fastest qualifier for this race as he set a one-lap record of 146.024 driving the #4 Bud Moore Mercury. He almost won the race, too. He was steadily pulling away from all challengers when he had to pit for fuel. The problem that hurt him was the engine stalled and the team couldn't get it to refire. He lost one lap in the pits, and winner Ned Jarrett got by. Rex made up his lap in the final stages of the race but ran out of time before he could catch Jarrett. The Fords entered this race with a bit of a problem and I believe Ned and James Hylton figured out a solution for it. Seems the valves were growing taller when they got hot and they would not completely close then. Freddy's engine blew on lap eight and the same thing happened to Junior Johnson, Marvin Panch, Larry Frank and Bobby Johns, who was also driving a Bud Moore Mercury.

Ned and James opened up their valve lash to about twice the recommended setting. This let the engine rattle quite a bit until it got hot. Then things began to go more smoothly. I don't remember exactly how I managed to do it, but I was standing right beside the victory podium when Ned drove that blue #11 Ford up and on top of it. I snapped a couple of photos of it for my scrapbook.

Ned won the race with Richard second and Paul Goldsmith third. Fourth went to Darel Dieringer in a Bill Stroppe Mercury as fifth position was taken by Rex White, who had truly driven a flawless race. Jim Paschal was sixth and Bobby Isaac drove the '64 Dodge that Louie was tuning home for a seventh-place finish. Eighth was Billy Wade in another Bud Moore Mercury and ninth went to Jimmy Pardue in his Plymouth. Tenth position was won by Larry Thomas in a '64 Ford. Wendell finished 12th, now driving the old Ned Jarrett '63 Ford that he had bought. Curtis Crider drove Rex and Louie's old '63 Merc home to a 15th-place finish as J.T. Putney brought that same old Chevy home in 16th place, still running at the end.

Opposite, bottom: It may sound macabre, but I trimmed down this picture and carried it in my wallet for years to remind me of my hero Fireball Roberts and the heroic efforts of Ned Jarrett in pulling Fireball from the flaming accident.

There were many very good short-track races that we just didn't get to attend this year. With Louie and Crawford working up in Highland, Indiana, we were just thankful when they could come home for a weekend. Our next big race which would involve the entire Nichels Engineering fleet was the July 4 Firecracker 400 at Daytona. Our whole family got to attend this one. We took the entire week and spent it all in Daytona. While my dad and uncle were at the track testing and qualifying, we were swimming in the motel's pools and playing on the beach. One afternoon, my oldest brother Lloyd took us all to the movies to see *How the West Was Won*, starring Debbie Reynolds. What a cool movie for its time! Then came the day for the qualifying races. As I remember, Lloyd drove the family wagon and took my other brother, me, and my cousin Gary, and we went back out to the track. For the only time in my life, I got to watch the Daytona qualifying races from the stands right at the start/finish line behind the tri-oval. It was awesome watching the cars from that perspective, which was new to all of us. A couple of things I remember about that day would be that Chrysler had just unveiled their new Plymouth Barracuda. It had the fastback rear glass and I believe they were equipped with the 318 engines. Anyway, they must have had at least twenty-five of them at the track, all in the same color of gold. Before the races got underway, they put the cars on the track and had them run wide open, bumper-to-bumper, in one big long draft. I believed they averaged about 125 mph. Not racing speeds, but not bad either.

Once the race itself started, from our vantage point in the front-stretch stands, right behind the flagstand, every time the cars came by, all the people would stand up to see if there was even any daylight between two cars drafting. It was indeed interesting to see from that angle. We did see a very frightening accident directly in front of us that day. I can't remember seeing what started this accident, but I certainly remember seeing the wreckage itself. Fred Lorenzen's white #28 Ford was somehow sideways in the track when Paul Goldsmith T-boned him right directly in his driver's door. The Ford spun around in the infield grass and soon after it came to a stop, Lorenzen climbed out of it in obvious pain. The race car was destroyed, as was Goldsmith's. But Freddy was bleeding extremely bad and we couldn't believe how long it took some help to reach him. These guys, all the drivers on the tracks, were our heroes. We didn't want to lose any of them. During the accident, Lorenzen had an artery cut in his left arm and hand. It was bleeding bad enough that he passed out and fell to the ground. Fireball had just died the day before. That made this accident even more scary for us boys to watch. (My uncle Crawford was the crew chief on the Plymouth for Goldsmith, and after that car was destroyed in this accident, Nichels asked him to handle those same duties for Super Tex, A.J. Foyt. Foyt was driving another Nichels Engineering '64 Dodge, red with gold #47 on it.)

Again, similar to the Atlanta incident, Foyt asked why his car wouldn't go through the corners on a rail like Isaac's could. The week before coming to Daytona, Chrysler engineer Larry Rathgab came to Nichels's shop and Louie showed him the problems with the front end steering geometry on the Chrysler cars. He put one of the cars on their in-ground front-end pit without front end sheet metal or an engine. He put the smallest torsion bars in it that they had in the shop. He then set the proper ride height on the car and set the toe to zero for a starting point. Then he asked Mr. Nichels and Mr. Rathgab to watch the screens on the alignment machine. Louie and Crawford jumped up and down on the cross member and the toe-in ran off each side of the screens. They were amazed. Louie had machined some slugs to go into the tie rod ends and/or the center drag link. With the right ones in there, that "bump steer" was then negligible. It cured a lot of evils in the way those cars drove.

Louie made the changes to Isaac's car while Nichels and Rathgab talked over what to do about Foyt's car. Crawford had also fixed the Plymouth for Goldsmith. Right at the race track in Daytona, they mentioned this to Foyt. Well, as with about anything, you have to show Foyt to get him to agree. Once he saw it, he requested that this modification be made to his car too. Daytona had a bear front end alignment pit so Louie and Crawford went over to use it and still be sly about what they were doing. Foyt drove the car in practice after that change and was all smiles then. He knew he had a horse that could win.

Naturally, for Gary and me to be standing up on top of my mom's car to see the finish of this race, it was a thing of sheer beauty to behold. Our daddies had set up the two cars that had just run first and second at Daytona. It still feels good talking about it today.

Out of the 34 cars, 13 were still running at the end in front of a crowd of almost 35,000 people. Foyt won the race by about three feet, or less than a fender's length. Isaac was on the outside making the pass that just couldn't be made in time for the win. Third place went to Jimmy Pardue, fourth was Buck Baker, and fifth was Paul Goldsmith (driving in relief of Jim Paschal). David Pearson, Johnny Rutherford, Earl Ballmer, Darel Dieringer, and Bunkie Blackburn rounded out the top 10. Nichels Engineering brought home $21,895 for the first- and second-place finishes. This had been race number 35 on this season.

We didn't attend the next race because we didn't have a dog in that fight. But it was a bit of NASCAR history being made that day in Manassas, Virginia, as Ned Jarrett won the 400-lap race in his #11 Ford and let James Hylton drive his backup car to make his first-ever NASCAR Grand National start. James dropped out after four laps, just as agreed. The next race was two nights later at Old Bridge Township for the Fireball Roberts 200. Billy Wade won the race in the #1 Mercury and Ned finished second. Once again, Hylton drove Jarrett's backup car for 22 laps and a 16th-place finish. Two nights later my dad and Bobby Isaac ran the race on the road course at Bridgehampton, New York. This race was a 50-lap contest over a 2.85-mile paved road course. Paul Goldsmith was there to drive the Plymouth tuned by my Uncle Crawford. Billy Wade won this one too. He didn't know it, but he was on his way to setting a NASCAR record. Buck Baker finished driving the Ray Fox Dodge that wasn't quick enough for Junior to drive. James Hylton finished 14th in this one, still nursing the Ned Jarrett backup car. Ned finished sixth. Both Goldsmith and Isaac were very fast and appeared to be in the hunt for a very good day, but those gremlins bit again. Isaac had the rear end gear burn up and Goldy lost a transmission. Isaac was 17th and Goldsmith was 19th.

Three days later the race was held in Islip, New York. And again, Billy Wade won it with Ned Jarrett finishing second. So the racers moved on to the big track at Watkins Glen, New York. And again, and for the fourth straight race, Billy Wade came home the victor. Ned finished eighth and Paul Goldsmith, despite being fast, lost oil pressure and finished 20th. Sophomore driver Billy Wade had just made a pretty good name for himself. He put on a fierce duel with Ned Jarrett at a few tracks but all ended well. Over the course of nine days of the Northern Tour, Wade brought in $4,625. I believe as of this writing, a run of four straight wins has only occurred four times in the history of the NASCAR Grand National/Sprint Cup series.

The race we drove to next would be the Volunteer 500 at Bristol Speedway. Again, Goldsmith and Issac were fast, but no cigar today. Richard Petty qualified for the pole and Goldsmith set second quick time for the outside pole. Eighth-place starter Fred Lorenzen once again won at Bristol in a lap by himself. Petty was second and Paschal was third. The cars that concerned us were still the two red Hemis of Goldsmith and Isaac. Goldy lost a transmission on lap 148 for a 21st-place finish. Isaac also lost his transmission on lap 74 for a 23rd-place finish. Of the 36 cars that took the green flag, only 14 were still running to accept the checkered flag at the end. Twenty-two cars were parked with mechanical problems. Not one accident happened during this race. The race required a little over three hours to complete and 25,500 people came out to watch.

Since Nichels Engineering was only interested in the larger races, we went from July 26 at Bristol until September 7 at Darlington without watching live at the races. We did listen to each race over the Motor Racing Network at the time, though. Now this 1964

Lined up before the start of the 1964 Southern 500, the #3 Dodge driven by eventual winner Buck Baker sits outside of #54 Plymouth driven by Jimmy Pardue. Later that year Jimmy lost his life in an accident while tire testing at Charlotte.

Darlington Southern 500 is a race that I will always remember. I remember it for some of the fine racing I saw that day. But mostly I remember it because I got to sit beside G.C. Spencer's daughter, Carolyn, all day. G.C. had three kids: Diane, Carolyn and Terry. Terry was G.C.'s son and he had a racing Go Kart just like my cousin Gary and I had. On occasion his mom would bring him over to our track, which was a dirt road behind our house, and all three of us boys could go at it. We were all close in age. But Carolyn was G.C.'s middle child and she was an absolute knockout! Both of my two older brothers and I all had a crush on her. During this race, we all got to park our family cars inside a new family "paddock" area inside the third and forth corners. Carolyn was about three or four years older than I was. So, a 13-year-old boy with a crush on a 17-year-old girl who could obviously have any movie star on the planet, well… let's just say I had my work cut out for me.

Not too many people sat in that new bleachers stand that day. We had the top right hand corner seats. I think Gary and Terry were running around the infield, no doubt chasing girls their own age. Any time I would get up I would ask Carolyn if she needed anything, and so on. She was really sweet to put up with a punk kid who was way out of his league. I spoke with her recently and she and her husband have a real estate office down in Surfside Beach, South Carolina. Terry now owns his own transmission shop back up in Inman, South Carolina. That is the town they grew up in and where G.C. had his shop.

The 1964 Darlington Southern 500 was the first race G.C. would run his new '64 Ford 427. He finally gave up on the old '64 Chevy with the 409, even though it did give him a few good finishes. It was just not fast enough to really run with the faster cars of the day. Buck Baker was there and he was set to drive Ray Fox's '64 Dodge Hemi #3. Buck was considered to be getting old at that time. Well, somebody forgot to tell Buck, because he flat-out whipped the field this day. Baker won the race by two full laps over Jim Paschal and four laps over third-place Richard Petty. Ned Jarrett was fourth and Jimmy Pardue was fifth. J.T. Putney had new sheet metal put on Rex and Louie's old '62 Chevy and drove the old 409 home in ninth place. Not bad at all. Spencer blew his engine on lap 186 and finished 18th. Bobby Isaac had kept the Hemi Dodge in the top 10 very solid for the first half of the race. Then he lost an axle on lap 176 for a 20th-place finish. Fred Lorenzen, Junior Johnson, Darel Dieringer, Bud Moore, and H.B. Bailey all crashed and were credited with positions 22 through 26. The red #25 of Paul Goldsmith began to suffer from a severe vibration on lap 129 so he parked it for the day and finished 28th. Goldsmith led the race on two occasions and looked to be a contender for the win before mechanical woes held him down. The race ran on for 4 hours and 15 minutes in front of a crowd of 65,000 spectators. Of the 44 starters, only 12 were still running at the end. Buck was 45 years old at this time and he brought home $21,230 for his third Southern 500 Victory.

Both Louie and Crawford were also assigned to work with Joe Leonard and A.J. Foyt for some USAC races. Joe Leonard had previously been an AMA Motorcycle champion. On one occasion my dad was crew chief for Leonard, and when the car came into the pits after practice laps, Louie asked Joe, "Well, what can I do to make it better for you?" Joe's answer was, "Just cut a big hole in my door so I can hang my leg out through the corners and we'll have this one nailed down." Joe Leonard and Foyt both ran very well for the Nichels team.

September 27 brought about the next chance we had to go racing. This time was back up in Martinsville, Virginia, for the Old Dominion 500, which called for 500 laps on the half-mile paved oval. This track was well known for being hard on equipment. Engines, brakes, trans, sheet metal, tempers, everything was on the line here. Fred Lorenzen took the pole with #27 Junior Johnson starting on the outside pole. Third on the grid went to Ned Jarrett and fourth quick was Bobby Johns driving the #7 Holman-Moody '64 Ford. Pole sitter Lorenzen won the race with Richard Petty and Junior Johnson on the same lap as the winner at the end. That made for a pretty good finish. Marvin Panch and Ned Jarrett rounded out the top five. Bobby Isaac brought the red #26 Dodge home in the seventh position. That was a good finish, as would be any finish inside the top 10. Paul Goldsmith qualified for the sixth starting spot and ran up front for most of the first half of the race. Then, his '64 Plymouth once again fell out due to the vibration gremlins. Spencer kept his new Ford running all day and finished 12th, one spot ahead of Buck Baker, who was still driving the Ray Fox Dodge. About 18,000 people came out to watch the 42 cars take the green flag. Twenty-two of the 42 starters were still running at the end. On a sad note, the night before this race, driver Jimmy Thompson suffered a fatal heart attack at his home in North Carolina.

The National 400 at Charlotte Motor Speedway would be the next event on our racing calendar. That was only about an hour from home and we could load the wagon and get a good seat for this one. Forty-four cars started this race with the Hemi Plymouth of Richard Petty on the pole. Outside front row was second quick qualifier Paul Goldsmith, driving that beautiful red-and-gold #25. Third on the grid was Fred Lorenzen in his white #28 Ford, and starting fourth was my dad's tuned '64 Dodge for Bobby Isaac. As far as horsepower went, Nichels's guys were pretty good. I remember seeing the engine dyno room at Nichels's shop when we were there. That was the first time I had ever seen an engine run on a dyno. It was one of those 426 Hemis too. And it sounded awesome.

The race got the green flag and all the cars roared down into turn one. It was more and more thrilling for me as I grew older and could better understand the work that went into it and the skills necessary to do this sort of thing. I was loving it. Of course, I still had my Pepsi and my fried chicken with me up on the roof of the wagon. From the start, Lorenzen and Goldsmith traded the lead back and forth several times. The top five cars were pretty much checked out in their own zone. But once again, those mechanical gremlins began to creep in. On lap 8, Billy Wade fell out with a crushed windshield. Then on lap 36, the #27 Ford driven by Junior Johnson suffered some suspension malfunctions. G.C. Spencer lost an engine on lap 64, and then Bobby Isaac lost a wheel bearing and spindle on lap 68. This left him with a 27th-place finish. A.J. Foyt was also driving a Nichels Engineering #47 Dodge Hemi when he, too, lost a wheel bearing on lap 127. Paul Goldsmith, who had started on the outside front row, blew an engine on lap 202 for an 18th-place finish. The #28 Ford of Fred Lorenzen won the race by one full lap over #41 Jim Paschal, driving a Petty Plymouth. Richard Petty finished third with #11 Ned Jarrett finishing fourth. Fifth position went to Lee Roy Yarbrough driving the #03 '64 Dodge of Ray Fox. Darel Dieringer was sixth, David Pearson was seventh and #3 Buck Baker was eighth. Ninth and 10th went to Earl Balmer and Bunkie Blackburn. Lorenzen earned $11,185 for his win and Petty Engineering won a total of $9,970 for their second- and third-place finishes. This race required about three hours to complete.

Around the last few races of 1964, Louie went to work for hometown racer Cotton Owens so he could be home more. Crawford came home too and opened his own automotive repair shop and racing engine business in Spartanburg, South Carolina. For the few races left at the end of the season, Louie was assigned to keep up and maintain the #5 Dodge for Earl Balmer to drive. Ned Jarrett's old crew chief from the '61 season was Bud Allman. Bud had also come to work for Cotton, who had Bud take care of the maintenance on the #6 Dodge for David Pearson to drive.

On November 1, 1964, Cotton wanted to run both cars down in Augusta, Georgia, for the Jaycee 300 race, which was a 300-lap contest on a half-mile track. Ned got the pole and Richard started outside front row. Third starter was David Pearson in the #6 Cotton Owens Dodge and fourth starter was #1 Billy Wade. Bobby Isaac was on hand this day to drive the #5 Cotton Owens Dodge. He and Louie had worked well before, so it stood to reason they had good communication and could run well again. When the 300 laps were completed, Darel Dieringer won the race in a '64 Mercury and Bobby Isaac finished second in the Louie Clements–tuned Dodge Hemi. Larry Thomas finished third in his '64 Hemi Plymouth, Billy Wade was fourth in his Bud Moore Mercury, and Doug Cooper brought home a well-deserved fifth-place finish in his '64 Ford. Finishing sixth was J.T. Putney, still driving Rex and Louie's old '62 Chevy, and finishing seventh was Curtis Crider, who was driving the '63 Mercury that had also been Rex and Louie's car. The #6 Dodge of David Pearson finished a disappointing 29th place after an accident on lap 9. Thirty cars started the race in front of 13,000 race fans.

Jacksonville, North Carolina, brought the site for race number 62 on the '64 season. This would be the last race of the season, and at 62 races a year, it was about time! Jacksonville was a half-mile dirt track, and 25 cars showed up for the last race before the new season would start. Doug Yates grabbed the pole in his '63 Plymouth with Ned Jarrett second quick. Starting third would be #55 Tiny Lund in his '64 Ford, and fourth-place starter was Richard Petty. Bobby Isaac qualified seventh in the #5 Dodge that Louie was working on and David Pearson qualified 10th in the #6 Dodge. When the 200 laps were completed, Ned had won the race by one lap over Richard. Third went to #49 G.C. Spencer in his new Ford. Fourth was Doug Cooper and fifth went to Larry Thomas. Twelve of the 25 starters were still running at the end. Pearson finished 10th, having burned down the ring and pinion gear on lap 172. Bobby Isaac, driving the #5, broke a torsion bar on lap 103 for a 17th-place finish. He had qualified seventh quickest this evening. About 3500 people came out to watch the two-hour event.

There were already dark clouds looming on the horizon concerning next year's rules. For 1965, NASCAR had announced that they would not allow the "superengines" in the intermediate-sized cars on the big tracks. Chrysler's racing chief had threatened to boycott the entire '65 season if NASCAR went through with its statement.

For the 1964 championship points race, Richard Petty brought home his first of what would become seven national championships. He earned a total of $114,771. Petty won with a healthy 5,000+ point lead over second-place Ned Jarrett. Third went to David Pearson and fourth was Billy Wade. Fifth in the points race was Jimmy Pardue.

Before the '65 season could get off to a start, we lost Billy Wade during a tire test at Daytona. Seems that when we lose someone we care about, we often work to try to prevent the same fate from taking someone else. All of us have noticed all of the changes that took

Louie's stopwatches that he bought at the Indy Speedway reside in my office today.

place in the name of safety after the tragic loss of Dale Earnhardt. Well, after the loss of Billy Wade, that anti-submarine strap that comes up between the driver's legs and holds the lap belts down into their proper position became mandatory. For years, we called it the "Wade Strap." The fuel cell was designed by Firestone Tire and Rubber Company because of the death of Fireball Roberts. Bill Simpson went to work much harder trying everything he could to produce better and safer fire suits. Goodyear worked a lot with Darel Dieringer on the development of the safety inner liners for the speedway tires. The driver's side window net came about because of Richard Petty's horrific flip on the front stretch at Darlington in '66 or '67. The videos of that crash clearly show the car gyrating wildly like a bucking bronco. Richard's arms were hanging outside the driver's window. It's a true shame that we have to wait until we lose someone we love before we can make a safety change. But sometimes, we just can't see into the future far enough to predict the next big gremlin.

One more thing about the '64 season: somehow, right during the middle of that summer, my dad got off from racing for a week to take us all to the 1964 New York World's Fair. Wow! That was a truly awesome experience for little hometown folks like us. We had a ball. We stayed at some friends' house out on Long Island, and one afternoon we listened to a Yankees game. Jim Bunning pitched a perfect game! You don't get one of those every day.

CHAPTER 10

1965: Chevy Is Back

NASCAR 1965 was, without a doubt, my favorite season of all. This would be our last full-time NASCAR season and it would be the best and most rewarding in terms of "feelgood."

During December of '64 and January of '65, Louie found a shop that would rent him a single car bay to work out of. Just down the hill, out back of that shop was another small shop where our friend Pop Eargle was working by himself. He was the guy who designed and built the first NASCAR- and Firestone-approved fuel check valve to stop the flow of fuel from the car in the case of a rollover. I still remember seeing the first one for the first time. My dad was taking in passenger cars for repair, building race parts for anyone who needed them, and on one Saturday I went with him and watched him do a

1963 Mercury #62 driven by Curtis Crider. Curtis bought the gold-and-white #4 Mercury from Rex and Louie at the end of the 1963 season.

tuneup on an outboard boat motor for a guy. The thing wouldn't run when it came in and it ran like a top when it left. After paying for all the necessary parts that went into the engine, he made $20 for his day's work. When we got home, I saw my dad hand that $20 bill to my mother. He said, "Here, babe, this is what I made today." That was for groceries or whatever we needed.

Once the race season started, Louie went to a couple of races to just walk around the pits and keep his face on the scene. At one of those races, J.T. Putney approached him and asked if he would be interested in being the chief mechanic and crew chief for the new '65 Chevy race car he just had built. Southeastern Aviation and the Beechcraft Company had invested into this sponsorship with Putney, who was a commercial pilot. They struck up a deal and we were racing again. With Louie turning the wrenches and J.T. doing the driving, Putney finished the '65 season seventh in the final points championship count. He finished second one time, third three times, fourth four times and fifth two times. He had 14 top tens for the season. That is actually pretty good for an underfunded, independent team with equipment that just wasn't up to par with the factory Fords or Chryslers.

They started the season with the '65 Chevy Impala Grand National car running the newly released Chevy 396-cubic-inch big block engine. I believe they got their hands on a couple of the L-78 motors that were advertised at 375 hp. That was for insurance purposes so that Chevrolet could sell these cars to the youth market looking for some excitement. In actuality, those engines made about 440 hp right from the factory. Problem was, the Fords and Plymouths and Dodges were making around 550 hp in NASCAR trim. So the Chevy teams had to get back to work. The best the factory had at this point was still

The General Motors Pavilion at the 1964 New York World's Fair.

100 horsepower shy of the 427 Mystery Motor they ran at Daytona in 1963. Within a couple of months, Chevy released the new 427s to the racers and they were able to pull closer to 500 hp from those in NASCAR trim. Still couldn't run with the big dogs on the super speedways, but they did OK against them on the short tracks. Several '65 Chevys were built too. Besides the #19 that Putney drove, Ray Fox built another white #3 Chevy for Lee Roy Yarbrough to drive. Curtis Turner took a couple of rides in a Chevy that year and Jim Paschal drove a #41 Chevy. Ned Setzer drove the #47 Chevy with the 427 engine and Smokey Yunick also built one. For the Charlotte World 600, Richard Howard had a few of these cars built and put some underfunded drivers in them to help entice a larger crowd to come out for the race. My Uncle Crawford was asked by Mr. Howard to serve as the crew chief on a white #34 Chevy for driver Wendell Scott to drive in that race. He and Wendell had some fun with that car. Crawford said he really enjoyed working with Wendell. There were a few more '65 Chevys built that year too. I remember that Buck Baker had a white one with large red #87s on it.

We didn't get to go as a family to many Grand National races that year. Ned Jarrett won his second Grand National championship in 1965 and he did it in a fine fashion, too. Fred Lorenzen won the Daytona 500 in '65 also. The only race that I remember seeing in person while Louie was working with J.T. was the World 600 in Charlotte. We had our family wagon down inside the fourth turn as we normally did. I remember very well counting the laps and always watching for that blue-and-white Chevy to come by us. Then, kabloom! Right in front of us was a pretty good-sized crash that took out a few

Louie started off the 1965 season as a chief cook, bottle washer and crew chief on the Southeastern Aviation 1965 Chevy "piloted" by J.T. Putney.

By spring of 1965 Rex and Louie had joined forces again, but this time to run the Sportsman Circuit, which kept them closer to home. Rex stands proudly beside the 1955 Chevy that carried him to 20 victories and 10 second-place positions out of 32 races he entered that summer!

cars. Putney was one of them. He hit the wall coming off the fourth corner and several other cars got a piece of him. It ripped all the front end and steering linkage from the car and made a mess of things. Once it was towed back into the garage area, Putney asked my dad if he could put it back together. Louie said, "Sure." So he walked over to their truck and grabbed some tie rods, an intermediate link and some hand tools and was walking back over to work on the car to get it back in the race. Right at that moment, Norris Friel, the NASCAR tech inspector, looked at Louie and said, "You know better than that." So the car was just shoved up onto the trailer and everything loaded up. Had it been Lorenzen or Petty or some other big-name driver, NASCAR would have let him repair the car. But no way for an independent.

There were several times when my dad would take the '65 Chevy to close dirt tracks for Putney to run it. If the race was Friday night I would ask him first thing Saturday morning, "So, how did it go?" Usually he would say something like "Old Putt ran pretty good last night." I specifically remember getting up early enough to go to the shop with him for a Saturday to work on that car, and when we got into the old truck my dad said,

Rex standing beside the 1955 Chevy Sportsman. The car sports an obvious Ralph Earnhardt signature caved-in driver's door.

"Old Putt dern near won us one last night." I believe that race had been in Columbia, South Carolina, and Putney qualified outside front row and ran very well all night.

One other good memory about Putney's driving that '65 Chevy came about at the first-ever race on the newly built North Carolina Motor Speedway, or Rockingham as we know it today. Bill France had just lifted the lifetime ban on Curtis Turner, and the Wood Brothers prepared him a new Ford with the #41 on it. Curtis won this race in fine fashion, which put his name in the record books forever. With the factory backing from Ford and Chrysler, it was tough for any independent to compete against them. However, for this race, J.T. Putney qualified that '65 Chevy as the first and fastest Chevy in the field, and there were many by this time. He was also able to run pretty close to the hot dogs for most of the day. It was just a treat for me to get to see an underfunded independent Chevy,

This is the notebook that Louie carried in his pocket that kept track of his chassis and engine settings and calendar appointments for the 1965 season.

MONMOUTH
ENGINE BEARINGS

NAPA

40TH ANNIVERSARY

GENUINE PARTS CO.
208 E. Daniel Morgan Avenue
Spartanburg, S. Carolina
Phone: 585-5221

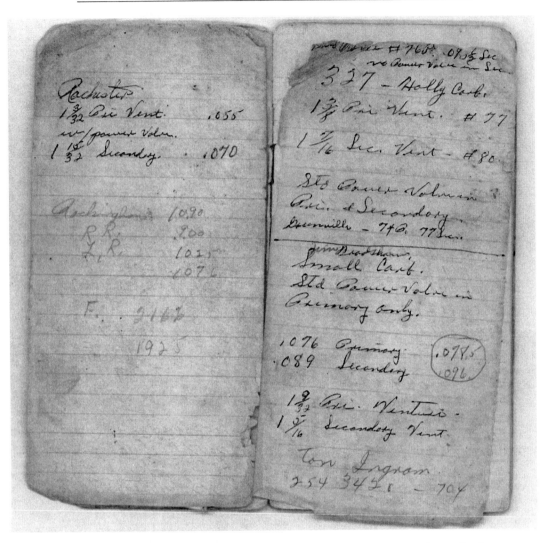

Example of an open page from the setup notebook showing carburetor jet sizes, wheel corner weights, gear ratios and a friend's phone number.

built and maintained in a single car stall, jump right in there and hang with the big boys. Putney was a driver sort of like Tiny Lund or Curtis Turner. He came to race and never showed one ounce of fear. Like Junior Johnson said, stand on it, go or blow!

About halfway through that summer of '65, Rex called Louie and spoke with him for quite a while one night. When he got off the phone, he was smiling. He and his old buddy, Rex White, were going to go racing together again. Rex had started up a new racing parts business in Spartanburg and racing a '55 Chevy Sportsman car at the area races was a large part of making sales for his parts. As long as he was winning, the other racers wanted whatever he had on his car. I believe Slick Owens and maybe Elmo Henderson may have been working for Rex at this time too. This go 'round would be a different arrangement from the last time Rex and Louie paired up. This time Rex offered Louie a salary of $125 per week to keep the race car in tip-top condition and ready and able to

In 1965 short dirt tracks were still part of the Grand National racing schedule (courtesy Ronnie Shelton).

win. In addition to that, Rex offered Louie all of the money he won when they qualified on the pole. Rex figured if the car was set up well enough to get the pole, he could win with it. Then he told Louie, on top of that, he'd even split the winnings right down the middle with him.

Well, this was too good a deal to pass up. That got Louie back into the same old shops where they had raced from in the past and it also got him off the grinding Grand National Series schedule. Or at least we thought at the time. As it turned out, he worked harder than he had to on the '65 Chevy for Putney, but he was home more often and made more money. Together, Rex and Louie ran that '55 Chevy Sportsman car (Nation-wide Series today) in 32 races that summer. My cousin Gary and I got to ride up in the tow truck with them to many of these races. Out of the 32 races they ran, Rex won 20 times! He ran second 10 times, too, and he got the pole just about every time they raced. No, they weren't racing against the Pettys or the Pearsons or the Allisons, but they did race heads-up against Ralph Earnhardt, Bosco Lowe, Jack Ingram, T.C. Hunt, Roy Tyner and Dickie Plemmons. All of these guys were the champions in their own back yards. And when they all came together at the same track, Rex whooped them all.

Rex did admit to me recently that whenever they went to Columbia, Ralph Earnhardt was real good there and tough to beat. There was a dark spot at the end of the back chute and the officials couldn't see that well down there. Ralph would always take a shot at Rex in that one position. Ralph was bad about mashing up the sheet metal on our '55 Chevy Sportsman car. NASCAR had rules about the appearance of the cars, and every time Earnhardt would run over Rex, it bothered Rex.

But it flat-out pissed off my father. That's because every time the body was torn up on that car, my dad would have to go back to the shop after having dinner with our family and he would have to beat out those dents or replace those body parts and then repaint the car. In his mind, my dad figured that Mr. Earnhardt was taking away his family time and he got to where it downright angered him to his limit. After Earnhardt had been knocking and beating on Rex's Chevy for 100 laps one night in Columbia, Louie was standing in Earnhardt's pit when he pulled in after the race. Louie climbed in the car with Ralph and got directly in his face and told him that the next time this happened, he would absolutely clean his clock with whatever was necessary to get his attention. Earnhardt said right back, "Get out of my face." And again, Louie warned him that enough was enough. Surprisingly, Earnhardt got the message and that stopped the slamming against that gold-and-white #4 Chevy. Sometimes a man's gotta do what a man's gotta do.

The best part of this summer of '65 for me came in two packages. First, I was playing guitar and started to play with a group in junior high school in Spartanburg. We were learning to play the #1 hit of the summer by the Rolling Stones, "Satisfaction." The Mamas and the Papas were also "California Dreamin'."

The next best part of the summer for me all played out in one week's time. Actually, it only took four days. Rex and Louie raced in Columbia on Thursday night, sat on the pole and won the race. Not bad. Then on Friday night, they raced at the Asheville River Bottom track, sat on the pole and won that one too. Then on Saturday afternoon, they ran a Sportsman race as a preliminary to the Sunday Grand National race at North Wilkesboro, North Carolina. Yep, sat on the pole and won that one too. They towed over to Shelby, North Carolina, for the Saturday night race and took the pole and won that race. This is getting to be fun, I'm thinking. So, just to cap off the weekend, we went up to Harris, North Carolina, for the Sunday afternoon race, took the pole and won it too. That's five poles and five wins in four days. They had to completely change the setup on the car for each race, too. Thursday night was a half-mile dirt and Friday night was a one-third-mile paved track. Saturday afternoon's race was on a five-eighths-mile paved track and Saturday night's race was another half-mile dirt track. Sunday's race was on a three-eighths-mile paved track. Before each race they had to change the oil and filter on the engine and run through the valve adjustments. They also changed all four springs before each race and changed the rear leaf springs too. Then, of course, all four shocks were changed before each race, as well as the rear end gear and one transmission. Tires and wheels being changed were a given. Also a new set of brake shoes, and, well... some food and rest would come in handy about now. I would have to say that all the work that went into winning all five races in the same weekend was the high point of my racing with my dad. The 1960 championship season was great, but at nine years old, I couldn't fully appreciate it. Winning the Atlanta Dixie 400 at the end of the '62 season was right up there because I was getting a little more mature and learning more about it. Watching that gold-and-white #4 Chevy lead the Daytona 500 in '63 was and still is a great memory. But these five victories in a row in the same weekend, well, for a 14-year-old racing fanatic like I was (and still am), that stands right up there at the top for me.

When the '65 racing season came to an end, we really didn't know what the next year would hold for us. Then, out of the blue, the phone rang and it was a group of engineers from the Chevrolet division of General Motors. They asked Louie if he might be interested in going with them to Daytona in January of 1966 to work on the Chevy cars that would be competing in the Pure Oil Performance Trials. All of the automotive magazines would have writers and photographers there and they needed to make a good showing to sell cars for the '66 model year. They made him an offer that was very substantial and he went down there with them to tune for performance, acceleration, handling, braking, stopping distances, fuel economy runs, and about every test you could put a new car through. They did extremely well and after that deal was over, my dad came back home to Spartanburg and asked us, "So, what do ya'll think about moving to Arizona?" That is where the GM Desert Proving Ground was and he had accepted a job working with the GM Engineering staff. He was excited because he would now have a retirement plan, warm weather in the winter and a nice home with a swimming pool to cool down in the summertime. We made the move. We didn't quit racing at all. Our racing expanded in several directions, but the rest of "Racing with the Clements Family" will require another book.

Index

LaVergne, TN USA
02 February 2011
214997LV00002B/1/P